COLONIAL BRAZIL

The complete *Cambridge History of Latin America* presents a large-scale, authoritative survey of Latin America's unique historical experience from the first contacts between the native American Indians and Europeans to the present day. *Colonial Brazil* is a selection of chapters from volumes I and II brought together to provide a continuous history of the Portuguese Empire in Brazil from the beginning of the sixteenth to the beginning of the nineteenth centuries. The chapters cover early Portuguese settlement, political and economic structures, plantations and slavery, the gold rushes, the impact of colonial rule on Indian societies, imperial reorganisation in the eighteenth century, and demographic and economic change during the final decades of the empire. Bibliographical essays are included for all chapters. The book will be a valuable text for both students and teachers of Latin American history.

D0011064

COLONIAL
BRAZIL

edited by

LESLIE BETHELL

Professor of Latin American History
University of London

CAMBRIDGE
UNIVERSITY PRESS

Published by the Press Syndicate of the University of Cambridge
The Pitt Building, Trumpington Street, Cambridge CB2 IRP
40 West 20th Street, New York, NY 10011, USA
10 Stamford Road, Oakleigh, Melbourne 3166, Australia

The contents of this book were previously published as part of
volumes I and II of *The Cambridge History of Latin America*,
copyright © Cambridge University Press 1984.

Printed in the United States of America

British Library cataloguing in publication data

The Cambridge history of Latin America. Vols. I and II. *Selections*
Colonial Brazil.
1. Brazil – History – 1549–1762   2. Brazil
– History – 1763–1821
I. Bethell, Leslie
981'.03 F2528

Library of Congress cataloguing in publication data

Colonial Brazil.
"Previously published as part of volumes I and II
of the Cambridge history of Latin America"
Includes bibliographies and index.
1. Brazil – History – 1500–1548. 2. Brazil – History –
1549–1762. 3. Brazil – History – 1763–1821.
I. Bethell, Leslie
F2524.C56 1987 981 87-31042

ISBN 0-521-34127-2 hardback
ISBN 0-521-34925-7 paperback

CONTENTS

v

MAPS

FIGURES

vii

NOTE ON CURRENCY AND MEASUREMENT

Various units of value and measurement are referred to in the text of the following chapters. It is not possible to give exact equivalents in modern terms, particularly as there were many local variations. The following explanations may prove helpful.

Réis (sing. *real*)	Smallest Portuguese monetary unit; existed only as money of account.
Milréis	1,000 réis, usually written 1$000; worth 12*s*. in the middle of the seventeenth century.
Cruzado	The Portuguese cruzado was equal to 400 réis (480 réis in the first half of the eighteenth century); originally of gold, later silver.
Conto	A conto equalled 1,000$000 réis (1,000 milréis).
Arroba	The Spanish arroba weighed about 11.5 kg (25 lb). The Portuguese arroba weighed 14.5 kg (32 lb).

PREFACE

The Cambridge History of Latin America (*CHLA*) is an authoritative survey of Latin America's unique historical experience during the five centuries from the first contacts between the native peoples of the Americas and Europeans in the late fifteenth and early sixteenth centuries to the present day.

Colonial Brazil brings together seven chapters from volumes I and II of *The Cambridge History of Latin America* in a single volume which, it is hoped, will be useful for both teachers and students of Latin American history. The chapters examine the early Portuguese settlement of Brazil in the sixteenth century, the political and economic structures of the empire, sugar plantations and African slavery, the Indians and the frontier, the gold rushes, imperial reorganisation in the second half of the eighteenth century, and demographic, economic and political changes during the final decades of the empire. Each chapter is accompanied by a bibliographical essay.

ix

1

PORTUGUESE SETTLEMENT, 1500–1580

Late medieval Europe had long been linked with Asia via tenuous land routes, as had Asia with America across the Pacific, but it was not until the Portuguese thrust into the Atlantic early in the fifteenth century that the last great oceanic hiatus in global intercommunication came to be closed. Paradoxically, this first stirring of what was to become modern European imperialism emerged from a society in contraction. Portugal, like the rest of Europe, had suffered a severe population decline in the middle years of the fourteenth century; the ensuing abandonment of marginal land along with the depopulation of towns and villages had created a classic 'feudal crisis' with the upper strata of society economically squeezed by the loss of much of their customary revenue. Elsewhere in Europe this pinch had the effect of sending forth members of the nobility on marauding expeditions in search of booty and new sources of income; the Portuguese conquest of the Moroccan seaport of Ceuta in 1415 (the same year as Henry V's victory at Agincourt) may well be viewed in this light. But Ceuta and the accompanying vision of a North African empire that it suggested turned out to be a dead end. It proved impossible to renew the peninsular reconquest in Morocco: the Berber population was too resistant, too deeply attached to its Islamic beliefs; Portugal's population was too small, its military resources too few.

Instead, the Portuguese thrust was deflected westward, onto the sea and down the coast of Africa. Here resistance was minimal. For centuries boats from the fishing villages along the southern coast of Portugal (the Algarve) had been drawn to the Moroccan coast by the natural action of the winds and currents in that part of the Atlantic, and there they found a variety of rich fishing grounds. Now, with internal pressures for outward expansion growing, these voyagers were stimulated to investigate the opportunities for trade and plunder that beckoned from the adjacent shores.

The traditional approach to this exploration has been to attribute it (at least before 1460) almost exclusively to the inspiration of Prince Henry 'the Navigator' (1394–1460) whose deeds in directing these discoveries were promptly preserved in chronicles which gave him quasi-heroic status. But these discoveries, though certainly stimulated by Henry's desire to create an overseas *appanage* for himself, involved other members of the royal family as well, in addition to numerous followers from their households. Equally important was the participation of members of the Italian merchant community in Lisbon (whether naturalized or not) who brought to the process their Mediterranean expertise and connections. Indeed, they may well have been the decisive factor in transforming these early forays for fishing and plunder along the African coast into organized expeditions for trade.

The Portuguese thrust outward, however, was not limited to pushing down the west coast of Africa, important though that finally proved to be. These sailings inevitably brought them into contact with the islands of the Atlantic – nearby Madeira and the Canaries to begin with, the Azores and the Cape Verdes later. It was the Portuguese experience here, even more than in Africa, that created the patterns later employed in the colonization of Brazil. Taken together, these islands, including the Canaries which gradually fell into the Spanish sphere, formed a kind of 'Atlantic Mediterranean' – a collection of lands whose economy was linked together by the sea.

Madeira was known to exist as early as the fourteenth century, but it was not exploited until the fifteenth. It was the French/Spanish occupation of the nearby Canaries in 1402 that stimulated the Portuguese to initiate serious exploration leading to settlement and agriculture. This began in the years 1418–26 under the leadership of two squires from the entourage of Prince Henry and an Italian nobleman from the household of his brother, Dom João. Development of the Azores lagged behind Madeira by several years. Discovered, or rediscovered in 1427, the Azores began to be settled only in 1439. Finally, much later, the Cape Verdes were explored in the years between 1456 and 1462, but their development and settlement progressed more slowly.

As these various islands or island groups were found, they were progressively incorporated into an economic system centred in Lisbon that was controlled jointly by the Portuguese court and the rich merchants (some of Italian origin) of the capital. This process of incorporation passed through at least three rather well-defined stages which prefigure certain aspects of the economic development of Brazil in the following century.

Since the islands were uninhabited when they were found, the first stage in their exploitation was of necessity extensive. In the earliest years, when there were few or no settlers, animals were put ashore to proliferate rapidly in the new surroundings. They could then be periodically rounded up for slaughter and the products taken back to Portugal for sale. The development of Madeira began with this stage and the first inhabitants brought with them sheep, pigs and cows, if indeed these had not, as it seems, already been put ashore to propagate by themselves. Likewise sheep and goats were set ashore in the Azores in 1431, four years after their initial discovery, to multiply at will. The first settlers arrived only later, in 1439, and for several years devoted themselves to tending the already existing herds before moving on to the next stage of development about 1442. The same pattern was repeated in the Cape Verdes where, before settlement began, goats especially were set ashore to multiply freely.

Since the Portuguese population, like that of most of Europe, was at a low ebb in the first half of the fifteenth century, it took some time before these island frontiers could attract enough people for settled agriculture. But whenever the influx had created a sufficient population density, a shift took place from the initial stage of extensive exploitation via cattle raising to the second stage of more intensive exploitation through the cultivation of cereals. In Madeira, this second stage followed only a few years after the first, due largely to an unexpected migration of disillusioned settlers who had abandoned the Moroccan outpost of Ceuta. The island (as its name 'wood' implies) was covered by immense forests and as these were burned to open areas for wheat, the enriched soil gave enormous yields: up to 50 times the seeding, or so the sources, with some probable exaggeration, claim. As the population expanded, however, the richness of the soil declined with successive harvests, the costs of wheat production rose, its market advantage shrank, and investment shifted to other more remunerative products.

In the Azores, the second or cereal stage began about 1442, some fifteen years after the discovery of the archipelago, and as the wheat exports of Madeira declined those of the Azores rose in compensation. Here, early in the wheat cycle, yields approximating to those of Madeira – 40 to 60 times the seeding – were reported. Unlike Madeira and the Azores, the Cape Verdes did not pass from a cattle stage into one of cereals. Rather the subsequent stage here was one of rice, cotton and fruit and sugar – clear evidence that these islands really lay outside the 'Atlantic Mediterranean' and formed, instead, a transitional region between the ecology of Madeira and the tropical ecology of the African coast.

Finally, a third stage of capitalistic agriculture appeared, but only in Madeira. As the grain yields fell off, capital tended to shift to the more lucrative crops of sugar and fine wine. From about 1450 onward, vineyards and cane-fields began to spread. Pre-Madeiran sugar production had centred in the Near East, Sicily and Spain; it was almost certainly from Sicily that it was introduced into the island. The Azores, however, never reached this stage due to climatological conditions. After Madeira, the next great area for sugar was to be Brazil. The spread of sugar cultivation thence, however, came belatedly, only after an initial generation during which the land was exploited in a manner that resembled, not the first or cattle stage of the Atlantic islands, but rather the factory system that the Portuguese had meanwhile developed along the coast of West Africa during the period after 1449.

Along this coast the Portuguese had avoided, as a rule, any attempt at significant settlement: the native populations were too dense to be easily subdued, the area was ecologically unattractive. Instead they chose to exploit the coast after a pattern adopted from the Italian trading cities of the late medieval Mediterranean. Here the key institution was the factory (*feitoria*), or fortified trading post. This was defended by the castle garrison headed by a knight and operated by a factor (*feitor*) or commercial agent who undertook to make purchases from the native merchants or chiefs. The merchandise he secured was stored in the factory and then sold to the Portuguese captains of the trading fleets that periodically visited the factory. These, however, were often attacked by foreign pirates who seized ships and cargoes when they did not make direct attempts to breach Portugal's fragile monopoly of trade with the natives. In practice the Portuguese crown responded with coast guard patrols to drive off unlicensed ships while juridically it sought and received recognition of its monopoly rights in a series of papal bulls

(1437–81) that formed the models for the later assignment of exclusive rights in America to Spain and Portugal.[1]

By 1500, then, the Portuguese had elaborated two basic patterns for empire in the South Atlantic, a repertoire to be applied as needed to the problems they encountered: (1) the uninhabited islands they regarded juridically as extensions of the mainland kingdom, to be granted to seigneurial lords by royal gifts (*doações*) similar to those made to lords on the mainland, and to be populated by Portuguese immigrants using a settlement system whose forms were borrowed from the medieval Reconquest; (2) along the African coast, where they did encounter native peoples, they opted, instead, for trade without settlement based on the factory system of the late medieval Mediterranean.

Upon finally reaching India (Vasco da Gama, 1498), it was the 'African' system the Portuguese imposed. Finding an age-old culture difficult to penetrate or conquer, they resorted to setting up an 'empire' based on factories, defended by sea patrols to control unlicensed shipping in their area. Brazil, 'discovered' in the course of the second voyage to India, presented a more ambiguous image. Geographically it resembled the Atlantic islands, but, like the African coast, it was populated by savages whom the first Portuguese often called 'negroes'.[2] Only with further exploration did Brazil's real nature gradually come into focus. Treated in the same fashion as the African coast during the first 30 years, it later came to be settled after the pattern of the Atlantic islands.

DISCOVERY AND EARLY EXPLORATION

Upon his return from India in 1499, Vasco da Gama, we are told, pleaded fatigue and recommended that the follow-up expedition of 1500 be entrusted instead to Pedro Álvares Cabral, a *fidalgo* and member of the king's household. Cabral's fleet of thirteen ships followed da Gama's route from Lisbon via the Canaries to Cape Verde, but after crossing the doldrums it was pulled westward by the winds and currents of the South Atlantic and came within sight of the Brazilian coast near present-day Porto Seguro on 22 April 1500. The eight days that the fleet spent refreshing itself in Brazil provided a first brief encounter between

---

[1] Charles-Mártial de Witte, *Les Bulles pontificales et l'expansion portugaise au XVe siècle* (Louvain, 1958), *passim*.

[2] On the indigenous peoples of Brazil in 1500, see Hemming, *CHLA*, I, ch. 5.

two civilizations, one recently embarked upon aggressive imperialism, the other a stone-age culture, virtually outside of time, living in the innocence apparently of Eden. The details of these first contacts were carefully related by the fleet scribe, Pero Vaz da Caminha, in a long letter to King Manuel of Portugal (the 'birth certificate' of Brazil, in the happy phrase of Capistrano de Abreu) that remains our principal source of information about the discovery. On 1 May, Cabral's fleet weighed anchor for its final destination, India, but the supply ship under the command of Gaspar de Lemos was detached to carry immediate news of the 'miraculous' discovery back to the Portuguese court. King Manuel I (1495–1521) promptly notified his Castilian relatives, Ferdinand and Isabella, of the discovery, emphasizing its strategic value to Portugal as a way-station for the India fleets, and organized another expedition the next year for further exploration of Caminha's 'Island of the True Cross'.[3]

This second fleet of three caravels left Lisbon in May of 1501 under the command of Gonçalo Coelho with Amerigo Vespucci aboard as chronicler. Our basic knowledge of this, as well as of the later voyage of 1503–4, comes from Vespucci's vain, if not mendacious, pen which has given birth to intricate and endless historiographical questions. Suffice it to say that the expedition of 1501–2 explored and named many points along some 500 leagues (*c.* 2,000 miles) of the Brazilian coast, from Cape São Roque in the north to near Cananéia in the south; these were soon incorporated into the Cantino map of 1502. Though Vespucci's mercantile sensibilities were not excited by what he saw, '...one can say that we found nothing of profit there except an infinity of dyewood trees, canafistula...and other natural marvels that would be tedious to describe . . .',[4] this second expedition brought back to Lisbon the first American samples of the brazilwood (*caesalpina echinata*) that was not only to provide the 'Island of the True Cross' with its permanent name (Brasil), but also the only compelling reason for its further exploration.

This second voyage also served to establish the sailing route between Portugal and Brazil for the remainder of the colonial period. Ships leaving Portuguese ports usually made for the Canary Islands (where

[3] On the seemingly endless debate regarding the 'intentionality' of Cabral's landfall, see the expert judgement of the late Samuel Eliot Morison, *The European discovery of America: the southern voyages, 1492–1616* (New York, 1974), 224.

[4] Carlos Malheiro Días, 'A Expedição de 1501–02', in *História da colonização Portuguêsa no Brasil*, ed. C. Malheiro Días (Porto, 1924), II, 202.

they often tarried to fish) and then headed for the Cape Verdes to take on fresh water and food; normally this leg of the voyage could last anywhere from fifteen to twenty days, depending upon weather conditions. From the Cape Verdes, ships steered south by southwest to cross the doldrums, a tiresome and tricky task that could easily fail, leaving the fleet to be swept up by the southern equatorial current into the Caribbean, as happened to Governor Luís de Vasconcelos on his outward voyage in 1571. Once safely across the doldrums, ships would veer westward, drawn naturally (like Cabral) in that direction by the winds and currents, until they touched Brazil somewhere between Cape São Roque and Cape Santo Agostinho, whence they could follow the coast all the way down to the Río de la Plata. A voyage, say, from Lisbon to Bahia required about a month and a half, if all went smoothly. If it did not (as with Padre Cardim in 1583), the outward voyage could take all of two months or more, even if the Cape Verdes were bypassed. Ships returning to Portugal steered north from Cape São Roque until they found the Azores whence they could ride the westerlies into Lisbon. This usually took longer than the outward voyage, often two and a half months or more.

THE FACTORY PERIOD

Once the initial phase (1500–2) of discovery and reconnaissance had been completed the Portuguese crown faced the problem of devising a system to exploit the new-found land. In the context of Portugal's prior Atlantic experience, the nature of Brazil was ambiguous. In most respects, it appeared to be simply another Atlantic island, but unlike Madeira or the Azores, it was populated by savage though comely natives. The island pattern of putting cattle ashore to multiply before the first colonists arrived was thus impossible in Brazil where the animals would rapidly fall prey to the Indians. Instead, the Portuguese felt obliged to treat Brazil like the coast of Africa and to exploit it via a system of trading factories.

To develop the few tradable commodities that were found (dyewood, monkeys, slaves and parrots) the crown opted to lease out Brazil to a consortium of Lisbon merchants headed by Fernão de Noronha, who was already important in the African and Indian trades. Unfortunately, the contract itself has not survived, but indirect evidence suggests that it resembled that by which the Guinea trade in Africa had been leased in 1469 to the merchant Fernão Gomes for a five-year period. The group, we are told, was granted a trade monopoly for three years with no payment to the crown the first year, a sixth of the profits the second, and a quarter the third. In return, the group agreed to send out six ships each year to explore 300 leagues (*c.* 1,200 miles) of coastline and to construct a fortified trading post or factory there.

We know of two fleets which the consortium sent out. Details of the first are sketchy: sailing under an unknown captain, it left Lisbon in August of 1502, made Brazil near Cape São Roque, visited the area of Porto Seguro and returned to Lisbon in April of the next year, bringing back a cargo of brazilwood and Indian slaves. The second voyage is better known, thanks to Vespucci who was in command of one of the five ships. He has left us an account of the voyage (his third and last) in his *Letters.* Departing Lisbon on 10 June 1503, the expedition ran into bad weather near the island of Fernando Noronha (named after the principal merchant of the consortium). Here Vespucci's ship, along with that of another captain, lost the fleet. The two went on together to Cabo Frio in Brazil where they stayed five months to erect the factory called for in the contract which they garrisoned with 24 men.[5] In June of 1504 the two ships returned to Lisbon with a cargo of brazilwood. It is likely that the consortium sent out a third voyage in 1504–5, but no evidence of it has survived.[6]

The profitability of these voyages is unknown, but, when the group's contract expired in 1505, indirect evidence suggests that the crown resumed direct control of the Brazil trade just as it did with regard to the India trade at the same time.[7] Thus re-established in 1506, direct crown control of Brazil was to last until 1534 when the land was again leased out, not, as earlier, to merchants for trade, but rather to territorial lords for purposes of settlement.

During the intervening years (1506–34) of royal exploitation, the Portuguese crown continued to adhere to the patterns worked out in Africa during the fifteenth century, i.e., it maintained royal factories at a number of strategic points along the coast (Pernambuco, Bahia?, Porto Seguro?, Cabo Frio, São Vicente?), but licensed private vessels to trade with the natives under its auspices. No yearly statistics for this trade

[5] The point of departure for Hythlodaeus in More's *Utopia.*
[6] Max Justo Guedes, 'As primeiras expedições portuguesas e o reconhecimento da costa brasileira', *Revista Portuguesa de História,* 12/2 (1968), 247–67.
[7] Rolando A. Laguarda Trías, 'Christóvão Jaques e as armadas Guarda-Costa', in *História Naval Brasileira,* ed. M. J. Guedes (Rio de Janeiro, 1975), 1/1, 275.

have survived, nor have we any record for most of these voyages. Good luck, however, has preserved for us a relatively detailed account of one expedition, that of the *Bretoa* in 1511, which reveals the essential nature of the system. The ship was financed by a group that again included Noronha, now in association with Bartolomeu Marchione, an important Florentine merchant settled in Lisbon who was already active in the Madeiran sugar trade. Carrying a complement of five officers and 31 crew, the *Bretoa* left Lisbon in February and arrived at Bahia in April where it remained about a month. In May it proceeded south to load dyewood at the factory established in 1504 near Cabo Frio. The factory had been sited on an offshore island (for safety against Indian attack) and contact between the crew and the natives was strictly forbidden, factory personnel being the sole go-betweens. Some 5,000 logs were cut and transported to the factory by Tupi Indians who were paid for their labour with gifts of trinkets and small tools. Members of the crew were also allowed to trade for their own account; thus, in addition to the main cargo of dyewood, 35 Tupi Indian slaves and numerous exotic animals were brought back. Sailing late in July the ship made Lisbon at the end of October. The overall profitability of the Brazil trade cannot be sensibly calculated from this one voyage, but it was evidently lucrative enough to attract at least occasional investors, especially those who were already involved in imperial trade or who had Antwerp outlets, as did Noronha.

Interest in Brazil was not exclusively economic, however. It also presented a geopolitical problem for the Iberian powers. If, as many still thought, it was really a large (but relatively poor) island, could it be rounded and a westward passage found to the much more lucrative spice islands of the East Indies? Though almost everyone agreed that the Brazilian bulge fell within the Portuguese sphere as defined by the Treaty of Tordesillas (1494), did the mouth of the Amazon and the Río de la Plata (the most likely routes around Brazil) fall on the Portuguese or Spanish side of the line? The search for answers centred largely on La Plata during most of the second decade of the century. A Portuguese expedition (the Fróis-Lisboa, financed by the Castilian-born Christóvão de Haro among others) had first discovered the Río de la Plata in 1511–12; Castile responded with the Solís expedition of 1515. This in turn helped trigger the Portuguese coastguard patrols probably begun in 1516 by Christóvão Jacques. These, however, did not prevent Spain

from sending Magellan to Brazil on the first leg of his search for a
westward passage in 1519. His subsequent discovery of the way around
'Brazil' to the Spiceries, though a spectacular feat of navigation, was
largely useless to Castile. The route proved too long to be practical;
and in the meantime Cortés had distracted the Spanish with his
discovery of the riches of the Aztecs. After years of desultory negotiations, Spain pawned her claim to the Spice Islands given her by
Magellan to Portugal for 350,000 ducats (Treaty of Zaragoza, 1529) and
Spanish pressure on Brazil came largely to an end.

More important in the long run than Spanish probing around the
fringes of Brazil was French poaching on the dyewood trade. Evidence
for this is haphazard: a ship seizure here, a protest there, but it was
growing, led by merchants operating out of northern French ports in
Normandy and Brittany. A French ship intent upon breaking into the
India trade had, like Cabral, drifted off course onto the coast of Brazil
in 1504, where it remained to load dyewood instead and then returned
to Honfleur. Appetites whetted, French merchants from other ports
(Dieppe, Rouen, Fécamp) began to seek dyewood in Brazil. They made
no attempt to establish factories after the Portuguese pattern, but traded
directly from their ships, sending agents to live among the Indians, with
whom good relations were developed. Not only did French competition
deprive the Portuguese crown of revenue, but it lowered the price of
brazilwood by increasing supplies on the Antwerp market. In addition,
French seizures of Portuguese ships drove up costs to such a point that
fewer and fewer merchants were willing to risk involvement in the trade.

The initial Portuguese response was to apply the tactics that had
worked so well in the Indian Ocean: to dispatch a fleet to police the
seas with instructions to seize or destroy unlicensed foreign ships. The
expedition of Christóvão Jacques, sent to the Brazilian coast in 1516,
was the first direct royal reaction in defence of Brazil. We have little
information on Jacques' activities during the three years his fleet
patrolled the coast (1516–19) but we know that he established a royal
factory at Pernambuco[8] and may also have attempted a limited
settlement there for growing sugar cane (if one can trust a document
– since disappeared – cited by Varnhagen). This first coastguard
expedition cannot be considered a complete success, however, for after
1520 there was a noticeable increase in French piracy which was no

---

[8] According to Laguarda Trías, he simply moved the factory Vespucci had established at Cabo
Frio (or Rio de Janeiro) to Pernambuco.

longer confined to Brazil. French privateers lay in wait about strategic rendezvous points such as the Azores and the straits of Gibraltar to seize Spanish and Portuguese ships. A recent rough calculation of Portuguese vessels seized by the French works out to an average of twenty per year for the decade 1520–30. There is some evidence that the Portuguese persisted in their attempt to contain this threat with coastguard patrols (in 1521–2 probably; in 1523–5 perhaps). In any case, Jacques was sent back to Brazil in 1527 at the head of a fleet of six ships with orders to eliminate the interlopers at all costs. Running into some French loading dyewood at Bahia, he seized their (three) ships, either hanged or buried alive numerous members of their crews and then proceeded to sweep the coast down to Cabo Frio. Ensuing protests from the French court brought issues to a head.

In contrast to the Castilians who accepted the juridical bases of the Portuguese claim and argued only over boundaries, the French presented a fundamental challenge to Portugal's exclusive rights to Brazil. These rested, as in Africa, on papal bulls that embodied the medieval canonistic tradition of universal papal jurisdiction over the world, a concept classically formulated by Hostiensis and Augustinus Triumphus in the thirteenth century. This gave the pope legitimate authority to assign monopoly rights over newly-discovered seas and lands to rulers who would undertake to evangelize them. But this thirteenth-century concept soon came under attack from Thomistic critics whose ideas had recently been reinforced by the Renaissance revival of Roman law, especially of the Code of Justinian. Indeed, the papal position was no longer accepted by progressive scholars even in Iberia (e.g. Francisco de Vitória). Armed, then, with a more 'modern' concept of empire based on the secular law of nations (*ex iure gentium*), the French court insisted upon its right to trade freely and declined to respect any title not backed up by effective occupation. The French considered their ships and merchants free to traffic with any area of Brazil not actually occupied by Portuguese – which meant, in fact, virtually the entire coast.

Under constant pressure during the 1520s, the Portuguese crown retreated on nearly all fronts. It found it impossible to drive out the French with sea patrols – the open coast was too long and royal resources too few. Juridically the papal bulls and the Treaty of Tordesillas were recognized only by Castile; and the intellectual acumen of the French lawyers made the Portuguese king uneasy. Unable to persuade the French king of his legal rights (he even argued, with a tinge of desperation, that he and his predecessors had 'purchased' Brazil through the Portuguese lives and money expended in the early expeditions), João III (1521–57) temporarily resorted to bribing Chabot, the admiral of France, in his attempt to control French piracy and poaching (1529–31).

This afforded a short respite and Portuguese policy now evolved rapidly. By 1530 João III and his advisers concluded that some kind of permanent colony would have to be planted in Brazil. This is one of the meanings of the expedition of Martim Afonso de Sousa (1530–3). His fleet of five ships carrying some 400 settlers really had three discernible aims, and in its variety of orientations looks both back to the earlier policy of royal coastguards as well as forward to the coming solution of settlement. Sousa's first charge – to patrol the coast – reveals that the crown had still not completely abandoned the view that the defence of its Brazilian interest was largely a question of clearing the seas of unlicensed ships, while his second charge – to establish a royal colony (São Vicente, 1532) through revocable (not hereditary) landgrants to settlers – adumbrates the emergence of a new policy in Brazil; lastly, in preparation for settlement, the expedition was instructed to explore the mouths of the Amazon and La Plata rivers to determine, among other things, their proximity to the meridian of Tordesillas.

The ambiguities in Portuguese policy were resolved while Sousa was still in Brazil. Prompted by Diego de Gouveia, the Portuguese principal of the college of Sainte Barbe in Paris, a fundamental shift in policy occurred which, in effect, moved the Portuguese line of defence from the sea to the land. Instead of attempting to keep French ships from reaching the Brazilian coast, the Portuguese would instead establish a number of settlements to prevent the Indian population from direct trading with the French. At the same time these settlements would answer the French juridical challenge: Portugal could now claim 'effective possession' of Brazil. Direct royal control would cease; instead of a single royal colony at São Vicente, a plurality of private settlements would blanket the coast from the Amazon to the Río de la Plata. Growing strains on crown income at this time made it useful to shift the costs of such extensive colonization to private investors, several of whom had already expressed interest in taking up New World lordships with the aim of growing sugar cane. Demand for sugar was booming in these years, and production had recently been greatly expanded on the island of São Tomé. The first tentative experiments with sugar in Brazil (Pernambuco, 1516, and São Vicente, 1532) had demonstrated the climatic and topographical suitability of large stretches of the Brazilian coast.

THE PERIOD OF PROPRIETARY SETTLEMENT

Grants were made to a group of twelve proprietary captains ranging from soldiers of fortune who had proven themselves in the Orient (Duarte Coelho, Francisco Coutinho) to a number of bureaucrats including a humanist historian of high intellectual distinction (João de Barros). What all of them had in common was court connections, especially with António de Ataíde, the Overseer of the Treasury (*Vedor da Fazenda*), who, in directing and co-ordinating Portugal's colonial enterprise, played a role similar to that of Bishop Fonseca in Castile until the death of Ferdinand in 1516. The fact that none of them came from the high nobility is hardly cause for surprise (as some historians have implied). João III was the heir of the New Monarchy created by João II and Manuel I and preferred to entrust power and bestow rewards on the university educated (*letrados*) and upwardly mobile servants of the crown whatever their birth.

The twelve grantees received fourteen captaincies in fifteen lots (one captaincy had two sections and two grantees got two captaincies each) by royal 'gift' (*doação*) – hence the terms 'donatary captain' and 'donatary captaincy'. The institution derived, slightly modified by circumstance, from the typical royal grant of lordship in late medieval Portugal. In essence it was the hereditary grant of a large portion of royal jurisdiction over a specified territory and its inhabitants to a lord who thereafter acted as the king's *locum tenens* to the extent spelled out in the gift. In a constitutional sense, land under the direct control of the crown (*reguengo*) was converted into a lordship (*senhorio*) in which royal rights were now restricted to certain attributes of 'greater lordship'. All twelve grants were similar in essentials; that made to Duarte Coelho will serve to illustrate them all.

Coelho received his captaincy of Pernambuco as an hereditary possession of which he and his successors were to be 'captains and governors'. Inheritance was more liberal than in the peninsula: the exclusion there of bastards and transverse or collateral relatives (the *Lei Mental*) was specifically disavowed. Coelho had the right to appoint all notaries, scribes and other subordinate officials in his captaincy, and he or his officials were granted most civil and criminal jurisdiction except for certain cases and persons reserved to the crown as evidence of its 'greater lordship'. He was also given the right to establish towns and to supervise the elections of their officials. In addition to these jurisdictional powers, Coelho was made a territorial lord by the gift of ten leagues of coast (in several parcels) of which he was direct owner. To attract settlers, the rest of the land was to be subgranted by him to colonists, in full ownership, obligated only to pay the tithe to the Order of Christ. Finally, as captain, he had the right to license all important capital improvements such as mills for grinding cane; these were the 'banal rights' commonly possessed by lords throughout medieval Europe.

As for the captain's rents, they were largely made up of taxes that would normally have gone to the king: a tenth of the tithe, a half of the tenth levied on fish caught by the colonists, a tenth of all royal revenues in the captaincy and a twentieth of the profits from the brazilwood cut; the latter was usually kept from the *donatário* and directly controlled by the king. Structurally these donations were indistinguishable from similar grants of royal authority made in Portugal as well as in the Atlantic islands in the late medieval period, and should be seen as adaptations of these. Attempts which have been made to force the institution into ideological categories (feudal or capitalistic) simply confuse its understanding.[9]

The letter of donation to the captain was complemented by a kind of mini-constitution (*foral*) for his lordship. This spelled out in some detail the relations between the settlers and the captain as well as the rights of the crown. In medieval Portugal the foral had usually been issued to his settlers by the lord himself, but the New Monarchy early in the sixteenth century had recovered this right from the donataries and royalized it, as it were. Coelho's foral exempted the inhabitants from the *sisa* and other royal taxes, but the crown retained its previous monopoly of the dyewood trade as well as its right to a tenth of the fish caught, a fifth of the minerals mined and a tenth on commerce in and out of the captaincy. Trade with the captaincies was open to both Portuguese and to foreigners, but only the captain and the Portuguese

---

[9] See H. B. Johnson, 'The donatary captaincy in historical perspective: Portuguese backgrounds to the settlement of Brazil', *Hispanic American Historical Review*, 52 (1972), 203–14.

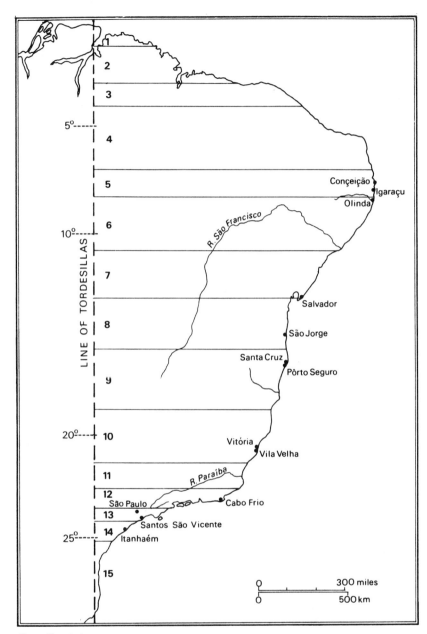

Captaincies of Brazil in the sixteenth century

residents were allowed to trade with the Indians. Finally, the king reserved the right to appoint officials directly concerned with the collection of his rents in the captaincy.

Only ten of the captaincies were settled in the sixteenth century; two (Ceará and Santana) were left abandoned by their lords. Of the ten that were settled only two (São Vicente and Pernambuco) could be termed genuinely successful before 1550. Of the remaining eight, five were moderately successful, for a time at least (Santo Amaro, Itamaracá, Espírito Santo, Porto Seguro, Ilhéus), while the remaining three rapidly became complete failures (São Tomé, Maranhão–Rio Grande and Bahia). Their various fates can be attributed in part to the capabilities of the individual captains; in this regard Duarte Coelho in Pernambuco stood out as exceptionally able, while Francisco Pereira Coutinho in Bahia was not. Still, the capability or even the presence of the captain cannot have been the decisive factor, since Martim Afonso de Sousa never bothered to visit his grant of São Vicente, yet it turned out, under able lieutenants, to be one of the two most successful of all. Evidently more important than the character of the donatary was the ability to attract the settlers and the capital necessary for success and to subdue the local Indians.

Obtaining sufficient settlers was not easy; the population of Portugal in the 1530s numbered no more than a million and a half at most, scattered over some 34,200 square miles of territory (*c.* 40–4 per square mile). With so little pressure for emigration, settlers often had to be sought instead from among the *degredados*, or exiles, who could be anyone from a political offender to a common criminal. With a few exceptions, they were on the whole undesirable, and many of the captains complained of them, sometimes bitterly. Coelho called them 'this poison' and tried instead, with considerable success, to attract sturdy peasants from his own region of the Minho. Lack of capital was another difficulty that could prove fatal. Some captains had good financial backing. Pero de Góis (São Tomé) was supported by Martin Ferreira, a businessman of Lisbon, while Coelho had connections with Florentine merchants, and Jorge de Figueiredo Correia (Ilhéus), scribe of the Treasury, could call upon the Giraldi, a family of Italian merchants settled in Lisbon. When Correia and Giraldi had problems getting the Indians to help set up sugar plantations in Ilhéus, they could afford to import 400 wage labourers and Guinea slaves during the years

1545–9 to defend the settlements and till the fields.[10] Reserves such as this often spelled the difference between success and failure. Others, on the other hand, like Pero de Campo Tourinho, could scarcely put together the amount needed to set off and had nothing to fall back on when circumstances turned adverse. The greatest challenge of all, however, came not from the problems of Europeans adjusting to a virgin land but rather from the hostility of the coastal Tupi-speaking and, to a lesser extent, Gê-speaking Indian population.

During the 'factory period' (1502–34), Portuguese relations with the Indians had been generally amicable. They furnished the Indians with technological artefacts that immensely increased the levels of productivity in their traditional economy, while in return the grateful Indians provided the labour necessary to fell and transport the brazilwood for loading on Portuguese ships, as well as the food required by the personnel of the factory. French incursions into this trade network may have been annoying to the Portuguese, but they did not seriously disturb their relations with the Indians.

Settlement, however, created a different situation. Given the intention of most captains to set up sugar plantations, Indian land rights were of necessity infringed. Though the migratory tendencies of Indian society blinded the Portuguese to it, the Indians did have a general sense of territoriality which the Portuguese plantations violated.[11] More importantly, sugar planting and sugar mills required a large and growing labour force that the settlers could not supply even had they been willing to do so, which they were not. The only recourse, therefore, was to Indian labour. But since work of the sort necessary to run a sugar plantation was unfamiliar to Indian culture, and (because of the often rigid schedule involved) antithetical to it, the two cultures – with their contrasting visions of the world – came into direct conflict. Tupi men were attuned to felling trees and had no difficulty satisfying Portuguese needs during the 'brazilwood' period, but field work was the traditional preserve of Indian women; Indian men refused to do it. They were profoundly unmaterialistic and unambitious, and in any case the settlers had little to offer which might make labour on plantations worthwhile. Given the recalcitrance of the labour force, the Portuguese settlers were soon driven to enslaving Indians for work on the growing

[10] *As Gavetas da Torre do Tombo* (Lisbon, 1962), II, 583.
[11] *As Gavetas da Torre do Tombo* (Lisbon, 1969), VIII, 512.

number of plantations and mills (*engenhos*). Slavery, of course, was an institution already known to Tupi culture, but largely in relation to ritual cannibalism. Enslaved Indians from neighbouring tribes were eventually sacrificed which usually led to a declaration of war by the kin of the enslaved. In this cultural context it is not difficult to understand how the growth of sugar planting and the slavery it entailed led to a state of constant conflict with the native population of the coastal area.

The Indians were always at a disadvantage in their struggle with the Portuguese. While the invaders had at their disposal arquebuses, swords and sometimes cannon, the Indians had to fight back with bows and arrows (though in their hands these were formidable weapons), wooden axes, as well as whatever guile and surprise they could add to the attack. Before disease had taken its toll, the Indians' main strength, however, lay in their numbers. At times they could simply overwhelm the Portuguese, who often had to take refuge in the fortified towers which formed the centre of most of their colonial settlements; they could then sometimes be worn down through starvation. On the other hand, if the Portuguese managed to hold out long enough (as they often did) the Indians usually became frustrated and went away. Another Portuguese tactic was terror: using the advantage of their technology they often frightened the Indians into submission, as did Jerónimo de Albuquerque in Pernambuco:

…after determining which [Indians] were the killers of the whites, he ordered some of them put into the mouths of cannon which he then had fired in front of the rest so that the culprits were blown to bits….[12]

Another weapon was fire which could be devastating against the palm thatch of the Indian *malocas*, as Mem de Sá demonstrated when he pacified the Indians around Bahia soon after his arrival by burning 60 of their villages. Finally, in addition to fire and gunpowder, the Portuguese had the weapon of bribery: defeated Indians who submitted could be rewarded with European artefacts such as fish hooks, scythes and metal axes.

Given the immense extent of the Brazilian coast that the Portuguese attempted to settle, from Cabo Santo Agostinho in the north to Cananéia in the south, these struggles were always local. The Indians' inability to overcome inter-tribal rivalries made it easy for the Portuguese

---

[12] Frei Vicente do Salvador, *História do Brasil, 1500–1627* (6th edn, São Paulo, 1975), 121.

to divide and rule; to make an alliance with one tribe against a second, and then to turn on their erstwhile allies at a later date was a standard Portuguese tactic.

During the first ten years after their arrival, the Portuguese settlers usually had either the co-operation of the Indians or the upper hand in the struggle with them; but in areas where settlement had failed to sink deep enough roots and was still fragile, native resistance, like the wave that swept the coast in the mid-40s (Bahia, 1545; São Tomé, 1546; Espírito Santo, *c.* 1546; Porto Seguro, 1546), could prove disastrous. It effectively wiped out the colonies of Bahia and São Tomé and severely crippled those of Espírito Santo and Porto Seguro. Only São Vicente, Ilhéus and Pernambuco/Itamaracá emerged intact, though the latter was seriously threatened in 1547–8. By 1548, the damage was clear; and the disappearance of effective Portuguese control in important centres such as Bahia and elsewhere increasingly exposed Brazil to the ever-present threat of French incursions and settlements. As Luís de Góis, brother of the donatary of São Tomé, summarized the situation in a letter to the king (1548): 'If Your Highness does not shortly aid these captaincies and coast of Brazil...You will lose the land.' Emphasizing the renewed threat of French invasion, he continued: 'But as long as these captaincies are standing with their inhabitants and Your Highness's aid and favour, the sea and coast will be rid of them.'[13] João III took Góis' advice and promptly decided to extend that 'aid and favour'.

THE ESTABLISHMENT OF ROYAL GOVERNMENT

The crown's decision to send a royal governor to Brazil was not intended to abrogate the donatarial grants. Most of these lasted through the next century and some of them into the eighteenth. Rather the king intended to resume, as it were, some of the authority that he had so generously given out at a time when royal resources were strained and rapid development had been sought. The Brazilian historian, Sérgio Buarque de Holanda, has related the establishment of the royal governorship to the Spanish discovery of silver at Potosí (1545); others, like Frédéric Mauro, have seen it as a decision to substitute Brazilian sugar for the waning spice trade of the Estado da India. On the other hand, one should not forget that the eventual resumption of royal control was a normal practice of *ancien régime* monarchies and the leasing

[13] As quoted in Serafim Leite, *Nóvas páginas de história do Brasil* (São Paulo, 1965), 261.

out of royal rights often a temporary expedient. This had been the case with the dyewood trade, farmed out between 1502–5 and royalized in 1506; it was now repeated with regard to the settlements that had been created between 1535–48. After private initiative had paved the way, the royal bureaucracy stepped in to appropriate a functioning enterprise. A glance at the Spanish parallels is instructive: only fourteen years passed in Mexico between Cortés' conquest and the arrival of the first viceroy; in Peru, the period between private conquest and the creation of a royal administration was no more than twelve years. If the donatarial captaincies are viewed as the phase of 'private conquest' in Brazil, then the arrival of a royal governor fourteen years later conforms perfectly to the general Iberian pattern. In a broader cultural sense one might view the royalization of both empires as a New World expression of the various 'closures' taking place in Catholic Europe about the middle of the sixteenth century: the definitive form given to dogma at Trent; the general retreat from Erasmian toleration; more specifically for Portugal, the final establishment of the Inquisition in 1547. In other words, it could be seen as part of a reaction against the ambiguity, openness and experimentation of the first half of the century, a move towards rigidity and codification, an exclusion of alternatives, demonstrating a new atmosphere of definite decisions having been finally made.

Whatever general interpretation may be preferred, immediate royal motivations are clearly revealed in the standing instructions (*regimento*) that accompanied the new governor, Tomé de Sousa (1549–53), another close relative of António de Ataíde, the Overseer of the Treasury. In the first place, he was charged to defend the weaker captaincies from possible attack and to revitalize those that had failed. These failures in every instance had been the result of Indian attack, not French conquest; yet, as Luís de Góis had written, the French threat was still alive, and captaincies weakened by Indian attacks were prime targets for possible French settlement. Secondly, the crown obviously wanted to increase the royal revenues from Brazil; not only was the king being cheated of what was due him, but the unsuccessful captaincies failed to provide him with the income he had expected from their development.

To deal with these problems João III chose three important officials: first, a governor to defend and bolster up the unsuccessful captains and to set general policy for dealing with the Indians; second, a *provedor-mor* of the Treasury to oversee the collection of crown revenues; and third, a captain-major of the coast to set up the policing of the littoral. Bahia was selected as the governor's seat; it was a central site with a potentially rich hinterland. And, due to the late donatary failing to deal with the Indians, it was possible to repurchase the captaincy from his heirs and re-incorporate it into the *reguengo* (land under the direct control of the crown). Tomé de Sousa (the first governor) was given detailed instructions for building a city of stone and mortar, centred on an impregnable fort, a worthy reflection of the royal determination to remain in Brazil. The sugar mills, satellite centres of Portuguese control, were also to be armed and fortified against possible attack. Once the governor's position in Bahia had been made strong, he was to visit the other captaincies to assess their needs and provide them with military assistance.

If increased military strength was one part of the solution of the Indian question, the other aspect was the elaboration of a workable Indian policy. Ultimately this would have to issue, as in the Spanish empire, from certain fundamental juridical decisions made by the crown. Brazil had been incorporated into the crown by the will of Manuel I,[14] but the native Indians (*gentio*) did not automatically, even by implication, become crown subjects. In contrast to the Spanish situation where Charles I simply succeeded to the thrones vacated by the Aztec and Inca emperors, the Portuguese could not discover any civilized structures in Tupi society – it appeared to lack identifiable laws and religious institutions. Indeed, the very innocence that had led Pero Vaz de Caminha in the beginning to see it as ripe for domination and conversion, was now revealed to be a frustrating obstacle. Tupi social organization did not fit any of the categories the Portuguese could comprehend; hence the crown's confused hesitation in defining the status of the Indians. In vain one searches contemporary documents for an unequivocal statement that the *gentio* are royal subjects. In short, the status of the Brazilian Indians within Portuguese colonial society was still to be worked out.

As early as the voyage of the *Bretoa* (1511), the crown placed the Indians under its legal protection, and the *regimento* given Tomé de Sousa emphasized that no harm should be done them as long as they were peaceful. Good treatment was essential if they were to be evangelized. That was the juridical justification for the whole enterprise,

---

[14] *As Gavetas da Torre do Tombo* (Lisbon, 1967), VI, 122.

whether derived from the papal bulls or Vitória's law of nations. On the other hand, rebellious Indians who resisted Christianity were equated with the Muslims of Africa and could thus be enslaved. So there gradually evolved in Brazil, as in the Spanish empire, the crucial distinction between peaceful Indians, minors to be protected by the crown while gradually being acculturated into full citizenship as Christians, and bellicose Indians against whom 'just wars' could be waged, who could be resettled by force if necessary and ultimately enslaved for use by the colonists. The crux of the matter, of course, was economic. Indiscriminate enslavements (*saltos*) were among the prime causes of Indian resistance, and this in turn made development of the economy impossible. Nevertheless, Indian labour for the developing sugar industry was essential and only enslavement could supply the workers required. The resolution of this contradiction was one of the principal tasks of the new generation of administrators.

As his special agents for converting and pacifying the Indians, the king chose the Jesuits, the missionary order founded only nine years before (1540) and brought to his attention by Diego de Gouveia in Paris. The first group of six (including Father Manuel de Nóbrega) came out with Tomé de Sousa; reinforcements arrived on subsequent voyages. But their total number was small; only 128 for the period up to 1598. The numerous diffuse letters they sent back to Europe reveal (as well as conceal) their work in Brazil. Up to 1580 Jesuit activity can be divided into five general stages: an initial period of experimentation (1550–3); an interlude of stagnation (1553–7); the full flowering of their settlement or *aldeia* system (1557–61); the crisis of the Caeté war and the ensuing waves of disease and famine (1562–3); and a final period of adjustment to the resultant decline of the Indian population (1564–74).

The initial period closely coincided with the term of the first royal governor; these were years of evaluation and experimentation. The Jesuits' aim was conversion, pacification and acculturation: the Indians' response, after some initial curiosity and acceptance, evasion, hostility and backsliding. Jesuit attitudes towards their task – the transformation of stone-age savages into quasi-European peasants living in settled villages practising the religion of an agrarian society – varied from dogged optimism to pessimistic self-pity. In contrast to Las Casas, few of them had much love or respect for their charges. Nóbrega compared the Tupi to dogs and pigs, and Anchieta described them as more like animals than men. Yet, in contrast to the colonists, they *did* believe in the possibility of changing Indian society. The Jesuits' reputation was at stake, and they applied themselves to their goal with a military determination.

At first they followed the methods of the Franciscans who always preferred to catechize Indians *in situ*, however slow the task might be. The Jesuits soon discovered, however, that the Indians they thought they had converted during their first visit to the village had gone native by the time they returned. To hasten the process and preserve their gains, they decided to remove Indians from their native villages and resettle them in aldeias whose large size was dictated by the scarcity of Jesuits to serve as supervisors. Here the Tupi could undergo intensive indoctrination. Nóbrega enunciated the plan of aldeias in 1550 and the first one was tried out near Bahia in 1552. They were not conspicuously successful; Indians often ran away: like minnows they wriggled through the net of Jesuit acculturation. Still, the determined fathers would have persisted but for political obstacles.

The settlers had never fully supported the Jesuit aldeias which removed so many Indians from the pool of potential slaves, and they soon found a powerful ally in the first bishop of Brazil, Dom Pedro Fernandes Sardinha. The crown's decision to create a royal governor was followed shortly after (1551) by the erection of a diocese for Brazil, located in Bahia, the extension to the *conquistas* of the metropolitan union of throne and altar. The king's choice of bishop, however, did not prove as happy as his choice of governor. Sardinha came with excellent credentials: trained as a humanist at the Sorbonne (where he had taught Loyola in the Portuguese-dominated college of St Barbe) his previous service as vicar general in Goa had been highly satisfactory. The Jesuits themselves had recommended him to the king. But once in Brazil contact with the savage Tupi seems to have stirred up his rigid moralistic tendencies. Not unreasonably, he did not share the Jesuit belief in the convertibility of the Indians; he insisted upon their full acculturation before baptism. Nor did he approve of the syncretic tendencies of Jesuit evangelization, the mere painting of a Christian patina over an obdurate Indian culture: e.g., tolerance of Indian nudity in Church, Indian songs and dances blended into the liturgy. As long as the Indians were cultural minors, they were not to participate in organized Christian life. In short, he envisaged in Brazil a dual society of the sort he had known in India, with a small 'republic' of Portuguese ruling over an alien world of mainly heathen natives.

His indifference towards the Indians was compensated by his fixation on the mores of the settlers. Their general adoption of Indian ways, a kind of ironic reverse acculturation that produced the proverbial squaw men such as João Ramalho in São Vicente and Caramurú in Bahia, drove him into a puritanical fury. Still, the settlers found his attitude towards the Indians and his non-support of the Jesuits congenial to their interests. The conflict between the bishop and the Jesuits gave them an opportunity to continue slaving and made it virtually impossible for the second governor, Duarte da Costa (1553–7), to exercise effective authority during his term of office. Because their work of evangelization was impeded by Sardinha's hostility and was not effectively supported by the harried governor, the Jesuits soon moved the centre of their activity to the southern captaincy of São Vicente where the Tupinikin Indians proved more receptive and malleable. Here they expanded on the aldeia system first conceived around Bahia, and established in 1554 an important Indian congregation (aldeia) at São Paulo de Piratininga. This site at the edge of the inland plateau commanded the basin of the Tieté river and formed the original nucleus for the future city of São Paulo.

Word of the conflict between the governor and the bishop in Bahia prompted the crown to recall the latter to Lisbon (1556) but his ship was wrecked along the coast of Brazil where, ironically, he suffered martyrdom, being killed and eaten by the Caeté Indians he so heartily disdained. Duarte da Costa's term of office ended the next year (1557) and with a new governor, Mem de Sá (1557–72), and a new bishop, Dom Pedro Leitão, royal consolidation of Portuguese Brazil entered a new phase.

Sá was, above all, a willing and enthusiastic collaborator of the Jesuits, who now returned to focus their activities around the royal city of Bahia. With the governor's military arm at their disposal, they made significant inroads into Indian paganism by sharpening the distinction, already adumbrated, between rebellious Indians, who might be enslaved, and peaceful, acculturating Indians, who were encouraged to accept the protection of the aldeias. Thus, the early period of Sá's long rule was the golden age of the aldeias. These now expanded from two or three to no less than eleven by 1561, with a total population of 34,000 at the beginning of 1562.[15]

Two developments brought this expansion to a halt. First, in 1562

---

[15] Alexander Marchant, *From barter to slavery* (Baltimore, 1942), 108.

Mem de Sá declared a 'just war' against the Caeté who had martyred bishop Sardinha six years before, declaring open season on that entire Indian nation. As retribution for the bishop's death this came a bit late; more likely this Caeté 'law' was conceived to placate colonists angered by the growth of the Jesuit aldeias which removed so many Indians from the slave pool. Unfortunately, the Caeté war overflowed even the lax conditions imposed by Sá; Caetés were not only seized *in situ*, but also in the Jesuit aldeias which they had earlier entered confident of Jesuit promises of protection. The effect on the aldeias was disastrous and Sá quickly revoked his 'law', but it was too late; the damage had been done.

On the heels of this uncontrollable war came another crisis to flagellate the colony: disease. It arrived in two waves: the first came in 1562 and struck the Indians in the area around Bahia; the second, in 1563, was more widespread. Together they may have carried off from one-third to one-half of the Indian population which, of course, lacked all immunity to European diseases, such as tuberculosis, influenza, smallpox and measles, brought by the Portuguese and others. The resulting decline in the Indian population not only reduced the number of aldeias from eleven to five, but significantly intensified the settlers' competition for the labour of those who survived.

One consequence was the transfer of physical control over the remaining aldeias to 'lay captains' for the next few years (*c.* 1564–*c.* 1572). This change was favoured by the General of the Jesuit Order in Rome who had never cared for the deep Jesuit involvement in the day-to-day administration of the aldeias. In practical terms, the result was to create a type of *repartimiento* of Indian labour (earlier rejected by Nóbrega) in order to ration their services among Portuguese claimants. At the same time the famine that followed the plague prompted many Indians to sell themselves or their relatives to the settlers for food or maintenance. These developments forced the crown and the Jesuits to focus their attention on fundamental questions about the Indian population in colonial Brazil. Many ambiguous questions left unanswered for years now came to the fore: under exactly what condition could Indians be 'justly' enslaved, if they could be enslaved at all? How were runaway Indians (both from aldeias as well as from sugar mills) to be treated? Could Indians legally sell themselves or their relatives into slavery?

The debate may be said to have begun in 1566 with the Junta charged by the king to make recommendations about Indian policy in Brazil. Mem de Sá, bishop Leitão, the Jesuits Grã and Azevedo as well as the crown judges (*ouvidores mores*) participated.[16] On the basis of recommendations hammered out by this Junta, King Sebastião (1554–78) enacted a law in 1570 on the status of the Indians. Born free, they could, nonetheless, be enslaved in two situations: (1) in the course of a 'just war' declared by the king or his governor; (2) if caught practising cannibalism. The system of *resgate* – the early practise of rescuing or ransoming Indians taken as captives in inter-tribal wars and about to be killed and forcing upon them in return a lifetime of servitude to the ransomer – was declared illegal. It had been widely abused: tribes were incited to fight one another for captives and soon any Indian seized and enslaved by the Portuguese was nominally 'ransomed'. Though King Sebastião's law could be, and was, interpreted very liberally, the settlers still sent violent protests to Lisbon, as the Peruvians had done after the New Laws of 1542. The law of 1570 was therefore revoked and replaced in 1574 by a modified code of Indian enslavement. Resgates were again permitted, but all Indians so enslaved had to be registered with the *alfândega* (custom house).

However, the final achievement of a *modus vivendi* with the Indian population came not so much from laws issued in Lisbon as from changes and developments in colonial society itself. Of these the most important was the increasing number of black slaves imported from Africa. When the first African slaves arrived in Brazil is unknown; a few were probably brought over by settlers in the early donatarial period. By the early 1540s it is clear that there were sizeable groups of them. In 1570 an early historian of Brazil, Magalhães de Gândavo, estimated that there were between 2,000 and 3,000 blacks in Brazil; seventeen years later, José de Anchieta put their number at 14,000. Though, on certain estates, Indian slaves still outnumbered Africans at the end of the century, the growing reliance on black slaves – about whom there were few if any moral qualms and no royal legislation – defused to a large degree the issue of Indian slavery. On the other hand, the years of attack on Tupi society by the Jesuits, the governors and the settlers had left their mark; traditional Indian culture was disintegrating in the settled areas of the coast. The remnants either blended into a new proletariat of *mameluco* half-breeds or else fled to

---

[16] Nóbrega would have participated, but was then in São Vicente. He later expressed his written opinion in an *Apontamento*: Leite, *Nóvas páginas*, 120.

the interior, the only place in which they might hope to preserve their cultural identity. Distance did not, however, provide absolute security. By the end of the century, the earlier occasional *entradas* into the interior gradually took on the character of the organized slaving expeditions (*bandeiras*) that were to develop into one of the dominant themes of Brazilian history in the next century. With increasing frequency governors declared 'just wars' on Indians of the *sertão*, or backlands, and issued licences for resgates, as Father Vicente do Salvador graphically describes in his account of the governorship of Luís de Brito (1572–8):

…the governor gave the settlers the licences they requested to send *mamelucos* to the interior (*sertão*) to bring back Indians. [The slavers] did not go so confident of their eloquence that they neglected to take along many white and friendly Indian soldiers, with bows and arrows, whom they used to bring back the Indians by force if they did not come willingly and peaceably. But in most cases the word of the *mamelucos* who told them of the abundance of fish and shellfish that they lacked in the interior, and the freedom they would enjoy if they did not resist, was sufficient. With these tricks and some gifts of clothes and tools to the chiefs (*principais*) or articles of barter (*resgates*) that they gave to those who held Indians enslaved and about to be eaten, they wiped out whole villages. When they got within sight of the coast, they separated sons from fathers, brothers from sisters and even, at times, wives from husbands, some going to the *mameluco* captains, some to the outfitters, others to those who sought the licences, or to those who granted them, and all made use of them on their plantations, or else sold them, with the declaration, however, that they were Indians 'of conscience' and that they were only selling their services. But the purchasers branded them on the face for the first fault committed or attempted escape, saying that they had bought them and they were their captives. Preachers banged their pulpits over the matter, but they were preaching in the desert.[17]

In short, epidemic disease, enslavement and religious proselytization by the well-meaning Jesuits effectively shattered the defeated Indian culture and societies, leaving the survivors to be re-integrated into a colonial society structured on Portuguese terms.

The French, the other threat to Portuguese permanence in Brazil, presented none of the religious and moral complications associated with the Indians. Though French attacks on Portuguese shipping continued after 1535 (as the creation of a captain-major for the coast in 1548 indicates) the donatary captaincies did effectively prevent French

[17] Salvador, *História do Brasil*, 180–1.

attempts at colonization in areas settled by the Portuguese. Nevertheless, the French had not abandoned the idea of founding a colony, and their attention was increasingly drawn to one extraordinarily attractive site (long important in the dyewood trade) at the northern edge of the captaincy of São Vicente that had never been occupied by the Portuguese: Rio de Janeiro.

It was here that Nicolas Durand, chevalier de Villegagnon, decided to locate his colony of *France Antarctique*. Growing religious strife in France had by 1550 produced groups (as later in England) who saw the New World as the perfect location for a new commonwealth, based on 'right' religion and free from the corrupt entanglements of European society. For an ambitious entrepreneur like Villegagnon, born to a bourgeois family but risen to be vice-admiral of Brittany, these religious dissenters formed a heaven-sent nucleus of willing immigrants for his purpose. He presented his plan to Admiral Coligny, a member of the high nobility who had gone over to the Reformed Church, and the latter in turn solicited the support of the king, Henry II. With additional backing from Norman and Breton merchants who had long been trading in Brazilian dyewood, Villegagnon and company set off in 1555 on three ships carrying some 600 persons for *la France Antarctique*. Though Villegagnon gave the impression of having Protestant leanings while attempting to recruit his colonists, he was compelled to accept Catholics as well as Huguenots to complete his expedition and some ex-convicts as well. After a difficult voyage, the little group reached Guanabara Bay where it finally built a fort and small settlement on Serigipe Island. The local Indians proved friendly, due to the Frenchmen's indulgent treatment and lack of demands, but Villegagnon's strict rule created discontent among the colonists, many of whom deserted to the mainland where they founded Henryville on the site of present-day Rio de Janeiro. His position precarious and in danger of Portuguese attack, Villegagnon solicited a second levy of immigrants from Calvin in Geneva, among them Jean de Léry who has left us one of the best accounts of the colony as well as of Tupi culture in general. These new arrivals were the seeds of the settlement's final destruction. Straight from Geneva, dogmatic, rigid and imbued with Calvin's steely will, they soon propelled the group into theological disputes that came to focus on the nature of the Eucharist: for Léry and his co-religionists, the Catholics' adherence to transubstantiation in the midst of a society of savage cannibals was too much to swallow. Angered by the disruptive activities of the Calvinists whose resistance he was unable to break,

Villegagnon suddenly reverted to an orthodox Catholicism, abandoned the colony and sailed back to France in 1559, where he finished his days as a member of the ultra-Catholic party of the Guises.

Antarctic France presented Portuguese Brazil with a serious threat, a base from which the French could support Indian opponents, expand their control down to the Río de la Plata and possibly raid Portuguese shipping lanes to India. To counter this threat governor Mem de Sá, as soon as he had re-established order around Bahia, turned his attention to Rio. Receiving naval aid from Portugal he gathered together a force of Indian allies and departed for Guanabara Bay early in 1560. The island fortress was taken by assault and the surviving French forced to flee for shelter to the Indian villages about the bay. But Sá lacked the personnel and material necessary to rebuild and occupy the fort, so it was abandoned, much to the concern of Nóbrega who sensed the importance of a permanent Portuguese presence there. As he feared, once the Portuguese left, the French survivors re-established themselves on various islands in the bay and a second expedition was required to dislodge them.

This second attack was led by Estácio de Sá, Mem de Sá's nephew, who arrived in Bahia in 1563 at the head of another fleet sent out from Portugal. Gathering together local reinforcements from Espírito Santo as well as São Vicente, Estácio sailed to Rio in 1565 where he first established a military base – the germ of the future city of Rio de Janeiro – at the foot of Sugarloaf Mountain. His position was strong enough to repel French attempts to dislodge him, but insufficient to take the offensive until additional reinforcements from Lisbon arrived under the command of Christóvão de Barros, the son of António Cardoso de Barros, donatary of the abandoned captaincy of Piauí and subsequently first *provedor-mor* of the crown in Brazil. As soon as Barros arrived, Estácio attacked the French on the west side of the bay (now Praia do Flamengo) with complete success. Sá was wounded in battle and died a few days later, but his uncle Mem de Sá now took the time to establish a permanent Portuguese settlement on the site of present-day Rio. Town officials were appointed, the bay and surrounding region separated from São Vicente and the area converted into the second royal captaincy in Brazil. With the appointment of Salvador Corréia de Sá, another nephew of Mem de Sá, as royal governor, there began the long and intimate association between Rio and the Sá family that was to last throughout most of the colonial period.

SOCIETY AND ECONOMY C. 1580

The end of Mem de Sá's heroic governorship (1572) brought Brazil's years of uncertainty to a close. Having survived two challenges to its continued existence – internally from native Indian resistance and externally from the threat of French conquest – Portugal's American 'conquest' had emerged intact from its precarious infancy. While neither problem completely disappeared (the French still attempted from time to time to establish colonies in sparsely settled areas and Indian resistance merely shifted to the interior), still, after 1580, neither was ever again strong enough to call into question the existence of a Portuguese Brazil.

Freed from these preoccupations the colony entered its first major economic 'cycle', based on the expanding sugar industry with its attendant population growth as well as social and administrative development. This shift from a concern with survival to concentration on consolidation and growth is clearly reflected in the historical sources. The first 70 years of Brazilian history provide little data that can be interpreted statistically. Rather, the story depends on a precise narration of events, descriptions of the institutions created and inferences regarding royal policy. But from 1570 on, our knowledge of the colony is greatly enriched by the appearance of a series of descriptive treatises written principally to excite interest in settling the new land. Used with caution and a tolerance for the inexactitude with which they were composed, they not only offer us our best information on the vicissitudes of the early settlements but also provide significant statistical information: i.e., rough estimates, captaincy by captaincy, of the Portuguese population plus occasional, less exact, estimates of Indians and Africans; and approximate figures for the number of *engenhos* (sugar mills) in each captaincy (see Table 1).[18] A rapid glance at the population figures indicates that of the eight settled captaincies, three – Pernambuco, Bahia and Rio de Janeiro – were growing, while the rest were in various stages of decline – Porto Seguro, Itamaracá and São Vicente rather rapidly; Ilhéus and Espírito Santo more gradually. The remaining captaincies had effectively been abandoned. How had these varying fortunes come about?

[18] Whilst, strictly speaking, the word *engenho* referred only to the mill for grinding the sugar cane, the term came to be applied to the whole economic unit: the mill itself, the associated buildings, the cane fields, pastures, slave quarters, estate house, etc. The term 'plantation' was never used by the Portuguese or Spaniards of this period.

Table 1 *Colonial Brazil: White Population and Engenhos, 1570 and c. 1585*

Captaincy (main towns)	1570 white population*	engenhos	c. 1585 white population*	engenhos
Itamaracá (Conceição)	600 (2.9%)	1 (1.7%)	300 (1.0%)	3 (2.5%)
Pernambuco (Olinda, Igaraçú)	6,000 (28.9%)	23 (38.3%)	12,000 (41.0%)	66 (55.0%)
Bahia (Salvador, Vila Velha)	6,600 (31.8%)	18 (30.0%)	12,000 (41.0%)	36 (30.0%)
Ilhéus (São Jorge)	1,200 (5.8%)	8 (13.3%)	900 (3.0%)	3 (2.5%)
Porto Seguro (P. Seguro, Santa Cruz, Santo Amaro)	1,320 (6.4%)	5 (8.3%)	600 (2.0%)	1 (1.0%)
Espírito Santo (Vitória, Vila Velha)	1,200 (5.8%)	1 (1.7%)	900 (3.0%)	5 (4.0%)
Rio de Janeiro (São Sebastião)	840 (4.0%)	0 —	900 (3.0%)	3 (2.5%)
São Vicente (São Vicente, Santos, Santo Amaro, Itanháem, São Paulo)	3,000 (14.4%)	4 (6.7%)	1,800 (6.0%)	3 (2.5%)
Totals	20,760 (100)	60 (100)	29,400 (100)	120 (100)

Sources: Pero de Magalhães Gândova, *Tratado da terra do Brasil e história da província de Santo Cruz* (*c.* 1570); Fernão Cardim, *Informação da província do Brasil para nosso padre* (1583); Fernão Cardim, *Narrativa Epistolar* (1583); José de Anchieta, *Informação do Brasil e de suas capitanias* (1584); Gabriel Soares de Sousa, *Tratado descriptivo do Brasil em 1587.*
* Calculated on the basis of six persons per household (*fogo*).

Espírito Santo, granted to Vasco Fernandes Coutinho, an old India hand and comrade of Duarte Coelho, had prospered in the beginning and some four sugar mills were in operation by 1540. But at this point, for reasons not entirely clear, the donatary decided to return to Portugal, leaving his colony in charge of subordinates who proved unable to hold out against the wave of Indian attacks that struck in the mid-1540s (native Tupi allied to the fierce Tapuia Goiticazes who had already wiped out São Tomé). When he finally managed to return, Coutinho found little more than one small surviving settlement in a state of constant siege. Old, ill and now impoverished, he was incapable of remedying the situation. The colony led a bare existence until 1560 when Mem de Sá, the new governor, decided to send his son, Fernão, with six ships and 200 men to subdue the Indians and incorporate the captaincy into the crown. Fernão lost his life in the struggle, but his cousin, Baltasar de Sá, continued the campaign and pacified the region. Although the colony never seemed able to attract many settlers (indeed its population declined some 25 per cent between 1570 and 1585), its sugar industry was expanding rapidly and by the 1580s the settlers who remained enjoyed one of the highest per capita incomes in Brazil.

Immediately to the north, the captaincy of Porto Seguro, granted to Pero do Campo Tourinho, an accomplished seamen from Viana do Castelo, had begun in a promising fashion. Nonetheless, it too succumbed to the general crisis of the 1540s which took the form here of a 'palace coup' over the question of the donatary's orthodoxy. Unpopular among the settlers, Tourinho was accused of heresy and blasphemy by a cabal of clerics and was soon hustled off to Lisbon (1546) to stand trial before the Inquisition. Though absolved, he never returned to Brazil. His colony was thenceforth administered by royal agents. After his death in 1556, it passed to his son Fernão, and then to his daughter, Leonor. She was granted a royal licence to sell it to the first duke of Aveiro who already had a sugar mill there; he converted it into an entail for the second sons of his house. In the process of further developing the sugar industry, however, Aveiro's agents exterminated or drove out most of the native Tupi, thus exposing the area to the incursions of the far more fearsome Tapuia Aimorés. They so terrorized the colony that only one mill was left standing by 1585 and two (Santo Amaro and Santa Cruz) of the three towns that had been established were virtually emptied of settlers.

Located between Porto Seguro and Bahia, Ilhéus also had an auspicious beginning, though the donatary, Jorge de Figueiredo Correia, secretary of the Treasury (*escrivão da fazenda*) never bothered to visit his grant in person. Rather he ran it through a Castilian agent, Francisco Romero. Although not above criticism, Romero did establish effective relations with the Tupi and even secured their aid in the construction of a number of sugar mills. After Correia's death in 1552, his heirs sold the captaincy (1561) to a merchant capitalist of Lisbon, Lucas Giraldi, who already possessed a land grant (*sesmaria*) in the colony. In spite of a sequence of events similar to that of neighbouring Porto Seguro (destruction of the Tupi tribes opening the way to attacks by the Aimoré who drove out many of the settlers), the sugar industry managed to survive on the offshore islands of Tinharé and Boipeba at the northern edge of the colony. Thus, in 1587 Gabriel Soares de Sousa could still call it a land 'rich in sugar'.

At the southern extremity of effective Portuguese settlement (the captaincy of Santana having gone unoccupied), São Vicente, along with its enclave of Santo Amaro, rode out the crisis of the mid 1540s virtually unscathed. Though it was never revisited by its captain, Martim Afonso de Sousa, after his epoch-making expedition of 1530–3, the colony made good progress under the administration of a sequence of capable lieutenants, including Brás Cubas, the founder of Santos (1543). In 1548 Luís de Góis was able to describe it to the king with pride, mentioning a population of 600 Portuguese, some 3,000 slaves and six sugar mills. From then on, however, expansion slowed down. São Vicente was farthest of all the settlements from Europe and was located in a harsher climate less suited to sugar cultivation. As a result its economy came to be increasingly oriented towards the interior settlement of São Paulo, the centre of a territory of wheat, barley and vineyards that soon became the principal base for slaving expeditions into the interior. The resulting decline in the export sector and contraction of the economy, plus a tendency towards quasi-subsistence agriculture produced an accompanying decline in both population and wealth. Beginning to be overshadowed by Pernambuco as well as the revitalized Bahia, its earlier success was still apparent in 1570. Fifteen years later, however, its population had dropped almost by half and its revenue value to the crown was no more than that of the fledgling colony of Rio de Janeiro, which after the expulsion of the French in 1565, blossomed under royal solicitude and a series of capable royal captains from the Sá family.

In contrast to these areas of settlement which, apart from Rio de Janeiro, were either declining or barely holding their own, the last quarter of the century was for Bahia and Pernambuco a period of unqualified success: these captaincies were to become the focal points of Brazil in the next century.

Bahia was settled in 1535 by Francisco Pereira Coutinho, an old warrior from the Orient where he had served as captain of Goa. The Bay of All Saints was already the home of Caramurú, a Portuguese castaway who, along with several others, had found a ready welcome among the uxorilocal Tupi of the coast. Thus Coutinho had expert assistance, at least in the beginning, in establishing good relations with the Indians of the region. The next year (1536) he was at work constructing his capital of Vila Pereira and by 1545 had managed to build two sugar mills (*engenhos*). Nonetheless, his northern neighbour, Duarte Coelho, described him as too old and ill to maintain the discipline necessary for an effective colony. And when the crisis of the mid 1540s struck Bahia, the colony succumbed; many of the settlers fled to Ilhéus in 1545. Coutinho joined them, only to be lured back to Bahia by the Indians and treacherously killed in 1547. The collapse of Bahia, exposing an important anchorage to French attack, was one of the most important reasons why it was decided to establish a royal administration there. And after 1549, Bahia's history becomes, in effect, that of the royal administration in Brazil. With royal support and organization, Bahia was rebuilt; by 1585 it had sufficient population (12,000 whites) to support nine parishes and 36 sugar mills.

Even more impressive than the resurrected Bahia was Pernambuco. Along with its satellite colony of Itamaracá, it marked the northern limit of effective Portuguese settlement before 1580. (Paraíba was not occupied until the 1580s, Río Grande do Norte in the 1590s: the northern coast remained to be conquered early in the seventeenth century.) Arriving in Pernambuco in person in March of 1535 with a host of followers, Duarte Coelho optimistically dubbed his grant 'New Lusitania' and built his first settlement near the site of the earlier royal factory. Subsequently Coelho scouted his territory for a more central location which he found at Olinda in 1537. There he constructed a tower for defence in case of siege, along with other essential buildings, and then made a tour (almost a royal 'progress') through his captaincy to expel any French interlopers he might find and to pacify the Caeté Indians of the area. His policy towards the Indians was a firm one, and he controlled them, as Vicente do Salvador put it, echoing Machiavelli, 'more through fear than good will'. What made this policy work, one suspects, was his equally firm control of the Portuguese colonists, the other facet of his outstandingly successful policy. The crisis of the mid-1540s did not damage Pernambuco, and this was crucial for its survival and prosperity. By 1546 five sugar mills had been built (compared to two in Bahia and six in São Vicente by that time) and more were under construction. When Coelho died in 1554, he bequeathed his two sons the best established colony in Brazil – so well established, in fact, that it was exempted from interference by the royal governor who had recently arrived in Bahia. In 1570 Pernambuco rivalled Bahia as the leading settlement; by 1585 it had clearly moved ahead, at least economically, with a per capita income almost double that of the governor's seat. Indeed the opulence of Pernambuco society was legend: when the lords of the sugar mills (*senhores do engenho*) came to town they were surrounded by a multitude of retainers, both Indian and African. They dined on foodstuffs imported from Portugal (wheat bread, olive oil and wine) instead of the native diet of manioc flour, palm oil and rum that was the lot of the ordinary settler, and they prided themselves on the conspicuous consumption, not to mention gaudy dress, of their women. It was, in fact, the possibility (or at least the belief in the possibility) of attaining a like opulence that constituted one of the main attractions for most of the immigrants who arrived during the last quarter of the century.

The majority of those immigrants were naturally Portuguese, but other Europeans, mainly Italian, could also be found in Brazil. And in contrast to the fifteenth century, when the Atlantic islands seem to have drawn the bulk of their population from the southern province of the Algarve, the majority of Portuguese emigrants to Brazil in the sixteenth century came from the populous northern province of the Minho as well as from the hinterland of Lisbon, which had by now supplanted the Algarve as the hub of the empire.[19] These immigrants joined some sixteen or seventeen fledgling settlements scattered along the vast eastern coast of Brazil (São Paulo alone was situated inland). Each captaincy had at least one main town and some also included several satellite communities, though in the declining captaincies these were shrinking (e.g., Santa Cruz and Santo Amaro in Porto Seguro). Most of these towns had been set up by the first donatary, as provided in his charter. He granted town lots to each settler with land to cultivate (*sesmarias*) in the surrounding territory (*termino*) – a replica of the system used to populate the reconquered areas of southern Portugal in the later Middle Ages. The captain usually had the power to nominate the members of the town council, at least in the beginning. Thereafter, according to the royal Ordinances, the councillors (in form at least) were

[19] Orlando Ribeiro, *Aspectos e problemas da expansão Portuguesa* (Lisbon, 1955), 24–7.

to be elected by the propertied citizenry (*vizinhos*), though the captain's right to supervise the process probably meant that his influence still predominated. In the crown captaincies (Bahia, Rio de Janeiro) municipal officers were almost always direct royal appointments.

Each colonial town drew most of its food as well as domestic labour from the surrounding pacified and (at least superficially) Christianized Indian villages (*aldeias*) whose existence was carefully noted by most of the writers as one of the captaincy's main forms of wealth. Colonists who did not live permanently in the towns were to be found on the sugar estates, small communities in themselves, where the lord (*senhor*) of the 'mill' (*engenho*) was surrounded by and ruled over his workers, free and slave, Indians and blacks who were being imported in increasing numbers from Africa. As the productive centres of the colony these estates were more significant than the towns and tended to overshadow them. It is revealing for example that clerics attached to the chapel of an estate were invariably better paid than those serving the town churches. Indeed, the growth in the number of sugar estates in a captaincy is probably a better indication of its 'success' than a growing population in the towns, for without the engenhos there would be little reason for the settlers to come or stay.

From 1570 to 1585 the white population grew from approximately 20,760 to some 29,400 (see Table 1), or at a rate of roughly 2.7 per cent a year. During the same period the number of engenhos doubled, from 60 to 120, thus increasing at a rate of 6.6 per cent per year.

Thus began the late sixteenth-century sugar boom and the rapid growth in per capita income of whites in Brazil. The principal source of revenue to the crown, the royal tithes, a 10 per cent levy on whatever the land produced – sugar, manioc, bananas, potatoes, sheep, goats, pigs, chickens, etc. – and theoretically (but not always in practice) intended for the support of the church, enables us (1) to estimate the gross product (minus services) of the Christianized (or colonial) economy, in addition to (2) the per capital income of the colonial population, captaincy by captaincy, as well as (3) of Brazil as a whole. Table 2, based on the royal tithe of 1593, indicates the gross product captaincy by captaincy, and Table 3 the average (white) per capita income (in milreis) by captaincy (except for Itamaracá, for which the data is inadequate).

These figures confirm all contemporary accounts of the colony which describe Pernambuco as by far the richest of the captaincies while

Table 2 *Colonial Brazil: Gross Product, 1593**
(in milréis)

Itamaracá	10,600$000	5%
Pernambuco	116,000$000	56%
Bahia	56,000$000	27%
Ilhéus	6,670$000	3.2%
Porto Seguro	1,800$000	<1%
Espírito Santo	6,000$000	2.9%
Rio de Janeiro	5,000$000	2.4%
São Vicente	5,000$000	2.4%
Paraiba	1,400$000	<1%
Total	208,470$000	100

* Calculated on the basis of royal tithes from the production (services omitted) of the 'Christian' sector of the economy.
Source: Francisco Carneiro, 'Relação de todas as rendas da coroa deste reyno de Portugal que nelle se arracadão de que procedem, modo, e lugar em que se pagão', ed. Francisco Mendes da Luz, *Boletim da Biblioteca da Universidade de Coimbra* (1949), 101–2.

Table 3 *Colonial Brazil: Average (white) per capita income in 1593*
(in milréis)

1. Pernambuco	9$660
2. Ilhéus	7$410
3. Espírito Santo	6$660
4. Rio de Janeiro	5$550
5. Bahia	4$660
6. Porto Seguro	3$000
7. São Vicente	2$770
Average	6$750

Source: see Table 2.

putting São Vicente logically last due to the low average income of the population in the inland settlement of São Paulo. At the top end of the scale, Mem de Sá's yearly salary as governor from 1557–72 was 600$000 and Fernão Cardim reported that 'more than 100' sugar-mill owners in Pernambuco had incomes of some 2,000$000 per year.

In contrast to the rapid growth in real income experienced by many of the settlers in the last quarter of the sixteenth century, the Portuguese crown seems to have shared far less in Brazil's development. Using data

on royal income assembled by the historian Vitorino Magalhães
Godinho, it is possible to estimate that Brazil, as a whole, provided some
1 per cent of the crown's income near the beginning of the century
(1506), compared to some 27 per cent coming from India at the same
time. Eighty-two years later, in 1588, Brazil still accounted for no more
than 2.35–2.5 per cent of the crown revenues, while India was still
furnishing about 26 per cent.[20] If the cost of maintaining control over
the Brazilian coast, as well as the expenditures necessary to reduce the
Indians to submission and drive out the French, are taken into account,
there must have been a deficit for long periods of time.

Thus, it is difficult to accept purely economic explanations either for
the crown's tenacious commitment to Brazil during the sixteenth
century or for its progression through four stages of ever-increasing
involvement: from leasing out the land (1502–5), to exploiting it
directly through royal trading factories (1506–34), to granting it out to
proprietary lords for settlement (1534), finally culminating in the
creation of a fully-fledged royal administration (1549). Instead, these
stages are more convincingly seen as so many necessary responses to
perceived threats of territorial loss. Once Brazil had been incorporated
into the Portuguese crown, it was not easily abandoned, however great
the burden. The royal attitude was well summed up by João de Barros,
historian of empire and donatary of Maranhão, in his *Decadas*,

...for a prince who prides himself on leaving a reputation of having done
glorious deeds, nothing, not even increasing the revenues of his kingdom nor
constructing great and magnificent buildings, can be compared to augmenting
the Crown of his kingdom or adding some new title to his Estate.[21]

Fundamentally seigneurial in its attitudes, the Portuguese crown found
its Brazilian rewards, at least in the sixteenth century, not in the
economic realm but rather in that of status and prestige. Indeed,
considering Portugal's record over the entire period, what strikes the
historian is not any 'neglect' of Brazil with which it has so often been
charged, but rather the tenacity with which this small European country
held on to its possession in the New World whose ultimate value was
so largely unknown, when its main colonial effort was being made in
India and the Far East.

[20] V. M. Godinho, *Ensáios II* (Lisbon, 1958), 57, 65–7. In 1593, Francisco Carneiro calculated that
Brazil contributed some 3.3 per cent of crown revenue (F. Carneiro, 'Relação de todas as rendas
da coroa deste reyno de Portugal que nelle se arracadão de que procedem, modo, e lugar em
que se pagão', ed. F. Mendes da Luz, *Boletim da Biblioteca da Universida de Coimbra* (1949), 53,
101.

[21] João de Barros, *Asia, primeira decada*, ed. António Baião (Coimbra, 1932), 216.

2

POLITICAL AND ECONOMIC
STRUCTURES OF EMPIRE, 1580–1750

Portugal in the sixteenth century was in the first place, to use João Lúcio de Azevedo's term, an 'agrarian monarchy'. Land, its major asset, was largely held in the form of the great manorial estate. The king himself was a landowner – *unus inter pares*. He could retract land grants made in the past. Moreover, lands bestowed by him could devolve only on the eldest legitimate son. These measures maintained the cohesion of the great estates and ensured the obedience to the king of their titular owners.

At the same time Portugal has also been called a 'maritime monarchy'. Endowed with a relatively long oceanic seaboard, Portugal had in the late Middle Ages made use of the sea for both coastal trading and long-distance voyages. Fishing was a significant resource and extended beyond the coastal waters as far as Newfoundland. The salt marshes of Aveiro, Lisbon and Setubal supplied not only Portuguese needs but also those of ships from the Mediterranean sailing to northern Europe and the Baltic. Thus was Portugal able to maintain a larger population than if she had merely depended on her agriculture and the export of corn. After the Great Discoveries in the fifteenth century the Atlantic island colonies – Madeira and the Azores – and the trading stations of Morocco, the Cape Verde islands and the Guinea coast brought products such as timber, sugar and wine to Portugal for re-export to Europe. Then gold from Guinea, spices from India and first brazilwood and, later, sugar from Brazil transformed the Portuguese economy.

The economic and social structure created by these developments was dominated by the merchant-king who possessed the monopoly of trade. As circumstances dictated he reserved it for himself or farmed it out,

* Translated from the French by Mrs Elizabeth Edwards; translation revised by Cynthia Postan; chapter reduced in length and partly reorganized by the Editor.

granting licences to private Portuguese or foreign merchants (*contra-tadores*) whom he was content to supervise. By the sixteenth century he was represented by agents in Antwerp and throughout his expanding maritime empire. Many foreign merchants, particularly Spaniards, Italians and Germans, were also established in Lisbon. The Spaniards were predominantly New Christians who had come to Portugal when the Jews and the Moors were expelled from Spain in 1492, a fortunate event for Portugal since for two centuries they were to form the backbone of the Portuguese trading class in Europe and overseas. The great landowners who composed the Portuguese nobility seemed more interested in colonial expansion because they needed land for their younger sons, although they did not hesitate to engage in trade. Overseas, first in the Atlantic islands, then in Brazil, the younger sons, titular incumbants of *sesmarias* (land grants) or even of *capitanias* (captaincies) became producers and exporters of agricultural products, of sugar in particular.

The social structure of Portugal was unlike any other in Europe not only because of the important part played by the king in the economy and the lack of a 'national bourgeoisie' in the accepted sense of the term but also because, as Albert Silbert has pointed out, Portugal had not experienced the feudal system. Apart from the fact that the 'property of the crown' was a much more important part of the economic power of the high and middle-ranking nobility than any patrimonial inheritance, the king had never surrendered his rights and powers (*direitos reais*) in the field of justice. Nor was the organization of military service founded on the feudal tie: it had always been both general and remunerated. The Portuguese crown also gained strength from its religious and cultural role. The king, for example, enjoyed considerable powers of patronage (*padroado real*), that is to say, the right to nominate candidates for ecclesiastical benefices, to present them, if priests, for the approbation of the bishop, or, if bishops, for the approval of the pope, at least in his overseas possessions. In addition, the king played a major part in the *Reconquista* and, after the death of King Sebastian at Alcacer Quibir in 1578, the myth of the Crusader King who had sacrificed himself for the Faith became a powerful element in the charisma attaching to the monarchy.

The financial position of the Portuguese crown was also relatively strong. The king derived his income from two sources, the traditional and the colonial, and the latter, of course, increased considerably in the fifteenth and sixteenth centuries. During the early decades of the sixteenth century receipts from colonial trade represented 65–70 per cent of the total revenues of the state. In turn, colonial trade stimulated agriculture and the economy of the towns and coastal regions of Portugal and further increased the fiscal revenue of the crown. In the early decades of its settlement Brazil made an insignificant contribution to royal income (less than 2 per cent compared with India's 26–27 per cent). But with the beginnings of the great sugar cycle in the 1570s and 1580s Brazil and especially Bahia and Pernambuco became and remained one of the keystones of the Portuguese empire.[1]

PORTUGAL AND BRAZIL, 1580–c. 1695

Any description of the administration of the world-wide Portuguese empire, including Brazil, from the late sixteenth to the late seventeenth century is complicated by the fact that Portugal was united with Spain in a dual monarchy during the first half of this period. In 1580 Philip II of Spain, nephew of João III (1521–57), became Philip I of Portugal. He was succeeded by Philip III (Philip II of Portugal) in 1598 and by Philip IV (Philip III of Portugal) in 1621. Only in 1640 did the Portuguese successfully revolt against Habsburg rule and proclaim the duke of Braganza João IV. During the union of the two monarchies, the Spanish Habsburgs on the whole respected the pledges made at Thomar in 1581 to allow considerable Portuguese autonomy and to maintain the two empires as separate entities. Public offices were reserved for Portuguese subjects at home and overseas. The king was represented at Lisbon sometimes by a 'governor' and sometimes by a viceroy. Important matters, however, were referred to Madrid, where they came before the Council of Portugal (which met in the same premises as a *Junta da Fazenda de Portugal*). And at least from 1631 one of the three Secretaries of State belonging to the Council bore the title of 'Secretary of State for India and the Conquered Territories'. Moreover, a commission of jurists set up to reform the legal system produced a new code for Portugal, the *Ordenações filipinas*, promulgated in 1603.

In Lisbon there was a Council of State without clearly defined administrative powers, and the Spanish kings maintained the system of two secretaries of state, one for the kingdom and the other for 'India',

---

[1] For a discussion of the early settlement of Brazil 1500–80, see ch. 1 above.

that is to say, for the colonies, despite several conflicts over jurisdiction, until the creation of the *Conselho da India* in 1604. In the same way they retained the *Mesa de Consciencia e Ordens*, which was both tribunal and council for religious affairs and was responsible for administering ecclesiastical appointments and for the property of the military orders in the colonies as well as in the mother country. Also preserved was the *Desembargo do Paço*, the supreme tribunal of the kingdom and of the empire, which on occasions advised the king on political and economic as well as judicial matters, and the court of appeal, the *Casa de Suplicação*.

Under Philip I (Philip II of Spain) in 1591 the four *Vedores da Fazenda* (overseers of the Treasury) were replaced by a *Conselho da Fazenda* composed of one Vedor da Fazenda presiding over four councillors (two of them lawyers) and four secretaries. One of the secretaries was responsible for colonial affairs, which occupied an important place in the deliberations of the council. Its meetings were frequent – every morning and twice a week in the afternoon as well. Moreover, from 1623 onwards, an additional afternoon each week was devoted solely to colonial affairs. From 1604 the newly created Conselho da India was invested with powers for all overseas affairs, apart from matters concerning Madeira, the Azores and the strongholds of Morocco. Colonial officials were appointed and their despatches handled by it. However, it was the Conselho da Fazenda which dealt with naval expeditions, the buying and selling of pepper and the collection of the royal revenues, in fact with all economic business. The Conselho da India, therefore, exercised only limited powers. As a creation of the Spanish king it was regarded with disfavour by the Portuguese and because of the jealousy of the Mesa da Consciencia disappeared in 1614.

After the Restoration, João IV preserved most of the administrative institutions which he found in existence on ascending to the throne and ratified the *Ordenações filipinas*. However, in the realm of finance, the king reverted to the former system of Vedores da Fazenda, while the Conselho da Fazenda appears to have continued only as a tribunal. A single Secretary of State was retained, but inspired by the Conselho da India (1604–14), the king created in 1642 a *Conselho Ultramarino* (Overseas Council). It was composed of a president, the *Vedor da Fazenda da repartição da India*, several councillors, a lawyer and a secretary. From November 1645 the council met on Mondays, Tuesdays and Wednesdays to discuss the business of India, on Thursdays and Fridays for Brazil and on Saturdays for the affairs of the other colonies, although Madeira and the Azores were outside its jurisdiction. There were inevitable conflicts over jurisdiction between the overseas council and the other councils.

In sixteenth-century Lisbon the major government offices, apart from the customs house (*alfandega*), primarily concerned with fiscal matters were the Casa da India and the *Casa da Guiné e da Mina*. Established on the river-bank at the western end of the present Terreiro do Paço, they occupied the ground-floor of the royal palace. Both were under the control of the same director and three treasurers, one for spices, one for the revenue from spices and the third for remaining business. Five secretaries shared the administrative work between them – three for the Casa da India and two for the Casa da Guiné. The Casas collected certain dues, ratified contracts with traders and explorers on behalf of the king, organized the fleet, supervised the loading and unloading of vessels and acted for the king in all the tasks which were necessary for the development of the colonies. A *factor* was in touch with *factores* in all the Portuguese trading-stations in the world. With them he conducted the business of the 'merchant-king' and from them he learned what merchandise the king and his subjects had at their disposal and what method of payment could be used. Lastly he kept a register of all the Portuguese ships which had set out from Lisbon and of the cargoes and passengers which they conveyed. During the union with Spain the *factor* was replaced by a *provedor* and the two Casas were fused into a single Casa da India, which from 1591 onwards came under the authority of the Conselho da Fazenda. In the seventeenth century the fiscal role of the Casa became relatively more important. Quite separate from the Casa da India, the *Armazem* (or *Armazens* – general stores or depot) *da Guiné e Indias* was in charge of all nautical matters, such as the construction and fitting of ships, the training of pilots and the issue of marine charts, master-copies of which were preserved by the depot itself. The naval dockyards came under its authority. The crews of the king's ships were appointed by the *provedor dos Armazens*, but they had to be registered with the Casa. Expenditure incurred by the Armazens, as for the purchase of materials or settlement of accounts, was defrayed by the treasurer of the Casa.

The colonial territories were lands belonging to the crown or to the crown's beneficiaries. In Brazil where royal government had been established in 1549 the first governor, Tomé de Sousa (1549–53), exercised authority over the settled areas of the country from Salvador da Bahia and was represented in each captaincy, either by a donatary captain or, if the captaincy had been redeemed by the monarchy, by a captain-general (sometimes a governor). The powers of Brazil's governor (sometimes styled governor-general) had been defined by the *regimentos* (standing instructions) of 1549. Like their Spanish counterparts, they might be subjected to an inspection (*visita*) during their tour of duty and to a final inspection (*residencia*) at the end of it. The governors-general, always drawn from the Portuguese nobility, but, at least from 1640, with some administrative experience, remained at their postings on average for six and a half years in the sixteenth century, for three and a half years in the seventeenth century and for a little less than six years in the eighteenth century. Many captains-general, the majority of whom were army officers, spent twenty or even 30 years in Brazil, changing from one post to another.

The authority of the governor-general gradually diminished as the Portuguese in the last decades of the sixteenth and the first half of the seventeenth centuries penetrated the interior of Brazil and expanded on the northern and southern extremities of the colony far beyond the line of Tordesillas, and as successive changes in the administrative structure of the colony were imposed from Lisbon.[2] The Portuguese, for example, with Spanish assistance, expanded north in the 1580s from Pernambuco into Paraíba at the expense of the French and the Indians – and later into Ceará. In 1614–15 they removed from Maranhão a French expedition under Sieur de la Ravardière which had arrived there in 1612. The Portuguese then moved to Pará and founded Belém at the mouth of the Amazon in 1616, although for more than a decade the occupation of the lower Amazon continued to be disputed by the French, the English, the Dutch and the Spanish. The captaincies of the south – Espírito Santo, Rio de Janeiro and São Vicente – were twice detached from Bahia (1572–8 and 1608–13) and administered separately. Even more significantly, in 1621 a separate *Estado do Maranhão* was formed from the recently established crown captaincies of Ceará, Maranhão and Pará and a number of small private captaincies, with its own governor-general in São Luís do Maranhão. There were sound geographical reasons for this division of Brazil: it was easier to travel from São Luís or Belém to Lisbon than to Bahia. The rest of Brazil, the crown captaincies from Rio Grande do Norte to São Vicente in the

---

[2] For a discussion of the territorial expansion of Brazil from the late sixteenth century, see chs. 3 and 4 below.

south and the remaining private captaincies, was now called the *Estado do Brasil*.

In 1652 the Estado do Maranhão was reunited with the Estado do Brasil, but separated once more two years later, and in 1656 Ceará was permanently transferred to the Estado do Brasil. In 1715 Piauí became a crown captaincy within the Estado do Maranhão, and in 1737 the capital was transferred from São Luís to Belém. Within the Estado do Brasil, after the recovery of Pernambuco from the Dutch in 1654 (see below) the new captain-general was concerned to assert his autonomy in relation to the governor-general in Bahia. Moreover, a conflict broke out between Salvador de Sá, who had been appointed governor and captain-general of the captaincies of the south, and the governor-general to decide which of them had authority over the captaincy of Espírito Santo. A viceroy had first been appointed in 1640–1, but the title had subsequently disappeared. The post was revived in 1663 in the person of Dom Vasco de Mascarenhas, count of Obidos, the king's nephew. He demanded that no royal decree should be executed in any captaincy without having been first passed by himself, and he sent a *regimento* to all the captains-general which redefined their duties and reminded them that they were subordinate to Bahia and to no other authority. There was a reminder also to the governors of Pernambuco and Rio de Janeiro of the exact limits of their powers. The governor of Rio deferred, at least on paper, but the governor of Pernambuco did not. In the late seventeenth and early eighteenth centuries there was a process of regrouping captaincies: those of medium size became subordinate captaincies and their captains-general were placed under the authority of their most important colleagues, who acquired the title of 'governor and captain-general' and administered a captaincy-general (Rio 1698, São Paulo 1709, Pernambuco 1715). The office of governor-general at Bahia appears to have been raised permanently to the rank of viceroy from 1720 onwards, but, although the viceroy henceforth enjoyed a higher stipend, he lost his powers over the internal administration of the captaincies-general, whose title holders dealt directly with Lisbon. Theoretically they remained subordinate but in fact the viceroy could intervene only in his own captaincy-general.

The original donatary captains of Brazil were assisted, in matters of justice, by *ouvidores* (crown judges) and in 1549 there arrived in Bahia, with the first governor, an *ouvidor-geral*. In 1588 the Spanish regime decided to set up in Bahia a *Relação* (High Court of Appeal) similar to the *Relação do Porto*, responsible for the north of Portugal, and the *Relação da India*. The magistrates sent to establish it were, however, thrown off course by winds and currents and their ship was finally discovered at Santo Domingo. The crown was unable to implement its plans for the establishment of the court until 1609. It was then suppressed in 1626, in part as an economy measure during the Dutch War (see below, p. 449) and was not restored until 1652. For the next century it remained Brazil's only high court. (Following the administrative division of Brazil into two estados in 1621, the Estado do Maranhão had remained directly responsible to the *Casa da Suplicação* in Lisbon.) *The Relação da Bahia* was presided over by the governor-general and was composed of a chancellor, three *desembargadores dos agravos* (high court judges), the *ouvidor-geral*, the *provedor-mor dos defuntos e residuos*, responsible for administering the property of deceased persons, and two *desembargadores extravagantes* (extraordinary judges). These crown judges were assisted by six secretaries, a doctor, a chaplain, an usher and a treasurer (*guarda mor*) charged with the collection of fines. The *ouvidores* continued to function in the captaincies as judges of the first instance, and they were often also *provedores de fazenda*, responsible for financial administration and collection of crown revenue.

The municipal organization of Salvador (Bahia) may be taken as typical of urban administration in Brazil. The first municipal council was created in 1549, at the time of the foundation of the city. The *mesa de vereação* was composed of three *vereadores* (councillors), two *juizes ordinarios* (elected magistrates) and a *procurador da cidade*, elected annually on a three-year basis, as in Portugal. After the Restoration (1640), at least in Bahia, the artisans of the city were represented by two *procuradores dos mesteres* and a *juiz do povo*. In 1696 the elective system was suppressed and it was the judges of the *Relação* who were responsible for choosing the municipal officers on the triennial rolls. The presidency of the municipal council was no longer assumed by each of the *vereadores* in turn but by a professional crown magistrate, the *juiz de fora* ('the judge from outside'). The appointment of ordinary judges was abolished and henceforward the *senado da câmara* was composed of the *juiz de fora*, three *vereadores* and the *procurador*. The secretary, or *escrivão da camara*, was, in practice, present and had a voice in the consultations. Although all these officers were paid by the crown, they preserved their freedom of speech in relation to the viceroy. The juiz do povo and the two *procuradores dos mesteres*, already objects of distrust, were finally suppressed by the king at the request of the *vereadores* in 1713. The *vereadores* appear to have been recruited almost invariably from among the *senhores de engenho* (sugar mill owners). However, the holders of office were often changed – an important difference from the *regidores* of Spanish America, whose responsibilities had come to be for life and were more or less hereditary.

For long periods during the second half of the sixteenth and the whole of the seventeenth centuries much of Europe was at war. Portugal and its empire was at first relatively secure, even after the union with Spain, although its shipping came under attack from Barbary corsairs in the Lisbon–Madeira–Azores triangle from the 1570s to the 1590s and, increasingly, from Dutch, English and French pirates around the turn of the century. However, with the end of the Twelve-Year Truce (1609–21), in the long and bitter struggle between the United Provinces and Spain, the newly founded Dutch West India Company looked on the Portuguese empire as a prime target for its military and naval operations. Salvador da Bahia was captured in 1624 and in March 1625 Salvador de Sá and Piet Heyn fought a battle off Espírito Santo. Bahia was recovered the following May by a joint Spanish and Portuguese fleet and expeditionary force led by Don Fadrique of Toledo. From March to June 1627 there were raids by Piet Heyn on the Brazilian coast after the Portuguese fleet was sunk in January in the Bay of Biscay. (In 1628 the same Piet Heyn captured the Spanish silver fleet at sea in the Caribbean.) The seizure of Recife by ships of the Dutch Company in 1630 marked a new stage in the conflict. It was the prelude to the conquest and occupation for a quarter of a century of the whole of the Brazilian north-east from the São Francisco river to Maranhão, including Pernambuco, one of the two most important sugar-producing captaincies. In 1637 the Dutch also occupied São Jorge da Mina on the West African coast. In 1638 a great Portuguese fleet under the command of conde da Torre left for Brazil but it was defeated by the Dutch off Itamaracá in 1640.

Portugal and Holland made peace in 1641 following the restoration of the Braganzas. But the war continued in Africa and Brazil, with the Dutch taking Luanda in August, Sergipe and Maranhão in November. In 1642 Maranhão revolted against the Dutch, and in 1644 the Dutch were obliged to withdraw. In June 1645 Pernambuco planters revolted against the Dutch, but in September a squadron under Serrão de Paiva was destroyed at Tamandaré. In 1647 van Schoppe occupied briefly the island of Itaparica at the entrance to the Bahian Recôncavo and the Dutch defeated a Portuguese expedition to Angola. The year 1648 was difficult, but eventually decisive. Two Portuguese fleets, under Villa-Pouca and Salvador de Sá, had left for Brazil in 1647. Meanwhile Spain had finally recognized the independence of the United Provinces and Witte de With's fleet reached Recife. However, in April (1648) near Recife, the first battle of the Guararapes gave the Portuguese a victory. Four months later, Salvador de Sá recovered Luanda, Benguela and São Tomé in Africa. In 1649 Francisco Barreto won another victory at the second battle of Guararapes. The Dutch increasingly lost control of the hinterland of Pernambuco and in 1654 the last Dutch strongholds fell. Brazil was once again fully under Portugal's control. Holland and Portugal made peace in 1661 and hostilities gradually subsided. In 1668 Spain also finally settled its differences with Portugal and recognized the Braganza Restoration.

Half a century of war – and more than a century of piracy – put an enormous strain on the administration and especially the defence of the Portuguese empire in Asia, Africa and America and exhausted Portuguese resources. Fortifications were built and rebuilt; the *Armada do Mar Oceano*, the fleet of the high seas, was reorganized in 1633; coastal defence fleets were created; naval squadrons and armies on several continents had to be provisioned; the navy shipyards worked at full strength; troops and naval crews were levied; even foreigners were conscripted, although certain traditionally overpopulated areas, such as the region between the Douro and the Minho, the Azores, Madeira and even Lisbon itself, supplied the majority of recruits. The war for Pernambuco alone cost 500,000 cruzados a year, and increased taxes and duties in Portugal and throughout the empire failed to provide the crown with the revenue it required. Recourse was had to other means for obtaining revenue including loans, both voluntary and forced.

Charts and log-books preserved from the sixteenth and seventeenth centuries show that most direct Atlantic routes between Europe and America had been discovered by the Portuguese at an early date. They were determined by climatic and hydrological factors, based on the trade winds in the tropics and the prevailing westerly winds in the northern and southern temperate zones. Latitude was calculated with the help of the astrolabe, the quadrant and other instruments which measured

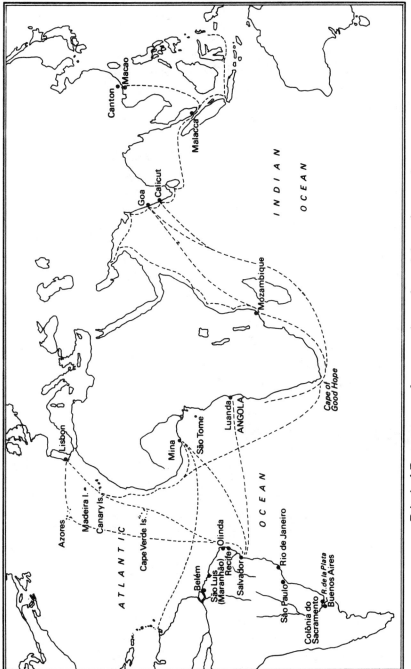

Principal Portuguese trade routes, sixteenth to eighteenth centuries

the height of the sun or of a star in relation to the horizon or to the pole, corrected according to the season of the year by tables which the cosmographers of King João II had formulated. However, navigation in the sixteenth and seventeenth centuries was far from reliable. And voyages were both long and uncertain: for example, it took from ten to fourteen weeks to sail from Lisbon to Bahia. Moreover, the voyage was uncomfortable for passengers, bundled together as they were with cargo and cannon. Food was bad and deteriorated, while storms and shipwrecks were frequent. The islands of Madeira and the Azores served as staging-posts; the former on the outward passage before the difficult stretch of the Atlantic where equatorial calms were encountered, and the latter before the last part of the voyage to Lisbon, where pirates and corsairs lay in wait.

Although the vessels carrying the Portuguese Atlantic trade were naturally ocean-going ships, they were certainly not as big as the ships reserved for the East India traffic. The caravel and the *navio*, built for heavy cargoes but slower and smaller, were the craft most commonly used. During the union with Spain, Portuguese galleons were, it appears, sometimes designed to imitate the gigantic lines of the Spanish galleons; one such was the *Padre Eterno* of 2,000 tons burden and armed with 114 pieces of cannon. It was built in Brazil – in the Bay of Guanabara (Rio de Janeiro) – and first visited Lisbon in 1665. The increase in the size of ships was a general phenomenon at this period, as Pierre and Huguette Chaunu have shown in their research on Seville's Atlantic trade.

Portugal's restriction of its colonial trade to its own nationals did not preclude the licensing and use of foreign ships nor the investment by foreigners in Portuguese colonial enterprises. Portugal never possessed a merchant fleet large enough to handle, in particular, the bulky Brazilian sugar trade. It was not possible for the *Mesa do Bem Commun dos Mercadores* (the corporation of Lisbon merchants) to maintain a strict monopoly of colonial trade. Dutch ships operating under Portuguese licence were prominent in the Brazil trade from an early date, as were English ships. Since the late Middle Ages the English had had a special relationship with Portugal, importing spices, salt, fruit and wine and exporting cloth (the balance of trade favourable to England). English merchants were already well established with special privileges in Lisbon when the development of the Portuguese colonial economy completely transformed English trade with Portugal. As early as 1595 the value of English sugar imports was already much higher than that of spice imports. After the union with Spain in 1580 which had a more 'closed' concept of empire, sporadic embargoes were imposed on Dutch and English shipping in the colonial trade (which served to increase the level of illegal trading). Licences were now granted more readily to Spanish merchants than to other nationalities. Eventually, however, the Portuguese became fearful that the Spaniards might take their trade with Brazil away from them, at a time when the Dutch had already partly appropriated the East Indian traffic and trade with northern countries was much reduced by reason of the taxes on salt. Spanish attempts to penetrate the Portuguese commercial system were thus largely rebuffed. At the same time the Portuguese themselves made good use of the loosening of political boundaries between the two empires. Contracts for the slave trade to Spanish America, in particular, opened up new markets to Portuguese merchants. In general, Portuguese merchants, often New Christians, established themselves in Lima, Potosí, Cartegena and Mexico City as well as Seville. Buenos Aires, above all, became in effect a Portuguese factory for illegal trade with Peru. The silver of Potosí became common coin in Brazil during this period. Meanwhile, Dutch interests were protected in Lisbon by the German, Conrat Rott, who acted as consul for both Germans and Flemish. During the first decade of the seventeenth century the number of Dutch ships in the Brazil trade more than doubled and it is estimated that during the Twelve-Year Truce (1609–21) one-half to two-thirds of the ships were Dutch.

The extension of hostilities between Holland and Spain to the Portuguese empire after 1621 led not only to the loss of the north-east of Brazil and its trade but also, especially after 1640 when the activities of Dutch privateers intensified, severely disrupted Portugal's trade with the rest of Brazil. Portuguese naval resources – eight galleons, part of the Portuguese-Spanish fleet, cruising off the coasts of Brazil – were totally inadequate for the protection of the sugar trade. Merchant shipping losses mounted: 108 ships were lost in 1647 and 141 in 1648, i.e. 249 ships out of a total of 300, or 83 per cent in two years. The king took a series of panic measures, such as despatching the royal fleet from the Tagus to Brazil, ordering ships in France, borrowing from New Christians to purchase ships in Holland, inviting foreigners to send vessels to Brazil, prohibiting the construction of small ships and even, in 1648, banning the transportation of sugar so long as the Dutch should continue at their existing strength at sea. Finally, at the initiative of the Jesuit Father António Vieira, the frequently-discussed idea of a monopoly trading company was revived and on 10 March 1649 the statutes of a *Companhia Geral do Comercio* were approved by the crown. Shipping between Lisbon and Brazil would for the first time be confined to a fleet (*frota*) system and provided with adequate escort vessels. The company would maintain 36 galleons for the protection of maritime trade.

The capital for the foundation of the company came from the property of New Christians condemned by the Inquisition and contributions from Lisbon merchants. The administration of the company was entrusted to a junta of deputies, elected for three years from among those merchants who had contributed at least 5,000 cruzados. The total subscribed was 1,255,000 cruzados (cruzado = 400 réis), which, when it came to the point, proved to be insufficient. The cost of a convoy (provided from the 36 galleons) was covered by the premiums paid against loss: 600 reis per case of sugar or tobacco to insure the ships and 1,400 réis per *arroba* of white sugar to insure the cargo. These premiums were to be paid to the agents of the company in the customs houses of the kingdom of Portugal when the vessels returned. The company had another source of revenue from the transport by warships of certain commodities, particularly the four over which it had a monopoly – wine, flour, oil and codfish. It also had the monopoly of brazilwood. In short, the company enjoyed a considerable number of privileges and exemptions.

Meanwhile the Anglo-Portuguese treaties of 1642 and 1654, besides re-affirming and extending the special status of the English factory in Lisbon, had conceded wide privileges to English merchants in the Portuguese colonial trade. For example, precedence was to be given to the English if additional ships were required by the company. Normal trading relations were re-established with the Dutch in 1661, the French in 1667 and the Spanish in 1668.

The company was well received and its early stages were full of promise. However, before long there was criticism that the capital of the company was Jewish, that it failed to maintain the 36 galleons stipulated in the charter and that it did not keep the Brazilians supplied with the four foodstuffs for which it held the monopoly. Between 1662 and 1664 it was gradually transformed into a state company, administered by a *Junta do Comercio*, which ultimately came under the authority of the Conselho da Fazenda. It continued, however, to pay dividends to the shareholders. As hostilities, privateering and piracy in the Atlantic all declined, the company became more effective and the frotas under escort regularly left Rio towards the end of March, picked up the sugar ships at Bahia in April and arrived safely in Lisbon in July or August. A separate trading company was established for Maranhão in 1678.

Although the Companhia Geral do Comercio was eventually abolished by King João V in 1720 the frota system was retained. In the eighteenth century there were separate fleets for each of five colonial ports, though outbound fleets often sailed together and two or more returned together. In addition, one or two supposedly swift vessels capable of eluding capture annually sailed from Lisbon to major ports as despatch boats (*naus de aviso*) or licensed priority cargo ships (*naus de licença*). São Luís and Belém were irregularly served by one or two ships a year until cacao generated more trade. The fleet system itself was abolished in 1765–6.[3]

The trade between Portugal, the rest of the Portuguese empire and Brazil was dominated east–west by slaves and west–east by sugar. Traders used two main regions of Africa as their source of slave supply. The first was West Africa, where the general term 'Sudanese' was used to describe several tribes, such as the Wolof, the Mandingo, the Songhai, the Mossi, the Hausa and the Peul. Generally speaking, men from these tribes were powerfully built, usually herdsmen, sometimes belonging to the Islamic faith; thus they tended to be independent and prone to revolt. The other region was Central and Equatorial Africa, where men from the Bantu tribes were small, more submissive, animist in religion and, for the most part, cultivators of the soil of settled habit. In the sixteenth and early seventeenth centuries most slaves were 'Sudanese'; by the eighteenth century the majority were Bantu. From the middle of the seventeenth century there were also contingents of Bantu from Mozambique in East Africa.

The slave trade was open to all Portuguese on payment of a due. The collection of dues was farmed out, by means of an *asiento* (contract), to a *contratador*, who delivered the *avenças* (agreements) to the traffickers. From being simply a contract, the asiento was to become, by the end

---

[3] For further reference to the fleet system in the eighteenth century, see chs. 6 and 7 below. In the final revision of this section of the chapter the Editor wishes to acknowledge the help of Professor Dauril Alden.

of the seventeenth century, an agreement under international public law. Although there were asientos for supplying slaves in Spanish America, there were none in Brazil, except perhaps late in the colonial period in Maranhão. The asiento merely constituted a permit for the shipment of slaves from Africa: there are examples for Angola dated 1573 and for Cape Verde dated 1582 or 1583. The purchase was conducted by intermediaries; in Guinea these men were *tangosmaus* or *lançados* (adventurers who lived like natives) and in Angola *pombeiros* (Africans who were already the slaves of white planters and who went off into the interior to look for slaves).

Conditions in the slave ships, or *tumbeiros* (literally 'hearses'), were appalling. They were overloaded, with as many as 500 slaves being stowed away in a single caravel. The length of the voyage varied, averaging 35 days from Angola to Pernambuco, 40 days to Bahia and up to 50 days to Rio. The unfortunate Africans were herded so closely together that epidemics broke out and many – sometimes half the total number – died. On arrival in Brazil the surviving slaves were given time to recover and were cared for in order to increase their value; they were then sold by auction. Owing to the high death rate and the perils of the voyage, there was not much profit for the transporters, especially when the price of slaves was low. In 1612, for example, a male slave in good condition and under 25 years of age, could be bought for 28$000 réis in Brazil. However, he had already cost 4$000 in dues and 9$600 to transport in addition to his purchase price in Africa, not counting his share of the cost of those who died on the voyage.

The number of Africans transported to Brazil is not easily calculated, as the Portuguese bureaucracy was not so highly organized as the Spanish and the slave trade was subject to very little control. Information is widely dispersed in various archives. Not much is known about Brazil's role in the slave trade during the sixteenth century.

Originally individual senhores de engenhos (mill owners) were authorized to bring over their own slaves from Africa, and in 1559 a royal decree limited the size of each contingent to 120. There were apparently from 2,000 to 3,000 black slaves in Brazil by 1570, and from then onwards the number increased rapidly. In 1575 Angola exported 12,000 '*peças*', 4,000 of whom died on the voyage. Between 1580 and 1590 there were, according to Father Anchieta, 10,000 black slaves in Pernambuco and 3,000 in Bahia. However, two other contemporary observers arrived at different figures. In the opinion of Fernão Cardim there were only 2,000 black slaves in Pernambuco and 3,000–4,000 in Bahia, while according to Gabriel Soares de Sousa there were 4,000–5,000 and 4,000 respectively. It is estimated that the number of black slaves living in Brazil in about 1600 must have been 13,000–15,000 distributed over 130 engenhos, where the labour force would already have been 70 per cent black. For the first half of the seventeenth century approximately 4,000 slaves were imported per annum. Between 1650 and 1670 this figure increased to 7,000–8,000 per annum and then declined. According to Philip Curtin, the Brazilian share represented 41.8 per cent of the total number of slaves imported into America between 1601 and 1700, while, for example, Spanish America took 21.8 per cent, the English colonies 19.7 per cent and the French colonies 11.6 per cent.[4]

By the end of the sixteenth century sugar had ceased to be a 'drug' in limited supply and had become a 'food'. And for a century from 1570/80 Brazil was by far the largest producer and exporter of sugar in the world.[5] Until the crisis of the 1680s the secular trend in Brazilian sugar production was upward (which is particularly remarkable since Dutch Brazil is excluded from the account). Moreover, against the general pattern of the seventeenth-century 'depression' abundant and increasing production did not affect the movement of sugar prices which was also upward, as was the price of slaves. The crisis of the seventeenth century did not seriously affect Brazil until towards the end of the century.

The century-long Brazilian sugar cycle can be divided into a number of phases:

(a) a period of expansion from c. 1570 to c. 1600; as the number of mills increased there was a corresponding increase in production and export and it is possible to discern behind the slow rise in the price of taxed sugar a more rapid upward movement of prices on the free market;

(b) a plateau with output at a high level (15–20,000 metric tons per annum from over 200 mills in the 1620s) until c. 1625; prices dropped slightly in the 1610s during the Twelve-Year Truce, but

---

[4] Philip Curtin, *The Atlantic slave trade. A census* (Madison, 1969), table 34, p. 119; for a further discussion of the slave trade to Brazil in the colonial period see Marcilio and Alden, CHLA, II, ch. 2 and 15.

[5] For a detailed discussion of the Brazilian sugar industry from the end of the sixteenth to the end of the seventeenth centuries, see ch. 3 below.

rose again in the 1620s as the war resumed and Dutch attacks
disrupted Portuguese Atlantic shipping and higher taxes were
imposed to pay for defence;

(c) a further phase of growth which lasted until shortly before 1640;

(d) a downturn in production and export *c*. 1640–60 following the
Dutch occupation of Pernambuco and the subsequent reorganization and relocation of the sugar industry by the Portuguese; prices,
however, continued to rise as a result of the war and the various
additional taxes imposed on Brazilian products including sugar;

(e) a resumption of growth in the 1660s following the creation of the
Companhia Geral do Comercio and the frota system, the ending of
the war and the recovery of Pernambuco production;

(f) the beginnings of a depression *c*. 1680 as prices on the international
sugar market fell during the 1670s and 1680s largely as a result of
increased production in the Antilles. (Sugar prices fell from 3$800
per arroba in 1654 to 1$300 in 1685.) As in previous periods of
commercial difficulty the senhores de engenho in both the north-
eastern captaincies and the more marginal south produced less,
stopped buying slaves and directed the existing labour force to other
commercial crops less vulnerable to international trade recessions,
to cattle raising and to subsistence agriculture. It would appear,
however, that, in spite of these vicissitudes and although the sugar
producers themselves were not doing well, substantial profits were
still being made by the merchants.

The sugar processed in the Brazilian engenhos was to a large extent
exported to Europe, consignments being despatched in the name of the
senhores de engenhos, the *lavradores* (sugar cane growers), or the
merchant-exporters. Until 1640 ships transported between 200 and 600
crates each, but after that date the ships were larger and therefore the
number of crates must also have increased. The call at Lisbon was often
part of a round trip; ships which had come from Africa with slaves
returned with sugar. The cost of transport (or *frete*) was high. During
the convoy period there were also the *avaria* duties, exacted to pay for
protection of the ships.

In addition to the legal trade through Lisbon by Portuguese
merchants and foreigners under licence from the king, there was the
lively contraband trade carried on by the English, the Spaniards (via
the Canaries), the French (through La Rochelle) and finally the Dutch,
who, as we have seen, had the lion's share of the illegal traffic.

Amsterdam became the entrepot for sugar and Dutch ships kept the market supplied by a combination of privateering, smuggling and licensing. The Amsterdam archives are full of sugar dealings which, like those in brazilwood, were quoted on the Bourse. Sugar arrived from all directions: the islands of the eastern Atlantic, Brazil and Central America, and, if not already refined, it was refined on the spot before being re-exported throughout northern Europe. This traffic reached its height between 1630 and 1654, when sugar from Pernambuco, under occupation by the Dutch, was transported direct to the United Provinces. By 1650 sugar-refining absorbed much of the available Dutch capital. A quarter of the customs duties collected were paid on sugar and a hundred ships were permanently engaged on its transportation. Jews, particularly Portuguese Jews, played an important part in this industry, although public opinion often favoured banning them from participating in it. By 1665 there were signs of a decline as a result of Colbert's efforts to create a French sugar industry. There were no refineries in Portugal in the seventeenth century. The mother country left sugar-refining to Brazil itself; indeed a royal mandate of 1559 had actually prohibited sugar-refining in Lisbon.

Among other commodities in the Atlantic trade, tobacco was the most important. In the first half of the seventeenth century Portuguese policy was to restrict the cultivation of tobacco at home and in the Atlantic islands in order to encourage Brazilian production. In 1674 a *Junta do Tabaco* was set up to supervise the tobacco trade and an unsuccessful attempt was made to have all taxes collected by a tax farmer appointed by the king. As the slave trade to Brazil grew, Brazilian tobacco and rum were the commodities chiefly used to barter for slaves on the coasts of Africa. On the other hand, cotton became less important during the seventeenth century. Antonil does not even mention it in his *Cultura e Opulencia do Brasil* (Lisbon, 1711). As early as the end of the sixteenth century the cost of transporting raw cotton to Lisbon equalled its production costs, probably about 2$000 milreis per arroba.

Imported into Brazil were many other goods apart from slaves and ivory from Africa. A number of ships travelling to Europe from Asia stopped at Bahia in the seventeenth and especially the eighteenth centuries, bringing silks and other luxury products. From Europe, of course, came all manufactures, including tools, materials for the engenho (particularly copper utensils), arms and textiles, for the most part made in France or England, with Lisbon serving only as an intermediary. There were also certain foodstuffs, such as salted meat which, like leather and silver, came from the Río de la Plata, salt-fish and wines, especially from Oporto and Madeira, which, it was alleged, were improved by the sea voyage. Lastly there were cereals, particularly wheat which reminded the Portuguese settlers of home. Finally, salt played a notable part in the Atlantic trade. It was not only essential for the diet of man and beast, but it was also indispensable for preserving fish and meat. Salt production was important to Portugal and other supplies were available from the Cape Verde Islands, Guinea and Angola. The Indians in Brazil used a vegetable salt and, along the São Francisco river, cattle found a briny soil which they were able to lick. The settlers created saltpans at Maranhão, between the Rio Grande and Ceará and between Paraíba and the Rio Grande, but the yield was quite insufficient and Brazil was obliged to import salt. In 1632 the supply of salt to Brazil came under state control, a monopoly which only ended in 1821. In 1665 and again in 1690–1 attempts were made to prohibit the production of salt in Brazil to prevent competition with salt imported from Portugal.

PORTUGAL AND BRAZIL, *c.* 1695–1750

The crisis in the Brazilian sugar industry in the 1680s after a century of growth and prosperity triggered off an economic crisis in Portugal. Revenue from colonial trade fell so much that Portugal was no longer able to purchase from abroad (especially England) manufactures for both the metropolis and the colonies. It is this fact which explains the economic policy of Count Ericeira, chief minister of Pedro II (1683–1706), who attempted to protect and promote Portuguese industry as a substitute for imports while also, in 1688, devaluing the currency. In order to earn Spanish silver piastres in the Spanish-American markets he created a joint stock company to carry on the slave trade on the Guinea coast. The silver piastre helped to some extent to redress the deficit in the balance of Portuguese foreign trade. Ericeira committed suicide in 1692 and his successor, the marquis of Fronteira, had little time to continue his policy before the Luso-Brazilian economy began to recover. One reason for this was increased demand and somewhat higher prices, for Brazil's agricultural products, above all sugar, but also cotton and hides as well as Portugal's own olive oil and wine. Exports of sugar from Brazil showed a temporary upward movement at the turn of the century although the long-term trend was now down. Antonil tells us that between 1688 and 1706 the price of white sugar rose first from 800 or 900 réis to 2$400 réis per arroba, declining afterwards to 1$600 réis. According to other sources, the price of white sugar is likely to have fluctuated between 1$200 and 1$400 réis between 1688 and 1743. It was, however, gold which transformed the Luso-Brazilian economy and initiated a new era. The economic crisis had stimulated the search for gold in the interior of Brazil. Expeditions of *bandeirantes* beginning with that of Fernão Dias Pais in 1674 became more numerous and determined. Finally, in 1695 at Río das Velhas between present-day Ouro Preto and Diamantina there occurred the first significant gold strike. During the next 40 years others followed in Minas Gerais, Bahia, Goiás and Mato Grosso.

Throughout the long reign of Dom João V (1706–50) production of gold in Brazil and its exportation to Portugal expanded. It increased five times between 1700 and 1720, grew steadily from 1720 to 1735, increased dramatically in the late 1730s and more modestly from 1740 until 1755 when it began to decline, although at first only slowly.[6]

The discovery of the diamond mines at Cerro Frio, north of Minas, should also be mentioned here. Their production very soon became sufficient to cause the value of diamonds to drop by 75 per cent on the international market. In all about 615 kg were extracted during the eighteenth century, and diamonds mined in Bahia, Mato Grosso and Goiás must be added to this figure. They remained an important item in Portugal's balance sheet.

Exports of gold and diamonds in such quantity allowed Portugal to cover its balance of payments in the short term. It also led to the abandonment of the early attempts to industrialize – and to modernize and diversify agriculture – with damaging long-term consequences. The reorganization of the Luso-Brazilian economy around gold in the first half of the eighteenth century also reinforced Portugal's ties with England. The Methuen treaties (1703) reaffirmed an already clearly defined commercial relationship in which the Portuguese provided wine and olive oil, the English textiles, other manufactured goods and wheat. Table 1 on p. 462 shows that wine constituted between 70 and 90 per

[6] For a full discussion of gold production, see Russell-Wood, *CHLA*, II, ch. 14. See in particular, Table 1 based on Virgílio Noya Pinto, *O Ouro brasileiro e o comércio anglo-português* (São Paulo, 1979), 114. For more detailed figures on gold exports, see tables in Michel Morineau, 'Or brésilien et gazettes hollandaises', *Revue d'Histoire Moderne et Contemporaine*, 25 (Jan.–Mar., 1978), 15–16, 18.

Table 1 *Patterns of Trade between Portugal and England: 1700–50*
(Annual Averages)

	Portuguese wines		English textiles	
Years	Exported to England (in thousands of £)	Percentage of Portuguese exports to England	Exported to Portugal (in thousands of £)	Percentage of English exports to Portugal
1701–05	173	71	430	71
1706–10	170	71	463	71
1711–15	217	86	488	77
1716–20	288	83	555	80
1721–25	326	84	620	76
1726–30	302	84	729	80
1731–35	287	88	744	73
1736–40	263	87	871	75
1741–45	367	86	882	79
1746–50	275	85	848	76
Total	2,668		6,630	

Source: H. E. S. Fisher, *The Portugal Trade 1700–1770* (London, 1971), Appendix I, 142–3, 'The Trade between England and Portugal, 1697–1773'.

Table 2 *Balance of Trade between Portugal and England: 1701–50*
(Average annual value in thousands of £s)

Years	Exports Portugal–England	Imports England–Portugal	Balance
1701–05	242	610	−368
1706–10	240	652	−412
1711–15	252	638	−386
1716–20	349	695	−346
1721–25	387	811	−424
1726–30	359	914	−555
1731–35	326	1,024	−698
1736–40	301	1,164	−863
1741–45	429	1,115	−686
1746–50	324	1,114	−790
Total	3,209	8,737	

Source: Elizabeth Boody Schumpeter, *English Overseas Trade Statistics (1697–1808)* (Oxford, 1960), pp. 17–18.

Table 3 *Slave Imports into Brazil, 1700–50*

| Years | Countries of Origin | | Total |
	Costa da Mina	Angola	
1701–10	83,700	70,000	153,700
1711–20	83,700	55,300	139,000
1721–30	79,200	67,100	146,300
1731–40	56,800	109,300	166,100
1741–50	55,000	130,100	185,100
Total	358,400	431,800	790,200

Source: Philip Curtin, *The Atlantic Slave Trade* (Madison, 1969), p. 207.

cent of Portuguese exports to England and textiles 70–80 per cent of English exports to Portugal. Table 2 reveals a huge and growing trade imbalance in England's favour. The balance was was made up by an outflow of gold and diamonds. It is also an undeniable fact that a large proportion of the Brazilian gold which entered Europe was clandestinely imported by the English. Trade between Lisbon and the Thirteen Colonies of North America was also far from negligible. Pitch, rice, tobacco and timber were among the American products which the Portuguese needed. Lisbon also served as a revictualling port on the route from London to the British Antilles. There was a considerable trade in cod between Newfoundland and Portugal, and there was free trade between the Thirteen Colonies, Madeira and Porto Santo, since the Portuguese islands, belonging as they did to Africa, did not come within the terms of the Navigation Laws. Salt was sent to Newfoundland from the Portuguese islands of Maio and Boavista in the Cape Verde group, and in 1713 120 vessels were needed for its transportation. Almost all Portuguese merchandise exported from Portugal was carried in English ships.

The Brazilian gold cycle had an important impact on one other aspect of the Atlantic trade – the slave trade from Africa. Demand for labour in gold-producing areas maintained the level of the slave trade despite the depression in the sugar regions. Table 3 shows that the number of slaves imported into Brazil actually increased from 1720 and even more after 1730. Angola was the main supplier of slaves to Brazil, as it had been since its recovery by the Portuguese in 1648. That part of the trade in slaves paid for directly by Brazilian products (mainly tobacco and rum), and therefore outside the triangular traffic between Europe, Africa and Brazil, seems to have grown in the course of the eighteenth century. The treaty of asiento signed between England and Spain in 1713 gave the English the idea of signing another similar treaty with Portugal. The Commissioners for Trade and Plantations, however, refused, on the grounds that the participation of England in the Brazilian slave trade could only serve to increase the number of slaves entering Brazil and would, in consequence, cause a reduction in their price and in that of the sugar which they still produced. There was a risk that Brazilian sugar might become a dangerous rival to sugar from the British Antilles which together with sugar from the French colony of Saint-Domingue, now dominated the international market.

The economic crisis of the 1680s, the end of the sugar cycle and the beginning of the gold cycle gave a new impetus to the expansion of the Brazilian frontier. Brazil was ceasing to be a coastal archipelago and was on the threshold of becoming a sub-continent. The far west in particular was opened up and settled during the era of gold and this is reflected in the major reorganization of colonial administration: in 1720 Minas Gerais was separated from the captaincy-general of Rio de Janeiro to form a new captaincy; in 1744 the captaincy of Goiás and in 1748 the captaincy of Mato Grosso were created from the captaincy-general of São Paulo. In the south, Salvador de Sá, to whom the king had in 1658 entrusted the captaincies of Espírito Santo, Rio de Janeiro and São Vicente, had had the idea of creating a 'captaincy of Santa Catarina' south of São Vicente, as a means of developing southern Brazil and perhaps of reopening the clandestine route for silver coming from Potosí by way of Buenos Aires, from which, at the beginning of the seventeenth century, Portuguese trade had profited considerably. But the idea was not taken up. In 1680 the Portuguese had founded the Colônia do Sacramento on the east bank of the Río de la Plata as a depot for the contraband trade with Buenos Aires, which was now becoming one of the chief ports of Spanish America. It was a vulnerable outpost, captured twice by the Spanish before Portuguese possession was upheld in the Treaty of Utrecht (1713) and even then subject to constant attack. Situated only fifteen miles from Buenos Aires across the estuary Colônia do Sacramento was hundreds of miles from Rio and the other major Brazilian ports. In the days of sailing ships it lay at less than a day's voyage from Buenos Aires, but seven days from Santa Catarina and no less than fourteen days from Rio de Janeiro. To offset this weakness, it would have needed an adequate population as well as strong defence. However, not until 1718 were families sent there to settle. The total population of Colônia do Sacramento probably never exceeded 3,000.

However, the Portuguese had begun to occupy the vast territories which separated them from Colônia and the Río de la Plata. By the end of the seventeenth century the coast of Santa Catarina had been occupied from the sea at three points: São Francisco do Sul, in the north (1653), Laguna, in the south (1684) and Nossa Senhora do Desterro in the middle of the island of Santa Catarina, opposite the continental mainland. And in 1738 a land route from São Paulo to Laguna was opened up. In the eighteenth century the coast was to be populated by settlers who came from the Azores under contracts resembling those for 'indentured servants' in the French and English Antilles. By 1749 there was a total of 4,197 inhabitants. During the first half of the eighteenth century the Portuguese also occupied the areas south of Santa Catarina. In 1737 the city of Rio Grande was founded at the entrance to the Lagoa dos Patos. The administration of southern Brazil was then reorganized and Santa Catarina and Rio Grande de São Pedro were detached from São Paulo, to become 'sub-captaincies' under the captaincy-general of Rio de Janeiro.

The decision to pitch the Portuguese tent on the lands to the south was a direct consequence of Portuguese-Spanish conflict on the Río de la Plata which broke out again in 1723. Since 1716 relations had been strained and the governors of Buenos Aires and Colônia do Sacramento watched each other closely and attempted to create posts and settlements at other points on the left bank of the estuary, to secure their own trade in meat, leather and pitch and to contain their enemy's expansion. In 1723 António Pedro de Vasconcellos, the governor of Colônia (1721–49), backed by the governor of Rio, Aires de Saldanha de Albuquerque, prepared a small expedition of 150 men commanded by Manuel de Freitas de Fonseca and established a settlement at Montevideo downstream from Colônia, but the following year they had to abandon the port owing to lack of resources. The Spanish quickly established themselves there and founded the port city of Montevideo in 1726. Their presence made communications between Colônia and Laguna, Santos and Rio very difficult for the Portuguese. The long-term consequences were momentous since, despite the fact that the original discovery (1513) and the first permanent settlement (1680) were both Portuguese, the *Banda Oriental* was henceforth largely populated by Spaniards and, instead of a Brazilian 'Cisplatine' province, eventually became the Spanish-speaking state of Uruguay.

By 1729, however, peace between Spain and Portugal seemed to have been restored. Dom José, the hereditary prince of Portugal, had married the Infanta of Spain, Mariana Vitoria, and the Prince of the Asturias, the future Ferdinand VI of Spain, had married the Infanta of Portugal, Dona Maria Barbara de Braganza, the daughter of João V. Then, in 1735, a sordid incident concerning the servants of the Portuguese ambassador to Spain, Pedro Alvares Cabral, provoked a rupture of diplomatic relations; it was an event which had no military consequences in Europe, but provided a good pretext for disturbing the *status quo* on the Río de la Plata. The governor of Buenos Aires attacked Colônia; António Pedro de Vasconcelos held out from October 1735 to September 1737 and only an armistice signed in Paris saved the Portuguese. The two countries were by now determined to settle their differences. Nevertheless, the dispute was to continue for a further thirteen years and was not resolved until the reign of Ferdinand VI in Spain (1746–59) – and then only temporarily. To make reconciliation possible, José de Carvajal y Lencastre, president of the Council of the Indies and principal minister in Spain, renewed his government's offer to exchange an equivalent piece of territory for Colônia do Sacramento. Carvajal had good reasons for these negotiations; in his view the trading-post at Colônia was responsible for the loss to Spain of much Peruvian silver. If the economy of the Río de la Plata was to be developed, Portuguese competition had to be eliminated. It was also important to avoid conflict with Portugal, for that automatically made England an enemy of Spain.

On the Portuguese side, too, there were many who wanted peace. Alexandre de Gusmão, a royal councillor of long standing and an experienced diplomat, had been born at Santos and knew Brazil well. Although he realized all the advantages which could be derived from peace with Spain, he wanted more than merely the settlement of the problem of Colônia; he sought a definitive solution to all frontier disputes between Portugal and Spain which would take into account the *de facto* possessions of both powers in South America. Although not believing that Colônia had a future under Portugal (a view not shared by the merchants of Lisbon), he still thought capital could be made out of its surrender. In his view the future of Brazil was to be identified with the Amazon, a region still little known but generally thought, in accordance with the preconceived notions of the times, to be potentially the richest simply because it was the hottest. Unlike, for example, the 'snowy acres' of French Canada, the vast region of the Amazon was thought to contain precious metals, rare plants or fruits and exotic animals. In the south, Rio Grande de São Pedro had all the advantages and economic potential and none of the inconvenience of Colônia do Sacramento and the left bank of the Río de la Plata. Portugal's title to the territories east of the Uruguay, like her title to the territories of the upper Amazon and, for that matter, Minas Gerais, Goiás and Mato Grosso, was dubious and confirmation of title could be exchanged for Colônia do Sacramento.

To Carvajal this seemed a high price to pay. Moreover, the territory claimed by Gusmão included the prosperous Seven Missions of the Jesuits, and he knew the Society of Jesus would oppose cession of this territory to the Portuguese. Nevertheless, desire for agreement was so strong in Madrid that the Portuguese conditions, subject to a small concession in the Amazon area and complete renunciation of all claims in the Philippines, were finally accepted by Ferdinand VI.

The Treaty of Madrid (1750), signed after three years of arduous negotiations, was the most important agreement about overseas possessions to be signed by the Portuguese and the Spanish since the Treaty of Tordesillas (1494). The two countries finally abandoned the underlying principle of Tordesillas which no longer bore any relation to reality and adopted that of the *uti possidetis*, that is, 'each of the parties retains that which it has occupied'. However, four key articles constituted exceptions. Under Articles XIII and XV Portugal renounced all claims to Colônia and recognized Spanish supremacy on the Río de la Plata, and under Articles XIV and XVI Spain abandoned all territory east of the river Uruguay and promised to evacuate the Seven Missions. The boundaries of the Spanish and Portuguese possessions – subject to precise definition in both the Amazon and the south by a mixed commission – were traced on the famous 'Map of the Courts'. The Treaty of Madrid, the 'Boundaries Treaty', gave Portugal sovereignty over vast areas (over half) of South America and Brazil the shape which to a large extent it has retained to the present day.[7]

---

[7] For further discussion of the Treaty of Madrid, see ch. 6 below.

The years 1580 to 1750 were decisive for the development of Brazil. First sugar and then gold, together with tobacco, cotton, livestock and diamonds, had shaped it and had finally given it pride of place in the Portuguese empire. The Portuguese imperial system, which had originally been based on Africa and the East, had come to be founded essentially on Brazil and the Atlantic. And it was Brazil which enabled Portugal to achieve a balance of payments with the outside world. It also gave Portugal the means and authority to defend itself against Spain, both in the peninsula and in South America, and reinforced the special relationship between Lisbon and London. Finally, it was increasingly Brazil which made it possible for Portugal to maintain her political – and cultural – influence in Europe, a remarkable position for a country so small, so backward and so poor.

In 1750 Dom José I came to the throne and brought to power the Marquis of Pombal, who was to play a dominant role in Portugal and its empire for more than a quarter of a century. At the same time the production of gold in Brazil, and therefore the income of the Portuguese crown, reached its peak and then began sharply to decline. It was the start of a new era for the Luso-Brazilian world.

3

PLANTATIONS AND PERIPHERIES, *c.* 1580 – *c.* 1750

SUGAR AND SLAVES

'A sugar mill is hell and all the masters of them are damned', wrote Father Andrés de Gouvea from Bahia in 1627.[1] Time and time again observers who witnessed the roaring furnaces, the boiling cauldrons, the glistening black bodies and the infernal whirling of the mill during the 24-hour day of the sugar *safra*, or harvest, used the same image of hell. Along with mining, the production of sugar was the most complex and mechanized activity that Europeans carried out in the sixteenth and seventeenth centuries, and its 'modern' and industrial nature shocked its pre-industrial observers. Yet it was from this nightmarish scene that the society and economy of Brazil grew. During the century from 1580 to 1680 Brazil was the world's largest producer and exporter of sugar. It was in the context of plantation agriculture and sugar that colonial society was formed. Like the sugar-loaf itself, society crystallized with white Europeans at the top, tan-coloured people of mixed race receiving lesser esteem, and black slaves considered, like the dark *panela* sugar, to be of the lowest quality.

By the final decades of the sixteenth century Brazil no longer resembled the trading-fort establishments of the Portuguese West African and Asian colonies. The shift from private to royal initiative in the exploitation and settlement of the vast Brazilian coastline, the creation of the captaincy system in the 1530s, the subsequent establishment of royal control in 1549, the elimination and enslavement of Indian peoples and the transformation of the principal economy from dyewood cutting to sugar-cane agriculture were all central elements in the

[1] Arquivo Nacional de Torre do Tombo (Lisbon) [ANTT], Cartório dos Jesuitas, maço 68, n. 334.

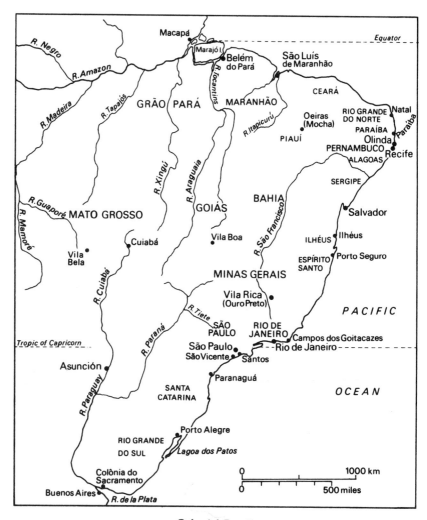

Colonial Brazil

colony's formation. Although missionaries and prospectors or slavers occasionally penetrated the interior, for the most part settlement remained concentrated along the narrow coastal strip, where good soils, adequate climatic conditions, labour supply, and cheap transport to ports favoured the sugar industry during a period of increasing demand in European markets. Effective governmental control was restricted to the coast and above all to the archipelago of ports and small agricultural towns along the eastern littoral from Pernambuco to São Vicente. By 1580 Brazil, with a population of some 60,000 of whom 30,000 were Europeans, had become a colony of settlement, but of a peculiar kind; a tropical plantation colony capitalized from Europe, supplying European demand for a tropical crop and characterized by a labour system based on the enslavement first of American Indians and then of imported African workers.

Climatic, geographic, political, and economic factors made the captaincies of Pernambuco and Bahia the centres of the colonial sugar economy. Successful cane cultivation depended on the right combination of soil and rainfall. Brazilian planters favoured the thick black and dark red *massapé* soils whose fertility obviated the need for fertilizer. Colonial authors spoke of lands planted in cane continuously for 60 or more years. It was said that a common planter's test was to stamp his boot into the ground: if his foot sank up to the ankle in the *massapé*, then the land was good for sugar. Over time much cane was also planted in sandier soils, the *salões* of the uplands, which while less suitable were adequate for sugar-cane. A reliable rainfall of 1,000–2,000 mm, needed for cane cultivation, was found along the coast.

As the sugar industry of the north-east was above all an export activity, the siting of the plantations in relation to the ports was the key factor in their precise location. Land transport depended on large ox-carts and their use was hindered by the lack of roads and bridges. The fact that the *massapé* turned into a quagmire after heavy rains made land transportation even more difficult. Water transport was therefore crucial. Mills (often driven by water power) on the *beira mar* (sea coast) or on rivers were always more valuable because of their location. In Pernambuco the industry developed particularly in the *massapé* of the flood plain (*várzea*) of the Capibaribe, Ipojuca and Jaboatão rivers. Here the soils were good and transport down river to the port facilities of Recife was relatively easy and inexpensive. In Bahia,

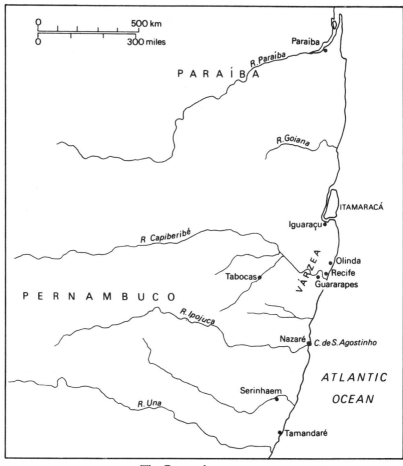

The Pernambuco coast

Source: C. R. Boxer, *Salvador de Sá and the struggle for Brazil and Angola
1602–1686* (London, 1952),

the Bay of All Saints was an excellent inland sea and even contemporaries
noted the particular Bahian dependence on boats for moving goods to
the *engenhos*[2] and sugar to the wharves of Salvador. The biggest and most

---

[2] The term 'plantation' was never used by the Portuguese or Spaniards of this period but
while, strictly speaking, *engenho* referred only to the mill for grinding the sugar cane, the term
came to be applied to the whole unit: the mill itself, the associated buildings for boiling and
purging the cane syrup, the canefields (*fazendas de canas*), pastures, slave quarters, estate house
(*casa grande*), slaves, cattle, and other equipment. In this chapter it is used to describe both
the sugar mill itself and the entire economic complex.

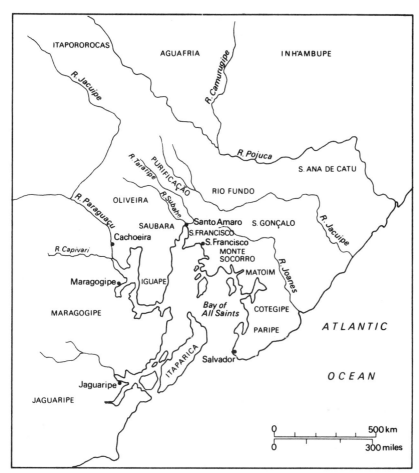

The Bahian Recôncavo

productive mills in the Bahian Recôncavo were at the water's edge. Some regions had adequate soil and rainfall but nevertheless failed to develop into major centres of production. Ilhéus provides a good example. Besides constant Indian attacks, the distance from a major port retarded the sugar industry throughout the colonial period. Some Ilhéus sugar was shipped to Europe from Salvador, but the area did not prosper.

Because the documentary record of Brazil's economic history in the sixteenth century is thin and because newly established engenhos were

Table 1 *Growth of the Brazilian sugar industry, 1570–1629*
(number of engenhos)

Captaincy	1 Gandavo 1570	2 Cardim 1583	% growth p.a. (1 to 2)	3 Campos Moreno 1612	% growth p.a. (2 to 3)	4 Cadena 1629	% growth p.a. (3 to 4)
Pará, Ceara, Maranhão							
Rio Grande				1			
Paraíba				12		24	(4.3)
Itamaraca	1			10		18	(3.5)
Pernambuco	23	66	(8.4)	90	(1.0)	150	(3.1)
Sergipe				1			
Bahia	18	36	(5.4)	50	(1.1)	80	(2.8)
Ilhéus	8	3		5		4	
Porto Seguro	5	1		1			
Espírito Santo	1	6		8*		8	
Rio de Janeiro		3		14*	(5.8)	60	(7.9)
São Vicente, Santo Amaro	4					2	
Totals	60	115	(5.1)	192	(1.8)	350	(3.6)

Sources: Frédéric Mauro, *Portugal et l'Atlantique* (Paris, 1960), 102–211. Column 1 based on Pero de Magalhães [de Gandavo], *The Histories of Brazil* (2 vols., New York, 1922). Column 2, Fernão Cardim, *Tratados da terra e gente do Brasil* (3rd edn, São Paulo, 1978). For a slightly higher figure (120) based on a synthesis of a number of sources (1583–5) see ch. 1 above, table 1. Column 3, Diogo de Campos Moreno, *Livro que dá razão do Estado do Brasil* [1612] (Rio de Janeiro, 1968). Additional figures (starred) from report of Jácome Monteiro [1610] printed in Serafim Leite, *História da Companhia de Jesus no Brasil* [HCJB] (10 vols., Lisbon, 1938–50), VIII, 393–425. Column 4, (Pedro Cadena de Vilhasanti), 'Descripción de la provincia del Brasil', in Frédéric Mauro (ed.), *Le Brésil au XVIIᵉ siècle* (Coimbra, 1963). See n. 4 below.

granted a ten-year exemption from the tithe by an *alvará* (royal decree) of 20 July 1551, thereby making tithe records unreliable for calculating the sugar economy's growth, it is difficult to trace the progress of the sugar industry. Between 1570 and 1630 various observers in Brazil did, however, leave descriptions of the colony which included estimates of the number of sugar mills in each captaincy. While these figures vary and are sometimes inconsistent, it is possible to establish from them a secular trend in engenho construction as an indication of the industry's growth (see table 1).

In 1570 Pero Magalhães de Gandavo reported that there were 60 engenhos in Brazil, of which two-thirds were located in the captaincies of Pernambuco (23) and Bahia (18) (table 1, column 1). During the next fifteen years the number of mills appears to have almost doubled, according to reports written between 1583 and 1585 (table 1, column 2). The rate of growth in Pernambuco, 8.4 per cent per annum, was considerably more than in Bahia, but the industry's growth in both captaincies was striking. The rapid growth seems to have resulted from continually rising prices for sugar in the European market and the availability of capital for investment in Brazil. Negative factors were overcome. For instance, the first legislation against Indian slavery appeared in 1570 but seems to have been successfully circumvented by the planters so that large numbers of Indians were still available as 'cheap' labour. It was also during this period that a regular slave trade from Angola and Guinea to Brazil was established.

The next period, between the mid-1580s and 1612 (table 1, columns 2 and 3), was one of much less rapid growth in the major sugar-producing captaincies, although the formerly undeveloped Rio de Janeiro area experienced considerable expansion. The whole colony's annual rate of new engenho construction dropped from 5.1 per cent to only 1.8 per cent. A report by Diogo de Campos Moreno of 1612 placed the number of mills in Pernambuco at 90, with another 23 in the neighbouring captaincies of Paraíba, Itamaracá, and Rio Grande. While this was a significant increase over the 66 mills reported for Pernambuco in 1583, the rate of growth was considerably less than in the previous period. The pace of increase in Bahia was even slower, going from 36 mills in 1583 to 50 in 1612, an annual growth rate of only 1 per cent. Brazil had by now almost 200 engenhos producing about 5,000–9,000 metric tons of sugar each year.

In the period following Campos Moreno's report engenho construction began to speed up again. Expansion in the post-1612 period seems to have been stimulated more by a new technical innovation than by favourable prices. European prices, in fact, were unstable in the 1620s and planters could not depend on a steadily rising curve as they had done previously. Sometime between 1608 and 1612 a new method of mill construction based on an arrangement of three vertical rollers was either introduced into Brazil or developed there. While it is not yet clear what effect this new system had on productivity, it does appear that the new mills were much less expensive to build and operate. The three-roller mill, the *engenho de tres paus*, eliminated some of the processes previously needed and reduced the complexity of making sugar. This innovation seems to explain the somewhat surprising expansion of the industry in the face of unstable market conditions.[3] Older mills were converted to the new system and many new ones were built.

Pedro Cadena de Vilhasanti's report of 1629 (table 1, column 4)[4] listed 150 mills in Pernambuco and 80 in Bahia, indicating a growth rate of 3.1 and 2.8 per cent per annum respectively between 1612 and 1629. Also striking was the effect of the invention on other captaincies, such as Paraíba, where the number of mills doubled to 24 (4.3 per cent per annum). The lands of Guanabara bay around Rio de Janeiro, which had previously been devoted mostly to manioc agriculture, were now also turned over increasingly to sugar. In 1629 there were 60 engenhos operating there, although most of these appear to have been small in scale. By the time of the Dutch invasion of Pernambuco in 1630 there were approximately 350 sugar mills operating in Brazil (table 1, column 4). The year 1630, in fact, probably marked the apogee of the engenho regime, for, while the number of mills was to expand and prices were occasionally to recover in the future, never again would Brazilian planters be as free from foreign competition, nor would Brazilian sugars dominate the Atlantic markets in the same way. Neither was the Brazilian sugar economy to be free of internal structural problems. Brazil's first historian, Fr. Vicente do Salvador, had complained in 1627 that the three-roller mill and the expansion it had engendered were a mixed blessing. 'What advantage is there', he asked, 'to making so much sugar if the quantity decreases the value and yields such a low price that it is below cost?'[5] It was a prophetic question.

How much sugar was produced? Just as it is difficult to establish with any certainty the number of engenhos, it is no easier to ascertain their size or productive capacity. It was said that a small mill could produce

[3] Antônio Barros de Castro, 'Brasil, 1610: mudanças técnicas e conflitos sociais', *Pesquiza e Planejamento Econômico*, 10/3 (Dec. 1980), 679–712.

[4] The anonymous report of 1629, 'Descripción de la provincia del Brasil', published by Frédéric Mauro in *Le Brésil au XVIIᵉ siècle*, 167–91, is the same as that of Pedro Cudena [*sic*] offered by him in 1634 to the count-duke of Olivares. Cudena is surely Pedro Cadena de Vilhasanti, Provedor mór do Brasil. His report is found in Martin Franzbach's bibliography published in *Jahrbuch für Geschichte von Staat, Wirtschaft und Gesellschaft Lateinamerikas* [*JGSWGL*] (1970), VII, 164–200.

[5] Fr. Vicente do Salvador, *História do Brasil* (4th edn, São Paulo, 1965), cap. 47, 366.

3,000–4,000 arrobas (43–58 metric tons) per annum and a large unit 10,000–12,000 arróbas (145–175 tons.)[6] Productivity in a given year depended on climate, rainfall, management, and exogenous factors such as the interruption of maritime trade. Thus estimates made by colonial observers vary widely from averages per mill of 160 tons in Bahia to 15 tons in Pernambuco. It appears that the average Brazilian production per engenho decreased in the later seventeenth century owing to the proliferation of smaller units in Rio de Janeiro and Pernambuco. Moreover, individual mill productivity also seems to have declined in the eighteenth century, although the reasons for this are not clear. Table 2, below, presents various estimates of productivity, among which those of Israel da Costa in 1623, the Junta do Tabaco in 1702, and Caldas in 1754 are noteworthy because they are based on actual counts, not estimates. Total Brazilian production rose from 6,000 tons in 1580 to 10,000 in 1610. By the 1620s a productive capacity of 1–1.5 million arrobas (14,545–21,818 tons) had been reached, although it was not always fulfilled. These levels do not appear to have been altered until the period after 1750. Even so there were changes within the structure of the industry that complicate calculations of production. It is difficult to estimate sugar production in Dutch Brazil (1630–54). Pernambuco and its neighbouring captaincies had 166 engenhos in 1630 but warfare and disruption had reduced that number to about 120 mills in operation by the end of the decade. The total productive capacity of Dutch Brazil probably never exceeded 600,000 arrobas despite the efforts of Governor John Maurits of Nassau to stimulate the industry. Dutch operations against Bahia destroyed engenhos there as well and the military campaigns and guerrilla operations in Dutch Brazil after 1645 devastated that sugar economy. Pernambuco took over a century to recover from the destruction of mills, cattle, and capital resources. In the later seventeenth century Pernambucan mills were smaller on the average than those of Bahia, which was by that time the leading Brazilian sugar producer. By the 1670s all Brazilian regions faced new competition from Caribbean production. When in 1710 André João Antonil published his account of Brazilian sugar production he estimated a total of under 18,500 tons, a figure falling within the range already reached in the 1620s.

[6] The Portuguese *arroba* = 14.5 kg. All weights here are given in metric units unless otherwise stated.

Table 2 *Estimates of sugar production, 1591–1758*

	Date	Region	Number of engenhos	Total production (arrobas)	Production per engenho (arrobas)	(tons)
A	1591	Pernambuco	63	378,000	6,000	87
B	1610	Bahia	63	300,000	4,762	69
C	1614	Brazil	(192)[a]	700,000	3,646	53
D	1623	Pernambuco	119	544,072	4,824	70
E	1637	Brazil	(350)[b]	937,500	2,678	39
F	1637	Brazil	350	900,000	2,571	37
G	1675	Bahia	69[c]	517,500	7,500	109
H	1702	Bahia/Sergipe	(249)[d]	507,697	2,039	30
I	1710	Brazil	528	1,295,700	2,454	36
		Bahia	146	507,500	3,476	51
		Pernambuco	246	403,500	1,750	26
		Rio de Janeiro	136	357,700	2,630	38
J	1751	Pernambuco	276	240,000	870	13
K	1755	Bahia	172	357,115	2,076	30
L	1758	Bahia	180	400,000	2,222	32

[a] Number of engenhos from Campos Moreno's account of 1612.
[b] Number of engenhos from Pedro Cadena; see source **G**.
[c] Number of engenhos is obviously too low.
[d] Number of engenhos is probably too high, since the production of all growers including those without mills was listed.
Sources: **A.** Domingos de Abreu e Brito, *Um inquérito à vida administrativa e económica de Angola e do Brasil* (Coimbra, 1931), 59; **B.** Father Jácome Monteiro in Leite, *HCJB*, VIII, 404; **C.** Report of André Farto da Costa, Arquivo Histórico Ultramarino (Lisbon) [AHU], Bahia, papéis avulsos, caixa 1*a*; **D.** Joseph Israel da Costa, in *Revista do Museu do Açúcar*, 1 (1968), 25–36; **E.** Geraldo de Onizio in Serafim Leite (ed.), *Relação diária do cerco da Bahia* (Lisbon, 1941), 110; **F.** Pedro Cadena in Mauro, *Le Brésil au XVII*ᵉ *siècle*, 170; **G.** Francisco de Brito Freyre. *História da guerra brasílica* (Lisbon, 1675), 75; **H.** ANTT, Junta do Tabaco, various maços; **I.** André João Antonil, *Cultura e opulência do Brasil por suas drogas e minas* [1711] (ed. Andrée Mansuy; Paris, 1968), 274–5; **J.** José Ribeiro Jr., *Colonização e monópolio no nordeste brasileiro* (São Paulo, 1976), 67, 136–7; **K.** José Antônio Caldas, *Noticia geral desta capitania da Bahia* (Salvador, 1951), 420–38; **L.** Coelho de Mello in *Anais da Biblioteca Nacional do Rio de Janeiro* [*ABNRJ*], 31 (1908), 321.

The engenho, the central feature of Brazilian life, was a complex combination of land, technical skills, coerced labour, management, and capital. Sugar production was a peculiar activity because it combined an intensive agriculture with a highly technical, semi-industrial mechanical process. The need to process sugar-cane in the field meant that each engenho was both a factory and a farm demanding not only a large agricultural labour force for the planting and harvesting of the cane but also an army of skilled blacksmiths, carpenters, masons, and technicians who understood the intricacies and mysteries of the sugar-making process. In order to understand the social organization of the Brazilian colony it is essential to know how sugar was transformed from the cane into its refined state.

Although there were regional variations in the seasons and intensity of the sugar-making cycle, the general process and technology was the same throughout Brazil. We shall use the cycle of Bahia as an example. Sugar-cane is a perennial plant and will yield crops for a number of years, although the yield of juice will gradually diminish. After planting, the cane needs fifteen to eighteen months to mature before being cut for the first time, but it can be harvested again after nine months. In Bahia there were two planting seasons. New fields planted in July and August could be cut between October and November the following year. The second planting cycle, in late February and March, was designed to provide cane in August and September of the next harvest. Once planted the cane needed to be weeded three times, an onerous task usually performed by gangs of 30 to 40 slaves. Timing the planting of fields to ensure a constant supply of cane during the *safra*, or harvest, required particular skill and foresight.

The sugar cycle in Brazil was determined by the *safra*. In Bahia it began in late July and continued until late May. This was a time of intense activity, for to obtain the highest yields of juice the cane had to be cut at exactly the right moment, and once cut it had to be processed quickly, otherwise the cane would dry out and the juice go sour. During the safra the engenho was alive with activity. Groups of two or three dozen slaves were placed in the cane fields in pairs, often consisting of a man and a woman. Each pair, called a *fouce* (literally, a scythe), was given a quota of canes to cut and bind which was expressed in 'hands and fingers'; ten canes to each bundle, ten bundles to each finger, and seven hands or 4,200 canes a day to be cut by the man and bound by the woman.[7] The canes were then placed in ox-carts, often driven by children or older slaves, or were loaded in boats to be brought to the mill.

The mills were of two types: those driven by water-wheels (*engenho*

---

[7] This is the quota reported in Antonil, *Cultura e opulência*. These quotas were subject to change according to time and place.

real) and those powered by oxen or, more rarely, horses. The original method of milling made use of large millstones or presses using a screw arrangement. A major technological advance was the introduction in the first decade of the seventeenth century of a mill press composed of three vertical rollers, covered with metal and cogged in such a way that it could be moved by one large drive-wheel powered by water or animals. The new mill arrangement was apparently cheaper to build and operate, especially for animal-powered mills. This innovation led to a proliferation of engenhos and, since water-power was no longer so essential, an expansion of sugar mills into areas farther from water courses. Aside from this innovation, the technology of the sugar mills changed very little until the late eighteenth century.

During the safra the pace of work was exhausting. The engenhos began operations at four o'clock in the afternoon and continued until ten o'clock the following morning, at which time the equipment was cleaned and repaired. After a rest of four hours, the mill began again. Slave women passed the canes through the rollers of the press and the juice was squeezed from the cane. The juice was then moved through a battery of copper kettles in which it was progressively boiled, skimmed, and purified. This was one of the most delicate stages of the process and it depended on the skill and experience of the sugar master and the men who tended each cauldron. The task of stoking the furnaces under the six cauldrons was particularly laborious and was sometimes assigned as a punishment to the most recalcitrant and rebellious slaves.

After cooling, the cane syrup was poured into conical pottery moulds and set into racks in the purging house. There, under the direction of the *purgador*, slave women prepared the sugar pots for draining the molasses, which could be either reprocessed to produce lower-grade sugar or distilled into rum. The sugar remaining in the mould crystallized and after two months was taken from the mould and placed for drying on a large raised platform. Under the direction of two slave women, the *mães do balcão* (the mothers of the platform), the sugar-loaves were separated. The higher-quality white sugar was separated from the darker, lower-quality *muscavado*. In Brazil the larger mills usually produced a ratio of two to three times the amount of white to *muscavado*. The sugar was then crated under the watchful eye of the *caixeiro* (crater), who also extracted the tithe and, when necessary, divided the sugar between the mill and the cane farmers. The crates were then stamped

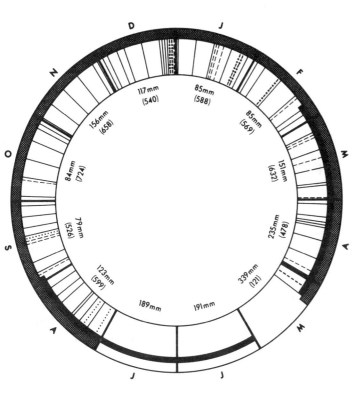

Safra

Planting

123mm Average rainfall

(526) Loaves of sugar
produced

Work stoppages

············ Weather

—————— Sunday or religious day

–··–··–··– Repairs

– – – – – – Lack of firewood

- - - - - - - Lack of cane

Fig. 1. Sugar plantation in Bahia: the agricultural cycle (based on the
Engenho Sergipe safra of 1650–1)

with marks indicating weight, quality, and ownership before being
transported by boat or ox-cart to the nearest seaport.[8]

The eight- to ten-months-long safra was a distinguishing feature of
the Brazilian sugar industry and its distinctive advantage. Records from

[8] The weight of the sugar crates varied over time. In the early seventeenth century, 15–20 arrobas
(480–640 lb) was common. By the eighteenth century, the average weight was calculated at
35–40 arrobas (1,120–1,280 lb).

the Jesuit-owned Engenho Sergipe do Conde in Bahia reveal an average safra lasting some 300 days. This figure compares favourably with the 120-day average of Jamaican sugar mills in the eighteenth century. There were, however, constant stoppages for Sundays, saints' days, poor weather, breakdowns, and shortages of cane and firewood. In Engenho Sergipe's 310-day safra of 1651, no cane was milled on 86 days: 56 for religious reasons, twelve for repairs, and eighteen for shortages.[9] Figure 1 represents the Bahian sugar year using the work stoppages of Engenho Sergipe in 1650–1 as an example of the interruptions experienced. Lay planters, it should be noted, were far less careful about observing Sundays and holy days, despite the denunciations and warnings of various churchmen. Thus, the Engenho Sergipe cycle represents a minimum number of working days. Finally, it should be noted that, despite costly interruptions, the Brazilian engenho enjoyed a favourable environment for sugar-cane cultivation and a comparative advantage in the length of its productive year. These were conditions especially conducive to slavery as a form of labour. The Brazilian sugar year had virtually no 'dead period', no time when slaves were unprofitably left without any useful occupation. Slaves could be used almost throughout the year, and they were. Given the length of the safra, the nature of the labour, and the rhythm of the working day, it is little wonder that high slave mortality was a constant feature of the Brazilian sugar industry.

Even this brief sketch of the sugar-making process makes clear its intensity and complexity. Given the existing technology, the peculiarities of sugar production imposed a certain rhythm and pace on the operations that made the period of the safra one of both exhausting labour and delicate precision. Integrating the sequence of planting, harvesting, milling, boiling, and purging demanded skilled management in order to avoid shortages or surpluses and to ensure a constant level of production. Technicians were needed to build and maintain the mill machinery, and at each stage of the sugar-making process skilled and experienced personnel were needed. The construction and supply of an engenho demanded a large capital outlay and access to credit in the face of the harvest's uncertainties. Engenhos often employed ten or twenty free men as artisans, managers, or skilled labourers. Salaries for such personnel could equal a quarter of the mill's yearly operating costs. Large quantities of firewood for the furnaces and great numbers of oxen

[9] *Documentos para a história do açúcar* (3 vols., Rio de Janeiro, 1954–63), II, 495–532.

for motive power were also constant items of expenditure. But, when planters discussed the operating cost of an engenho, it was the slaves who demanded their attention above all else. An average engenho needed 60–100 slaves, but a large estate producing over 100 metric tons a year could have 200 or more. Above all, the nature and organization of the labour force of the engenho determined the pattern of Brazilian society.

'The most solid properties in Brazil are slaves', wrote Governor Luís Vahia Monteiro in 1729, 'and a man's wealth is measured by having more or fewer... for there are lands enough, but only he who has slaves can be master of them.'[10] By 1580 slavery was already firmly established as the principal form of labour in the colony. The early expansion of the sugar industry took place with Indians working both as slaves and as contract workers drawn from Jesuit-controlled villages. In the 1560s the Indian population was devastated by a series of epidemics. Thereafter demographic collapse combined with physical resistance and aversion to plantation labour to make the use of Indian slaves less desirable for the Portuguese planters. In addition, under pressure from the Jesuits, the crown began to turn against the enslavement of Indians. The first prohibition was issued in 1570 and after the Iberian union further laws were promulgated in 1595 and 1609. Although this legislation did not eliminate Indian slavery entirely, in conjunction with high mortality, low productivity, and the general resistance of the Indian peoples, it made the seemingly stronger and more easily controlled African labour more attractive even though more expensive. The Portuguese had already made use of African bondsmen at home and in the Atlantic sugar colonies of Madeira and São Tomé. There is some evidence to show that the first Africans introduced as plantation labour had already been trained in the complexities of sugar-making and were placed in the more skilled positions where the planters' investment in training was less likely to be lost through disease. Europeans generally considered the value of Indian labour to be less than that of African, a situation which was reflected in the pricing of Indian slaves at one-third to one-quarter of the value of Africans. Even as free workers, Indians were paid less than free blacks and mulattos performing similar tasks.

The transition from Indian to African labour, although under way from the 1570s on, was slow and not fully achieved in the plantation

[10] *Publicações do Arquivo Nacional* (1915), xv, 364–5.

areas until the third decade of the seventeenth century. In Pernambuco, where there were 66 engenhos in 1585, Father Cardim reported 2,000 African slaves. Assuming an average of 100 slaves on each engenho, it would appear that two-thirds of the slaves were still Indians. Cardim also reported that Bahia had some 3,000 Africans and 8,000 slave and free Indians on its engenhos. At the Engenho Sergipe the transition can be plainly seen. Its slave force in 1574 was only 7 per cent African, but by 1591 it was 37 per cent African, and by 1638 totally African or Afro-Brazilian.

Statistics on the slave trade and general population figures are lacking for the period under discussion, so it is difficult to ascertain the size of the slave population. The best estimates at present are that about 4,000 slaves a year were imported between 1570 and 1630 and that there was a total African slave population of 13,000–15,000 in the colony by 1600. The level of imports rose to 7,000–8,000 a year until 1680, when the total slave population was about 150,000. Imports probably declined over the next two decades until the need for slaves in the gold-mining areas created a vast new demand. In the first half of the eighteenth century Bahia took some 5,000–8,000 slaves a year. Rio de Janeiro received 156,638 from Luanda alone between 1734 and 1769. By the eighteenth century slaves composed about half of the population in the north-eastern captaincies, but in sugar-growing regions they often constituted between 65 and 70 per cent of the inhabitants.

Slave trade figures were particularly important in the Brazilian case because it appears that natural increase in the slave population was negligible, if it existed at all. High levels of infant and adolescent mortality and a marked sexual imbalance were the major factors responsible for this situation. A survey of agricultural slaves in the Bahian Recôncavo reveals a sex ratio of two men to every woman.[11] This imbalance was continually exacerbated by the tendency within the slave trade to favour men over women and adults over children. Brazilian planters became particularly tied to the Atlantic trade and tended to reject natural growth as a viable alternative because child mortality rates were high and raising a slave child for twelve or fourteen years until maturity was a risky investment. Less than 20 per cent of the slave force was under the age of fourteen. The low fertility and high

---

[11] These figures and those that follow in this section are based on preliminary analysis of 1,740 slaves listed in Bahian inventories of agricultural properties between 1689 and 1826 drawn from Arquivo Público do Estado da Bahia (Salvador) [APB], secção judiciária.

Table 3 *Slave productivity in relation to original purchase price* (réis)

Date	1 Price per arroba of white sugar	2 Price per male slave	3 Annual value of slave output (col. 1 × 40)[a]	4 Monthly value of slave output (col. 3 ÷ 12)	5 'Replacement life' in months (col.
1608	1$080	30$000	43$200	3$600	8.3
1622	556	29$000	22$290	1$860	15.6
1635	812	39$000	32$749	2$730	14.3
1650	1$125	49$000	45$151	3$760	13.0
1670	1$177	45$000	47$080	3$923	11.5
1680	1$109	43$000	44$360	3$696	11.6
1700[b]	1$600	80$000	64$800	5$400	14.8
1710[c]	1$200	120$000	48$000	4$000	30.0
1751[d]	1$400	140$000	56$000	4$666	30.0

[a] Estimate of one crate of 40 arrobas per slave from José da Silva Lisboa (1780).
[b] Values represent averages from 1698 to 1704.
[c] Figures based on Antonil, *Cultura e opulência*.
[d] AHU, Bahia, caixa 61 (paper submitted to Mesa da Inspeção). All other figures based on accounts of Engenho Sergipe, Bahia.

mortality rates, estimated by planters at 5–10 per cent a year, could be offset by the high sugar prices and the readily available replacements through the slave trade. Throughout the first half of the seventeenth century a slave could produce enough sugar to recover his original cost in between thirteen and sixteen months, and, even after the steep rise of slave prices after 1700, replacement value could be earned in 30 months (see table 3).[12] Thus there was little incentive to ameliorate the conditions of labour or to change the existing manner of slave management. The engenhos consumed slaves and the slave trade replaced them.

Finally, the pattern of the slave trade had two other effects: one demographic and the other cultural. Because mortality seems to have been particularly high among the newly-arrived (*boçal*) slaves, high levels of importation, together with the sexual imbalance, tended to

[12] Table 3 presents a calculation of slave productivity in sugar in relation to the original purchase price of a male field hand. The calculations are based exclusively on the higher-priced white sugar, which was produced in ratios of 2 : 1 or 3 : 1 over *muscavado* on most Brazilian engenhos. This method of calculation probably lowers the estimate of months for replacement by one-third. At present it is not possible to calculate slave maintenance costs, although a report of 1635 set these at about 2 milréis per slave a year. Since slaves also produced food crops which also cannot be measured, I have left both the maintenance costs and non-sugar production out of the table.

create a self-perpetuating cycle of importation and mortality throughout most of the period under discussion. Moreover, the constant arrival of newly enslaved blacks tended to reinforce African culture in Brazil. There were regional variations. Rio de Janeiro, for example, was closely tied to Angola and Benguela, while Bahia traded intensely with the Mina coast. While a great deal is known about the Yoruba traditions introduced in the late eighteenth century, it is more difficult to say much about the African cultural elements brought by the earlier slaves. Planters and administrators complained about 'witchcraft' in a general fashion. *Calundus*, or ceremonies of divination accompanied by music, were reported in the early eighteenth century by one observer, who complained that planters ignored these rites in order to get along with their slaves, and that the latter then passed them on to freedmen and even to whites.[13]

While slaves were used for all kinds of labour, most could be found working on the engenhos and cane farms. The majority of these were field hands, 'slaves of sickle and hoe' (*escravos de fouce e enxada*), but those who had artisan skills and those who worked inside the mill house as kettlemen were more highly valued by the masters. House slaves, often mulattos, were favoured but relatively few in numbers. Occasionally an engenho would employ slaves in managerial roles, as drivers, for instance, or (more rarely) as the sugar master. In the Bahian survey mentioned above, 54 per cent were listed as field slaves, 13 per cent worked in the mill; 13 per cent were house slaves, 7 per cent were artisans; 10 per cent were boatmen and carters; while slaves in managerial roles constituted only 1 per cent of those listed with occupations. Brazilian-born blacks (*crioulos*) and mulattos were preferred as house slaves and mulattos were often chosen for artisan training.

The occupational distribution of the slave force reflects the hierarchies of the slave society. Distinctions were made between the *boçal*, newly arrived from Africa, and the *ladino*, or acculturated slave. In addition, a hierarchy of colour was also recognized in which mulattos received preferential treatment. The two gradations of colour and culture intersected in a predictable fashion, with Africans tending towards one end of both scales, mulattos at the other and *crioulos* between. The preference shown towards mulattos, and their advantages, were accompanied by prejudice against them as inconstant, sly, and 'uppity'. These hierarchies of colour and culture were, of course, created by the

[13] Nuno Marques Pereira, *Compendio narrativo do peregrino da America* (Lisbon, 1728), 115-130.

slaveowners, and it is difficult to know how far they were accepted by the slaves themselves; but the rivalry between Africans and *crioulos* in militia units and the existence of religious brotherhoods based on colour or African 'nationhood' indicate that these distinctions were maintained by the coloured population.

The once popular myth of the benign nature of Brazilian slavery has to a large extent been laid to rest by scholarship in the last two decades. Most contemporary observers commented that food, clothing, and punishment were the essentials of slave management. There seem to have been generous portions of the last, but provisions for slaves in the plantation zones were minimal. While there were considerable efforts to convert slaves to Catholicism and to have them participate in the sacraments of the church, the reality seems to have been quite different. High rates of illegitimacy among the slave population and low birth rates indicate that legal marriage was infrequent. Rather than viewing slaves as members of an extended family, it would seem that a natural hostility born of the master–slave relationship was paramount. The administrator of Engenho Santana in Ilhéus complained that the 178 slaves under his care were 'so many devils, thieves, and enemies'.[14] The counterpoint of plantation life was formed by the master's demands and the slave's recalcitrance – expressed by flight, malingering, complaint, and sometimes violence. Planters cajoled and threatened, using both punishments and rewards to stimulate effort. Slaves in the mill were given sugar juice or rum, slaves might receive extra provisions, 'gifts', or even the promise of eventual freedom, in order to coax them into co-operating. The following statement made by an engenho administrator in the 1720s describes vividly the texture of Brazilian plantation slavery and the slaves' ability to manoeuvre within their subordinate position:

the time of their service is no more than five hours a day and much less when the work is far off. It is the multitude that gets anything done just as in an anthill. And when I reprimand them with the example of whites and their slaves who work well, they answer that the whites work and earn money while they get nothing and the slaves of those whites work because they are given enough clothes and food... It is sometimes necessary to visit the quarters two or three times a day to throw them out,...those that are only feigning illness. God knows what I suffer by not resorting to punishment in order to avoid runaways. And when I complain, they point to their stomach and say, 'The belly makes

[14] ANTT, Cartório dos Jesuitas, maço 15, n. 23.

the ox go', giving me to understand that I do not feed them. It is my sins that have sent me to such an *engenho*.[15]

There were a limited number of responses to the conditions of slavery, ranging from acquiescence to rebellion. The most common form of resistance was flight, which was endemic in the plantation areas. Inventories of properties almost always list one or two slaves who had escaped. Planters hired slave-hunting 'bush captains' (*capitães do mato*), themselves often free blacks, to hunt down the fugitives. In 1612 'bush captains' were created in the eight parishes of Pernambuco for slave control and by 1625 the town council of Salvador was setting fixed prices for the capture of fugitive slaves. When they could the escapees formed themselves into exile communities (*mocambos* or *quilombos*), in inaccessible areas. Usually small in size (under 100 people), they survived by a combination of subsistence agriculture and raiding. Expeditions were organized to destroy them, led by 'bush captains' in command of Indian auxiliaries. While most of the *mocambos* were short-lived, usually a few fugitives would escape recapture, and a new community would spring up.

In the period under discussion the most important escapee community was the great group of villages located in present-day Alagoas and known collectively as Palmares. The first *mocambos* in this region were probably formed around 1605 and the number of inhabitants swelled during the period of the Dutch invasion of Pernambuco. Expeditions were sent out periodically by both Portuguese and Dutch authorities to destroy Palmares, but all of them were unsuccessful. By the 1670s, the number of escaped slaves in Palmares was reported at over 20,000, probably an exaggeration since such numbers would have equalled all the slaves on Pernambuco's engenhos. Nevertheless, Palmares was by all accounts a very large community, containing thousands of escaped slaves and encompassing several villages and at least two main towns, called by this time by the Kimbundu term *quilombo* (*ki-lombo*). Major Portuguese punitive expeditions were carried out in 1676–7 under Fernão Carilho, followed in 1678 by fruitless treaty negotiations. After a heroic defence in 1695 the *quilombo* of Palmares was finally destroyed and its leaders executed. But *quilombos* died hard and as late as 1746 slaves and Indians were still gathering at the site of Palmares.[16]

The other major outlet from slavery was provided by manumission.

[15] Jerónimo da Gama (Ilhéus, 1753), ANTT, Cartório dos Jesuitas, maço 54, n. 55.
[16] AHU, papéis avulsos [PA], Alagoas, caixa 2 (2 August 1746).

Iberian traditions of slavery provided some basis for the phenomenon of voluntary manumission. Slaves who had performed long and faithful service or children raised in the plantation house were singled out for awards of liberty, but just as important was the process of self-purchase, in which slaves raised funds to buy their own freedom. A study of Bahian manumission charters from 1684 to 1745 reveals that women were freed twice as often as men.[17] Males had their best opportunities for freedom as children. *Crioulo* and mulatto slaves were freed far more frequently than Africans relative to their numbers in the population. The proportion of purchased to free manumissions rose during the eighteenth century to a point in the 1740s when the two forms of grant were made in almost equal numbers. The large numbers of purchased manumissions must discount to some extent the arguments sometimes made about the humanitarian aspects of manumission in Brazil, as does the fact that about 20 per cent of the charters were granted conditionally dependent on further service by the slave.

The patterns of manumission once again reveal the hierarchies of colour and acculturation that characterize other aspects of Brazilian slavery. As a group mulattos were the smallest sector of the slave population, but in manumission they were particularly favoured. Brazilian-born blacks followed and Africans, in this period, came last, receiving the fewest number of charters while composing the largest segment of the slave population. The manumission process was itself a complex mixture of Iberian religious and cultural imperatives and economic considerations, but it is clear that the more acculturated the slave and the lighter his or her colour, the better the chances for obtaining freedom. During the course of the seventeenth century manumission slowly began to produce a class of freedmen, former slaves who filled a series of low and intermediate roles in Brazilian economic life. The pattern of freeing women and children also tended to increase the reproductive capacity of the free coloured population while depleting that capacity among the slave population, thereby adding another reason for the negative natural growth rate of the Brazilian slave population.

Since the engenhos formed the core of the colony's economy, it is not surprising that the planters (*senhores de engenho*) exercised considerable social, economic, and political power. While some titled nobility in

---

[17] Stuart B. Schwartz, 'The manumission of slaves in colonial Brazil: Bahia, 1684–1745', *Hispanic American Historical Review* [*HAHR*], 54/4 (Nov. 1974), 603–35.

Portugal, like the duke of Monsanto, owned mills in Brazil, they did not come in person to administer them and were content to depend on agents and overseers in the colony. Most of the early *sesmarias* (land grants) went to commoners who had participated in the conquest and settlement of the coast. In general, then, the planter class was not of noble origin but was composed of commoners who saw in sugar the means to wealth and upward mobility. The title of *senhor de engenho* in Brazil was said to be like that of *conde* (count) in Portugal, and Brazilian planters tried to live the part. Their wealth and luxury drew the notice of visitors. And while they also made a great display of piety and some maintained full-time chaplains at their engenhos, ecclesiastical observers were often not impressed. Father Manuel da Nóbrega wrote, 'this people of Brazil pays attention to nothing but their engenhos and wealth even though it be with the perdition of all their souls'.[18]

The striving for social status and its recognition through the traditional symbols of nobility – titles, membership in military orders and entails – must be seen as a predominant mark of the planter class. A government report of 1591 suggested that the planters' aspirations could be manipulated for royal ends since the *senhores de engenho* were 'so well endowed with riches and so lacking in the privileges and honours of knighthoods, noble ranks, and pensions'. Eighteenth-century genealogists constantly strove to blur the distinction between families of noble origin and lineage and those whose claim to high status rested simply on longevity or success. In works like that of the Pernambucan Borges da Fonseca, planter families become 'noble' by 'antiquity' and even Indian origins are explained away.[19] A family like the Monteiros could be described as 'having maintained itself pure and finding itself today with sufficient nobility'. In fact, although the Brazilian planter class exercised considerable influence in the colony, it did not become a hereditary nobility; titles were not given, entails of property (*morgados*) were awarded only in a few cases, and even membership in the military orders was not granted often. The *senhores de engenho* were a colonial aristocracy, invariably white or accepted as such, locally favoured and powerful, but not a hereditary nobility. Lacking the traditional privileges and exemptions of a hereditary estate, the planters were relatively weak in their access to royal power.

The traditional historiography of colonial Brazil has tended to

---

[18] Serafim Leite (ed.), *Cartas do Brasil e mais escritos do Padre Manuel da Nóbrega* (Coimbra, 1955), 346.

[19] António José Victoriano Borges da Fonseca, 'Nobiliarchia pernambucana', *Anais da Biblioteca Nacional de Rio de Janeiro [ABNRJ]*, 47 (1925) and 48 (1926) (Rio de Janeiro, 1935), 1: 462.

encrust the planter class with a romantic patina that makes it difficult to perceive their social characteristics. Genealogists emphasizing the antiquity of important planter families projected a false impression of stability among the planter class. The sugar industry, in fact, created a highly volatile planter class, with engenhos changing hands constantly and many more failures than successes. Stability was, in fact, provided by the engenhos themselves, for the same mill names and properties appear continuously for hundreds of years. The owners and their families seemed to be far less stable. Undue emphasis on the few dominant families that survived the vicissitudes of the colonial economy has clouded this point.

There has in fact been little serious research on sugar planters as a social group. The main exception is a detailed study of 80 Bahian *senhores de engenho* in the period 1680–1725.[20] A century or more after the establishment of the industry almost 60 per cent of these planters were immigrants or the sons of immigrants, a pattern that indicates considerable mobility and flux within the planters' ranks. While the great families like the Aragão, Monis Barreto, or Argolos were third- or fifth-generation Brazilians, there were patterns of behaviour that allowed entrance to immigrants. The Portuguese-born merchant who acquired a mill and who himself (or whose son) married the daughter of a Brazilian planter family was a common phenomenon. While the old planter families tended to intermarry, room was always found for sons-in-law who were merchants with access to capital or high-court judges and lawyers bringing prestige, family name, and political leverage. Obviously, the arranged marriage was a key element in the strategy of family success.

The common pattern seems to have been for planters to live on their estates. In fact, the lack of absenteeism has been suggested by some as a major feature in the development of a patriarchal relationship between masters and slaves. While it is true that Brazilian planters resided in the *casa grande*, most of the engenhos of Bahia and many of those in Pernambuco were quite close to the port cities, so that constant interchange and movement between the engenho and the city was possible. Many planters kept urban residences and transacted their business in the city in person. Ownership of more than one mill was

---

[20] Rae Flory, 'Bahian society in the mid-colonial period: the sugar planters, tobacco growers, merchants, and artisans of Salvador and the Reconcavo, 1680–1725' (Ph.D. thesis, University of Texas, 1978). The period covered by this study was a time of crisis and thus the findings must be used with care, but it remains the only study to date.

also not uncommon and some engenhos were owned by religious establishments and administered for them by majordomos. The picture of the resident planter family must thus be modified somewhat. Neither were the sugar planters akin to feudal barons living in isolation, surrounded by their slaves and retainers and little interested in the outside world. Planter investment in cattle ranches, shipping, and urban properties was common, and often a merchant who had acquired a sugar mill continued his mercantile activities. The latest quotation on the Lisbon or Amsterdam sugar market was of constant interest. One viceroy in the eighteenth century, homesick for the salons of Europe, complained that the only conversation he heard in Brazil was on the prospects for next year's harvest.

From its origins the sugar industry of Brazil depended on a second group of cultivators who did not own their own mills but who supplied cane to the engenhos of others. These cane farmers were a distinctive stratum in colonial society, part of the sugar sector and proud of their title *lavrador de cana* yet also often at odds with the *senhores de engenho*. In the seventeenth century there were perhaps, on average, four to seven cane farmers for each engenho, supplying cane under a variety of arrangements. The most privileged *lavradores de cana* were those who held clear and unencumbered titles to their own land and were thus able to bargain for the best milling contract: When cane was scarce these growers were much pampered by the *senhores de engenho*, who were willing to lend slaves or oxen or provide firewood in order to secure the cane. Many growers, however, worked *partidos da cana*, that is land that was 'obligated' to a particular mill. These *lavradores* of 'captive' cane might be sharecroppers working an engenho's lands on a shares basis, or tenants, or those who owned their own land under conditions such as a lien on their crop in return for money or credit. Contractual arrangements varied from place to place and at different times, but the standard division was one-half of the white and *muscavado* sugar to the mill and one-half to the grower, with all lower grades the property of the mill. In addition, those with 'captive cane' then paid a rent in the form of a percentage of their half of the sugar. This, too, varied from one-third to one-twentieth depending on time and place, but the *senhores de engenho* preferred to lease their best lands to growers of considerable resources who could accept the one-third obligation. Contracts were commonly for nine or eighteen years, but a parcel was sometimes sold with an obligation for 'as long as the world shall last'.

In theory, the relationship between the *lavrador de cana* and the *senhor de engenho* was reciprocal, but most colonial observers recognized that ultimate power usually lay in the hands of the *senhor*. The *lavrador de cana* accepted the obligation to provide cane to a particular mill, paying damages if the cane went elsewhere. The *senhor de engenho* promised to grind the cane at the appropriate time, so many *tarefas* per week. While these arrangements sometimes took the form of written contracts (especially when part of sales or loans) they were often oral. Ultimate power usually rested with the mill owner, who could displace a grower, refuse to pay for improvements of the land, give false measure of the sugar produced or, even worse, refuse to grind the cane at the appropriate time and ruin a whole year's work. This unequal relationship caused tension between the millowners and cane farmers.

Socially, the *lavradores de cana* came from a spectrum that was economically broad but racially narrow. Humble men with two or three slaves and wealthy growers with twenty or 30 slaves could be found as cane farmers. Merchants, urban professionals, men of high military rank or with claims to noble status, could all be found among the *lavradores de cana* – people in every respect similar to the planter class in origin and background; but alongside them were those for whom the growing of a few hectares of cane exhausted all their resources. Thus, once again, as with the *senhores de engenho*, there was a certain instability in the agrarian population, people taking a chance, planting a few *tarefas* and then failing. In eighteen safras at Engenho Sergipe between 1622 and 1652 almost 60 per cent of the 128 *lavradores* appeared in less than three harvests. In this period, however, *lavradores de cana* were, almost without exception, European or Brazilian-born whites. Few people of colour could overcome the disadvantages of birth or the prejudice of creditors against *pardos* and enter the ranks of the sugar growers. In short, the *lavradores de cana* were 'proto-planters', often of the same social background as planters but lacking the capital or credit needed to establish a mill. The value of the average cane farm was perhaps one-fifth of that of the average engenho, surely a reflection of the relative wealth of the two groups.

The existence of a large class of cane farmers differentiated the colonial Brazilian sugar economy from that of the Spanish Indies or the English and French Caribbean islands. In the early stages of the industry it meant that the burdens and risks of growing sugar were widely distributed. It also meant that the structure of slave-owning was complex since large numbers of slaves lived in units of six to ten rather than the hundreds of the great plantations. Evidence from the late colonial period suggests that perhaps one-third of the slaves who worked the sugar were owned by *lavradores de cana*. Finally, the existence of *lavradores de cana* added to the problems of colonial Brazil when the sugar economy entered hard times in the late seventeenth century. Various attempts were made to limit the construction of new mills, but limiting the opportunity for *lavradores* to become *senhores de engenho* was perceived as even more injurious to the health of the industry than the proliferation of mills. It was felt that the industry had to hold out at least the hope of social mobility to attract cane growers, even though increasing output had an adverse effect on the price of sugar, already falling through foreign competition.

Despite the natural antagonisms between the *senhores de engenho* and the *lavradores de cana*, these two groups are best viewed as substrata of the same class, mainly differentiated by wealth but sharing a common background, aspirations, and attitudes. Conflicts between them might be bitter, but together the two groups constituted a sugar sector with similar interests in matters of taxation, commercial policy, and relations with other groups and both enjoying the highest political and social positions in the colony, dominating the town councils, prestigious lay brotherhoods, and militia offices.

Of considerably lower social status were the whites and free people of colour who performed a variety of tasks as wage labourers on the plantation. Records from the seventeenth century rarely speak of the attached agricultors, the *agregados* or *moradores*, who are common in the eighteenth century, but engenhos regularly employed woodmen, boatmen, carpenters, masons, and other craftsmen. There were, in fact, two kinds of employees on the plantations: those who received an annual salary (*soldada*), and those who were paid a daily wage or for each task carried out. The former generally included the sugar master, crater, overseers, boatmen, and sometimes kettlemen. Carpenters, masons, and woodcutters were employed as needed. Once again, hierarchies of colour and race emerge from the records. In this case Indians, no matter what their occupation, were invariably paid less than whites or free blacks performing similar tasks. Moreover, Indians were usually hired by the job or by the month and paid in goods rather than cash, indications that they were not wholly integrated into a European wage-labour market. Artisan occupations were one area where free people of colour could hope to find some opportunity for advancement. But, as in other productive activites, artisans on the engenhos often owned their own slaves.

Despite a historiography that has emphasized the seigniorial aspects of the planter class, sugar-growing was a business greatly concerned with profit and loss. By contemporary standards the establishment of an engenho was an expensive operation. An average engenho in the mid seventeenth century required about 15,000 milréis of capital investment. Lands were acquired by grants of *sesmaria* or by purchase, but in this period land does not seem to have been the most important factor of production, since transactions and wills rarely specified its extent or value. Much more care was devoted to the identification and evaluation of the labour force. It was estimated in 1751 that slaves were the most expensive factor of production, constituting 36 per cent of a plantation's total value. Land was valued at 19 per cent, livestock at 4 per cent, buildings at 18 per cent, and machinery equipment at 23 per cent. Yearly operating costs were high and once again labour topped the list. Salaries for free labourers were calculated at 23 per cent of the total annual costs, slave maintenance at 16 per cent, and the replacement of slaves at 19 per cent for an estimated loss of 10 per cent of the slave force each year.[21] Labour-related costs, then, were almost 60 per cent of annual expenditure. Firewood was the other major item of expense, 12–21 per cent of costs, depending on its availability and the plantation's location. With so few plantation records available, the profitability of the industry is difficult to establish in any but the most general terms. Early observers of Brazil always commented on the opulence and luxury of the planter class, while the planters themselves were continually seeking exemption from taxes or a moratorium on debt payments on grounds of poverty.

Credit and capital for the establishment and operation of *engenhos* came from a variety of sources. In the sixteenth century some direct investment from Europe seems to have been made in the Brazilian sugar industry, but there is little evidence of this in the seventeenth century. One method of raising funds for investment in a sugar mill might be called the 'Robinson Crusoe' pattern, since Defoe's hero practised it

---

[21] Câmara of Salvador to crown, AHU/PA/Bahia, caixa 61 (1751). Cf. Frédéric Mauro, 'Contabilidade teórica e contabilidade prática no século XVII', *Nova história e novo mundo* (São Paulo, 1969), 135–48.

during his stay in Bahia (1655–9?) and it was reported by other sources
as well. This was the growing of manioc, tobacco, or some other crop
with the hope of accumulating enough capital or credit with a local
merchant to permit the building of a sugar mill. Probably the best
opportunities for this approach were to be found in raising sugar-cane
for processing at someone else's engenho. Loans came from various
religious institutions such as the charitable brotherhood of the Misericórdia and the Third Orders of St Francis and St Anthony. The interest
rate charged by these institutions was fixed by canon and civil law at
6.25 per cent and thus their loans tended to be low-yield, low-risk
contracts made with members of the colonial elite, many of whom were
members of these bodies. These institutional lenders favoured the sugar
industry. The 90 loans of the Misericórdia of Salvador secured by
mortgages on agricultural properties in 1694 included 24 on engenhos
and 47 on cane farms. One suspects that institutional lenders preferred
to make loans for the original capital expense in setting up a mill or
cane farm, but that loans for operating expenses were much more
difficult to obtain.

For the operating costs, and for those who could not gain access to
the sources of institutional credit, the next alternative was private
lenders, principally merchants. While also constrained by laws against
usury, merchants found ways of extracting much higher interest rates,
often by lending funds against a future crop at a pre-determined price.
Further sources of credit were urban professionals or other *senhores de
engenho*, but the study of Bahia's engenhos between 1680 and 1725
indicates that almost half the money lent came from religious institutions
and another quarter from merchants.[22] Despite social fusion between
planters and merchants, the debtor–creditor relationship created
antagonism and tension between them and at many junctures caused
them to take hostile – one might say class – positions towards each other.

In the long run, questions of finance and profitability cannot be
viewed in static terms. International political events, the price of sugar,
and local conditions in the colony all produced changing patterns of
profit and loss. In general, it can be said that during most of the period
under discussion Brazil was faced with rising costs and falling prices
for its sugar. The rising cost of slaves, who as we have seen were a major
item of expenditure, signalled to the planters the problem that they

[22] Flory, 'Bahian society', 71–5.

faced. We can make the same calculation that the planters made: how much sugar did it take to replace a slave? The answer provided in table 3 above is that it was about four times as much in 1710 as it had been in 1608.

It was on the wharves of Amsterdam, London, Hamburg, and Genoa that the ultimate success of the Brazilian sugar economy was determined. The European price for sugar rose sharply throughout the last half of the sixteenth century. After a slight drop in the 1610s price levels rose again in the 1620s, owing in part to the disruption of the sugar supply to Europe caused by Dutch attacks on Brazil and the losses suffered by Portuguese shipping. With the end of the Twelve-Year Truce between Spain and the United Provinces in 1621, Brazil became a major target for attack, and from 1630 to 1654 the Dutch held most of north-east Brazil, half of the colony, including Pernambuco, the major sugar-producing captaincy. Sugar continued to be produced in this area by Luso-Brazilian planters, but the Dutch West India Company began to call in the loans it had made to those persons who had acquired engenhos during the period of Dutch rule. The Luso-Brazilian rebellion, which erupted in 1645, was in part a response to the falling price of sugar and the straits in which the planters found themselves. During the war, between 1645 and 1654, production in Brazil was disrupted; while the price of sugar rose on the Amsterdam exchange it fell in Brazil.

The Dutch period was, in terms of the social and political development of the north-east, a historical hiatus. After the 30 years of Dutch rule few tangible vestiges of their presence remained. In broader economic terms, however, Brazil's place within the Atlantic system was never the same again, nor was the regional concentration of economic resources within the colony ever to be as it had been before 1630.

First, the destruction and disruption caused by the fighting seriously impaired the production and export of sugar. The seizure of Salvador in 1624 resulted in the loss of much of two safras and the capture of many ships. Similar losses resulted from the expeditions against Bahia in 1627 and 1638. The Dutch attack on the Recôncavo in 1648 brought the destruction of 23 engenhos and the loss of 1,500 crates of sugar. During the war, Portuguese shipping was decimated: between 1630 and 1636 199 ships were lost, a staggering figure except when compared with the 220 vessels lost in 1647–8. After the beginning of the Luso-Brazilian revolt of 1645 both sides burned engenhos and canefields as a matter of course.

Within the captaincies under Dutch control the confiscation of property and the flight of owners meant that 65 out of 149 engenhos were inactive (*fogo morto*) in 1637. During the revolt of 1645–54, one-third of the engenhos were out of action. While, around 1650, estimates of Pernambuco's capacity were set at about 25,000 crates, the captaincy actually produced only 6,000. Planters from Pernambuco fled southward to Bahia or even Rio de Janeiro, bringing slaves and capital with them. After 1630 Bahia replaced Pernambuco as the captaincy with the most slaves and as the centre of the Portuguese-controlled sugar economy. Rio de Janeiro's sugar economy was characterized by smaller units often producing rum for export. By the 1670s it was expanding northward into the area of Campos de Goitacazes.

While the sugar economy of Pernambuco suffered badly in the 1640s, Bahia and its surrounding captaincies did not enjoy the new leadership without problems. Brazilian sugar production had begun to level off in the 1620s and the fighting of the following decade simply intensified a process already begun. During the Dutch occupation of the north-east, the Portuguese crown sought to generate funds in order to carry out the war and meet its defence needs, but found that the slackening in Brazilian sugar production made doing so ever more difficult. Its response was to tax sugar production and trade ever more heavily. In 1631 a tax of one cruzado (= 400 réis) per crate was imposed followed by another of ten cruzados per crate in 1647. It was only natural that the crown should hope to finance its defence of the colony by taxing sugar. In Pernambuco about 80 per cent of government receipts resulted from various sugar taxes. Planters, of course, complained loudly about these imposts and other wartime measures such as requisitioning boats and quartering troops.

The damage to the sugar economy, the lower world price for sugar as a result of competition from the Caribbean, and the War of Restoration in Portugal all prevented the crown from abolishing the imposts on the sugar industry. But continuing taxes impeded rebuilding and expansion of the industry. In turn, the fall in output meant lower revenues from the tithe and other normal imposts, thus making the extraordinary taxes still necessary. Attempts to break this vicious circle were unsuccessful. For example, a proposal to declare a moratorium on all debts contracted before 1645 and thereby enable the planters to accumulate capital met with stiff resistance from Portuguese merchant-creditors.

By the end of the war in 1654, when Brazil was once again fully under Portuguese control and a return to its former prosperity might have been expected, the Atlantic community's sources of sugar and Brazil's share of them had changed considerably. The English, Dutch, and French colonies in the Caribbean which had begun to grow sugar during the favourable price conditions of the 1630s now began to compete heavily with Brazil. Increased production from these new suppliers tended to keep prices low, especially during the 1670s and 1680s, when a period of general European peace after 1675 permitted a regularization of the slave trade and an unrestrained growth of tropical agriculture. On the Lisbon market the price of an arroba of sugar fell from 3$800 réis in 1654 to 1$300 in 1688.

The 1680s, in fact, marked a low point in the fortunes of the Brazilian sugar economy. The colony was hit by a severe drought lasting from 1681 to 1684, there were smallpox outbreaks from 1682 to 1684, and a yellow fever epidemic that first struck Recife in 1685–6. Added to these problems was a general economic crisis in the Atlantic world after 1680. In 1687 João Peixoto Viegas penned his famous *memorial* identifying the problems of Brazilian agriculture and forecasting the ruin of the colony, but events in 1689 quickly turned the situation around. The outbreak of war between France and England disrupted the supplies of those nations and offered Brazil higher prices and increased opportunities for its sugar. Planters who, like Peixoto Viegas, had prophesied doom in 1687 could by 1691 think of regaining their former prosperity, despite the rising cost of slaves and other imported commodities. However, the recovery of the 1690s was short-lived. The uncertainties of war made sugar prices fluctuate wildly until 1713, when the earlier decline was resumed. Despite occasional recoveries the secular trend was downward into the middle of the eighteenth century.

Meanwhile, the discovery of gold in Minas Gerais after 1695 created a vast new demand for labour in Brazil and drove slave prices up to unprecedented peaks, reaching a rate of increase of over 5 per cent per annum in the decade between 1710 and 1720. The discovery of gold was itself certainly not the cause of export agriculture's problem. As we have seen, the sugar industry had suffered bad times intermittently since 1640, especially in the 1670s and 1680s, but the gold rush created new pressures on coastal agriculture. As early as 1701 attempts were made to limit the slave trade to the mines and after 1703 planters' complaints about labour shortages and the high cost of slaves were continuous. By 1723 the municipal council of Salvador complained that 24 engenhos had ceased to function and that sugar production had fallen because of the high price of slaves and the planters' inability to compete with the miners for the purchase of new labourers. After 1730 the north-eastern sugar economy entered a period of depression reflected in a declining annual production.

The unhappy history of sugar just outlined made difficulties for planters, merchants, and Portuguese crown alike. Planters complained of excessive taxes, high prices for slaves, droughts, and extortion by merchants; royal officials laid the blame on the planters' profligacy and lack of foresight; and merchants claimed that planters overspent and that their fraudulent weighing and quality-marking on Brazilian sugar crates had lowered the value of sugar in European markets. More perceptive observers realized that foreign competition and English and French protectionism had also cut deeply into the available market for Brazilian sugar. Such steps as were taken by the crown and by the planters themselves to meet the crisis had only limited effect. The Brazilian sugar industry in the eighteenth century steadily lost ground to its Caribbean rivals.

SUBSIDIARY ECONOMIC ACTIVITIES

The cutting and export of wood, so important in the early years of the colony's development, continued throughout the colonial period, although the emphasis shifted from dyewood to varieties used for furniture or shipbuilding. A new royal monopoly on brazilwood was established in 1605 in which contracts for cutting and shipping the wood were granted to private individuals. Contraband was always a special problem because some of the best wood was to be found in Porto Seguro, Ilhéus, and Espírito Santo, captaincies far from the centres of government control. Similar royal monopolies were established over whaling and salt, in which contractors would lease the rights to exploit those resources. While these activities undoubtedly generated funds for the crown, agriculture remained the basis of the colony's economy.

An agricultural hierarchy ranged according to the export possibilities of the crops prevailed in the colony. The best and most valuable lands were always given over to export crops, preferably sugar-cane but also tobacco. Subsistence farming, especially growing manioc, was considered to be the 'least noble' occupation, and was usually relegated

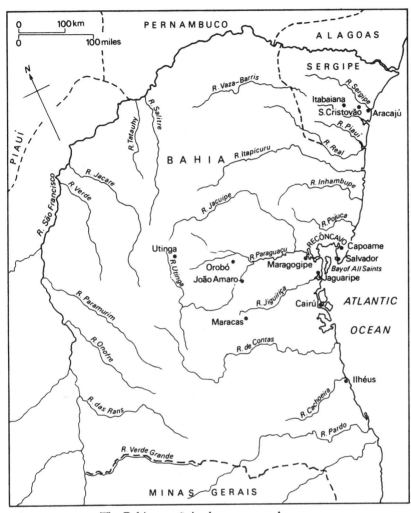

The Bahian *sertão* in the seventeenth century

Source: Stuart B. Schwartz (ed.), *A governor and his image in Baroque Brazil*
(Minneapolis, 1979).

to marginal lands and often left to the humblest cultivators. Cattle-
raising, at first for internal consumption and later for export, differed
somewhat from the general pattern not only because it could be carried
out effectively on land unsuited for export crops but also because the
mobility of cattle on the hoof made it unnecessary for the ranches to
be near the coast.

The agricultural hierarchy was closely paralleled by a hierarchy of colour amongst agriculturalists, and this in turn was matched by differences in the numbers of slaves they employed. Sugar planters and cane farmers were almost invariably white, tobacco farmers nearly always white, whereas manioc farmers included *pardos, mestiços* and free blacks. The number of slaves in each branch of agriculture, as well as the average number per holding, decreased according to the type of farming. A *senhor de engenho* might own a hundred slaves, a tobacco farmer fifteen or twenty on average, and a manioc grower only two or three, or even none at all. Clearly the highest return on investment in slave labour was in the export sector.

Tobacco

After sugar the most important export crop grown in Brazil up to the mid eighteenth century was tobacco or, as the Portuguese so poetically and accurately called it, *fumo* (smoke). Some tobacco was grown in Pará, Maranhão, and the captaincy of Pernambuco, but by far the most important centre of this husbandry was Bahia south and west of Salvador, especially the area around the port of Cachoeira at the mouth of the Paraguaçú river. It is not clear when tobacco cultivation in this zone began. Gabriel Soares de Sousa's description of the Recôncavo in 1587 does not mention the crop, but by the 1620s some tobacco was clearly being grown and exported from the Brazilian north-east. While the sandy and clay soils of the fields (*campos*) of Cachoeira were the focal point of production in Bahia, smaller zones could be found around Maragogipe and Jaguaripe in the Recôncavo, Inhambupe towards the *sertão*, the arid backlands, and to the north-east of Salvador on the Rio Real and in Sergipe de El-Rei. It is estimated that these Bahian regions produced nine-tenths of the tobacco exported by Brazil in this period.

Tobacco growing had some special features that influenced its social organization and its position in the Brazilian economy. Its six-month growing season was shorter than that of sugar and under proper conditions offered the possibility of double cropping. Its cultivation demanded intensive care: the seedlings had to be transplanted and then kept constantly weeded and protected from pests until the harvest, when the leaves had to be picked by hand. The gang labour of the canefields was not well suited to this activity. In fact, tobacco could be grown as efficiently on small family farms of a few acres as on larger units with twenty to 40 slaves. The scale of operations varied widely. Mixed cattle and tobacco farms were common, because the best-grade tobacco was produced using manure as fertilizer. But lower grades could be produced without the benefit of fertilizer. After the harvest the most difficult task was the preparation of the crop for sale. Brazilian tobacco was usually twisted into ropes, treated with a molasses-based liquid, wound into rolls (of eight arrobas for the Portuguese trade and three arrobas for the African coast) and then placed in leather casings. The onerous yet precise process of twisting and rolling had usually to be given to skilled slaves and was thus an item of some expense, but the poorer growers did not need to maintain their own processing unit; they simply paid *enroladores* to do this task.

Opportunities for profit, then, existed at various levels of production. Small family farms of four to seven acres existed alongside much larger slave-based units, although a survey of land sales at the turn of the eighteenth century placed the average unit at around 100 acres.[23] While cattle and a processing unit were essential for large producers, tobacco generally needed a smaller capital outlay and labour force than sugar and its preparation was a less complicated and costly process. The Bahian Superintendent of Tobacco wrote in 1714: 'There is much land that does not produce any other fruit, inhabited by many people who have no other means of support, since this agriculture is among the least costly and thus the easiest for the poor who practise it.'[24] In fact, in 1706, it was reported in Pernambuco that slaves themselves were producing low-grade tobacco in their free time.[25]

As in sugar agriculture, a variety of social types and classes were associated with tobacco, but in comparison with sugar they tended to be concentrated at a somewhat lower social level. While it might be profitable, the title of tobacco grower did not bring great social prestige or political power. Evidence drawn from notary records indicates that the average tobacco–cattle *sítio* was worth only about one-third of the value of the average cane farm and less than 1 per cent of that of an engenho. Thus, former manioc farmers and poor immigrants from Portugal were attracted to this crop, although there were also wealthy producers who combined tobacco cultivation with other activities. In the Cachoeira region families like the Adornos and Dias Laços had received enormous *sesmarias* when the area was first opened to European settlement. Some dozen families who raised sugar in Iguape (a zone of

23 *Ibid.*, 172.
24 ANTT, Junta do Tabaco, maço 97A.   25 *Ibid.*, maço 97 (21 Jan. 1706).

transition), ran cattle in the sertão, and also grew tobacco were the political and social elite of the area. Large growers like these might produce 4,000 arrobas a year, while there were others who grew less than 100 arrobas. Types of tenure varied and renting of tobacco lands was common. During the eighteenth century the number of small growers rose. Moreover, as a group their complexion darkened. Whereas a sample of 450 *lavradores de tabaco* between 1684 and 1725 revealed that only 3 per cent were *pardos*, a similar study for the late eighteenth century raised that figure to 27 per cent.[26] Tobacco, then, was a less prestigious, less expensive, and less exclusively white branch of export agriculture than sugar. However, tobacco agriculture was firmly based on slave labour and the census returns of tobacco-growing parishes at various points of time always show at least half the population to be slave – a lower proportion than in the sugar zones, to be sure, but one large enough to dispel any illusions that tobacco growing was based on yeoman husbandry.

The fortunes of tobacco as an export commodity were closely tied to those of Atlantic commerce and to the rhythm of Brazil's own economic development. The Dutch seizure of the Portuguese slaving station at São Jorge de Mina in 1637 disrupted the normal pattern of slave supply to Brazil. This, plus the loss of Angola in 1641, led to royal legislation in 1644 allowing direct trade between Brazil and Africa without any benefit to the metropolis. The Dutch limited Portuguese trade to four ports on the Mina coast and prohibited the introduction of any goods except Brazilian tobacco. This stimulated the expansion of tobacco cultivation in Brazil. The creation of a royal monopoly administration, the Junta da Administração do Tabaco, in 1674 was an attempt to control this product, but its major efforts were aimed at limiting production and contraband in Portugal itself.[27] While Brazilian planters complained about the monopoly, they continued to derive regular profit from the sale of tobacco to both Africa and Europe. Their position was considerably strengthened by the discovery of gold in Minas Gerais in 1695 and the resultant soaring demand for slave labour in the colony. Brazilian tobacco and gold became the items necessary for the slave trade in the eighteenth century.

[26] Cf. Flory, 'Bahian society', 158–217; Catherine Lugar, 'The Portuguese tobacco trade and the tobacco growers of Bahia in the late colonial period', in Dauril Alden and Warren Dean (eds.), *Essays concerning the socioeconomic history of Brazil and Portuguese India* (Gainesville, 1977), 26–70.

[27] Carl Hanson, 'Monopoly and contraband in the Portuguese tobacco trade', *Luso-Brazilian Review*, 19/2 (winter, 1968), 149–68.

Two curious paradoxes marked the Brazilian tobacco trade. First, in order to make sure that it had a supply of the best-quality tobacco, Portugal had prohibited the export of either of the first two grades to Africa. The third grade, *refugado*, had to be liberally treated with molasses syrup, a sugar by-product, so that it could be wound into cords, but it was exactly this treatment that gave it the sweet taste and aroma that made it so popular on the African coast and as a major trade item with the Indians in the Canadian fur trade. The Portuguese monopoly also attempted to fix the price of high-quality tobacco to ensure a profit to metropolitan merchants. This situation led planters to concentrate on growing lower grades for sale in Africa or to enter the thriving contraband trade in tobacco. By the 1730s the crown was trying various measures to control the trade to Mina and to sustain the amounts going to Portugal, but, as figure 2 demonstrates, they had little effect. Finally, in 1743, the Mina trade was reorganized in favour of the Brazilian merchants. Only 30 ships a year – 24 from Bahia and six from Pernambuco – were allowed to trade on the Mina coast, thereby guaranteeing limits on supply and high prices for Brazilian goods. In 1752 it was estimated that a Mina slave could be bought at Whydah for eight rolls of tobacco or 28$800 réis, transported for another 26$420 réis, and sold in Bahia for 100$000 réis, yielding a profit of almost 45 per cent.

It is difficult to establish the levels of tobacco production and export and almost impossible to do so for the period prior to the creation of the Junta da Administração do Tabaco in 1674. Not only are statistical series lacking, but contraband was always rife, especially after the creation of an *estanque*, or monopoly, on tobacco sales in Portugal in the 1630s. Despite prohibitions and stiff penalties, the crop was grown in Portugal and, even more important, sailors and masters in the Brazil fleets seemed to be involved in smuggling on a grand scale. Occasionally contemporary estimates can be found. Antonil placed Bahian annual exports at 25,000 rolls in the first years of the eighteenth century. An estimate of 1726 placed levels of exports from Cachoeira alone at 20,000 rolls to Portugal and another 20,000 to Mina in the slave trade.

The best figures for the period under consideration here can be obtained from the lists kept by the Junta do Tabaco. This board, which controlled the importation and sale of tobacco, rented the regional monopoly contracts, licensed sale in Portugal and set prices recorded each year, the size of the annual cargo of tobacco and sugar in the Bahia

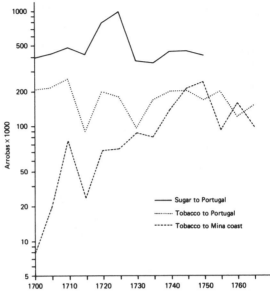

Fig. 2. Bahian sugar and tobacco exports, 1698–1765 (based on a five-year moving average)

Source: ANTT, Junta do Tabaco, maços 96A–106 *passim*.

fleet and the amount that was shipped to Africa. Records for the period before 1700 are incomplete, but for the seven years between 1680 and 1686 total annual imports averaged around 20,500 rolls. After 1700, a rather full record of the Bahian trade to both Portugal and Africa can be compiled until the end of the fleet system in 1765. If we assume that Bahian production was 90 per cent of the total output, then these figures provide the best available estimates. Figure 2 demonstrates that the highest levels of Bahian production, about 400,000 arrobas a year, were reached in the 1740s and that the percentage of production destined to the Mina coast as part of the slave trade rose sharply over the first half of the century.

Livestock

Various types of European domestic animals had been introduced into Brazil in the sixteenth century. Horses thrived in Bahia and by the 1580s there was a trade in horses from Bahia to Pernambuco and even to Angola, where mounted troops were used with success against the

Africans. However, cattle were more important. The engenhos required large numbers of oxen for carts and, in the smaller mills, as the motive force. It was estimated that an engenho needed between 30 and 60 oxen at any one time and their mortality rate during the safra was apparently high. In addition, engenhos needed tallow, hides, and beef in quantity. Most engenhos maintained some pasture for their resident herds, but the presence of grazing cattle near agricultural land always caused trouble. Cattle-raising was restricted by custom to the margins of the settled coastal areas. Eventually in 1701 cattle grazing within 50 miles of the coast was prohibited by law.

Forced out of the better agricultural zones, cattle herds began to grow rapidly in the interior sertão, north of Pernambuco, in the captaincies of Paraíba and Rio Grande do Norte (conquered in the 1580s), and especially in the region of Sergipe de El-Rei between Pernambuco and Bahia along the banks of the São Francisco river. This region was opened up in the 1590s with the aid of government-sponsored expeditions against the Indians. Ranchers, some of them also planters or related to planter families, and their herdsmen pushed their cattle out along both banks of the São Francisco river and by 1640 there were over 2,000 corrals in this region. The history of much of the interior of the north-east can be summarized as exploration, extermination of the Indians, large land grants, and the establishment of cattle ranches. By the first decade of the eighteenth century, there were over 1,300,000 head of cattle in the north-east, supplying the needs of the sugar and tobacco industries and the coastal cities.

Landholding in the sertão was truly extensive. Although there was legislation limiting the size of *sesmarias* to three square leagues, this restriction was simply disregarded. The *sesmarias* on which cattle ranches (*fazendas de gado*) were established sometimes exceeded hundreds of thousands of acres. At the close of the seventeenth century there were landholdings in the Bahian sertão larger than whole provinces in Portugal. Domingos Afonso Sertão, one of the great lords of the interior, owned 30 cattle ranches and another 30 farms totalling over 1,206,000 hectares. A great ranching family like Garcia d'Avila of Bahia, or a merchant turned rancher like João Peixoto Viegas, whose herds were on the upper Paraguaçú, might run over 20,000 head on their scattered ranches, but such 'potentates of the sertão' were the exception and ranches of 1,000 to 3,000 head were more common. As a rule, the interior cattle-ranching zones tended to be divided into large estates, sparsely populated by cowboys and subsistence farmers and dominated by great rancher families who were often linked to the planter elite of the coast. Farther from the centres of royal government, less constrained by municipal institutions, and controlling vast tracts of land, the cattle ranchers wielded more unrestrained power than did the sugar planters.

The great age of cattle expansion into the sertão in conjunction with the sugar industry dates between the opening of Sergipe de El-Rei in the 1590s and the creation of Piauí in the first decade of the eighteenth century. During this period a distinctive social organization and life-style developed. The missionary orders, especially the Jesuits, often played a crucial role in the opening up of new areas and the pacification of the Indians. Eventually, conflicts between ranchers and Jesuits developed because the Jesuits controlled Indian labour and owned extensive herds. The contact between cattlemen and Indians eventually produced a mixed-race population, regionally called *cabras* or *caboclos*. Miscegenation was common and the population of the sertão was composed principally of people of colour, Indians, *caboclos*, and blacks. Despite claims sometimes made that the cattle frontier was too free and uncontrolled to make much use of slaves, more recent studies have revealed that slavery was also a characteristic labour form in the sertão. The common pattern was to use both slaves and free workers as *vaqueiros* (cowboys), placing them on a distant ranch with their families and leaving them to guard the stock fairly independently. Periodically accounts were made and workers were sometimes allowed to keep a portion of the yearly increase in calves as an incentive to good service. There was nothing incompatible between cattle ranching and slavery.

Loosely structured and free of much direct interference from the crown, the society of the sertão developed its own peculiar characteristics. The *fazendeiros* exercised broad social and political power over their slaves and *agregados* (retainers). Control of river banks and waterholes was essential for success. The great ranchers apparently left broad expanses of their territory unused and refused to sell or rent any of it, in order to ensure that they themselves had adequate pasture and to deny the peasants and *agregados* alternative opportunities. In the scrub brush of the arid sertão the horse became a way of life and milk and beef the daily fare. Materially poor, the people literally lived on hides. Everything was made of leather – clothing, household utensils, saddles, window coverings, and tools. This was a society poorer than that of the coast, but more mobile and less constrained by metropolitan law;

but it was also totally dependent on the dominant economy, ranching, which was in its turn linked to the sugar industry.

From the sertão, herds of cattle (*boiadas*) covering up to 40 miles a day were brought down to fairs on the edges of the sugar districts and coastal centres of population. The system seemed to work well from the planters' viewpoint. The price of a team of oxen in the 1690s was about half what it had been in the 1590s, despite a general inflationary trend in the colony. Only after 1700, when the herds were diverted towards Minas Gerais, did the coastal population complain of shortages. Two other movements could also be noted in the eighteenth century: the expansion of the cattle frontier northward into the Maranhão and westward into Goiás, and the development of cattle products for export. By 1749 Pernambuco alone had 27 tanneries employing over 300 slaves and both Pernambuco and Bahia were exporting large quantities of hides and leather.

Manioc

Manioc, the Indian staple, had been quickly adopted by the Portuguese, who found that their familiar wheat and other grains did not flourish in the tropics. Manioc was relatively easy to grow and it could be prepared in a number of ways. Ground into flour it was easy to transport and store and it became the bread of everyday life. In the sugar-growing regions manioc and subsistence farming in general were pushed onto the most marginal lands. Peasant cultivators were allowed to grow foodstuffs on their *roças* on lands that could not be planted to cane. Along the roadways or on hilly uplands in the plantation zones the *lavradores de roça* eked out their humble lives, growing food for themselves and selling a very small surplus in local markets. But, in general, sugar planters disliked the presence of subsistence farming in the same region both because of their desire to use all good land for sugar cane, and because the manioc *roça* tended to destroy the forest which supplied the firewood so essential to sugar production. The result of this hostility was the development of a regional specialization with some areas devoted to sugar and others to manioc.

There were, in fact, two kinds of food-crop agriculture in colonial Brazil. One was the subsistence farming of peasant cultivators producing mainly for themselves and their families and selling a very small surplus in local market fairs, and the other was the production of large quantities of manioc flour destined to be sold to the engenhos and cities of the coast. In Pernambuco, the parishes of Una, Porto Calvo and Alagoas were important provisioning grounds for the captaincy. In Bahia, Maragogipe and Jaguaripe in the southern Recôncavo and towns southward along the coast, like Cairú and Camamú, were the major producers. While little is known about the internal organization of manioc agriculture for market, it is clear that foodstuff production was not necessarily a peasant family husbandry. Cairú and Camamú, for example, were manioc-producing regions of great fame, yet an ecclesiastical census of 1724 revealed that about half the population of these parishes were enslaved. This situation seems to indicate a slave-based economy of production for the supply of internal markets. A somewhat later account, of 1786, listed 188 manioc farmers in Cairú, of whom 169 owned a total of 635 slaves.[28]

Planter hostility towards subsistence agriculture and regional specialization in foodstuffs meant that the populations of cities and the inhabitants of sugar estates were dependent for their daily bread on sources of supply often beyond their control. Shortages, high prices, and near-famines were endemic in the plantation regions. One problem was the attraction which export agriculture held for manioc farmers. As early as 1639 attempts were made to force colonists in Cairú and Camamú to plant manioc instead of tobacco, and in 1706 residents of Maragogipe and Cachoeira sought to be released from prohibitions against growing tobacco or sugar-cane. A similar situation developed somewhat later in Pernambuco as farmers sought to plant cane, a more 'noble occupation', rather than grow manioc. Again, with the expansion of the slave trade, Brazilian manioc producers found that even their crop could be exported. By the 1720s, over 6,000 *alqueires* a year were being shipped in the Mina trade alone, to say nothing of what was shipped to Angola. Then, too, producers of foodstuffs could hold back supplies in order to maintain high price levels, a ploy made possible by the ease with which manioc flour could be preserved. Complaints against the cupidity of the manioc farmers and their regulation of supply were continually voiced in the coastal cities.

Colonial government took various measures to ensure adequate food supplies, but with very limited success. The first measure, already discussed above, was the requirement that certain regions be excluded from practising any agriculture except the growing of foodstuffs. This

[28] Lista das mil covas de mandioca, Biblioteca Nacional de Rio de Janeiro [BNRJ], 1–31, 30, 51 (Cairú, 25 Oct. 1786).

approach was unsuccessful because the growers were reluctant to comply and because they could control supply and thus raise prices. A second approach was to require sugar planters and cane farmers to plant enough manioc to support their own slave force. In Dutch Brazil, Count Maurits of Nassau had imposed this law in 1640. In 1688, at the urging of the *câmara* (city council) of Salvador, a similar law was issued in Bahia, requiring each *senhor de engenho* and *lavrador de cana* to plant 500 *covas* of manioc per slave. In 1701 further steps were taken. Cattle (except those needed by the growers) were prohibited from grazing within 50 miles of the coast and any cultivator with fewer than six slaves was prohibited from growing sugar-cane, a provision that brought heated complaints from the small-scale cane farmers of Rio de Janeiro. The idea behind these measures was that one-third of the manioc produced would feed the grower and his slaves while the rest would reach the market. Finally, merchants in the Mina trade were also required to maintain manioc farms to supply their needs. This last provision caused considerable tension between the merchants of Salvador, who argued that the roles of merchant and manioc farmer were incompatible, and a city council tired of the constant shortages and high prices.

One final response to the problem of food supply deserves to be mentioned. Caribbean sugar planters spoke of the 'Brazil system', by which planters allowed slaves to maintain their own plots, growing their own food supply and sometimes marketing the surplus in local fairs. While this system was reported in various places and usually evoked comment by travellers to Brazil, it is not clear how widely it was practised. It was reported in Bahia in 1687 that 'there are many engenhos that do not have their own lands to plant manioc and ... the owners who do have them usually rent them out'.[29] It has been suggested that the system of slave plots was a 'peasant breach' in Brazilian slavery. There is evidence that the privilege of maintaining a *roça* was desired by the slaves. From the planters' viewpoint the system shifted the burden of sustenance to the slaves themselves. Moreover, it could have direct benefits to estate management. The overseers of Fazenda Saubara were instructed to allow slaves and poor people in the area to plant their *roças* in scrublands, but never in the same place for more than a year so that new lands for pasture would be continually cleared.[30] At Engenho Santana in Ilhéus, manioc was bought from

[29] AHU/PA/Bahia, caixa 15 (9 Aug. 1687).
[30] Regimento que ha de seguir o feitor de Fazenda Saubara, Arquivo da Santa Casa de Misericórdia da Bahia (Salvador) [ASCMB], B/3a/213. Saubara was a manioc-producing parish in the

slaves at 20 per cent below the rate paid to freemen. However, the complaints of shortage and famine indicate overall that slave plots were inadequate as a major source of food. As Antonil noted, for the slaves of the many engenhos near the sea and rivers, 'shellfish was their salvation'.

PERIPHERIES OF NORTH AND SOUTH

At the northern and southern extremes of Portuguese colonization along the Brazilian littoral, settlements took shape that differed considerably from the plantation zones on the humid north-eastern coast. São Vicente in the south and Maranhão-Pará in the north were peripheral areas throughout the seventeenth century, lacking a European population of any size and only marginally integrated into the export economy of the rest of the colony. Geography, climate, difficulties of communication, and the nature and distribution of the local Indian populations propelled these regions along distinctive economic and social trajectories. While the far north and the far south were dissimilar in many ways, both were poor frontiers with few white men, fewer white women, little wealth, and hardly any black slaves. The institutions of Portugal were reproduced in these areas, but existed in an attenuated form. Culturally and ethnically both regions were markedly Indian in character. A relatively large mestizo population developed and in both São Vicente and in Maranhão-Pará exploitation of the resources of the sertão and of the Indian population became a way of life.[31]

The southern extremes

The origins of São Vicente and its neighbouring areas to the south were much like those of the other captaincies. Portuguese and Spanish voyages had passed along the southern coast in the early sixteenth century; a few castaways had settled there among the Indian population and a few small landing points had been established. Granted to Martim Afonso de Sousa in 1533, the captaincy of São Vicente at first centred on the port from which it took its name, but during the next two decades other settlements were established. São Vicente proved to

Recôncavo. This *fazenda* worked by slaves produced manioc for the hospital of the Misericórdia of Salvador.

[31] For further discussion of the northern and southern peripheries, see ch. 4 below.

be unsuitable as a port and it was replaced in importance by Santos, a town founded in 1545 by Bras Cubas, a wealthy and energetic royal official. Along the humid coast behind these small coastal settlements sugar mills were established; the most famous of them was originally built by Martim Afonso but eventually came into the hands of the Schetz family of Antwerp. Sugar was produced for export, but the added distance from Europe and the lack of suitable land put São Vicente at a disadvantage in competition with Pernambuco and Bahia. Nevertheless, these coastal settlements looked much like poorer reproductions of those further to the north.

The future of the southern captaincies did not, however, rest with the ports. Behind the coastal strip, the Serra do Mar range rises steeply to a height of 800 metres. Beyond lies a plateau formed by the Tietê and others rivers, whose rolling hills dotted with trees, temperate climate, and relatively dense Indian population attracted the Europeans. A small settlement developed at Santo André da Borda do Campo, but it was soon surpassed in importance by São Paulo de Piritininga, originally a Jesuit village established in the midst of the Indians of the plateau. The two settlements were merged in 1560 and in the following year São Paulo was raised to the status of a township (*vila*). The Jesuits continued to play an important role in the pacification of the local Indian groups in the next two decades, and by the 1570s São Paulo's existence was secure. Separated from the coast as São Paulo was by the Serra do Mar, the 50 miles between it and Santos could be travelled only by footpath and goods had to be transported on the backs of human porters. São Paulo became the point of control and contact with the Indian population of the interior, serving both as a forward base against the hostile Tamoio to the north and the Carijó to the south and as a supplier of Indian captives to the engenhos of the coast.

By the end of the sixteenth century, the coastal settlements of São Vicente were in decline but on the plateau the basic social and economic features of São Paulo for the next century or so were already well established. Despite the remarks of Jesuit observers who felt that the town and its regions greatly resembled Portugal, São Paulo did not become an Iberian peasant community. From the beginning the Portuguese lived in a sea of Indians as Jesuit missionaries and military expeditions subdued the tribes of the immediate vicinity.

The community was poor and modest. The town had less than 2,000 inhabitants in 1600. Few Portuguese women were attracted to the area and the Portuguese households and farms were filled with captive and semi-captive Indians. Illicit unions between Portuguese men and Indian women were common and a large number of *mamelucos* (the local term for *mestiços*) resulted. Well into the seventeenth century the wills of *Paulistas* (residents of São Paulo) listed Indian slaves, and despite the anti-slavery legislation beginning in 1570, loopholes were always found. Many Indians who were legally free but held in a form of temporary 'tutelage' as *forros* or *administrados* also appear in the wills, passed along like any other property. Indians were used as servants and labourers but also as allies and retainers, linked to the Portuguese by the informal unions and the ties of kinship that resulted from them.

Indians also served as the principal resource in the captaincy. The Portuguese of São Paulo measured their wealth by the number of slaves and supporters they could call upon. 'Rich in archers' was a common description of the most prominent citizens of the plateau. The frontiersman Manoel Preto, for example, was reported to have almost 1,000 bowmen on his estate and, while such numbers were surely an exception, units in the hundreds were not uncommon. While the hierarchical distinctions of noble and commoner were transposed from Portugal, the general poverty of the region, its small European population, and the need for military co-operation against hostile tribes tended to level social differences among the Europeans, who included a relatively large number of Spaniards, Italians, and Germans. In the early period of São Vicente's history, little distinction was made between *mamelucos* and Portuguese so long as the former were willing to live according to what passed in the region for European norms.

The extent of cultural fusion, in fact, was notable. Indian material culture – tools, weapons, handicrafts, foods, and agricultural practices – were widely adopted and used by the Portuguese. The Paulistas were often as skilled with the bow as they were with firearms. The principal Indian language, Tupí, was spoken at all levels of society until well into the eighteenth century. The Portuguese, surrounded by Indian servants, slaves, allies, and concubines, spoke it as a matter of convenience and necessity, and at least some Paulistas were more fluent in it than in their native Portuguese. European forms and institutions were always present, especially in matters of government and religion, but they were limited by the poverty, the sparse European population, and the relative isolation of the region, far from the centres of colonial and metropolitan control.

Throughout the sixteenth and much of the seventeenth centuries the town of São Paulo itself remained small and poor. The most important families lived on their *fazendas* and either maintained a second residence in the town or simply came in periodically to serve on the municipal council or to participate in religious processions. Material possessions were few: a shirt or a musket were highly valued, a pair of boots or a European-style bed a real luxury. The local economy often suffered from a lack of coinage and much trade was done by barter. But by the mid-century some of the rusticity had gone from São Paulo. The Carmelites, Benedictines, and Capuchins of Saint Anthony had built churches, joining the Jesuits, whose college was one of the town's major buildings. Wills and testaments from the mid-century also seem to reflect less poverty than earlier ones. European crops grew well on the plateau. Grapes and wheat were cultivated alongside cotton, small amounts of sugar, and vegetables. Cattle were also raised. By 1614, a flour mill was operating in São Paulo and eventually flour, wine, and marmalade were exported to other captaincies. In 1629 the town's external commerce was estimated to be one-third that of Rio de Janeiro, although only one-fortieth that of Bahia.[32] By the mid seventeenth century the captaincy of São Vicente was no longer isolated from the rest of the colony, although its role was primarily that of a supplier to other captaincies more closely linked to the export sector.

The decline of the local Indian population and rumours of gold, silver, and emeralds in the interior led the Paulistas to turn their ambitions towards the sertão. The Tietê, Paranaíba, and other rivers that flowed westward towards the Paraná system were natural routes to the interior. By the 1580s mobile columns led by the Portuguese and *mamelucos*, but composed mainly of Indian allies, struck westward or southward in search of Indian captives and mineral wealth. These expeditions were organized into quasi-military companies called *bandeiras* (banners), and their participants often spent months or even years in the sertão, preferring to do that, said one governor, rather than serve someone else for a single day. At times the town of São Paulo was half deserted because so many men were absent. Those who stayed behind often acted as outfitters, providing supplies and arms in return for a share of the Indians captured. The sertão and the bandeiras became a way of life. In the forest, the Indian background of the Paulistas was

---

[32] 'Descripción de la provincia del Brasil' [1629], in Mauro, *Le Brésil au XVIIᵉ siècle*, 167–91.

invaluable: they dressed, spoke, ate, and lived more or less like the Indians they led and hunted.

While there is an extensive and often laudatory literature on the Paulistas and their bandeiras, the economic aspects of their operations are both poorly documented and often confusing. Earlier writers such as Alfredo Ellis and Afonso de Escragnolle Taunay continually emphasized the poverty and isolation of São Paulo and ascribed to these causes the thrust into the sertão. However, even if we accept these authors' descriptions of the scope and success of the bandeiras, we are then presented with some puzzling questions about the Paulista economy. Jesuit observers estimated that over 300,000 Indians were taken from the Paraguay missions alone, to say nothing of those captured in the sertão. While such estimates may have been an exaggeration, other observers also provide high figures. Lourenço de Mendonça, prelate of Rio de Janeiro, claimed that in the decade prior to 1638 between 70,000 and 80,000 Indians had been captured.[33] According to Taunay there was a great migratory wave of Indian captives from São Paulo[34] to the engenhos of Bahia and Pernambuco, but there is little documentary evidence to support this view.

Rather than the north-east, it was probably Rio de Janeiro and São Vicente that absorbed the majority of the Indian captives. As we have seen in table 1, the sugar industry in Rio was expanding in this period, reaching an annual growth rate of about 8 per cent between 1612 and 1629. The demand for labour was met to some extent by Indian slaves. Slaves were brought to Rio from São Paulo by sea and also marched overland. As late as 1652 one-third to one-quarter of the labour force on the Benedictine engenhos in Rio de Janeiro was Indian.[35]

It well may be that the *fazendas* of São Paulo itself were the major consumers of Indian labour. Wheat, flour, cotton, grapes, wine, maize, and cattle were all produced on the plateau and some of these products

---

[33] *Memorial*, Biblioteca Nacional de Madrid, Códice 2369, fos. 296–301. Mendonça reported that of 7,000 Indians taken near Lagoa dos Patos in 1625, only 1,000 arrived in São Paulo. High mortality rates then may provide an explanation of what was happening to the captured Indians, but at the same time they provoke questions about why the Paulistas continued to engage in such a risky and uncertain enterprise.

[34] For the arguments against the traditional view, see Jaime Cortesão, *Introdução à história das bandeiras* (2 vols., Lisbon, 1964), II, 302–11, and C. R. Boxer, *Salvador de Sá and the struggle for Brazil and Angola, 1602–1686* (London, 1952), 20–9; see also the curious appendix in Roberto Simonsen, *História económica do Brasil (1500–1820)* (4th edn, São Paulo, 1962), 245–6.

[35] Arquivo Distrital da Braga, Congregação de São Bento 134 (1648–52).

were sent to other captaincies or to the Río de la Plata. A Spaniard long resident in São Paulo estimated wheat production at 120,000 *alqueires* in 1636 and also placed the number of Indian slaves on Paulista estates at 40,000.[36] This estimate seems to be supported by the many references by the eighteenth-century genealogist Paes Leme, who often spoke of large *fazendas* with hundreds of Indians in the seventeenth century. Given the small population of the captaincies, units of this size make sense only if they are producing for more than the local market. Thus, by the export either of Indians or of foodstuffs, São Vicente was drawn into increasing contact with the rest of the colony. Indian labour and the enslavement of Indians remained central aspects of the Paulista economy throughout much of the seventeenth century and a matter of vital concern in the captaincy.

The isolation that had characterized São Paulo in the sixteenth century and contributed to its social and cultural formation began to change after 1600. While São Paulo remained a relatively small town and never achieved the wealth of Salvador or Olinda, it was by the end of the seventeenth century a reasonable facsimile of those centres. It dominated the plateau and was increasingly surrounded by smaller settlements like Mogi das Cruzes (1611), Taubaté (1645), and Itu (1657), the results of bandeira activity and agricultural expansion. In 1681 São Paulo was made the capital of the captaincy and in 1711, two years after the creation of the enlarged captaincy of São Paulo e Minas de Ouro, its status was raised from town to city.

A few great families dominated São Paulo's social life and municipal institutions. For much of the seventeenth century the Pires and Camargo clans carried on an intermittent feud which had originated in a point of family honour but later took on political overtones. Royal control in the region was minimal. In 1691 the governor-general of Brazil wrote that the Paulistas 'know neither God, nor Law, nor Justice'. A few years later they were described by another crown officer as 'deeply devoted to the freedom in which they have always lived since the creation of their town'.[37] São Paulo was called a veritable La Rochelle in 1662, but in fact its loyalty to the crown of Portugal was constant. When in 1640 a small pro-Spanish faction tried to separate the captaincy from the rest of Brazil, it was frustrated by the majority of the population and by the loyalty of Amador Bueno, who refused its offer of leadership.

[36] Cortesão, *Introdução*, II, 305.
[37] Charles R. Boxer, *The Golden Age of Brazil, 1695–1750* (Berkeley and Los Angeles, 1964), 34.

At the same time, any interference in matters directly affecting Paulista interests was strongly opposed. Royal magistrates who meddled in 'matters of the sertão' (i.e. Indians) were often subjected to threats or violence. In 1639 the Spanish Jesuits, objecting to the raids against Guairá and Tape, obtained the bull *Commissum nobis* from Pope Urban VIII, which reiterated the prohibitions against Indian slavery and specifically mentioned Brazil, Paraguay, and the Río de la Plata. This document and the accompanying royal law of March 1640 caused a furore among the principal consumers and suppliers of Indian labour. There was rioting in Rio de Janeiro and the Jesuits were physically expelled from Santos and São Paulo in 1640. Although the Jesuits were allowed to return in 1653, the truculent independence of the Paulistas caused the crown to move cautiously in the captaincy. It was not really until their defeat in the War of the Emboabas in Minas Gerais (1708–9) that the Paulistas' 'pretensions' were brought under control.

While the crown often found the peculiar qualities and attitudes of the Paulistas a nuisance or a problem, it began to call increasingly on their skills and abilities to further royal aims. Expeditions were still often privately organized, but the Portuguese crown and its representatives in the colony began to find definite uses for the bandeiras. The great bandeira of Antônio Rapôso Tavares (1648–52) which crossed the Chaco, skirted the Andes northwards, and followed the river system of the continent's interior to emerge at the mouth of the Amazon was apparently commissioned by the crown and had a geopolitical purpose. Other uses were found for the Paulistas in the arid sertão of the north-east, especially in southern Bahia. From the 1670s onwards, groups of Paulistas could be found in the sertão, ranching on their own lands, Indian-slaving when they could and willing to be employed by the state. Paulistas and Bahians were principally responsible for opening up the area of Piauí to settlement in the 1680s. The Paulista Domingos Jorge Velho helped to open up Piauí and then joined another Paulista, Matias Cardoso de Almeida, in resisting a major Indian rebellion, the *Guerra dos Bárbaros*, which erupted in Rio Grande do Norte and Ceará (1683–1713). Participation in these government-backed actions was particularly attractive because they were considered to be 'just wars' and therefore the Indian captives taken could legally be sold as slaves. Indians captured during the *Guerra dos Bárbaros*, for example, were sold in the city of Natal.

The crown derived increasing benefit everywhere from using the skills and bellicosity of the Paulistas for state purposes. Fighting the

Indians was a primary employment, but other threats to internal security could also be met by the Paulistas. After years of intermittent warfare, it was the same Domingos Jorge Velho who between 1690 and 1695 led the final campaign against the escaped slave community of Palmares. In the far south also, traditional Paulista interests and activities naturally led to state sponsorship in the Portuguese push into the debated frontier with Spanish America.

Both the Paulistas and their traditional rivals, the Spanish Jesuits of Paraguay, had been involved in the opening up and settlement of the lands that lay to the south of São Vicente. Gold had been reported near Paranaguá in the 1570s, and although a town was not established there until 1649, the region was already well known by that time. Further to the south the Jesuits had apparently hoped to extend their Tape missions all the way to the sea at Lagoa dos Patos, but the bandeiras of the 1630s had forced their retreat. The Jesuits returned after 1682 and between that date and 1706 they established seven missions east of the Uruguay river in what was to become Rio Grande do Sul. The cattle introduced into the region from São Paulo and those left to roam by the Jesuits multiplied on the temperate plains into great feral herds. The upland pastures of Santa Catarina were known as the *vaqueria dos pinhais* and those of Rio Grande do Sul and the Banda Oriental as the *vaqueria do mar*. By the 1730s there were Portuguese cattle hunters who exploited these herds for the hides.

The creation in 1680 of a Portuguese outpost at Colônia do Sacramento on the banks of the Río de la Plata was a move with geopolitical and economic motives, designed to stake Portugal's claim to the region and to serve as a base for trade with Upper Peru (and the flow of silver). The subsequent history of the far south was a filling-in of the territory that lay between the small settlements of Paraná and the outpost at Colônia. It was also a story of the interplay between the actions of government and private enterprise. Settlements were made in Santa Catarina in the 1680s, the most important being Laguna (1684), which was settled by Paulistas and Azorean couples sent by the crown. By 1730 the discovery of gold in Minas Gerais had created a strong demand for the livestock of the south and a road had been opened from Laguna to São Paulo by way of Curitiba and Sorocaba, over which mules and horses destined for the mining region were driven.

Early penetration of the lands further to the south had been made by various bandeiras, but by the 1730s there was royal interest in occupying these lands. In 1737 Rio Grande do São Pedro was founded, and in the following year, it and Santa Catarina were made sub-captaincies of Rio de Janeiro. By 1740 more Azorean couples were arriving to serve as frontier settlers. Between 1747 and 1753 about 4,000 couples arrived, joining the Paulistas who also began to move into the region.

Society in the regions lying to the south of São Paulo varied to some extent according to the major economic activities in each. The region of modern Paraná, with its settlements of Paranaguá and Curitiba, was an extension of São Paulo. Early mining activity was characterized by the use of Indian slaves, and by the middle of the eighteenth century blacks were being used in increasing numbers. Eventually, the cattle *fazendas* that developed in the region were also based on slave labour, as the early *sesmarias* make clear. Further to the south life was organized around the scattered military posts and the exploitation of the cattle herds. The horse was an essential element of life, as was maté tea and barbecued beef. Small settlements developed around military posts or at river crossings. In general, it was a simple pastoral society in which cattle-rustling, smuggling, and hunting were the major activities.

The equatorial north

The northern periphery, although separated from São Paulo and the plains of the southern frontier by thousands of kilometres, and despite a strikingly different climate and geography, exhibited many parallels in the development of its society and economy with the extreme south. In the north the failure to create a suitable export economy, the sparse European population (especially the lack of women), the few black slaves, the independent attitude of local government, the cultural and biological fusion of Europeans and Indians, and, most of all, the central role of the Indian in the region's life all duplicated the patterns of the far south.

Although hereditary captaincies had been created for the northern coast of Brazil in the 1530s, these had not been occupied by the Portuguese. Instead, the French were the first to take an active interest in the 'east–west coast' of the north. Only after a group of French nobles led by the Sieur de la Ravardière established a settlement around a fort on Maranhão island in 1612 did the Portuguese show any interest in the area. And only after the surrender of St Louis (São Luís) in 1615 did they expand their control to the Amazon, establishing the town of Belém in 1616. Belém then served as a base of operations against small Dutch and Irish trade forts on the lower Amazon, which the Portuguese destroyed. In 1621 the vast region of northern Brazil was created as a separate state of Maranhão, with its own governor and administration and São Luís as its first capital, although after the 1670s governors began to spend much of their time at Belém, which became the capital in 1737.

Given the meagre population and resources of the state of Maranhão, the crown once again created hereditary captaincies as a means of shifting the burden of colonization into private hands. Cumá, Caete, and Cametá were created in the 1630s, as was Cabo do Norte (present-day Amapá), which in 1637 was given to Bento Maciel Parente, a courageous but rapacious Indian-fighter and backwoodsman (*sertanista*). Eventually, in 1665, Marajó island (Ilha Grande de Joanes) was also made a hereditary captaincy.[38] None of these grants proved particularly successful and they were eventually abolished in the mid eighteenth century. Until the 1680s, effective Portuguese control was limited to the areas around the two cities São Luís and Belém and a few river outposts designed to control canoe traffic and Indian slaving. Of these, Gurupá, which served as a toll station and control point some ten or twelve days' journey up the Amazon from Belém, was probably the most important.

As in São Vicente, the colony in the north was oriented towards the interior. Belem and São Paulo stood symbolically at the extremes of effective settlement. Both lay at the entrance to major river systems that facilitated movement into the interior, and both were bases for continual expeditions.

In the north, the Portuguese and their *caboclo* sons, accompanied by Indian slaves or workers, organized *entradas*, or expeditions, up the rivers in search of forest products like cacao and vanilla or Indians who might be 'rescued' from their enemies and made to serve the Portuguese. The life of these *sertanistas* was difficult and dangerous. Their river expeditions often lasted for months at a time. In the interior, the Europeans adopted many aspects of Indian life. The hammock, the canoe, manioc flour, and forest lore were all copied from the Indians among whom the Portuguese lived. A form of Tupí was spoken as a *lingua franca* throughout the state of Maranhão and remained the

[38] A sixth captaincy, Xingu, was created in 1685 but was never occupied.

dominant language of the area until well into the eighteenth century. The steel axe and the Catholic Church symbolized the cultural influences moving in the other direction, but in the far north, as in the south, the Indian impact was much greater and lasted longer than in the plantation zones of the coast.

The frontier nature of the state of Maranhão was underlined by its tiny European population. In 1637 the Jesuit Luíz Figueira complained of the lack of European women and decried the sins that resulted from illicit unions with Indians in terms exactly like those used almost a century earlier by Jesuits in Bahia and São Paulo. Efforts to rectify this situation had been made as early as 1619, when Azorean immigrants were sent to São Luís. We have already seen how this technique of sponsored immigration from the Atlantic islands to the frontiers was used in the far south, and it was to be employed again at later times in the Amazon region. But despite such measures, the European population remained small. In 1637 São Luís had only 230 citizens and Belém only 200. By 1672 the whole state of Maranhão was thought to contain no more than 800 European inhabitants. However, Belém began to grow in the eighteenth century. From about 500 in 1700, its population reached 2,500 by 1750. By that time the total population of Pará and Rio Negro was estimated at 40,000, including the Indians under Portuguese control.

As in the south, the small number of Europeans, the physical isolation from the centres of colonial government, the high percentage of Indians in the population, and the economic opportunities presented by the exploitation of the sertão and the Indians combined to create conditions in which Portuguese institutions were attenuated and European culture was deeply penetrated by indigenous elements. The two cities housed the senior government officers, a few merchants, and, eventually, the main establishments of the missionary orders. The wealthier colonists lived there, often combining interests in agriculture with the financing of slaving expeditions to the interior. The *entradas* were usually led by Europeans, but the canoes were paddled by Indians. In the scattered forts and outposts that were eventually established up the rivers, small garrisons of poor conscripts lived in isolation. Soldiers, frontiersmen, and deserters became *cunhamenas* ('squawmen'), fathering *mestiço* children and often living as agents for missionaries or government-sponsored *entradas*.

Royal control over the region was tenuous. The colonists of Pará and

Maranhão proved to be as truculent and as independent as the Paulistas had been. The municipal councils of Belém and São Luís forced governors to appear before them to explain policy until the crown put an end to the practice. Royal officers who favoured the settlers' interests in matters of taxation or the use of Indian labour were supported; those who favoured the missionaries' efforts to limit the use of Indians were opposed. Curiously enough, António Vieira, the great Jesuit missionary, called Maranhão 'Brazil's La Rochelle', the same term used to describe São Paulo's resistance to royal authority. As in São Paulo, it was usually 'matters of the sertão' (i.e. Indians) that provoked the strongest reactions on the part of colonists. The Jesuits were expelled from the main cities on two occasions and in the 1720s a campaign of vilification and complaint against them was mounted that eventually contributed to their ultimate expulsion from Brazil. The colonists sometimes found considerable support from those governors who were themselves violators of the laws against Indian slavery. This could be said of Cristóvão da Costa Freire (1707–18), or Bernardo Perreira de Berredo (1718–22), whose *Anais historicos* is still a major source for the region's history. The virulence of the struggle between the colonists and the missionary orders sprang ultimately from the economy and the central role of Indian labour within it.

From the beginning, the Portuguese had attempted to create an export-oriented economy in the north. In the immediate vicinity of Belém and São Luís both crown and colonists tried to develop sugar plantations like those of Pernambuco or Bahia. As early as 1620 privileges were given to those who promised to build engenhos in Maranhão.[39] Some sugar was eventually produced, especially near São Luís, but there were serious problems impeding the industry's growth, such as a persistent shortage of artisans and technicians, despite efforts to attract and maintain them. In 1723 the town council of Belém complained that there was only one blacksmith to serve the twenty mills of the area. Even more serious was a chronic shortage of labour. The importation of Africans prior to 1682 was sporadic. In that year the Companhia de Commercio de Maranhão was formed to supply slaves to the region. Its failure to do so, along with mismanagement and price-fixing, contributed to a settler revolt in 1684 that was also directed against the Jesuits. The crown suppressed the revolt, but it loosened the restrictions on using Indian slaves. The colonists continued to

[39] AHU, cod. 32, fos. 58–60.

agitate for the importation of Africans and, with local private capital in short supply, the crown itself sponsored a new company, the Companhia de Cacheu e Cabo Verde, to supply at least 145 slaves a year to the state of Maranhão. This trickle of slaves did little to stimulate production and caused much grumbling. Colonists complained of the high prices charged and the settlers of Pará claimed that the ships unloaded the best slaves at São Luís. Prior to 1750 probably only a few thousand Africans reached the north of Brazil.

Sugar production suffered from other problems as well. Shipping to the north was often irregular. In 1694 only one ship called at Belém. The sugar, already inferior in quality to that of Bahia, often lay for long periods on the docks, where its value fell even lower. Increasingly, the colonists and the missionary orders who owned engenhos turned to the production of rum for local consumption rather than sugar for export. Despite royal attempts in 1706 to stop distilling, production continued. By 1750 there were 31 engenhos and 120 small-scale *engenhocas* in the state of Maranhão.[40] While a few of these estates were large operations like those of the Carmelites and Jesuits, the majority were small units producing rum for local use.

Other cash crops were also produced. Cotton was grown, especially in Maranhão. It was used to make homespun cloth throughout the north and it also circulated widely as a form of currency, but did not figure as an important export until the late eighteenth century. Attempts were made to develop other crops. Indigo and coffee were introduced or sponsored by the crown, but with little success. Faced with the general failure to develop any export crop, the colonists depended increasingly on the products of the forest: vanilla, sarsparilla, anatto dye all found markets in Europe, but of all these so-called *drogas do sertão* none was so important as cacao.

The crown tried with little success to stimulate cacao production between 1678 and 1681 by offering tax exemptions and other advantages to producers. The colonists preferred to send their Indians after the wild cacao of the Amazonian forest rather than cultivate the sweeter domesticated variety. Cacao grew wild throughout the region and little capital was needed to gather it. *Tropas* of canoes paddled by Indians would move upriver, set up temporary bases while they gathered the fruit, and then return down river to Belém after about six months. Desertion,

---

[40] *Relatório* of Ouvidor João Antônio da Cruz Denis Pinheiro (1751), printed in J. Lucio de Azevedo, *Os Jesuitas no Grão-Pará* (2nd edn, Coimbra, 1930), 410–16.

Indian attacks, and the lack of commercial opportunities all presented difficulties to the cacao trade. Slowly, however, as markets for Amazonian cacao developed in Italy and Spain, the trade increased. In the mid-1720s about 100 licences a year were granted to canoes going to gather cacao. By the 1730s this figure had risen to 250 and by 1736 it stood at 320. During this era of open but licensed exploitation, before 1755, cacao was Pará's major export. Between 1730 and 1744 it constituted over 90 per cent of the captaincy's exports. Between 1730 and 1755 over 16,000 metric tons of cacao were exported from the Amazon region, and it was the major attraction for ships calling at Belém. At times Amazonian cacao fetched higher prices on the Lisbon market than Bahian sugar, but after 1745 exports became more irregular because of scarce labour, shortage of shipping, and a drop in cacao prices.

The failure to develop a dependable export crop during most of the seventeenth century underlined the essential poverty of the north. The settlements ran at a deficit. The tithe collected in Maranhão usually failed to cover the costs of government and it was the same in Pará until 1712. Government licences and the tithe on forest products were the principal sources of government revenue. Belém and São Luís were poor towns. As in São Paulo, imported goods were a rarity and the population depended on rough, locally-made products. There was little capital available for investment and a chronic shortage of coinage. Until 1748, when Lisbon minted coins specifically for Maranhão-Pará, almost all transactions were carried out by barter or by using cotton cloth or cacao as a means of exchange. What currency did exist circulated at twice its face value and the commodities used for exchange were often given an official rate of exchange different from their market value, thus making business difficult.

Ultimately, it was the Indian who became the key to the development of the north. The crown, the colonists, and the missionary orders all sought, for various reasons and under various pretexts, to bring Indians under European control. Almost from the beginning of the northern settlement this issue brought the colonists into direct conflict with the missionary orders, especially the Jesuits, and often with the crown and its representatives as well.

Northern Brazil became a great mission field. The Franciscans were established in Pará as early as 1617, but by the 1640s the Jesuits had replaced the Franciscans as the major missionary order in the north. With the arrival in 1653 of the remarkable and energetic Father António

Vieira as Provincial, the Jesuits' attempts to protect the Indians and to bring them under their control intensified. Vieira used the power of pulpit and pen to condemn the many abuses committed against the Indians in Maranhão and Pará, and his advocacy eventually resulted in a new law of 1655 against Indian enslavement. This legislation followed the lines of the early laws of 1570, 1595, and 1609 mentioned above, but it did leave loopholes that permitted defensive expeditions against hostile Indians and allowed those who 'rescued' Indians to exact five years of personal service, after which those Indians would become part of the general free labour pool. The law was, in reality, a compromise: the crown wanted to respond to the arguments of the Jesuits, but was unwilling to eliminate completely colonists' access to Indians because of the unrest it would create and because it had itself begun in 1649 to tax all slaves brought in from the interior. The Jesuits were given free rein to bring Indians from the interior by peaceful means and to establish them in mission villages where they would provide a pool of labour the colonists could draw upon.

The law of 1655 did little to eliminate the Indian slave trade and the Jesuits soon discovered that bringing in Indians by peaceful persuasion was also very difficult. Moreover, such limitations as the law imposed were the cause of continual complaints by settlers against the Jesuits, who were even expelled from São Luís and Belém in 1661–2 as a result of their Indian policy. A further law of 1680 which prohibited all Indian slavery and increased Jesuit control over Indian souls and Indian labour provoked even more virulent reactions from the colonists and contributed to the expulsion of the Jesuits from Maranhão in 1684. The Jesuits were reinstated with royal support and a new ordinance, the *Regimento das Missões* of 1686, was issued to regulate Indian affairs and to grant the missionary orders even greater powers. But two years later a further law also provided for government-sponsored *tropas de resgate* ('rescue troops') to bring in Indian slaves and distribute them among the colonists. In this arrangement, the Jesuits were to accompany each troop to ensure its compliance with the rules for slaving. To decide whether Indians captured by the state-sponsored *tropas* were taken under the limitations of the law, a Junta das Missões (Board of Missions) composed of representatives of the missionary orders and a royal judge met periodically in Belém. While the Jesuits were reluctant to co-operate with this legalized slaving, they were astute enough to realize that some compromise was necessary. The legislation of 1686–8 remained the basic law governing Portuguese–Indian relations until the middle of the following century.

The state of Maranhão, then, depended on a variety of forms of Indian labour, all based more or less on coercion. Indian slaves acquired legally or illegally were used everywhere and could be found in the governor's household, on the plantations of the Jesuits, and on the estates of the settlers. In addition, 'rescued' Indians and those who had come in of their own free will were placed in *aldeias* (villages) under missionary control. By 1730 the Jesuits alone had over 21,000 Indians in 28 mission villages and the Franciscans controlled another 26 aldeias. It is estimated that by the 1740s about 50,000 Indians lived under the missionaries. The aldeias were of various types. Those near the centres of Portuguese population provided labour under contract to the colonists. A few were royal villages used exclusively by the government to provide canoemen or workers in the salt-pans. The missionary orders were also entitled to the exclusive use of some villages for the upkeep of their establishments. Deep in the interior were frontier aldeias whose labour was only occasionally called on when a *tropa de resgate* passed by.

It was the success of the aldeias and the missionaries' interference in the colonists' access to Indian labour, together with the economic activities of the religious orders, that brought ever more vehement complaints from the settlers. The Jesuits were as always the prime target. They had acquired and developed extensive holdings in the north: cattle ranches on Marajó island, engenhos, cotton and cacao plantations. They had introduced new crops into the region and were also very active in gathering the *drogas do sertão*. In 1734 over one-third of the wild cacao registered at the Gurupá customs station belonged to the Jesuits. While the Mercedarians and Carmelites also had extensive properties, it was always the Jesuits who drew the sharpest criticism, probably because of their unaccommodating attitude on the issue of Indian slavery. Their greatest critic was Paulo de Silva Nunes, a retainer of Governor Costa Freire, who held some minor posts in the colony and later became the settlers' official representative in Lisbon. His angry petitions eventually led to a royal investigation in 1734 which exonerated the Jesuits, but the inquest itself indicated a stiffening of royal policy towards the religious orders which eventually resulted in the expulsion of the Jesuits and the secularization of the missions.

We should keep in mind that, from the Indian perspective, the problem was not one of labour but of survival. The demands made by the Portuguese and the mistreatment they meted out took their toll. In addition, epidemic diseases periodically decimated the Indian population. There were smallpox epidemics in 1621 and 1644 and then a region-wide outbreak in 1662. The following century brought no relief, with smallpox again in 1724 and a devastating measles epidemic in the 1740s. Each outbreak was followed by a shortage of labour that led to renewed slaving. Regions were depopulated by disease or were 'slaved out'. As the Portuguese penetrated the region of the Negro, Japura, and Solimões rivers, they found it increasingly difficult to trade for captives with the river tribes who already had access to steel tools and weapons acquired by trade with peoples in contact with the Dutch on the lower Essequibo. Faced with this situation the *tropas* depended increasingly on direct force.

North-western Amazonia was opened up in the late seventeenth century. By the 1690s a small outpost had been established near Manaus at the mouth of the Rio Negro and after 1700 Portuguese slaving on the Solimões river and the Rio Negro was common. These activities eventually led the populous Manao people to resist. They were defeated in a series of punitive campaigns in the 1720s, the survivors being sold as slaves in Belém. The region was given to the Carmelites as a mission field. They established some missions, but their efforts were often directed more towards economic gain than spiritual care of the Indians. Finally, it was also on this far frontier that, as in the south, the interests of Portugal came into direct conflict with those of Spain. Beginning in 1682, the Bohemian-born Jesuit Samuel Fritz, working out of the Spanish province of Quito, had established missions among the Omagua people along the Solimões river. Eventually, after diplomatic manoeuvring and some fighting, the Spanish Jesuits were forced to withdraw from the region. In 1755 north-western Amazonia became a separate captaincy, Rio Negro, establishing Portuguese authority well beyond the line of Tordesillas.

To summarize: the northern and southern extremes of Portuguese America seemed in many ways to lag behind the centres of settlement. The life and concerns of Belém and São Paulo in 1680 were much like those of Salvador or Olinda in 1600: the role of the missionaries, access to Indian workers, tapping the Atlantic slave trade. The relative racial proportions of the population – small numbers of whites, few Africans, many *mestiços* and a high percentage of Indians – in both peripheries also recalled earlier periods in the plantation zones of the coast. The differences, however, were not chronological but structural. They were related to the way these peripheries were integrated into the export economy of the colony. São Paulo first began to grow as a supplier of labour and foodstuffs to other captaincies. Then, with the development of mining in the captaincy, especially after 1700, the early pattern began to change; and, as it was drawn into the supply and exploitation of the mines, São Paulo came increasingly to resemble the captaincies of the north-east. In Amazonia change came more slowly. The failure to develop an export crop was the main reason. Although by the 1730s cacao and other forest products found some outlet, it was only after 1755 with state intervention in economy and society that the northern periphery was also drawn into the Atlantic commercial system.

THE URBAN FABRIC

The cities of Brazil, whether in the zones devoted to plantation agriculture or at the extremities of Portuguese settlement, were essentially a creation of the export economy. All the major centres were ports, points of exchange between the products of Brazil and the incoming flow of manufactures, immigrants, and slaves from Europe and Africa. The few secondary towns that existed were usually small riverine agricultural settlements or minor ports, tied by coastal trade to the maritime centres. In the north-east, secondary towns were few and slow to develop because of the attraction of the engenhos. Populations and economic resources tended to concentrate on the sugar plantations, so that during the safra the engenho, with its hundreds of labourers, its artisans, its chapel, and sometimes even its resident priest, provided many of the functions and services of a town. Noticeably absent were the small peasant villages on the Portuguese model; but in the context of slave-based plantations they would have made little sense. Only São Paulo and the towns of the plateau developed as inland settlements relatively free of the export orientation of the rest of the colony; they were of course small and unimportant throughout much of this period and were greatly overshadowed by Olinda and Recife, Salvador, and Rio de Janeiro.

Between 1532 and 1650 six cities and 31 towns or *vilas* were established in Brazil. The first foundations were concentrated along the coastal strip between Olinda and Santos, but after 1580, with the northward expansion of the colony, there was a new wave of foundations as Natal (1599), São Luís (1615), and Belém (1616) were established. Once again all these cities were ports and it was not until the second quarter of the eighteenth century and the opening of Minas Gerais that the urban network began to spread inland. In fact, it can be argued that Brazil had no network of cities, but only an archipelago of ports, each surrounded by its own agricultural hinterland and in closer contact with Lisbon than with each other. This was the result of the export orientation of the economy and of the Portuguese imperial structure, which sought to keep each captaincy directly dependent on the metropolis. The coastal location of Brazilian cities made fortification and defence matters of constant concern and expense. Dutch and English interlopers regularly attacked Brazilian ports in the period 1580–1620 and after 1620 these cities became vulnerable to attack as part of wider conflicts, as in the Dutch seizure of Salvador in 1624 or the French attack on Rio de Janeiro in 1710.

By contemporary European standards Brazilian cities were small and unimposing. The population of Salvador, the largest, grew from about 14,000 in 1585 to 25,000 in 1724, and reached nearly 40,000 by 1750. About half its residents were slaves. Olinda, the capital of Pernambuco, had a population of perhaps 4,000 in 1630 and only 8,000 in 1654. (Its port facility, Recife, did not really take form as a separate municipality until the Dutch made it their capital.) The cities of the north were even smaller. In the 1660s São Luís contained only 600 *moradores* (white inhabitants) and Belém only 400. Rio de Janeiro remained small throughout the seventeenth century, growing to 40,000 by the middle of the eighteenth after the opening up of Minas Gerais. These cities served as civil and ecclesiastical centres. The governor-general and the High Court sat in Salvador and after 1676 that city was also the archepiscopal see. In the capital city of each captaincy resided the governor and chief magistrate as well as the principal fiscal officers. Export cities, cities of ships, docks, and warehouses, cities of stevedores, sailors, and slave markets, the Brazilian ports acquired a certain similarity of plan born of necessity and function. Business concentrated near the wharves and warehouses where the sugar, tobacco, and hides were gathered, weighed, and taxed. The wealthy residents, planters or merchants often sought to remove themselves from the world of the wharves – hence the separation of the docks from the residential areas. In Salvador there was an upper city of government buildings and homes and a lower city of commerce. In Pernambuco, the port facility developed at Recife a few kilometres away from Olinda. High ground was preferred for public buildings and churches, usually the best constructions in a city. Cut stone and tile had been shipped from Europe in the 1570s and 1580s as ballast, and by 1600 impressive civil and religious buildings were being raised in the major cities. Many of these were then replaced, rebuilt, or improved in the mid seventeenth century. The Jesuit colleges built in the main cities at the close of the sixteenth century were among the most important buildings, as were the Franciscan churches and monasteries. The churches defined the quarters of the cities, for the parish was also the neighbourhood and reference point for civil and religious purposes.

One distinguishing characteristic of the Brazilian city of this period was the absence of its wealthiest and most prominent citizens for much of the year. The sugar planters and ranchers maintained urban residences but spent much of their time on their estates. Much has sometimes been made of the 'rural dominance' of Brazil's social and economic life. While this is true, it is misleading. City and plantation, or port and hinterland, were not polar opposites but part of an integrated continuum. Interaction between city and countryside was continuous and was faciliated by the fact that the vast majority of the rural population lived within a few days' journey of the coastal cities.

The cities had come to life under a variety of political conditions. Where the original donataries were weak, private power did not greatly constrain municipal authority. In Pernambuco, however, the Albuquerque Coelho family exercised its authority well into the seventeenth century, while in Rio de Janeiro the Correa de Sá clan remained predominant until the 1660s. In Salvador the presence of the chief royal officials of the colony also hampered the local exercise of political authority by the municipality. Smaller, more remote towns were less inhibited and tended to advocate without restraint the interests of the locally dominant economic groups expressed through municipal institutions.

Political life centred on the *senado da câmara*, the senate or town council, usually composed of three or four councillors, one or two municipal judges, and a city attorney. The voting members of the council were chosen by a complicated system of indirect elections from lists of men with the proper social qualifications. These *homens bons* were expected to be men of property, residents of the city, untainted by artisan origins or religious or ethnic impurity. While there were exceptions to these requirements, especially in frontier communities, they were generally honoured. Not so, however, the prohibitions against consecutive terms and relatives serving together, which were usually ignored, with the excuse that there were not enough men qualified to hold public office.

All aspects of municipal life and often those of the surrounding countryside fell under the control of the câmaras. The minutes of a typical month's activities in the mid seventeenth century might include regulating sanitation, fixing the price of sugar, municipal taxes, awarding the slaughterhouse contract, and organizing an expedition to hunt down runaway slaves. In time, and to the displeasure of royal governors, magistrates, and prelates, the town councils sought to extend their authority. Câmaras often wrote directly to Lisbon and some maintained attorneys in Portugal to look after their interests. When legislation or royal policy seemed to threaten the interests of the local elite, opposition coalesced around the câmara. Prohibitions against Indian enslavement provide a case in point in the seventeenth century. In Salvador (1610), Rio de Janeiro (1640), São Paulo (1640), and Belém (1662), the câmaras spearheaded resistance to royal policy and led movements that resulted in the arrest or expulsion of governors or Jesuits who were held responsible for anti-enslavement legislation.

It is clear that, while the câmara sought to promote the welfare of the municipality in general, these bodies represented most actively the interests of the locally dominant groups. In Salvador, the one city where the lists of councillors are almost complete, it can be seen that the câmara members were most often drawn from the *senhores de engenho* and *lavradores de cana* of the region. Of 260 men elected to voting office on the câmara of Salvador between 1680 and 1729, over half were mill owners, cane farmers, or large landowners; if the merchants and professionals who had acquired lands by the time of their election are added, the proportion rises to over 80 per cent.[41] Membership in the municipal council, then, was not the exclusive domain of one group, but the sugar sector clearly dominated and the same family names appear year after year. If this was the case in a large city with a high degree of social differentiation, then we can assume that the pattern of limited representation was even more intense in smaller places where the

---

[41] Cf. Charles R. Boxer, *Portuguese society in the tropics* (Madison, 1965), 72–110; Flory, 'Bahian society', 139–44.

number of potential councilmen was reduced. The câmaras tended to define the common interest in terms of the interests of the economic groups from which they were drawn. Thus, the councils of Belem and São Paulo ardently sought to ensure the right to send out Indian slaving expeditions, while those of Rio de Janeiro and Bahia were often concerned with establishing a moratorium on debts incurred by sugar planters or combating a royal trade monopoly.

Within the context of urban political life it is appropriate to discuss two social classes, the artisans and the merchants, whose political fortunes varied greatly in the cities of colonial Brazil. In contrast to Portugal, where artisan representation in town councils was a permanent characteristic of urban life and where artisan corporations (*bandeiras*) and the artisan council (*casa do vinte-quatro*) had exercised considerable influence, the Brazilian senates were usually without such representation. When artisans did participate in the town councils it was usually only in matters of direct interest to the crafts and trades, such as licences or price-fixing. The artisan crafts had not been well represented in Brazil in the early years of settlement, and even in the mid seventeenth century their numbers were small. Salvador, the largest city, had only 70 registered artisans in 1648. Artisan organizations became more active in the years after 1640, electing judges for each trade in Salvador and advising the senate of Rio de Janeiro on certain issues. In Salvador artisan representatives led by a *juiz do povo* (people's tribune) had formal representation in the town council from 1641 to 1711, but their position was so secondary that they were forced to sit out of earshot of the main table to prevent their participation in matters that did not concern them. Artisan complicity in the project to limit the number of new engenhos and in a tax riot in 1710 won them the enmity of the planters and brought their representation to an end.

The small number of urban artisans and their relatively weak political position was due to a number of related phenomena. First, the demand for many artisan skills on sugar plantations drew men in these occupations to the countryside, lessening their numbers and power in the cities. 'Mechanical office' was an 'ignoble' profession according to traditional concepts of society and artisans suffered discrimination on that ground. Royal office, membership in knightly orders, and other such honours were beyond their reach. In the Misericórdia of Salvador artisans were relegated to secondary status as brothers of lower condition and in the militia regiments artisans rarely received commissions. Contributing to their lowly status was the influence of slavery. Many slaves learnt to perform the 'mechanical offices' with skill. In addition, free people of colour looked upon the skilled trades as a step upward and set up shop whenever they could. Slave labour tended to depress wages and weaken the traditional qualitative distinctions of master (*mestre*) and apprentice of the Portuguese guild system. The existence of a small but growing percentage of *pardo* artisans lessened the prestige of the craftsmen as a group. In short, artisan status, never high in Portugal, was further lowered in Brazil within the context of a slave society. But this is not to say that artisans were unimportant in Brazilian cities. In the building and clothing trades, goldsmithing, tanning, and many other occupations, artisan brotherhoods, organized under the protection of a patron saint, assumed their obligations in municipal processions and festivals. Still, their power as trade guilds was weak and they remained for the most part under the thumb of the town councils or governors.

As for the political and social position of the merchants, it can be said that the Portuguese maintained a Ciceronian attitude towards business. Cicero had written: 'Commerce, if it is on a small scale, is to be considered mean; but if it is large-scale and extensive, importing much from many places and distributing to many without misrepresentation, it is not to be greatly censured.'[42] This was exactly the sentiment in colonial Brazil, where real distinctions existed between the export–import merchants, the *homens de negócio*, and the retail traders or shopkeepers, the *mercadores de loja*. In theory, any commerce in one's own name was considered a non-noble occupation, and mercantile origins were, like artisan background, cause for exclusion from honour and civil distinction. To this disability was added the fact that merchants were considered to be mostly of New Christian (i.e. Jewish) stock and thus suffered discrimination on that ground as well. While this New Christian connection has sometimes been overstated, a study of Salvador reveals that in the seventeenth century about half the resident merchants were New Christians.[43] But in the context of an export-oriented economy in which commerce was an essential element of life, such disabilities did not remain unchallenged or, at least, immutable. The

[42] Cicero, *De officiis*, I, 150–1. This work was known in Brazil. A copy appears in the inventory of *senhor de engenho* João Lopes Fiuza, APB, secção judiciária, maço 623, 4.

[43] Much of this section is drawn from Rae Flory and David G. Smith, 'Bahian merchants and planters in the seventeenth and early eighteenth centuries', *HAHR*, 58/4 (Nov. 1978), 571–94.

shopkeepers found their upward mobility continually blocked but the export merchants, who were involved in trade with Africa and Europe and, during the Iberian union, in a brisk contraband with Spanish America, could not be excluded from social and political advancement.

Though never great in absolute numbers, the merchants had some attributes that facilitated social advancement. The overwhelming majority of them were Europeans, many often coming to Brazil as agents for merchants at home or brought over by some uncle or cousin already doing business in Brazil. It is not surprising that many married Brazilian women, often daughters of the landed elite, who were willing, in some cases, to overlook the New Christian 'taint'. Success also cleared its own trail, as wealthy merchants were able to buy engenhos or ranches and gain membership in the prestigious Misericórdia or Franciscan tertiary brotherhoods. In many ways, the merchant class was absorbed into the landed elite in a gradual process that by the late seventeenth century blurred the social distinctions between the two groups.

Such fusion, however, did not eliminate the inevitable antagonism between merchants and producers born of their economic relationship. Planters' complaints against the merchants' 'extortion' persisted throughout the period in all the captaincies. The planters' habit of buying necessary equipment on credit for 20–30 per cent above the Lisbon price by mortgaging the next harvest at a set price below its market value was the cause of endless acrimony and remonstrance to the crown. In 1663, and periodically thereafter, planters managed to stop engenhos and canefields from being sold piecemeal to satisfy debts, but the mercantile interest was always strong enough to prevent the realization of the planters' dream – a complete moratorium on debts. The merchants' dictum, as expressed by Francisco Pinheiro – 'Do everything possible to obtain the highest price' – did nothing to mitigate the economic antagonism between them and the agrarian groups in the colony.[44]

The social and political rise of the merchants signalled by their increasing participation in town councils, commissions in militia regiments, membership in prestigious lay brotherhoods, and absorption into the planter aristocracy seems to have begun in the mid seventeenth century and intensified in the first decades of the eighteenth century. This was an epoch of severe strain in the Portuguese Atlantic empire,

[44] The most complete set of merchant records are those of Francisco Pinheiro (1707–52) contained in Luís Lisanti (ed.), *Negócios coloniais* (5 vols., Brasilia, 1973).

to which the crown responded with a series of mercantilist measures designed to shore up the flagging economy. The creation of the Brazil Company in 1649 (transformed into a government agency in 1663) with monopoly rights over the trade in certain commodities and the responsibility to provide a well-protected fleet was a wartime measure. It was followed in 1678 by the creation of a similar Maranhão Company designed to provide slaves to the north and granted control of commerce in that region. Such measures, while they sometimes struck at the interests of Brazilian merchants, were viewed with particular dislike by the planters and other colonists and tended to intensify the traditional planter–merchant conflict. Thus, during a period in which merchants were becoming increasingly important and prominent as a class, resistance towards them and towards royal mercantilist measures became intense.

In two places this conflict erupted into a violent confrontation. In 1684, the colonists of São Luís, led by a sugar planter named Manuel Beckman, rose against the company, declared its monopoly void, and took control of the city. The revolt petered out and Beckman was captured and executed. More serious was the civil conflict that broke out in Pernambuco, where the planter aristocrats of Olinda resisted the rise of neighbouring Recife as an independent city and suppressed the Portuguese-born merchants who resided there and to whom they were often indebted. The merchants, for their part, objected to their lack of representation in the câmara of Olinda, which levied the taxes on Recife. Matters came to a head in 1710–11 in a bitter but not particularly bloody civil war between the two factions of Olinda planters and Recife-based *mascates*, or merchants. This War of the Mascates revealed the natural tensions between merchants and planters and also the fact that within the colony's increasingly mercantilist orientation the merchant class would play an important role.

The turn of the century had brought not only more active merchant participation in Brazilian social and political life, but an intensification of the crown's role in municipal government as part of a new state activism. A major alteration in local government occurred between 1696 and 1700, with the creation of *juizes de fora* in the major Brazilian cities. These royally appointed professional magistrates presided over the câmaras and exercised authority in the preparation of electoral lists. The crown's justification for their use in Brazil was the elimination of favouritism and nepotism in the town councils, but their ultimate effect was to diminish the local autonomy of the câmaras. In addition, the expansion of settlement into the interior and the growth of secondary towns near the coast led in the first decades of the eighteenth century to the establishment of new municipal senates, a development which diminished the former authority of the coastal centres. For example, planters elected to the town council of Salvador increasingly declined to serve, preferring to attend to their engenhos or to take office on the senate of the new rural câmaras like those of Cachoeira or Santo Amaro, founded in 1698 and 1724 respectively. While planters continued to dominate Salvador's senate throughout the colonial period, there were increasing opportunities in other port cities for the merchants. The positions that they acquired by the middle of the eighteenth century, however, were in less powerful institutions.

SOCIAL STRUCTURE

Brazil was from its early period of settlement too large an area with too complex and diversified an economy for its social and political forms to become simply the sugar plantation writ large, but as we have seen, the demands of sugar agriculture and the peculiarities of its organization contributed in no small way to the ordering of society. The Portuguese had brought with them an idealized concept of social hierarchy buttressed by theology and a practical understanding of social positions and relationships as these functioned in Portugal. These concepts and experiences defined the terminology of social organization and set the parameters within which society evolved. But export agriculture and the plantation created their own hierarchies and realities.

As early as 1549 Duarte Coelho, donatary of Pernambuco, described his colonists in a way which unconsciously outlined the social hierarchy of his captaincy:

some build engenhos because they are powerful enough to do so, others plant cane, others cotton, and others food crops, which are the principal and most important things in the land; others fish, which is also very necessary; others have boats to seek provisions...Others are master engenho builders, sugar masters, carpenters, blacksmiths, masons, potters, makers of sugar forms, and other trades.[45]

Here was a natural social order in an economy based on commercial agriculture. Mill owners came first, followed by cane farmers. Next,

[45] Letter of 15 Apr. 1549, *Cartas de Duarte Coelho a El Rei* (Recife, 1967), 71.

those engaged in other export activities were mentioned. Men in subsistence farming or other such activities received special mention just as peasants in Europe were usually singled out for praise as the foundation of all else, but they were mentioned last among the agricultors. With a bare mention of commerce and merchants, Duarte Coelho then turned to the artisans, listing them roughly in the order of their importance in the sugar-making process, or, put another way, according to the annual salary that each would expect to earn on an engenho.

Duarte Coelho's description is revealing both in what it includes and what it omits. The hierarchy described is a functional–occupational order directly linked to export agriculture, primarily sugar. While reflecting an essential reality, it is incomplete in that it describes only the free population. The vast majority of the colonial population – the Indians and, later, the African slaves – do not figure here. In reality, in addition to this agrarian occupational hierarchy, Brazilian society was ordered by two other principles: a juridical division based primarily on distinctions between slave and free, and a racial gradation from white to black.

In the sixteenth century some attempt had been made to maintain the traditional legal distinctions between noble and commoner and the divisions of a European society of estates or orders. But the planter class failed to evolve into a hereditary nobility and all whites tended to aspire to high rank. *Fidalgos* (nobles) and churchmen continued to enjoy certain juridical rights and exemptions. On solemn or important occasions representatives of the traditional estates were convoked. Such was the case, for example, when, in reaction to a property tax in 1660, the câmara of Rio de Janeiro was joined by representatives of the nobility, clergy, and people, or when, at the founding of the town of Cachoeira, 'men of the people' and 'serious men of government' met to establish the town ordinances.[46] In Brazil, however, other forms of social organization made these traditional principles of stratification less important.

Juridically, Brazilian society was divided between slave and free status. Because of the large numbers of unfree labourers, Indian and African, the distinction between slave and free was crucial. But even

[46] Cf. Vivaldo Coaracy, *O Rio de Janeiro no século XVII* (Rio de Janeiro, 1965), 161; Arquivo Municipal de Cachoeira, Livro 1 de Vereação (1968). See also José Honório Rodrigues, *Vida e história* (Rio de Janeiro, 1966), 132.

within the clear legal separation of slave and free status there were intermediate categories. Indians who had been captured and placed under the tutelage of colonists, the so-called *forros* or *administrados*, were legally free but treated little differently from slaves. Moreover, those slaves who had arranged to make payments for their freedom or who had received their liberty on condition of future services or payments apparently enjoyed as *coartados* a legal position that distinguished them from slaves. Thus, while the juridical divisions of a European society of estates existed in Brazil they were of less importance in a colony where the distinctions of a slave society exercised great influence on social stratification.

Moreover, the existence of three major racial groups – Europeans, American Indians, and Africans – in a colony created by Europeans resulted in a colour-based hierarchy with whites at the top and blacks at the bottom. The place of people of mixed background – the mulattos, *mamelucos*, and other such mixtures – depended on how light or dark in colour they were and on the extent of their acculturation to European norms. To the free people of colour fell the less prestigious occupations of small trade, artisan craft, manual labour, and subsistence agriculture. Despite their legally free status they suffered from certain disadvantages. They were excluded from municipal office or membership in the more prestigious lay brotherhoods such as the Third Order of St Francis. Occasionally municipal councils passed sumptuary legislation. Slaves were prohibited from wearing silk and gold in Salvador in 1696 and by 1709 the restrictions were expanded to include free blacks and mulattos, as was done, it was argued, in Rio de Janeiro. There were other restrictions, too. According to a law of 1621 no black, Indian, or mulatto could be a goldsmith in Bahia, and in 1743 blacks were prohibited from selling goods on the streets of Recife.[47] The fact that such discriminatory laws were sometimes circumvented does not negate the limitations under which the free coloured population lived. That they realized their disadvantage and tried to do something about it is made clear by incidents such as that of 1689, when mulattos had sought to be admitted to the Jesuit College in Bahia where they wished to 'improve the fortune of their colour' by education and had been denied admission.[48]

[47] BNRJ, II–33, 23, 15, n. 4 (20 Feb. 1696); *Documentos históricos da Bibliotica Nacional de Rio de Janeiro* [*DHBNRJ*] 95 (1952): 248; Biblioteca Geral da Universidade de Coimbra [BGUC], Códice 707.

[48] AHU/PA/Bahia, caixa 16 (30 Jan. 1689). The crown ordered that the Jesuits admit them.

The antipathy towards people of colour was profound and penetrated all aspects of life. In Ceará in 1724 and in Rio Grande do Norte in 1732 it was suggested that, although mulattos and *mamelucos* had held public office when there had been a shortage of whites, there should now be restrictions on their service, 'since experience has demonstrated that they are less able because of their inferiority and because unrest and trouble is more natural to them'.[49] They were, as the câmara of Salvador put it, 'low people who have no honour nor reasons for the conservation and growth of the kingdom and seek only their own convenience'.[50] The ultimate comment on their disability is the fact that the freedom of a former slave could be revoked for disrespect towards a former master.

Among the free people of colour institutions developed, paralleling those of white society, which provided a sense of community and pride. Black militia regiments, named the *Henriques* after Henrique Dias, a leader against the Dutch, existed throughout much of Brazil. Distinctions were maintained between black and mulatto regiments and there were even attempts in some black units to limit officer status to the Brazilian-born *crioulos*. Still, the militia units provided a point of cohesion and eventually a platform from which grievances could be expressed. Perhaps of even greater importance were the lay sodalities of blacks and mulattos that existed through the colony. Providing social services, alms, dowries, burials, and organized religious observance, the brotherhoods became a fixture in urban life and sometimes on the engenhos as well. Although some may have existed as early as the sixteenth century, it was not until the eighteenth century that they began to proliferate. Bahia, for example, had six black and five mulatto brotherhoods dedicated to the Virgin at the beginning of that century. Although some of the brotherhoods were open to men and women of all races, others were limited by colour or by African nation of origin. While such institutions did offer paths to participation in the dominant culture, separation by colour and nation also reflected the realities of a slave-based society and the disabilities suffered by people of colour, both slave and free. The blacks of the brotherhood of the Rosary, which had been housed in the see of Salvador, had left and built their own church because of the insults they had suffered from the white brotherhoods, which had treated them poorly 'because they were

---

[49] *Ibid.*, Ceará, caixa 1; Rio Grande do Norte, caixa 3.
[50] Arquivo da Câmara Municipal do Salvador [ACMS], 124.7 Provisões, fos. 171–3 (3 Dec. 1711).

blacks'.[51] For people of colour election to the board of a brotherhood or the winning of a militia commission was undoubtedly a matter of social achievement and success but within a limited and always restricted range of opportunities offered by colonial society.

In addition to the fundamental distinctions of civil status and race, there were others, particularly important among the white population. Married men with a fixed residence were the preferred colonists and were favoured for municipal office and rights. Ethnic or religious origins were also used as a social gradient. Those with 'New Christian' – that is, Jewish – ancestors or relatives were considered religiously and culturally suspect and suffered legal and financial disabilities. In Brazil, however, these were often overcome by economic achievements.

New Christians played a major role in the colony throughout the seventeenth century. The forced conversion of all Jews in Portugal in 1497 had produced a large group who were suddenly plunged into a new faith. In theory, religious distinctions had been eliminated at a stroke, but differences of custom, attitude, and thought could not be so easily obliterated. New Christians bore the stigma of their birth from generation to generation, and even those who were devout Catholics could suffer, under discriminatory legislation and practice, exclusion from office or honour because of a New Christian somewhere in the family tree. Both crypto-Jews and those who had not the slightest attachment to Judaism were lumped together by the society as a suspect group. However, New Christians had been involved in the Brazilian enterprise from its origins and the fact that the Portuguese Inquisition was not established until 1547 meant that the colony's early years were relatively free from the watchful eye of orthodoxy. In Brazil New Christians became not only merchants but artisans, sugar planters, and *lavradores de cana*, holding civil and ecclesiastical offices. In 1603 the Board of Conscience in Lisbon ordered the bishop of Brazil to appoint only Old Christians to religious offices in Pernambuco because the majority of the churches in that state were served by New Christians. A study of Bahia from 1620 to 1660 revealed that while 36 per cent of the New Christians were in commerce, 20 per cent were in agriculture, 12 per cent were in professions, and 10 per cent were artisans. Another 20 per cent held civil, military, or religious office.[52]

---

[51] 'Pellos desgostos que padecião com os Brancos...e por serem pretos os maltratavão'. AHU/PA/Bahia, caixa 48 (8 July 1733).

[52] Anita Novinsky, *Cristãos novos na Bahia* (São Paulo, 1972), 176; ANTT, Mesa da Consciência, Livro de registro 18, fos. 8v–9.

The period of the Iberian union (1580–1640) brought the New Christians to the centre of the stage in the colony. The Inquisitorial visits to Pernambuco and Bahia in 1591–5 and 1618 created great consternation in the New Christian community, but the inability of the Inquisition to establish itself permanently in Brazil may have been due to the influence of that group in the colony. Bishops had inquisitorial powers and used them on occasion, but persecution of New Christians was less efficient in Brazil than in Spanish America and the levels of New Christian immigration to Brazil rose during the early decades of the seventeenth century. Pressures on the New Christians in Brazil and opportunities for trade created by the union with Spain caused many to emigrate or establish trading ventures in Spanish America, especially in the viceroyalty of Peru. The *peruleiros* were thoroughly resented on national, economic, and religious grounds. The term 'Portuguese' became a synonym for Jew in Spanish America and with the separation of Spain and Portugal in 1640 a series of *autos-da-fé* were held in Lima, Mexico, and Cartagena, aimed primarily at Portuguese merchants.

Controversy rages among specialists over the extent to which the Brazilian and Portuguese New Christians were or were not Jews and whether the Inquisition's efforts were designed to promote religious orthodoxy or were simply a tool of the nobility to break, by persecution and confiscation, the back of a growing bourgeoisie. The Inquisitorial visits do certainly suggest that there were practising Jews among the sugar planters of Bahia and Pernambuco. Moreover, under the policy of religious toleration advocated by Count Maurits of Nassau in Dutch Brazil, those who were crypto-Jews were able to come into the open, and they were soon joined by Jews from Holland. Two synagogues were operating in Recife in the 1640s. Those who fought with the Dutch were allowed to leave Brazil as part of the surrender terms, emigrating to Surinam, Jamaica, or New Amsterdam or returning to Holland. New Christians in Portuguese Brazil were apparently divided in their loyalties, but all were considered potential traitors. The fall of Salvador in 1624 was attributed by the *vox populi* to a New Christian 'stab in the back', although subsequent historiography has proven this to be untrue.[53] Attempts made by the Jews of Dutch Brazil to contact the New Christians in Portuguese territory were generally unsuccessful, but

---

[53] Cf. Novinsky, *Cristãos novos*, 120; Eduardo d'Oliveira França, 'Um problema: A traição dos cristãos novos em 1624', *Revista de História* 41 (1970), 21–71. For an economic interpretation of the Inquisition, see Antônio José Saraiva, *Inquisição e cristãos-novos* (Oporto, 1969).

the cosmopolitan connections of New Christians with Italy, France, and Holland were considered cause for suspicion. Episcopal investigations were made in Bahia in 1635, 1640, 1641, and 1646, the last being particularly extensive.

After 1660 the concern with New Christians as a group seems to have diminished until the beginning of the following century. Arrests of judaizers were made throughout the century from Maranhão to São Paulo, but in small numbers. The traditional discrimination against New Christian membership in public office, the Misericórdias, or the more prestigious lay brotherhoods continued. With the discovery of gold the arrests and confiscations of the Inquisition intensified. Most of those arrested were from Rio de Janeiro and Minas Gerais. The Lisbon *auto-da-fé* of 1711 included 52 prisoners from Brazil. In all, about 400 Brazilian New Christians were tried by the Inquisition. By the eighteenth century, under the watchful eye of the Inquisition and their neighbours, the cultural and religious distinctiveness of the New Christians faded away, although they remained a disadvantaged segment of Brazilian society.

Finally, there was in Brazilian colonial society, in addition to the burdens of colour, creed, and origin, that of sex. Brazilians shared the typical European attitudes of the time towards women but with an intensity that made even their Spanish neighbours comment. In theory, women were to be protected and secluded from the affairs of the world and expected to be devoted to the life of an obedient daughter, submissive wife, and loving mother. A rigid double standard of female chastity and constancy and male promiscuity was condoned to the point of the law's permitting an offended husband to kill his wife caught in an act of adultery. Various institutions existed in colonial society to aid or to ensure compliance with expected norms of behaviour for women of 'good family'. Benefactors of the Misericórdias left funds for the dowries of orphan girls. Retirement houses were established for young women whose chastity was endangered by the loss of a parent. As early as 1602 residents of Salvador sought to have a convent established in their city. The request was finally successful in 1677, when the Convento do Destêrro was founded, and by 1750 most of the major cities had convents.[54] As in other areas of life, admission to these depended on 'purity of blood', and since the 'dowry' needed for admission was large,

---

[54] ANTT, Mesa da Consciência, Livro de registro 17, fos. 158–9; Susan Soeiro, 'A baroque nunnery: the economic and social role of a colonial convent: Santa Clara do Desterro, Salvador, Bahia, 1677–1800' (Ph.D. thesis, New York University, 1974).

the daughters of planters and merchants held most of the positions available. If we can believe the complaints made about the scandalous life in the convents and the boastful observations of French travellers like Foger and Dellon, the ideals of seclusion and chastity were in reality often circumvented.

In fact, the role of women in colonial society was more complex than is usually portrayed. While in a legal dispute a party might argue that his property had been endangered because it had been in the hands of his wife, and women were 'by nature ... timid and unable to care for such matters, surrounded by tender children and lacking protection ...', many women, in fact, assumed the role of household head in their widowhood or because of desertion.[55] Women were to be found as plantation owners, *lavradores de cana*, and owners of urban real estate. To some extent this situation resulted from the Portuguese laws of inheritance, which assured all heirs of an equal portion and provided that a surviving spouse should inherit a major portion of the estate. Moreover, as we descend through the layers of class and colour, women become increasingly obvious in active economic roles. For instance, the small-scale ambulating retail trade in the colonial cities was almost exclusively in the hands of women of colour, both slave and free.

Government and society in Brazil formed two interlocking systems. Government sought to bind individuals and corporate groups to the formal political institutions of the state and to create conditions that facilitated and maintained the productive capacity of the colony; while the principal factors which motivated society and held it together were personal relations based on the extended family and on kin groups, shared social status and goals, and common economic interests. Throughout the colonial period state and society were so linked as to ensure the survival of the colony and the social and economic dominance of those groups which controlled the production and distribution of Brazil's major exports.

There were at least three levels of government within the colony. Royally appointed officers – the viceroy, governors, *disembargadores* (high court judges), and other crown magistrates – were the direct representatives of Portuguese authority. They were, in theory at least, a bureaucracy of professionals. Those in the higher executive positions were usually drawn from the Portuguese nobility, who were supposed, by inclination and training, to be soldiers. Magistrates were *letrados*,

---

[55] APB, Ordens régias (royal dispatches), 86, fos. 234–6.

university-trained lawyers, who formed a growing class of professional royal administrators. Together, soldiers and lawyers filled the highest offices in the colony. Beneath them was the second level of government, a myriad of minor offices, treasury officials, customs collectors, market inspectors, probate judges, scribes, and watchmen. Originally, these positions had been filled by European-born Portuguese, but by the mid seventeenth century colonials held many of these offices, some of which were bought and others held by inheritance. Finally, there was, as we have seen, a third level, formed by the offices of municipal government, the elected judges and *vereadores* (councillors) of the câmaras and the many lesser positions appointed by these local colonial bodies. In the countryside government was often in the hands of the senior militia officers, who served paramilitary functions as policemen, tax collectors, and, eventually, census-takers.

From the time of the donatary captaincies private power had played an important role in the colony's organization and, while the crown continually asserted its authority, the dominant groups in the colony found ways to make government respond to their needs. Municipal offices were usually in the hands of the local economic elite, which also came to control many of the lesser offices of justice and the treasury. In rural areas it was rare to find a militia colonel who was not also a planter or rancher. Even the ranks of the most highly professionalized royal officials, the magistrates, were penetrated by and incorporated into the Brazilian elite. Despite a strict prohibition on Brazilians serving in high government positions in the colony, and against family ties that might influence a magistrate's impartiality, webs of kinship and association between crown officers and local society were formed. Between 1652 and 1752 ten Brazilian-born judges were appointed to the Relação of Bahia, and when a new high court was created in Rio de Janeiro in 1752, its first chancellor was a Bahian by birth. Twenty-five high court judges married Brazilian wives, usually the daughters of sugar planters, and others became linked to the colonial elite by godparenthood, business dealings, or common participation in lay confraternities. In short, the colonial elites sought and found ways to make royal and municipal government responsive to their interests and goals. Government was often ineffective, sometimes oppressive, and usually corrupt, but it was rarely viewed as an external and foreign force, even though Portugal tried to put its own interests first.

Quite clearly the family played a major political and social role in the colony. The predominance of the donatarial families in Rio de Janeiro and Pernambuco was paralleled by the more restricted but still extensive powers held by interconnected, but sometimes quite hostile, kin groups of sugar planters, cattle ranchers, and other rural magnates. The struggles between the Pires and the Camargos in São Paulo in the 1650s or the Vieira Ravascos and Teles Meneses in Bahia in the 1680s reflect the importance and power of the family as an institution in the colony. The extended patriarchal family, with its many members linked by blood, marriage, and godparenthood and including dependants and slaves, was an ideal concept cutting across the social hierarchies described above. The formation and maintenance of these elite families, their strategies of inheritance, linkage, and continuity are topics that greatly merit attention. Unfortunately, the study of the family in Brazil is still in its infancy and the lack of any census data earlier than 1750 makes the task a hard one.

The relationship of state and society must finally be looked at in the context of Brazil's economy and its dominant form of labour relations – slavery. The Portuguese state and law provided a framework for the control of property, commercial transactions, and the distribution and control of labour power. Once the colony was launched as a producer of export crops based on enslaved African or coerced Indian labour, the state intervened very little in the internal aspects of the economy, the ordering of the factors of production, or the relationship between master and slave. So long as the major economic inputs came from the planter class, they were given free rein and the crown was content to collect its tithe and the various taxes on imports and exports. After 1650, when prices for Brazil's agricultural exports fluctuated, the crown took a number of measures to stimulate and improve the position of the sugar planters, often to the detriment of the mercantile groups in Portugal and the colony. By the beginning of the eighteenth century, however, changing European conditions, a Colbertian approach to political economy, the growing importance of mercantile groups within Brazil and the metropolis, and the discovery of gold all combined to bring about a change in the relationship between the Portuguese state and its American colony. That the Brazilian agrarian elite was able to absorb the newly important mercantile and mining classes and to adjust itself to a more active and interventionist state was mainly because both it and the colonial state were so firmly based on the institution of slavery and its concomitant social distinctions.

4

INDIANS AND THE FRONTIER

The 'frontier' in this chapter is the European boundary, the limit of colonial expansion into Brazil. Each of the hundreds of native American tribes also had its own frontier, sometimes fluid and shifting but more often geographically defined and well known to every member of the tribe. Tribal frontiers were the boundaries between often hostile, warring groups, or were the limits of each people's hunting forays or annual collecting cycle. The European frontier was a sharper division: the limit of penetration or permanent occupation by an alien culture. It marked a divide between peoples of radically different racial, ethnic, religious, political and technological composition. To European colonists, the frontier was the edge of civilization. Beyond it lay the barbaric unknown of the *sertão* – the 'wilds', the bush or the wasteland of the interior – or the impenetrable *selva*, the Amazonian rain forests.

In practice, the frontier was less precise than it may have been in the colonists' perception. The men who explored, exploited or attacked the frontier were often *mamelucos* of mixed European and Indian blood. Many of them spoke Tupi-Guaraní or other Indian languages. They were almost invariably accompanied by Indian guides, auxiliaries or forced labourers, and they adopted efficient Indian methods of travel and survival. Even when European colonists were firmly established on conquered tribal lands, the frontier was not necessarily the boundary between civilization and barbarism. It was often the Indians beyond the frontier who were more civilized. In most forms of artistic expression and often in political organization and social harmony, the Indians had the advantage over the frontiersmen, who were usually tough, brutal, ignorant, greedy, and uncultured.

There was little to attract Europeans to the Brazilian frontier. There was a complete lack of precious metals among the tribes of the Atlantic seaboard, and there were few rumours or signs of any advanced civilizations in the interior. There seemed to be no chance of discovering any rich empires comparable to those of the Incas, Aztecs, or Muisca in the *campo* of the Brazilian plateau or the forests that lay beyond. Spanish adventurers, more determined or more self-deluding than their Portuguese counterparts, made the explorations that quickly established that there was no wealth to be looted in the heart of Brazil. Sebastiano Caboto, Juan de Ayolas, Domingo Martínez de Irala, and Alvar Núñez Cabeza de Vaca explored far up the Paraguay and Paraná rivers in the 1520s and 1530s, and Aleixo Garcia, a Portuguese working with the Spaniards, accompanied a group of Guaraní right across the continent to be the first European to see outposts of the Inca empire. During the 1530s, some of Pizarro's lieutenants led disastrous expeditions from the Andes to explore the western edges of the Amazon forests. During those same years, gold-hungry Spaniards and Germans were marching deep into northern South America, up the Orinoco and onto the headwaters of the north-western tributaries of the Amazon. As early as 1542, Francisco de Orellana made the first descent of the Amazon from Quito to the Atlantic Ocean; and it was another Spanish expedition, that of Pedro de Ursúa and the infamous rebel Lope de Aguirre, that in 1560 made the only other descent during the sixteenth century. The survivors of these expeditions emerged broken and impoverished; and Amazonia acquired a terrible reputation. Lope de Aguirre summed up contemporary thinking when he wrote to the king of Spain: 'God knows how we got through that great mass of water. I advise you, great King, never to send Spanish fleets to that cursed river!'[1]

There were desultory attempts to discover gold, silver, and precious stones in the endless expanses of central Brazil but until the last decade of the seventeenth century very little came of them. At the same time land was not an attraction sufficient to lure people to the frontier. There was no lack of land along the thousands of kilometres of the Brazilian coast. The idea of scientific discovery came only with the age of enlightenment at the end of the colonial period. Very few explorers achieved any fame or reward for their efforts: Pedro Teixeira was praised for his journey up and down the Amazon in 1638–9, but only because it was a geopolitical venture to push Portuguese frontiers far up the river.

[1] Lope de Aguirre to King Philip [V], in C. R. Markham (trans.), *Expeditions into the Valley of the Amazons* (Hakluyt Society, 24; London, 1859) xii.

The Brazilian interior had only one commodity of interest to Europeans: its native inhabitants. The rivers, plains, and forests of Brazil were full of tribes of robust men and relatively attractive women. This great human reservoir was an obvious target both for colonists desperate for labour and for missionaries eager to spread their gospel and swell their personal soul-counts.

The Indian population of the Brazilian coast and interior was, however, at the same time being annihilated during the sixteenth, seventeenth, and every subsequent century by imported diseases against which it had no genetic defence. Smallpox, measles, tuberculosis, typhoid, dysentery, and influenza rapidly killed tens of thousands of native Americans who were otherwise in perfect health and physically very fit. It is impossible to quantify the extent of this depopulation, but there are many clues in the chronicles. There are early references to dense populations and large villages close to one another in all parts of Brazil and Amazonia.[2] The chronicles are also full of references to depopulation and disease. The Jesuits are, as usual, our best informants: they wrote accurate descriptions of disease symptoms and provided numerical data on the decline in the numbers living in their missions. Whatever the actual figures, there can be no question that a demographic tragedy of great magnitude occurred.

THE SIXTEENTH AND SEVENTEENTH CENTURIES

There were four main theatres of expansion of the frontier during the period up to the discoveries of gold at the end of the seventeenth century: (1) the south – the area penetrated by Paulistas, embracing the modern states of Rio Grande do Sul, Santa Catarina, Paraná, São Paulo and southern Mato Grosso; (2) the centre, inland from Salvador da Bahia; (3) the interior of the north-east; (4) the Amazon, which was exploited from Maranhão and Pará.

The south

João Ramalho, a Portuguese who was shipwrecked on the coast of São Vicente in about 1510 and who managed to marry a daughter of the powerful chief Tibiriçá of the Goianá Tupinikin living on the

---

[2] For a discussion of the population of Brazil *c.* 1500, see John Hemming, *Red Gold. The Conquest of the Brazilian Indians* (London, 1978), appendix, 487–501.

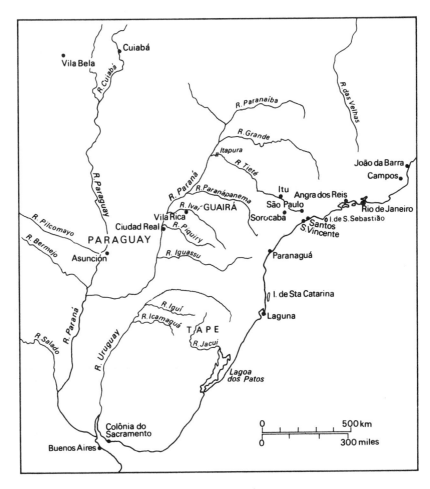

Southern Brazil

Piratininga plateau, fathered many sons and these in turn produced a
sizeable *mameluco* offspring from many Indian women. By the time of
the first Portuguese colony at São Vicente in 1532 and the founding
of the Jesuit college and reduction at São Paulo de Piratininga in 1553,
Ramalho's descendants were described by the Jesuit Manoel da Nóbrega
as 'going to war with the Indians, their festivals are Indian ones, and
they live like them, as naked as the Indians themselves'. Such racial
intermingling was characteristic of São Paulo, where a century later
children still spoke Tupi as their first language and went to school to

learn Portuguese. By identifying themselves so closely with one Indian tribe, the Paulistas embroiled themselves in intertribal wars: the early history of their town was marked by bitter fighting against the Tamoio (allies of the French at Guanabara) and excursions down the Tietê against Gê-speaking tribes then known as Bilreiros ('wooden lip discs') or Coroados ('crowned', from their haircuts), who were presumably precursors of the modern Kaingáng and the now-extinct Southern Caiapó.

It was at the start of the seventeenth century that the tribes of southern Brazil began to feel the impact of two distinct European frontiers: Spanish Jesuits were pushing their missionary thrust east-wards across the Paraná and upper Uruguay from their bases near Asunción in Paraguay; and the Paulistas were beginning to make excursions into the forests in search of slaves. It was no accident that the Jesuits were more successful with the Guaraní of Paraguay and the closely related Carijó and Tape of southern Brazil than with any other South American tribes. These Guaraní-speaking peoples were deeply spiritual and were excellent farmers living in populous villages. They responded readily to the two benefits that the Jesuits had to offer: a well-disciplined existence regulated from cradle to grave by religious precepts, and plenty of food from efficient plantations and ranches. Alonso de Barzana, one of the first Jesuits in Paraguay, understood the potential of these Guaraní when he wrote in 1594:

All this nation is very inclined to religion, whether true or false... They know all about the immortality of the soul and greatly fear the *angüera* [devils] which are souls emerged from dead bodies that go about terrifying people and causing harm. They have the greatest love and obedience for the [Jesuit] Fathers if these give them a good example... These tribes are great farmers: they have vast quantities of food, especially maize, various kinds of manioc and other fine root crops, and a great amount of fish.[3]

In the last decade of the sixteenth century and the first decade of the seventeenth, Spanish Jesuit missionaries moved into an area they called Guairá – east of the Paraná and between its tributaries the Iguaçu and Paranapanema, roughly midway between Asunción and São Paulo and therefore, the Portuguese reckoned, on their side of the Line of Tordesillas. Their missionary activity was successful, and a series of *reducciones* (villages of Indians 'reduced' to Christianity and 'civilized' society) were soon full of Guaraní–Carijó converts. By 1594, the Spanish

---

[3] Alonso de Barzana to Juan Sebastián, Asunción, 8 Sept. 1594, in Marcos Jiménez de la Espada, *Relaciones geográficas de Indias* (Madrid, 1965), 85.

Jesuit Barzana was complaining that the greater part of his Society's original converts in Paraguay were dead from alien diseases or had fled to avoid persecution by settlers. Baffled by these epidemics and impotent to prevent the decline, the Jesuits did not desist from their proselytizing but merely looked hungrily at large native populations to the east and north-east.

The Paulistas were looking in the same direction, for less exalted motives. The town council of São Paulo explained the problem in 1585, in its first open reference to Indian slavery:

This land is in great danger of being depopulated because its inhabitants do not have [Indian] slaves as they used to, by whom they have always been served. This is the result of many illnesses... from which over two thousand head of slaves have died in this captaincy in the past six years. This land used to be ennobled by these slaves, and its settlers supported themselves honourably with them and made large incomes.[4]

São Paulo was a small hilltop town of only 2,000 white inhabitants in 1600. And yet the Paulistas, the citizens of this frontier town, embarked on a series of audacious expeditions that explored thousands of kilometres of south and central Brazil. These expeditions were called *bandeiras* (probably from the flag carried by a small company of troops), and the tough woodsmen who marched on them were *bandeirantes*. Although the bandeirantes hoped that they might possibly find precious metals or stones, their true purpose was to capture Indians. In the 1590s Jorge Correia, captain-major of São Paulo, and Jerónimo Leitão led slaving expeditions against the Carijó along the coast south to Paranaguá, and then for six years down the Tietê. Spanish Jesuits claimed that these Tietê campaigns destroyed 300 native villages and caused the death or enslavement of 30,000 people. Other expeditions 'raided and roamed the country' north to the Jeticaí (now called Grande) and Paranaíba rivers. In 1602 Nicolau Barreto led 300 whites and many Indians – a large proportion of the adult men of São Paulo – north for hundreds of kilometres to the Velhas and upper São Francisco rivers: they returned after two years of marching and many deaths, bringing 3,000 Temimino prisoners. Each year, bandeiras struck the Carijó and other tribes within easy reach of São Paulo.

It was inevitable that these expeditions would soon clash with the Spaniards pushing north-eastwards from Asunción. This was during the

[4] Acta da Câmara de São Paulo, 1585, in Afonso de Escragnolle Taunay, *História geral das bandeiras paulistas* (11 vols., São Paulo, 1924–50) I, 156.

60-year union of the crowns of Spain and Portugal (1580–1640), when
many Portuguese felt their country to be occupied by Spain and there
was no love lost between subjects of the Catholic dual monarchy of the
Iberian peninsula. Paraguayan Spaniards tried to establish two towns
in Guairá: Ciudad Real at the junction of the Piquiri and the Paraná,
and Villa Rica on the lower Ivaí. Between 1607 and 1612, the Preto
brothers led raids from São Paulo that captured hundreds of Indians
working for the settlers in these towns. It was now that the Jesuits
opened their missionary province of Guairá. For twenty years after
1610, Jesuit fathers under Antonio Ruiz de Montoya created fifteen
villages or 'reductions' in the Paranapanema, Tibagi and Ivaí valleys.
Indians flocked into these reductions to escape severe oppression from
the Spanish settlers of Ciudad Real and Villa Rica.

The spectacle of large mission villages full of thousands of docile
Guaraní was too tempting to Paulista bandeirantes. The bandeirantes
and their bands of trained Indians and *mamelucos* had become expert
woodsmen and trackers. They lived rough on their expeditions, eating
a little roast manioc or any game or fish that their men could catch. If
possible, they raided Indian villages and stole their stores of food. They
were heavily bearded and wore high boots, skin or hide suits, padded
cotton armour, and broad-brimmed hats as protection against strong
sun or rains, or the insects and detritus that fall from tropical forests.
Apart from food, swords, and firearms, their baggage included ropes
and shackles to secure their victims, and some mining implements in
case they might come across mineral deposits. One Jesuit marvelled at
the effort that the bandeirantes expended on slaving expeditions that
might last for several years. 'They go without God, without food, naked
as the savages, and subject to all the persecutions and miseries in the
world. Men venture for 200 or 300 leagues into the sertão, serving the
devil with such amazing martyrdom, in order to trade or steal slaves.'[5]
The Jesuit Diego Ferrer admitted that 'these Portuguese do and suffer
incomparably more to win the bodies of the Indians for their service
than I do to win their souls for heaven'.[6] To such desperadoes, it was
infinitely easier to round up the inmates of a Jesuit reduction than to
hunt hostile uncontacted or nomadic tribes in the depths of the forests.

[5] Anon. Jesuit, 'Sumário das armadas que se fizeram e guerras que se deram na conquista do
rio Paraíba' [*c.* 1587] in *Revista do Instituto Histórico e Geográfico Brasileiro* [*RIHGB*], 36/1 (1873),
13–14.
[6] Diego Ferrer, Carta Anua of 21 Aug. 1633, in Jaime Cortesão, *Jesuítas e bandeirantes no Itatim
(1596–1760)* (Rio de Janeiro, 1952), 45.

The first Paulista attack on outlying Indians of a Guairá reduction was by Manoel Preto, in 1616. He was back for another attack in 1619, and in 1623–4 his bandeira led over 1,000 Christian Indians from Guairá to slavery on plantations near São Paulo. Other attacks took place in ensuing years. The Jesuits sent furious complaints to King Philip of Spain and Portugal. They fulminated against 'Portuguese pirates... more like wild beasts than rational men... Men without souls, they kill Indians as if they were animals, sparing neither age nor sex.'[7] They reported that the bandeirantes killed babies or the elderly because they slowed down the marching column, and they killed chiefs to prevent them inspiring their people to rebel.

In 1628 an enormous bandeira of 69 whites, 900 *mamelucos*, and over 2,000 Indians left São Paulo under the command of the most famous of all bandeirantes, Antônio Rapôso Tavares. The Portuguese on this raid included two justices of São Paulo, two aldermen, the public prosecutor, and the son, son-in-law, and brother of the town's senior judge. The bandeira marched to the Ivaí valley and camped outside the reduction of San Antonio. Four months of uneasy calm ensued, with quarrels between bandeirantes and Jesuits over the ownership of various Indian groups. Finally, on 29 January 1629, the bandeirantes entered the mission to seize a particular chief. The spell was broken: this was the first time that Portuguese had penetrated within the walls of a reduction. They went on to round up 'all the others whom the Father was instructing. They themselves admit that they took 4,000 Indians from it... and they destroyed the entire village, burning many houses, plundering the church and the Father's house...'[8] The Portuguese regarded themselves as devout Christians, so they had to fabricate elaborate excuses for this violation of a Christian sanctuary – a negation of all the proselytizing claims advanced to condone Spanish and Portuguese colonizing of the Americas. Some claimed that the catechumens they led off to slavery were being taken into the bosom of the church; others pleaded that their country faced ruin without a supply of 'free' labour and that the Indians were technically free. Rapôso Tavares is said to have sounded a patriotic note, exclaiming: 'We have come to expel you from this entire region. For this land is

---

[7] Ruiz de Montoya to Nicolas Durán, Carta Anua of 1628, in Jaime Cortesão, *Jesuítas e bandeirantes no Guairá (1594–1640)* (Rio de Janeiro, 1951), 269.

[8] Justo Mancilla and Simón Masseta, 'Relación de los agravios que hicieron algunos vecinos y moradores de la Villa de S. Pablo de Piratininga...' in *ibid.*, 315.

[9] Antonio Ruiz de Montoya, *Conquista espiritual hecha por los religiosos de la Compañía de Jesús en las provincias de Paraguay, Uruguay y Tape* (Madrid, 1639), 35.

ours and not the king of Spain's!'[9] His bandeira went on to sack another empty village and to invade a flourishing mission on the Tibagi, shackling its entire population of 1,500 men, women and children. Two Jesuits accompanied the bandeira on the 40-day march back to São Paulo with thousands of captives herded along by the Paulistas' own Indians. The Jesuits were appalled to see the ease with which the slavers bribed the town's authorities with presents of captured Indians. 'Thereupon, after committing so many abominations, they were well received...No one who had not seen it with his own eyes could imagine such a thing! The entire life of these bandits is going to and from the sertão, bringing back captives with so much cruelty, death and pillage; and then selling them as if they were pigs.'[10]

Once Rapôso Tavares had destroyed and enslaved a Jesuit reduction with impunity, the Guairá missions were doomed. Two more villages were sacked by André Fernandes in 1630, and another by another bandeirante in 1631. The Jesuit fathers decided that their position was untenable. They assembled 10,000 Indians from their remaining Guairá reductions and sailed them down the Paraná in a convoy of hundreds of canoes. Spanish settlers tried in vain to prevent this exodus of what they regarded as their pool of labour. In 1632 the Paulistas turned against these settlers' towns, and Villa Rica and Ciudad Real were abandoned for ever. The refugees from Guairá were relocated in a region that the Jesuits were just beginning to penetrate. Four years earlier, two reductions had been established east of the upper Uruguay river, in what is now the Brazilian state of Rio Grande do Sul. After spiritual conflict with powerful shaman-chiefs – and some physical fighting by newly converted Indians against those who resisted the new faith – the Jesuits won over thousands of eager Guaraní. As always in Brazilian history, the missionaries used gifts of trade goods and the prestige of an advanced technology to buttress their proselytizing.

Having established reductions on the Ijuí and Ibicuí tributaries of the Uruguay, the Spanish Jesuits pushed on to the east. In 1633 they crossed the plain, in the territory of Tape Guaraní, to reach the Jacuí, a river that flowed directly into the Atlantic through the Lagoa dos Patos. They were coming close to achieving a stated geopolitical aim: the creation of a continuous belt of missions across the middle of South America, from the silver mining city of Potosí on the altiplano, across the Chaco and the Paraguay–Paraná basin to the Atlantic Ocean. This eastward push by Spanish Jesuits brought them into conflict with Portuguese

[10] Mancilla and Masseta, 'Relación de los agravios', 335–6.

interests in this section of the Atlantic seaboard. In the early sixteenth century, these southern coasts had been occupied only by occasional Spanish visitors. They lay on the Spanish side of the Line of Tordesillas. But with the failure of the Spaniards to make a permanent occupation, and with the growing Portuguese claim that Tordesillas ran from the mouth of the Río de la Plata to that of the Amazon, Portuguese from São Vicente and São Paulo were increasingly active in this southern region. By 1576 a chief of the Carijó of Santa Catarina complained that ships from São Vicente were coming twice a year to barter for slaves. With the dearth of slaves in and near São Paulo in the early seventeenth century, the traffic in slaves moved further south. Native middlemen called *mus* rounded up captives who were sold to Portuguese slavers and carried off in ships or overland. In 1635 the governor of São Vicente licensed a huge seaborne expedition to the Lagoa dos Patos. There was now no pretence to barter for slaves: the expedition was equipped for war, not trade. A Portuguese Jesuit saw the slavers' base in the lagoon, with fifteen seagoing ships and many large war canoes. He was shocked that the authorities had licensed 'ship after ship full of men with powder and shackles and chains, to make war on the heathen of the Patos, who had been at peace for so many years and some of whom were Christians'.[11]

In the year after this brazen raid on the lagoon, the bandeirante Antônio Rapôso Tavares marched south with a mighty expedition of 150 whites and 1,500 Tupi. He struck the northernmost of the Jesuits' new Tape reductions in December 1636. There was now no hesitation or delay. The Paulistas attacked at once, with drum and battle trumpet and banners unfurled. The Jesuits were also less timid. They had secretly started to arm and train their native converts, so the Portuguese were held off for a time by arquebus fire. That mission was destroyed. Another large bandeira spent the years 1637 and 1638 rounding up thousands of Christian Indians from the Jesuits' new villages on the Ibicuí. Finally, in 1639, the Spanish authorities in Asunción officially permitted the Jesuits to arm their converts to defend themselves against these outrages. Some Jesuit Fathers had had military experience before joining the Society, and these supervised the fortification of the remaining reductions and the training of their inmates. The result was the defeat of the next large bandeira, in March 1641. In a series of battles in canoes on the Mboreré tributary of the upper Uruguay, and in pitched

[11] *Registro geral da Câmara Municipal de São Paulo* (Arquivo Público Municipal de São Paulo, 1917–ꞏ), I, 500.

battles at palisaded missions, the Paulistas were routed. The pursuit lasted for days, through the rain-soaked pine forests of Santa Catarina and Paraná, and there was fierce hand-to-hand fighting. The victories of Mboreré put a stop to Paulista aggression against the Paraguayan missions, and affected the eventual boundary between Portuguese and Spanish possessions in southern Brazil.

At the time of the dispersal of the Guairá missions in 1631, one group of Jesuits moved westwards across the Paraná to establish a missionary province on the left bank of the Paraguay, north of Asunción. Although this new Jesuit province, called Itatín, lay far to the west of the Paraná and the Line of Tordesillas, and although it was protected by hundreds of kilometres of arid forests – the great dry forest or *mato grosso* that gave its name to the modern Brazilian state – it was soon attacked by bandeirantes. Spanish colonists conspired to help the Paulistas enter reductions of the hated Jesuits; until, having destroyed the missions, the Portuguese raiders attacked and demolished the Spanish settlers' own town, Jérez. There were bandeirante attacks on Itatín in 1632, 1638, and 1637; and the new missions were also harassed by fierce Guaicurú and Paiaguá warriors who controlled the banks and waters of the upper Paraguay. The final blow came in 1648 with a raid by António Rapôso Tavares at the start of an epic 12,000-kilometre journey that the bandeirantes' apologist Jaime Cortesão has called 'the greatest bandeira of the greatest bandeirante'. Leading 60 whites and relatively few Indians, Rapôso Tavares marched along the watershed between the Paraguay and Amazon basins, across the Guaporé and northern Chaco to the eastern foothills of the Andes, then down the Mamoré and Madeira in the first descent of that great river, and on to Belém at the mouth of the Amazon. When he returned to São Paulo after many years' absence, his family scarcely recognized the ravaged old man. The Jesuit António Vieira deplored the bandeirantes' cruelty, but could not but admire this feat of exploration: 'It was truly one of the most notable [journeys] ever made in the world up to now!'[12] But at its outset, this bandeira had dealt the final blow to the Jesuit province of Itatín, destroying a mission on the Tare river that now forms the boundary between Brazil and Paraguay. A Jesuit father was shot and killed during this attack, and hundreds of Christian converts were again packed off to slavery.

The raids of the bandeirantes checked Spanish expansion from

---

[12] António Vieira to Provincial of Brazil, Parrá, Jan. 1654, Alfred do Vale Cabral (ed.), *Cartas Jesuíticas* (3 vols., Rio de Janeiro, 1931), I, 411.

Asunción and thus laid the foundations of Brazil's southern and western frontiers. But the great Brazilian historian Capistrano de Abreu asked: 'Are such horrors justified by the consideration that, thanks to the bandeirantes, the devastated lands now belong to Brazil?'[13]

The sugar engenhos of the captaincies of Rio de Janeiro and São Vicente and the *fazendas* around São Paulo were the major consumers of Indian labour. Many new towns, notably Parnaíba, Sorocaba, and Itú, were founded in the seventeenth century by bandeirantes and based on Indian labour. The leading citizens of São Paulo itself held 'administrations' over hundreds of Indians and boasted private armies of native bowmen. The captive Indians far preferred the manly pursuit of warfare – either on slaving expeditions or in the periodic feuds that occurred between Paulista families – to ignominious and abhorrent plantation labour. In Indian societies, men were traditionally responsible for clearing forest and for hunting and fishing; but agriculture was women's work. Members of a tribe helped one another and often shared the game they caught. The ideas of working for someone else, either for reward or from coercion, and the production of a surplus beyond the immediate needs of a man's family, were utterly repugnant to them.

Portuguese law required that Indians who had not been legally enslaved should live in mission villages or *aldeias*. The Jesuits in São Paulo attempted to administer a few such aldeias near the city, but these regimented missions, which functioned well enough when they were remote from frontier society, were unworkable when surrounded by colonists. The mission aldeias became lay parishes and their lands were constantly invaded by colonists and their cattle. The greatest problem was a legal requirement that mission Indians must work for part of the year – how many months varied with successive legislation – for adjacent colonists in return for 'wages' expressed in lengths of coarse cloth. The result was that the aldeias were often denuded of their menfolk. They were dismal places, constantly dwindling despite efforts to replenish them with a proportion of the Indians brought back by bandeirantes.

The mission aldeias were the subject of frequent dispute between Jesuits and citizens of São Paulo. The settlers' view of mission Indians was demonstrated in a declaration from a public meeting in 1611: 'There should be orders that the heathen work for the citizens for hire and payment, to tend their mines and do their labour. This would result

13 João Capistrano de Abreu, *Capítulos de história colonial* (5th edn., Brasília, 1963), 115–16.

in tithes for God, fifths for the king, and profit for the citizens. It would give [the Indians] and their wives utility and the advantages of clothing themselves by their work. It would remove them from their continual idolatry and drunkenness...'[14] Although some Jesuits stoutly resisted such pressures, others wanted to abandon the thankless task of administering the aldeias because, in the words of Francisco de Morais, 'our presence in them serves only to affront and discredit the [Jesuit] Society...[and leads to] the ignominies and vituperation we suffer.'[15] During the 1630s a torrent of righteous protest by Spanish Jesuits led to Papal condemnation of Paulista slavers. The citizens of São Paulo were affronted. Matters came to a head with the expulsion of the Jesuits from Rio de Janeiro and then from São Paulo in July 1640. Mission villages were entrusted to the care of lay administrators, which ensured their rapid decline and exposed their remaining inhabitants to constant abuse. There were more strident protests from colonists and missionaries. But it was not until 1653 that the Jesuits returned to São Paulo, and then only on condition that they share the administration of the aldeias with laymen. During their absence, Governor Salvador de Sá testified that the populations of the four main villages of Marueri, São Miguel, Pinheiros, and Guarulhos had declined by almost 90 per cent, from a total of 2,800 families to 290.

The centre

Citizens of Rio de Janeiro and of the small towns of the long coastline between there and Salvador da Bahia were less concerned with the frontier than were the tough backwoodsmen of São Paulo. The reasons were both geographical and historical. Geographically, Rio de Janeiro was cut off from the interior by the granite pinnacles of the Serra dos Orgãos and the Serra da Mantiqueira. Similar coastal ranges and dense forests trapped the colonies of Espírito Santo, Pôrto Seguro and Ilhéus along a narrow belt of coastline. They were more concerned with maritime trade than exploration of the interior. Rio de Janeiro was a later foundation than São Vicente and São Paulo and its early years were spent in battles against the French and their Tamoio allies. It was not

---

[14] Declaration of 10 June 1612, São Paulo, in Pedro Tacques de Almeida Paes Leme, 'Notícia histórica da expulsão dos Jesuítas do Collegio de S. Paulo', *RIHGB*, 12 (1849), 9.
[15] Francisco de Morais to Simão de Vasconcelos, in Serafim Leite, S.J., *História da Companhia de Jesus no Brasil* (10 vols., Lisbon and Rio de Janeiro, 1938–50), VI, 97.

until 1567 that Estácio de Sá finally defeated the French in Guanabara; and 1575 before the Tamoio of Cabo Frio were subdued and forced to flee inland. There was a little slaving activity in the latter part of the century – the shipwrecked Englishman Anthony Knivet was employed by the governor of Rio de Janeiro on such ventures in the Paraíba valley in the 1590s – but nothing on the scale of the bandeiras. As late as the 1630s, the lethargic citizens of Rio de Janeiro were just moving into the fertile plains of the Waitacá, at the mouth of the Paraíba a mere 200 kilometres north-east of the city.

The stagnation of the colonies along the north–south coastline between the Paraíba and the Bahia de Todos os Santos was due to the success of the Aimoré tribes as much as to geographical constraints. The Aimoré were a Gê-speaking tribe with the usual Gê skills in archery, running, and forest tracking. According to Knivet – who may have been mistaken in this – they had adopted the Tupi practice of eating their enemies; but Knivet said that they did it for nourishment rather than for ritual vengeance in intertribal feuds. In battle, the Aimoré baffled the Portuguese by their use of camouflage, ambush, deadly accuracy with bows and arrows, and rapid dispersal after an attack. They did not mount the set-piece battles that made the Tupi vulnerable to European horses, swords, and firearms. Physically powerful, brave, and implacable, the Aimoré shrewdly resisted attempts to subdue or seduce them with trade goods. In 1587 Gabriel Soares de Sousa complained that 'There occurred in this land a plague of Aimoré, so that there are now only six [sugar] mills and these produce no sugar... The captaincies of Pôrto Seguro and Ilhéus are destroyed and almost depopulated from fear of these barbarians... In the past 25 years these brutes have killed over 300 Portuguese and 3,000 slaves.'[16] Pero de Magalhães Gandavo lamented that the Aimoré 'are so barbarous and intractable that we have never been able to tame them or force them into servitude like the other Indians of this land, who accept submission to captivity'.[17] A partial pacification of the Aimoré took place at the beginning of the seventeenth century. The governor of Brazil, Diogo Botelho, brought hundreds of newly pacified Tobajara and Potiguar warriors south from Ceará and Rio Grande do Norte, and was amazed when these achieved some military successes against the Aimoré. The ravages of disease and the

[16] Gabriel Soares de Sousa, *Tratado descriptivo do Brasil em 1587* (São Paulo, 1938), 57.
[17] Pero de Magalhães Gandavo, *Tratado da terra do Brasil*, trans. John B. Stetson (Cortes Society; 2 vols., New York, 1922), II, 110.

deceptive lure of 'civilized' society also helped persuade that fierce tribe to stop fighting. But despite this success there was no drive to push the frontiers of these captaincies inland throughout the colonial era.

The middle sector of the Brazilian frontier was inland from Bahia, up the Paraguaçu, Jacuípe, and Itapicurú rivers towards the great arc of the São Francisco river. Once Mem de Sá had defeated the tribes near the Recôncavo and their lands had been occupied by sugar plantations, excursions inland were in search of Indian labour. Movement into the interior of Bahia is relatively easy: the country is often open enough for movement by horse. The main impediment for expeditions into the sertão was lack of water or game.

In the 1550s the first wave of Jesuits settled thousands of Indians in missionary aldeias near Salvador da Bahia. Manoel da Nóbrega, Luís de Grã, José de Anchieta, and other Jesuit leaders were jubilant about the numbers of natives who accepted baptism. Two things destroyed these initial successes. One was the killing of the first bishop, Pero Fernandes Sardinha, who was shipwrecked north of Bahia in 1556 and eaten by pro-French Caeté. In an emotional reaction to this outrage, Mem de Sá permitted open war on the Caeté and enslavement of any captives. Settlers, desperate for labour, abused this edict to enslave any Indians they could catch. The other disaster was a wave of epidemics in the early 1560s that annihilated the missions. The most lethal disease appears to have been a form of haemorrhagic dysentery. One Jesuit said that 'the disease began with serious pains inside the intestines which made the liver and lungs rot. It then turned into pox that were so rotten and poisonous that the flesh fell off them in pieces full of evil-smelling grubs.'[18] Another described it as

a form of pox so loathsome and evil-smelling that none could stand the great stench that emerged from them. For this reason many died untended, consumed by the worms that grew in the wounds of the pox and were engendered in their bodies in such abundance and of such great size that they caused horror and shock to any who saw them.[19]

Whatever the diseases may have been, there is no question about the depopulation they caused. The Jesuits kept records of 30,000 dead in their missions near Bahia. Leonardo do Vale spoke of 'so much

[18] Simão de Vasconcelos, *Chronica da Companhia de Jesus*, bk 3 (Lisbon, 1663), 285.
[19] António Blásques to Diego Mirón, Bahia, 31 May 1564, in Serafim Leite, *Monumenta Brasiliae* (*Monumenta Historica Societatis Iesu*, 79–81, 87; Rome, 1956–60), IV, 55.

destruction along the coast that people could not bury one another. [In tribes] where previously there were 500 fighting men, there would not now be twenty.'[20] Such epidemics spread far beyond the frontier: this same Jesuit admitted that 'the Indians say this was nothing in comparison with the mortality raging through the forests'[21] beyond European control.

The immediate aftermath of this demographic disaster was a famine caused by the Indians' inability to grow their food. In desperation some Indians sold themselves or their families into slavery in return for emergency supplies of food; the Mesa da Consciência in Lisbon issued rulings on whether this was morally and legally acceptable. Other Indians followed tribal shamans on messianic quests for a 'land without ills': they developed curious mixtures of Christian and Tupi spiritual beliefs and fled inland beyond the frontier to illusory sanctuaries known as *santidades*. During the decades after the great epidemics, there were campaigns to conquer or win over these *santidades*, and this helped to push the frontier up the rivers that drained into the Bahia de Todos os Santos.

The other factor responsible for pushing the frontier inland from Bahia was the perennial shortage of labour. As in São Paulo, this shortage was heightened by the deaths of subject Indians, the influx of European colonists eager to enrich themselves and unwilling to perform manual labour, and the boom in sugar prices. The traffic in African slaves was in its infancy. African slaves were worth far more than Indian – when he wrote his will in 1569, Governor Mem de Sá valued his African slaves at from thirteen to 40 escudos each, whereas unskilled Indians were valued at only one escudo – but there was still intense demand for Indian labour, whether technically 'free' or slave. This inspired efforts to conquer uncontacted tribes of the interior or to lure them down to the coast by false promises. The governor who succeeded Mem de Sá in Bahia, Luís de Brito de Almeida, had no scruples about fighting Indians or taking slaves by any possible means. During his governorship, there were slaving expeditions such as that of António Dias Adorno, who was sent inland nominally to search for minerals but brought back 7,000 Tupiguen, or Luís Álvares Espinha,

[20] Leonardo do Vale, letter, in João Fernando de Almeida Prado, *Bahia e as capitanias do centro do Brasil (1530–1626)* (3 vols., São Paulo, 1945–50), I, 219.
[21] Leonardo do Vale to Gonçalo Vaz de Mello, Bahia, 12 May 1563, in Leite, *Monumenta Brasiliae*, IV, 12.

who marched inland from Ilhéus to punish some villages and 'not content with capturing those villages he went on inland and brought down infinite heathen'.[22] Other slavers used more cunning methods: they dazzled tribes with boasts of their military prowess, bribed them with trade goods and weapons, and deceived them with stories of the wonderful life that awaited them under Portuguese rule. The Franciscan historian Vicente do Salvador described how

with such deceptions and some gifts of clothing or tools to the chiefs,...they roused up entire villages. But once they arrived with them in sight of the sea they separated children from parents, brother from brother and sometimes even husband from wife... They used them on their estates and some sold them...Those who bought them would brand them on the face at their first [attempted] flight or fault: they claimed that they had cost money and were their slaves.[23]

When the Holy Inquisition visited Brazil in 1591, it investigated a number of professional slavers and its records contain interesting details of their activities. In order to gain the confidence of the tribes they planned to betray, these slavers would do things that disturbed the Inquisition – they ate meat during Lent, had numerous native women, traded weapons to the Indians, or smoked 'holy grass' with the shamans. The most famous of these professional slavers was Domingos Fernandes Nobre, whom the Indians called Tomacauna. The governor of Brazil employed Tomacauna as a slaver, and the Holy Office of the Inquisition was told how, in the course of his nefarious trade,

he sang and shook rattles and danced like [the Indians], and went naked like them, and wept and lamented just like them in their heathen manner...and he plumed his face with gum and dyed himself with the red dye *urucum*, and had seven Indian wives whom they gave him to keep in the Indian manner.[24]

Official wars against the Caeté and other tribes of the lower São Francisco, epidemics, and the activities of the slavers all combined to denude the sparsely populated sertão to the west of Bahia. One Jesuit was soon writing that 'the Portuguese go 250 or 300 leagues [1,500–2,000 kilometres] to seek these heathen since they are now so far away. And because the land is now deserted, most of them die of hunger on the

---

[22] Vicente do Salvador, *Historia do Brasil*, bk 3, ch. 20, in *Anais da Biblioteca Nacional do Rio de Janeiro [ABNRJ]*, 13 (1885–6), 85.

[23] Salvador, *História do Brasil* (São Paulo/Rio de Janeiro, 1931), 92.

[24] Heitor Furtado de Mendonça, *Primeira visitação do Santo Officio às partes do Brasil: confisões de Bahia, 1591–92* (Rio de Janeiro, 1935), 172.

return journey.'[25] Another Jesuit marvelled at the 'boldness and impertinence with which [the slavers] allow themselves to enter the great wilderness, at great cost, for two, three, four, or more years'.[26] It was the same story as the bandeirantes, except that the men of Bahia were less determined woodsmen and they had fewer Indians to harass in their hinterland. They also lacked the lure of Jesuit reductions full of partly acculturated Christian converts.

The sertão that had been largely stripped of native inhabitants was found to be good cattle country. A map from the end of the sixteenth century showed a cattle corral at the mouth of the Paraguaçu, and during the ensuing decades cattle ranches spread up along this and the parallel rivers, across the Jacobina sertão towards the upper São Francisco, and along both banks of that great river. Some families became powerful cattle barons, *poderosos do sertão*, with lands stretching across many hundreds of kilometres of scrubby *campo* country. The descendants of Garcia Dias d'Ávila developed a ranch called the Casa da Torre, and they often quarrelled with another *poderoso*, António Guedes de Brito, and his heirs. Although a few acculturated Indians and half-castes made good cattle hands, most Indians were incompatible with cattle. They could not resist the temptation of hunting this large and easy game. The ranchers would not tolerate such killing, and were determined to clear all natives from lands they wanted for pasture. The result of this need for land for cattle was a series of campaigns against Indian tribes during the seventeenth century. This was warfare similar to the battles of the American West two centuries later. The opponents were plains Indians, generally Gê-speaking and as cunning as the dreaded Aimoré. In the 1620s Indians wiped out all settlers on the Apora plain; they moved on to evict those of the *chapada* of Itapororocas and to attack ranches on the lower Paraguaçu. It was not until after the Dutch wars that the authorities in Bahia resumed the offensive. In the 1650s there were military expeditions to destroy villages up the Maraú river and against the Guerens tribe of Aimoré. A lonely fort was established on the Orobo hills 250 kilometres west of Bahia, and there was an uneasy alliance with the Paiaiá of the Jacobina sertão to the north of these hills. The men of Bahia had little stomach for this tough, dangerous, and unrewarding

[25] Anon. Jesuit, 'Informação dos primeiros aldeiamentos da Bahia', in *José de Anchieta, Cartas, informações, fragmentos históricos e sermões*, ed. António de Alcântara Machado (Rio de Janeiro, 1933), 378.
[26] Anon. Jesuit, 'Sumário das armadas', 13–14.

fighting. Successive governors therefore turned to the Paulistas, whose bandeirantes had a reputation as Brazil's best Indian-fighters. Shiploads of Paulistas sailed north and were sent into the sertão with bloodthirsty orders to fight Indians, 'defeating and slaughtering them by every means and effort known to military skill...sparing only Tapuia [non-Tupi] women and children, to whom you will give life and captivity'.[27] Little was achieved during the 1660s, for the Paulistas were often outwitted by the 'Tapuia' tribes and they suffered in the dry interior of Bahia. Governor-General Afonso Furtado de Castro (1670–5), however, imported more Paulistas to lead bandeiras into Espírito Santo, present-day Minas Gerais, and especially the southern sertão of Bahia. He declared that hostile Indians must 'suffer stern discipline...Only after being completely destroyed do they become quiet...All experience has shown that this public nuisance can be checked only at its origin: by destroying and totally extinguishing the villages of the barbarians!'[28] The Indians fought hard. A campaign of 1672–3 brought back only 750 live captives (700 also died on the march to the coast), but its Paulista leader Estevão Ribeiro Baião Parente was authorized to found a town with the boastful name Santo António da Conquista, 260 kilometres from Bahia.

Some tribes avoided extinction by submitting to white conquest. They entered the service of the private armies of the cattle barons, or they accepted Christian missionaries and settled in mission aldeias. There was some activity by Franciscans, and the Jesuits had some missions on the middle São Francisco; but the most famous missionaries in the hinterland of Bahia and Pernambuco were French Capuchin (Hooded) Franciscans. One of these, Friar Martin de Nantes, wrote an account of his experiences among the Cariri between 1672 and 1683. He did his utmost to protect his native flock against oppression by the cattle barons.

At the beginning of the seventeenth century, settlers avoided the *cátinga* – dense, dry woods full of thorn bushes – that grew near the São Francisco river. But they later learned to clear and burn the *cátinga* and discovered that it contained stretches of good pasture. The result was the creation of immense cattle ranches along both banks of the river, and along the adjacent Vasa Barris, Real, Itapicurú and Jacuipe. By 1705

[27] Francisco Barreto, instructions to Bernardo Bartolomeu Aires, Bahia, 1 Feb. 1658, in *Documentos históricos da Biblioteca Nacional do Rio de Janeiro* [*DHBNRJ*] (1928–), IV, 71–2.
[28] Report by Alexandre de Sousa Freire, 4 Mar. 1669, in *DHBNRJ*, V, 213–14.

an author claimed that there were cattle ranches extending uninterrupted along 2,000 miles of the river. And a governor-general wrote in 1699 that the Paulistas had, 'in a few years, left this captaincy free of all the tribes of barbarians that oppressed it, extinguishing them so effectively that from then until the present you would not know that there were any heathen living in the wilds they conquered'.[29] All that was left of the original Gê and Tupi tribes were some groups in mission aldeias: Pancararú at Pambú island on the São Francisco (some of whose descendants survive at Brejo dos Padres, Tacaratú, Pernambuco); Ocren and Tupi-speaking Tupina and Amoipira upstream of them on the main river, and a mixture of tribes in the Jesuit aldeias of Pilar, Sorobabé, Aracapá, Pontal, and Pajehú towards its mouth; Cariri tribes at Caimbé and Massacará (where Garcia d'Ávila later kept part of his private native army), Jeremoabo on the Vasa Barris and Canabrava (now called Pombal) and Sahy (now Jacobina) on the Itapicurú.

Towards the end of the seventeenth century, saltpetre or nitrate was found on the river now called Salitre, and mission Indians such as the Paiaiá and Sacuriú – and soon the newly-pacified Araquens and Tamanquin – were forced to labour in the dangerous saltpetre quarries. At the beginning of the eighteenth century, the wild and nomadic Orí of the forested Cassuca hills near the headwaters of the Vasa Barris were pacified with the aid of Christianized Caimbé Indians. The civil authorities appointed a Cariri chief from Pontal aldeia to be governor of the Indians of the São Francisco, and he duly led his men into battle on behalf of the Portuguese against other Indians.

The north-east

The Indian frontier in the north-east – the interior of Pernambuco, Paraíba, Rio Grande do Norte, and Ceará – followed a similar pattern to that of Bahia and the São Francisco valley. In the sixteenth century the Tupi tribes of the Atlantic littoral were consumed and destroyed by warfare, imported disease, and forced labour in sugar plantations. The frontier then moved inland to the territories of more resilient Gê-speaking 'Tapuia' tribes, and sugar gave way to cattle in the dry sertão. There was the usual conflict between cattle barons and Indian tribes over land. But in one respect, Indians found it easier to come to

[29] João de Lancastro to Fernando Martins Mascarenhas de Lancastro, Bahia, 11 Nov. 1699, in *DHBNRJ*, xxxix (1938), 88–9.

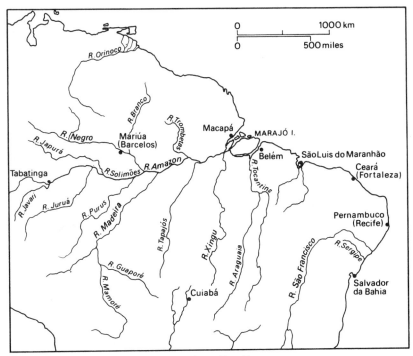

Northern Brazil

terms with a society based on cattle: they preferred the tough, lonely, mobile work of cattle hands to back-breaking, ignominious labour in sugar plantations.

Two factors made the north-east different from Bahia in its Indian affairs. One was the intrusion of other powers – the French and then the Dutch – and the attempts by rival European nations to manipulate Indian allies. The other was the existence there of large and cohesive native peoples: the Tobajara of Paraíba, the Potiguar of the long east–west coast from Rio Grande to Maranhão, and Chief Jandui's Tarairyu in the interior.

The fact that Pernambuco was the most successful of the captaincies that the Portuguese created in Brazil in the 1540s was due to the energy of the first donatory, Duarte Coelho, and to the suitability of the region for sugar planting. It was also due to an alliance with the Tupi-speaking Tobajara, which followed heavy fighting during the first years of the colony and which was sealed by the marriage of the donatory's brother-in-law Jerónimo de Albuquerque to a daughter of a Tobajara chief. Jerónimo de Albuquerque sired such a large family of *mamelucos* by his Indian wife that he became known as 'the Adam of Pernambuco'.

The Portuguese had more difficulty with the tribes to the south and north-west of Pernambuco. To the south, between the Cabo de Santo Agostinho and the mouth of the São Francisco, were the Caeté, the tribe that killed Bishop Sardinha and that welcomed French logwood traders. The Jesuit Jácome Monteiro complained that French Huguenots had made a 'La Rochelle' on the Sergipe river; but between 1575 and 1590 successive Portuguese campaigns ruthlessly destroyed the tribes of this stretch of coast. In the 1575–6 campaign, Governor Luís de Brito de Almeida himself led an attack from Bahia that 'gave such punishment as had never before been seen in those parts'.[30] The French, as usual, failed to reinforce or protect tribes that accepted their alliance. The Portuguese were thus able to crush the last native resistance in the Baepeba hills, when a force led by Cristóvão Cardoso de Barros in 1590 killed 1,500 Indians and captured 4,000, and founded the town of São Cristóvão at the mouth of the Sergipe river.

The large and bellicose Potiguar tribe successfully repelled Portuguese advances to the north of Pernambuco during the 1570s and early 1580s. Various Portuguese expeditions were defeated or left after only limited success. A Portuguese fort was established at São Felipe near the mouth of the Paraíba in 1584, but whenever its garrison ventured inland it was routed by Potiguar ambushes or attacks. A Jesuit complained of the Potiguar that 'none can resist the fury of this nation of victorious heathen. They are personally more spirited than any others, and so brave that they do not fear death.'[31] It was a judge from Recife called Martim Leitão who began to gain ascendancy over this formidable tribe. In expeditions in 1584 and 1585 he penetrated into the heart of Potiguar territory in Paraíba, and won some victories in heavy hand-to-hand fighting. By 1590 there was a Portuguese town on the Paraíba, with Jesuit and Franciscan missions among its Tobajara Indians. French ships were destroyed throughout these years and any Frenchmen caught on land were executed. By 1597 the Portuguese were ready to push northwards to Rio Grande, where the Potiguar had for many years been intermarrying with Frenchmen. Their expedition advanced by land and sea, and the land column contained a powerful force of Tobajara

---

[30] Soares de Sousa, *Tratado*, 43–4.
[31] Anon. Jesuit, 'Sumário das armadas', 25.

warriors. It also brought smallpox, which wrought havoc both on the Tobajara but even more on their Potiguar enemies. A fort called Reis Magos (Magi) was established on the Potengi and it resisted furious Potiguar attacks. In the end, a solemn peace treaty was concluded at Paraíba on 11 June 1599; a subsequent attack on the Reis Magos fort by 40,000 Potiguar was defeated, and by 1601 the Potiguar finally came under Portuguese control.

The next frontier was westwards along the coast of Ceará, towards Maranhão and the mouth of the Amazon. An Indian-fighter called Pedro Coelho de Sousa led an expedition of Tobajara and Potiguar across Ceará in 1604 and successfully attacked some French-influenced Tupinambá in the Ibiapaba hills near Maranhão; but he alienated his native allies by attempting to enslave both friendly and hostile Indians, and an attempt to colonize Ceará was ended by a disastrous drought. Jesuit missionaries were equally unsuccessful, when one of them was killed by 'Tapuia' tribes beyond Ibiapaba. It was a young Portuguese officer, Martim Soares Moreno, who succeeded in colonizing Ceará where warfare and religious proselytizing had failed. He succeeded by becoming a close friend of the Indians, adopting many of their customs and impressing them as a warrior. Martim Soares Moreno was in command of the fort of the Reis Magos at Natal, and he occupied Ceará 'with only five soldiers and a chaplain, trusting in the affection and friendship he had made with all the Indian chiefs on both banks [of the Jaguaribe]'.[32] The Portuguese frontier in Brazil was now close to Maranhão, approaching the Amazon and about to cross the Line of Tordesillas in northern Brazil just as it was in the south.

When the French made their last attempt to colonize Brazil, with the landing of three ships of colonists under the Sieur de la Ravardière on the island of Maranhão in 1612, the Portuguese, who had themselves failed to establish settlements there, dealt swiftly with the threat. The French tried to win over the Tupinambá of Maranhão by taking six chiefs to Paris, where they enjoyed lavish hospitality and a royal christening in Nôtre Dame. Such wooing was no match for Portuguese military skill and Indian alliances. The Portuguese mobilized the recently pacified Potiguar of Rio Grande under their chief Poti or Camarão ('Shrimp' in Tupi and in Portuguese), the 65-year-old *mameluco* Jerónimo de Albuquerque as commander with his Tobajara relatives, and the Ceará Indians of Martim Soares Moreno. The

---

[32] Diogo de Campos Moreno, *Livro que da razão do Estado do Brasil* [1612] (Recife, 1955), 211.

Portuguese sailed north-west with their Indians and established themselves in a fort at Guaxenduba, opposite Maranhão Island. Here, on 19 November 1614, they annihilated a larger and better-equipped force of French and Tupinambá; and within a year the French were gone for ever.

The frontier in the north-east would doubtless have advanced in a similar pattern to that of Bahia. The lands of the Rio Grande Potiguar who accepted the peace treaty of 1599 were rapidly parcelled out into cattle ranches. Cattle ranching would have spread into the dry interior – which was inhabited by Gê-speaking 'Tapuia' Indians, as was the interior of Bahia – during the first half of the seventeenth century. Such expansion was, however, delayed for a quarter-century by the advent of another European power: the Dutch. The Dutch wars (1624–54) halted expansion into the interior of the north-east and enhanced the standing of Indian tribes in the disputed areas. Both European powers enlisted native troops in their battles, and both regarded good relations with the Indians as important in ensuring control of the region. The struggle between Portuguese and Dutch was in part a war of religion, so that Catholic and Protestant missionaries redoubled their efforts to convert tribes and enlist them in the fighting. The Portuguese were lucky to have the young Potiguar chief Poti-Camarão, who turned into a formidable guerrilla leader, harassing the Dutch throughout the conquered provinces and deploying a force of Indians who had mastered all forms of European fighting. His men combined native skills in tracking and woodcraft with proficiency in handling European firearms. For their part, the Dutch had Indian warriors fighting under another Potiguar called Pieter Poti. The two native commanders were distant cousins and they corresponded in an unsuccessful attempt to persuade one another to change allegiance and religion.

Meanwhile, Calvinist pastors moved into the few remaining Indian villages and sought to convert the inhabitants to the Protestant faith. After initial superficial success they found, like the Jesuits before them, that the Indians had failed to grasp the finer points of Christianity. The Indians responded more enthusiastically to the great Dutch governor of Brazil, Count Johan Maurits of Nassau. Count Maurits had a genuine affection for the Indians. He wrote to his superiors that

the quiet and preservation of the colony of Brazil depends in part on the friendship of the Indians. With this in mind they should be permitted to enjoy their natural freedom...Orders should be issued that they are not to be outraged by their administrators, hired out for money, or forced to work in sugar mills against their will. Each should, on the contrary, be allowed to live in the way he understands and to work where he wishes like men of our nation.[33]

When Johan Maurits was recalled in 1644 a crowd of Indians insisted on accompanying him to his ship and demanded that he take them to Holland. A year later, in April 1645, the Dutch authorities organized an assembly of chiefs of the twenty Indian aldeias under their rule. The meeting was docile enough, but it made a powerful plea for Indian freedom to be observed in practice and not just in theory or in paper legislation. This meeting was unique in Brazilian history: not until the late twentieth century has there been a comparable gathering of tribal leaders in European-occupied Brazil.

For all their good intentions and their desire to win Indian allegiance, the Dutch proved little better than the Portuguese when it came to forcing Indians to labour for derisory pay expressed in lengths of cotton cloth. They sought to impose their Protestant religion and to eradicate 'heathen' practices with just as much vehemence as the Portuguese. They also unwittingly brought deadly diseases, such as smallpox or measles, which raged through the colony. As a result, when the Dutch began to be defeated most Indians turned against them. Many Dutch were massacred in a native rising in Maranhão and Ceará, and the survivors concluded that this was because 'instead of finding relief from us Dutch, the Indians are subjected to greater captivity'.[34]

One by-product of the Dutch invasion was increased knowledge of the Indians of the north-east. Contemporary accounts show terrible depopulation. Domingos da Veiga had reported that in 1627 there were 'little more than 300 bowmen divided among four villages [in Rio Grande]. There used to be such a quantity of them here that their numbers were not known.'[35] Twelve years later, Adriaen van der Drussen listed five villages in Rio Grande, five in Paraíba, five in Goiana, and four in Pernambuco, with a total of less than 2,000 men of all ages between them. Johannes de Laet gave a measure of the decline when he reported that in Ceará, where the Potiguar had once had 8,000 warriors, there were only 105 by 1635. In addition to the usual

---

[33] Johan Maurits van Nassau, report to States General, 27 Sept. 1644, in José António Gonçalves de Mello Neto, *Tempo dos Flamengos* (Rio de Janeiro, 1947), 234–5.
[34] Gedeon Morris de Jonge to Supreme Council, São Luís do Maranhão, 29 Jan. 1643, *RIHGB*, 58/1 (1895), 307.
[35] Domingos da Veiga, description of Rio Grande, 1627, in Barão de Studart (ed.), *Documentos para a história do Brasil e especialmente a do Ceará* (4 vols., Fortaleza, 1908–21), IV, 35.

epidemics and deaths in battle, there had also been widespread flight into the interior to avoid colonial oppression. According to Laet's figures, there was a total Indian population of only 9,000 in the 800 miles of coast between Ceará and the São Francisco river.

The Dutch also spread their influence inland, to try to bring the Gê-speaking tribes of the interior into the fighting on their side. Their emissary, Jacob Rabe, visited the Tarairyu of the hinterland of Rio Grande–Ceará and established excellent relations with the tribe's aged chief Nhandui or Jandui. Rabe and his successor Roulox Baro left careful descriptions of the society and religion of the Tarairyu, which reveal that they were very similar to modern Canela or Timbira of Maranhão or to the Krahô of northern Goiás. They were plains Indians, swift runners who maintained their agility through frequent log races between the two moieties of the tribe. Their marriage customs, religion, and even their physical appearance and bonnet-like haircuts were identical to those of their modern Gê-speaking counterparts. Thanks to Rabe's influence, the Tarairyu and other 'Tapuia' joined the Dutch and were particularly ferocious in the fighting against Portuguese settlers. In revenge, the settlers were merciless in slaughtering any Indians who fought with the Dutch, even when these surrendered under negotiated truce.

When the Dutch finally abandoned their Brazilian forts in 1654, 4,000 native people from the aldeias of Itamaracá, Paraíba and Rio Grande marched north-westwards to take refuge in Ceará. They were furious that the Dutch, whom they had served so faithfully for many years, had deserted them. They fortified themselves among the Tobajara in the Ibiapaba hills and sought to create an independent enclave which they called Cambressive. They even sent a Dutch-educated chief to Holland to beg for Dutch military assistance, as a reward for past services and to preserve the Protestant religion. This chief pleaded, in vain, that 'if help fails them, our people must inevitably finally fall into the clutches of the cruel and bloodthirsty Portuguese, who since the first occupation of Brazil have destroyed so many hundreds of thousands of people of that nation...'[36]

With the expulsion of the Dutch, Brazil was never again seriously threatened by a rival European invasion. The settlers of the north-east

[36] Appeal by Antony Paraupaba, The Hague, 6 Aug. 1654, in Pedro Souto Maior, *Fastos Pernambucanos* (Rio de Janeiro, 1913) and *RIHGB*, 76 (1913), 191.

were therefore able to push their frontier inland during the second half of the seventeenth century. Their frontier was similar to that of the Bahia hinterland: vast expanses of barren sertão good only for cattle ranching. After the Dutch wars the Tarairyu of Chief Janduí (whom the Portuguese continued to call 'Janduin' in his memory) were at peace for some years until their territories began to be invaded by cattle ranchers. Sporadic outbursts of fighting occurred during the ensuing decades. In the mid-1660s the Tarairyu and their allies the Paiacú attacked domesticated Tupi in the Jesuit missions of the Rio Grande and Paraíba coast. There were reprisal expeditions. But the explosion that had long been threatening finally occurred in 1687, when these Cariri tribes swept through Rio Grande slaughtering over 100 colonists and their retainers on isolated ranches and killing over 30,000 head of cattle. The governor reported that the settlers retreated into Natal and almost abandoned the captaincy.

At this time a few tough cattlemen had crossed the middle São Francisco and moved northwards into the valley of the Parnaíba, in what is now the state of Piauí. One of these pioneers was Domingos Afonso, nicknamed 'Mafrense' or 'Sertão', who pushed the frontier deep into this sparsely inhabited wilderness. The eighteenth-century historian Sebastião da Rocha Pitta told how he 'entered lands not previously penetrated by Portuguese and inhabited only by wild heathen, with whom he had many battles, emerging dangerously wounded from one but victorious in them all, killing many heathen and making the rest retreat to the interior of the sertão'.[37] Domingos Afonso died leaving the Jesuits 30 huge ranches stretching over almost 400 miles. Another pioneer of Piauí was Domingos Jorge Velho, who conquered territories to the west of Domingos Afonso; for a time the two cattlemen campaigned together. Each of these frontiersmen enlisted private armies of conquered Indians. Jorge Velho wrote to the king excusing his raids and conquests as being a way of 'domesticating' the tribes to a 'knowledge of civilized life' and introducing them to the mysteries of the Catholic church. He admitted that few missionaries were involved in this altruistic endeavour. Instead,

we enlarge our troops from those thus acquired and brought into settlements. With them we wage war on those who are obstinate and refractory to

---

[37] Sebastião da Rocha Pitta, *História da América Portugueza* (Lisbon, 1730), VI, 385.

settlement. If we later use them in our fields we do them no injustice, for this is to support them and their children as much as to support us and ours. Far from enslaving them, we render them a gratuitous service by teaching them to till, plant, harvest, and work for their livelihood.[38]

Despite this glowing account of his civilizing mission, the bishop of Pernambuco was appalled when he met Domingos Jorge Velho, describing him as

one of the worst savages I have ever met...He is no different from the most barbarous Tapuia, except in calling himself Christian. Although recently married, seven Indian concubines attend him – from which one can infer his other habits. Until now...he has roamed the forests hunting Indian men and women, the latter to exercise his lusts and the former to work on the fields he owns.[39]

As so often in Brazilian history, the Indians responded well to such a man and, once defeated by him, were willing to follow such a successful warrior. It was men like him, uncouth but brilliant woodsmen, who expanded Portugal's frontier in Brazil.

It was to Domingos Jorge Velho that the authorities turned when confronted by the Tarairyu war of 1687. He and his rugged army performed an extraordinary march across hundreds of miles of sertão. His 600 exhausted men engaged the Tarairyu or Janduin on the Apodi and many were killed on both sides in a fierce four-day battle. The Janduin had already shattered an expedition of 900 men sent against them from Pernambuco. There were the usual urgent appeals to the Paulistas, who were still rightly considered to be the only 'men accustomed to penetrate the sertão and endure hunger, thirst, and inclemencies of climate and weather. The regular infantry have no experience whatsoever of such conditions; nor do the local militia, who lack discipline and endurance.'[40] A Paulista commander, Matias Cardoso de Almeida, made an incredible 1,500-mile march north from the São Francisco and then led three years of campaigns against these Gê tribes. It was a ruthless war, in which the Portuguese commanders were ordered to slaughter all adult Indians they could catch, and in which

---

[38] Domingos Jorge Velho to king, Serra da Barriga, Palmares, 15 July 1694, in Ernesto Ennes, *As guerras nos Palmares* (São Paulo, 1938), 206; Eng. trans. in Richard M. Morse (ed.), *The Bandeirantes: the historical role of the Brazilian pathfinders* (New York, 1965), 118.

[39] Bishop of Pernambuco to Junta das Missões, 18 May 1697, in Edison Carneiro, *Guerras de los Palmares* (Mexico, 1946), 133–4.

[40] Archbishop-Governor Frei Manoel da Resureição to Câmara Coutinho, governor of Pernambuco, in Afonso de Escragnolle Taunay, *História das bandeiras paulistas* (2 vols., São Paulo, 1953), I, 175.

they launched murderous surprise attacks on native villages. The Janduin, in return, twice besieged Natal and mustered large armies of fearless warriors. As always, most of the fighting was done by rival Indians marching for or against the Portuguese. In the end, the Janduin achieved something that was common in North America in later centuries but rare in Brazil: a formal peace treaty with the king of Portugal that recognized their chief Canindé as an autonomous ruler and granted the tribe independence and large tracts of land within Portuguese sovereignty. The treaty was signed at Salvador da Bahia on 10 April 1692; but it was soon violated by ranchers' invasions of Indian territory and aggressions by Paulista commanders who remained in this part of the north-east.

The Amazon

It was very difficult to reach the mouth of the Amazon by ship from the north-east of Brazil: contrary winds, currents, and shoals meant that it was easier to sail from Maranhão and Pará to Lisbon than to Bahia. This isolation, together with the different vegetation and climate of the Amazon basin, meant that this frontier developed distinctly from the rest of Brazil. There was the added factor that even by the most pro-Portuguese interpretation of the Treaty of Tordesillas, the entire Amazon river lay within the Spanish rather than the Portuguese sphere.

With the failure of the Portuguese attempt to colonize Maranhão in 1535, and the failures of two Portuguese expeditions up the Amazon, that great river was visited only by Spaniards during the sixteenth century. Contact was made with hundreds of its tribes by the first discoverer, Vicente Yáñez Pinzón, in 1500; by Amerigo Vespucci, sailing under Gonçalo Coelho two years later; by Diego de Ordaz in an abortive attempt at settlement in 1531; and most notably during the first descent of Francisco de Orellana in 1542. The largest attempt to colonize the upper Amazon – in the mistaken belief that the lands of the Tupi-speaking Omagua of the Solimões-Amazon were the legendary kingdom of Eldorado – was the great expedition of Pedro de Ursúa of 1559–60, which ended in mutiny by the Basque traitor Lope de Aguirre. After this disaster the tribes of the Amazon were not molested by Europeans for a further half-century.

In January 1616, within two months of their eviction of the French from Maranhão, the Portuguese founded a fort 400 miles west on the

Pará river, which forms the southern mouth of the Amazon. This fort was to develop into the town of Belém do Pará. After initial calm, fighting soon erupted with the Tupinambá of the forested coast between Pará and Maranhão. During the ensuing decade there were savage wars of annihilation that left this region almost depopulated. Even the Tupinambá of Maranhão Island, whose populous villages had welcomed the French and who refused to join their compatriots in fighting the Portuguese, were not spared: for in 1621 they were struck 'by an epidemic of smallpox of such virulence that any who caught it – most of whom were Indians – did not survive for more than three days'.[41]

There is relatively little documentation of the first 35 years of Portuguese occupation of Pará and the lower Amazon: histories by the contemporary Vicente do Salvador and the later Bernardo Pereira de Berredo, a few official papers, and brief accounts by Capuchin missionaries or such explorers as Simão Estácio da Silveira. The picture that emerges from these sources is one of near-anarchy, a lawless time during which the Indians suffered. The settlers of the tiny town of Belém conquered the tribes on rivers flowing north to the Pará, on the lower Tocantins, and on other rivers between it and the Xingu. There was particularly heavy fighting against the Pacajá on the river of that name. Some tribes were lured down to Belém with promises of trade goods. Others were seized in surprise attacks by flotillas of canoes full of Portuguese and their Indian allies armed with firearms. Contemporary accounts speak of the destruction of hundreds of villages and heavy depopulation of all exposed coasts and rivers near Belém. The few missionaries in Pará at this time fulminated against the oppression of nominally free Indians who were 'forced to do very heavy labour such as making tobacco, in which they work for seven or eight months on end by day and night'.[42] Payment was in trivial lengths of coarse cloth, which the Indians themselves made; failure to work was punished by flogging in the stocks. The Indians had an obvious remedy in this forested land. As the Jesuit Luis Figueira wrote, 'Because of this oppression, they flee into the forests and depopulate their villages. Others die of despair in this labour without remedy.'[43] Any protest against violations of Pro-Indian legislation was greeted by howls of

---

[41] Bernardo Pereira de Berredo, *Annaes historicos do Estado do Maranhão* (Lisbon, 1749), bk 6, 211.
[42] Luís Figueira, 'Memorial sôbre as terras e gentes do Maranhão e Grão-Pará e rio das Amazonas', Lisbon, 10 Aug. 1637, in *RIHGB*, 94 (vol. 148) (1923), 431.   [43] *Ibid.*

indignation from the colonists, and most of the early governors of Maranhão and Pará were themselves involved in raiding for slaves.

The most ferocious killer of Maranhão Tupinambá was a captain called Bento Maciel Parente. Yet this same Indian-fighter was appointed captain-general of Ceará in 1626 and a Franciscan complained that his treatment of its Indians was appalling even by contemporary standards: he kept the men constantly at work in his mills, without pay and with no breaks on Sundays or saints' days, and allowed no time for Indians dying of hunger to provide for their families. This Bento Maciel Parente was given royal authorization to make expeditions up the Amazon: and in 1637 he was given a hereditary captaincy of Cabo do Norte, which included the north shore of the Amazon as far upstream as the Paru river, a vast area corresponding to the modern territory of Amapá. This was the first time that a Spanish king of Portugal made an award to a Portuguese that was clearly west of the Line of Tordesillas; and the award was a licence to a notorious Indian-fighter and slaver to exploit at will its thousands of native inhabitants.

In that same year, the settlers of Pará were surprised by the arrival of a canoe containing two Spanish friars and some soldiers that had descended the Amazon from Quito. This inspired an expedition of great geopolitical importance in shaping the Brazilian frontier. The governor, Jacomé Raimundo de Noronha, determined to claim nothing less than the main Amazon river for Portugal. He sent Pedro Teixeira up-river with an important expedition of 70 Portuguese soldiers, with 1,100 mission Indians to paddle 47 canoes and to supply food by hunting and fishing. The governor gave Teixeira sealed orders to plant Portuguese boundary markers when he reached the lands of the Omagua, no less than 1,500 miles west of the Line of Tordesillas! The expedition was a triumphant success, thanks to the endurance of the Indians, who paddled upstream for months on end and eventually carried the flotilla up to Quito. The Spaniards sent observers to accompany the return journey and one of these, the Jesuit Cristóbal de Acuña, wrote a splendid account of his descent. He strongly urged the king of Spain to make an effective occupation of the Amazon: but his advice was ignored, and the boundary of modern Brazil is now far up the river, close to the place where Teixeira placed his marker.

Acuña observed the large and prosperous tribes that still existed on the Amazon. He was particularly impressed, as Orellana's men had been a century earlier, by the Omagua, who kept ponds stocked with thousands of turtles alongside their villages, and by the Curucirari, whose delicate polychrome pottery rivalled Chinese ceramics. But as the expedition descended the Amazon, Acuña witnessed increasing destruction by Portuguese slavers from Belém do Pará. He watched in horror while one of Bento Maciel's sons rounded up Tapajós men at gunpoint while permitting his own gang of Indians to rape their women and pillage their town. As he approached Pará, he saw increasing destitution and depopulation, with riverine settlements abandoned and no one left to cultivate the land. The small and primitive settlement of Belém was an incubus that steadily destroyed and denuded the Amazon and all its accessible tributaries. Pedro Teixeira's brother, the vicar-general of Maranhão, Manoel Teixeira, reckoned that in the first three decades after their arrival on the Amazon, the few hundred settlers of Maranhão and Pará were responsible for the deaths of almost two million Indians through their 'violent labour, exhausting discoveries, and unjust wars'.[44]

The Jesuits planned to operate in Pará, but their hopes were frustrated when a ship carrying their Provincial Luís Figueira and eleven Fathers foundered in full view of Belém in 1643 and the missionaries were captured and killed by hostile Aruan Indians of Marajó Island. It was ten years before the Jesuits returned; but they did so in 1653 in the towering person of António Vieira. Vieira was a Brazilian-born Jesuit who had risen to be the close confidant and confessor of Dom João IV of Portugal. He was famous for the brilliance of his sermons at a time when the pulpit was the most potent medium of communication. Vieira had been entrusted with secret diplomatic missions in Europe, and his was the most influential voice in shaping Portuguese foreign policy. It came as a surprise when this powerful man suddenly vowed to take up missionary field work, and actually sailed for the backwater of the Amazon.

António Vieira was appalled by the conditions he found in Maranhão and Pará. He preached fiery sermons against expeditions to 'rescue' or 'ransom' Indians which were really slaving expeditions and condemned any settlers who kept Indian slaves: 'All of you are in mortal sin; all of you live in a state of condemnation; and all of you are going directly

---

[44] António Vieira, 'Reposta aos capítulos que deu... Jorge de Sampaio' [1662, reply to ch. 24], *Obras escolhidas* (12 vols., Lisbon, 1951–4), V, 280.

to Hell!'[45] But his eloquence was wasted on colonists who had no intention of giving up any Indians and who were constantly clamouring for more native labour. After a journey up the Tocantins, Vieira returned to Portugal and persuaded the vacillating king to enact new legislation (1655) against Indian enslavement. The Jesuits were entrusted with the task of bringing the Indians from the interior by peaceful means and establishing them in mission villages under their control. Five years of euphoric activity ensued for the Jesuits. The Fathers accompanied expeditions up all the main tributaries of the lower Amazon and far up the Negro, and they had soon 'descended' some 200,000 Indians into 54 mission aldeias. The tribes came willingly, impressed by the reputation of the Jesuits and by their promises of material prosperity and religious enlightenment. The descents were, however, murderous deceptions. Many Indians died of alien diseases during the voyages down to Belém; but the missionaries consoled themselves that these victims of their misguided policy had at least received baptism before dying. Once settled in aldeias near Portuguese towns, the Indians were exposed to constant demands for their labour. Crowded into these settlements, they were particularly vulnerable to smallpox and measles, epidemics of which occurred with dismal regularity. The Jesuits could not reconcile the fundamental contradiction that stifled any royal wish for humane treatment of the Indians. The small European colonies in Brazil could not prosper without native labour and could not ward off attack by hostile tribes or rival colonial powers without docile native auxiliaries. The settlers knew that they could make the Indians work for them only by force; and in the impoverished Amazon they were too poor to afford African slaves. Life in this region depended on river transport and on fish and game, gums, fruits, and resins extracted from the forests. For such activities local Indians were far better than imported Africans. The Jesuits deluded themselves that the Indians in their missions would become loyal Christian subjects of Portugal. But they knew in practice that they were condemning them to forced labour and rapid destruction from disease, demoralization, malnutrition and social disruption.

Vieira himself performed two missions of which he was proud. In

---

[45] A sermon given by him at Maranhão, Lent 1653, can be found in Leite, *História da Companhia de Jesus*, IX, 211; Eng. trans. in E. Bradford Burns, *A documentary history of Brazil* (New York, 1966), 83.

1659 he undertook an embassy to the tribes of Marajó Island, who were
known collectively as Nheengaíba (Tupi for 'incomprehensible
languages'). These tribes had successfully resisted repeated Portuguese
punitive expeditions, usually by disappearing into the labyrinth of
channels on their island. Forty thousand of them now surrendered,
accepting Vieira's assurances that Portuguese attitudes had changed
with the new law of 1655. The Jesuits established themselves on Marajó,
where their huge cattle ranches prospered, to the envy of the colonists
and eventually of the government in Lisbon. In 1660 Vieira made a
difficult journey to the remote Ibiapaba hills on the border between
Maranhão and Ceará. He confronted the remnants of the north-eastern
Indians who had fled there after the departure of the Dutch. All but
the oldest accepted conversion to Catholicism and the presence of Jesuit
missionaries.

The Jesuits' efforts to accommodate settlers' demands for Indian
labour were in vain. Colonists who had hoped to make their fortunes
in the Amazon were defeated by the difficult conditions and climate.
As they saw their riverside clearings fail, they vented their frustration
on the Jesuits, pious busybodies who seemed to be thwarting their
supply of fresh Indian labour. Their fury erupted in May 1661 with a
rising in São Luís do Maranhão against the Jesuit Fathers. Vieira and
most of his men were arrested and shipped off to Portugal. A new law
of 12 September 1663 installed lay *repartidores* in Indian villages to
oversee the allocation of men to work on settlers' holdings. It was
seventeen years before Vieira was able to influence a new king, Pedro
II, to reinstate the Jesuits in full control of Indian aldeias and to forbid
all forms of Indian slavery. During those years irreparable damage had
been done to the Indians under Portuguese rule. The liberal law of 1
April 1680 awarded land to the Indians, since they were 'the original
and natural lords of it'[46] – an important concept and a phrase still being
quoted by pro-Indian activists in modern Brazil. But this law brought
a reaction almost as swift as that to similar legislation in 1609 and 1655.
In February 1684 the colonists of Maranhão rose in a revolt led by
Manoel Beckman and Jorge Sampaio and again expelled the Jesuits. The
revolt was soon crushed and the ringleaders hanged; but the Jesuits
were alarmed and decided, albeit reluctantly, to compromise on two
important issues. They were granted full temporal and spiritual control

[46] Law of 1 April 1680, in Agostinho Marques Perdigão Malheiro, *A escravidão no Brasil* (Rio de
Janeiro, 1867), II, 70.

of the mission aldeias, although they agreed to increase the time that their charges must work for settlers to six months a year, and they undertook to administer these labour levies at wages to be agreed with the colonial governor. Not surprisingly, this wage was fixed at the derisory figure of two and a half yards of cloth for a month's work, and this wage remained in force for a century, even though it was only a fifth of the amount paid during the Dutch occupation. The cloth was almost valueless as an item of barter and could not purchase the tools or fish-hooks needed by the Indians; it was also produced from cotton worked by the Indians and was spun and woven by their women. The other terrible surrender was the reintroduction of legalized Indian slavery. As often throughout the colonial period, slavery was permitted for *índios de corda* – Indian prisoners of intertribal wars supposedly bound and ready for execution – and captives taken in 'just wars', which could now be waged on any tribe about which there was 'certain and infallible fear' that it might threaten Portuguese rule. Both these definitions were open to flagrant abuse. Official annual slaving (euphemistically called 'ransoming') expeditions were resumed, although they were accompanied by Jesuits to guarantee 'legality' and subject to a Junta das Missões composed of missionaries and a royal judge sitting in Belém. Contemporary documents are full of descriptions of slaving activities carried out against any tribes caught on the banks of the Amazon or its navigable tributaries. The traffic died down only when such areas were denuded, when tribes had retreated into the forests or up the tributaries beyond barriers of rapids, or when a few large tribes organized themselves for defence.

António Vieira himself drew up regulations for the daily conduct of life on Jesuit missions on the Amazon, the Regimento das Missões (1686) in what was now called Maranhão and Grão Pará. These regulations were later adopted for the rest of Brazil and with a few modifications remained in force until Pombal's secularization of Indian affairs in the 1750s. In 1693 the whole area was divided among the religious orders for missionary purposes. The Jesuits restricted their own activities to the south bank of the Amazon upstream to the mouth of the Madeira. The north shore of the Amazon to the Paru fell to Franciscan Capuchins of Santo António, as far as the Trombetas to Franciscans of Piedade and Conceição, to the mouth of the Rio Negro to the Mercedarians, and, later, the Negro itself and the Solimões to Carmelites. The missionary orders now adopted a policy of creating aldeias along the banks of the rivers, close to the original habitats of the tribes, rather than bringing Indians down-river in disastrous 'descents' for resettlement near Portuguese towns. This new policy provided a thin Portuguese presence along the Amazon, Solimões and Negro rivers. The existence of these aldeias (which were to become secular villages with Portuguese names under Pombal's legislation) was recognized in the Treaty of Madrid of 1750, which scrapped the Line of Tordesillas and awarded most of the Amazon basin to Portuguese Brazil.

THE EIGHTEENTH CENTURY

By the end of the seventeenth century the Brazilian frontier was static or in retreat except in Amazonia. Cattle ranching in the interior of Bahia and the north-east was reaching the limit beyond which animals could not be profitably driven to coastal markets. Bandeirante activity in the south was subsiding, with the disappearance of most Indians in the hinterland of Paraná and São Paulo and the realization that Indian captives were scarcely worth the effort now needed to capture them. Spanish Jesuits responded by pushing their Paraguayan missions back across the Uruguay river. Between 1687 and 1706 they established seven reductions on the east bank of the Uruguay and on its Icamaguá and Ijuí tributaries. These missions flourished, because of the industry of their Guaraní Indians and the immense herds of wild cattle that had bred during the half-century since the earlier missionary activity in the region. Such was their prosperity that Italian architects were imported to build great churches, and the Indians became highly proficient in performing sacred music or carving baroque sculpture.

New impetus to the expansion of the frontier, however, came from the discoveries of gold, in quick succession, in what are now Minas Gerais, west-central Mato Grosso, and Goiás. The upper Velhas river, which contained the largest gold deposits around Ouro Preto, had already been largely denuded of Indians by bandeirante raids. But the rush of miners seeking their fortunes in this area largely destroyed the remaining aldeias near São Paulo itself. Many Paulista families also used their private contingents of Indians to help on journeys to the mining area and to work in the mines themselves. Few of these ever returned.

The gold discoveries of Goiás involved the local Goiá and Araé tribes, for the bandeirante Bartolomeu Bueno da Silva, son of the original 'Anhangüera', recalled having seen gold ornaments on these

Indians. After repeated quests, he found the tribe again and persuaded its members to reveal where they had obtained their gold. Anhangüera the younger took a mass of his Carijó from São Paulo to work on the new deposits; but the brunt of the ensuing gold rush fell on the Goiá, who were forced to work with the miners and were soon extinguished. The long trail inland from São Paulo to the mining camp of Sant'Anna (Vila Boa de Goiás) was exposed to attack by groups of Gê-speaking Southern Caiapó, who mounted a determined and effective campaign to drive the Portuguese out of their forests and *campos*. After the failure of various punitive expeditions, the authorities called on António Pires de Campos, a Paulista who had gained the friendship of some of the Caiapós' traditional enemies, the Bororo of central Mato Grosso. Panic-stricken Goiás miners subscribed to bring this mercenary woodsman and his Bororo warriors to try to destroy the Caiapó. Between 1742 and 1751 Pires de Campos mounted a series of long raiding expeditions that, despite some Indian victories, eventually destroyed most Caiapó villages in a broad arc to the south and west of Goiás.

It was this same Pires de Campos who in 1719 had been one of the discoverers of gold in the depths of the South American continent, on the Coxipó river near Cuiabá. The long journey by flotillas (*monções*) of canoes from São Paulo to Cuiabá exposed adventurers on this gold rush to attack by three formidable Indian groups. After descending the Tietê and crossing the Paraná, the fleets portaged across onto the Paraguay watershed at a place called Camapuã. This place was exposed to ambushes by the same Southern Caiapó who harassed the Goiás miners. Further west, as the canoes descended the Aquidauana and paddled up the Paraguay, they were attacked by two of the most formidable nations of Indian warriors; the riverine Paiaguá and the Guaicurú of the Chaco and the Bodoquena hills. The Paiaguá were brilliant canoers and fearless fighters. They hid in the swamps and inlets of the Pantanal and sped out in light canoes to ambush passing Europeans. They had been opposing intruders ever since the first Spanish explorers of the sixteenth century, and it was they who killed many members of Rapôso Tavares' bandeira of 1648. They thus had no illusions about Portuguese intentions. António Pires de Campos described the Paiaguás' devastating fighting methods:

They were very highly skilled in handling their arrows and lances – they fired several shots during the time the bandeirantes took to fire one. Extraordinary swimmers, they advanced in their canoes and leaped into the water, tipping a side of their boat to act as a shield against musket balls. They would suddenly right the canoe again and fire another volley. If they felt they could not overcome the whites' resistance they submerged their boats; and before long dived and raised them again, and fled with such speed that they seemed to have wings.[47]

Paiaguá victories included the destruction of an entire flotilla of 200 people in twenty canoes in 1725; the destruction of most of the 1726 flotilla; and the capture of 900 kilos of gold and annihilation of most of its escort of 400 whites, blacks and Indians, in 1730. The Portuguese responded in 1734 with a formidable expedition of over 800 men in 100 canoes that ambushed and destroyed the main Paiaguá village; but fighting with this valiant tribe continued for some decades.

Part of the Paiaguá success was due to their alliance with the equally formidable Guaicurú. This tribe had also been fighting Europeans since the 1540s, and it gained a mastery over horses rivalling that of the North American plains Indians. A nomadic people, the Guaicurú lived only for their 7,000 or 8,000 horses, which they bred, trained, and tended with the utmost care. They considered themselves as an aristocratic people and dominated or terrorized neighbouring tribes. In order to remain mobile, Guaicurú women aborted most of their infants, so that the tribe had to raid to capture children from other tribes. Their superb horsemanship made the Guaicurú almost invincible in battle, and their lightning attacks could have destroyed all Spanish and Portuguese settlements in what are now northern Paraguay and southern Mato Grosso had they followed up their victories in sustained military campaigns; but they lacked the necessary will or leadership.

The Cuiabá goldfields lay in the territory of the Bororo; but although most of that nation were hostile to the Portuguese, they tended to avoid contact. Another large tribe affected by the discoveries of gold at Cuiabá and Vila Bela were the Arawak-speaking Parecis who lived north-west of Cuiabá near the upper Guaporé. This populous, docile, and civilized tribe was regarded as perfect potential labour by the miners. These unwarlike people were rounded up in hundreds to toil in the mines or to be shipped back to replenish the vanished stock of Indian labour at São Paulo itself.

[47] Antonio Pires de Campos, 'Breve noticia...do gentio bárbaro que ha na derrota...do Cuyabá', *RIHGB*, 25 (1862), 440.

The opening of the goldfields of Minas Gerais had an impact on the cattle areas of Bahia and the north-east. Hungry miners provided a splendid new market for cattle. With the peace treaty of 1692 that ended the Tarairyu (Janduin) wars there was a period of ugly violence as ranchers moved deeper into the interior of the north-eastern provinces. Official papers contain reports of atrocities against Indians on this nominally peaceful frontier. A Paulista commander, Manoel Álvares de Morais Navarro, slaughtered a village of peaceful Paiacú in 1699 during a parley; the primitive Tremembé, one of the few surviving tribes on the Atlantic coast, were annihilated by a punitive expedition from Maranhão; another Paulista, Francisco Dias de Siqueira, in 1692 ravaged the *corso* or roving tribes of the Maranhão interior but also attacked peaceful missions, and at the end of the century this old rascal was attacking uncontacted tribes in Piauí with a private army; in the final years of the seventeenth century there were slaving raids and Indian counterattacks on the Mearim and Itapicurú rivers of Maranhão; and between 1702 and 1705 the Vidal and Axemi of the Parnaíba valley were wiped out in a series of disgraceful violations of truces with them. One of the cruellest ruffians was António da Cunha Souto-Maior, who terrorized tribes from a camp on the Parnaíba. One 'barbarous entertainment'[48] devised by him and his brother was to release Anaperu prisoners one by one, ride them down on horses, and decapitate them with machetes. A rebellion by his own Indians in 1712 killed Cunha Souto-Maior and his Portuguese soldiers, and then spread rapidly into the most serious and widespread of all Indian rebellions. The insurrection was led by a mission-educated Indian called Mandu Ladino and it raged throughout southern Maranhão, Piauí and Ceará for seven years. It cost the Portuguese the loss of many lives and the destruction of hundreds of ranches. For a brief time Mandu's Gê tribes were allied to their traditional enemies, the Tupi tribes of Ceará. Had this alliance lasted, it could have expelled all Portuguese from Ceará; but the Tupi were placated by the authorities, and it was a force of Tobajara from Ibiapaba, fighting 'without any whites whatsoever, who were only an embarrassment to them in the forests',[49] who in 1719 caught and killed

[48] Antonio de Sousa Leal, report in Virginia Rau and Maria Fernanda Gomes da Silva (eds.), *Os manuscritos do arquivo da Casa de Cadaval respeitantes ao Brasil* (2 vols., Coimbra, 1956–60), II, 386.
[49] Father Domingos Ferreira Chaves to king, Ceará, 23 Nov. 1719, in Rau and Gomes da Silva (eds.), *Manuscritos*, II, 248–9.

Mandu and exterminated his 'Tapuia'. In 1720 the king called for a report on the situation of tribes in the north-east following the cattle boom. The resulting document was a litany of murders and outrages against its Indians during the preceding twenty years.

In north-western Amazonia the river Solimões ('poisons', because its tribes used curare), the main stream of the Amazon between the mouths of the Negro and the Javari at the modern boundary with Peru and Colombia, was scarcely claimed by either Spain or Portugal. In 1689 a Spanish Jesuit, Samuel Fritz, was active among the Yurimagua, who then lived near the mouth of the Purús. The Portuguese made occasional expeditions to this river in search of sarsaparilla, cacao or slaves. Fritz was taken to Belém and detained briefly in 1689 but was returned to his mission three years later. In 1697 Portuguese Carmelites appeared with a military escort to claim this stretch of river and expelled Fritz. During the ensuing decade the Iberian kingdoms disputed this long stretch of the Amazon, with Portuguese incursions upstream to the Napo and the arrest of a Spanish Jesuit near modern Iquitos in 1709. The result of all this was that the Portuguese eventually established a mission at Tabatinga, at what is now the frontier; but the Amazon was denuded by the squabbling. The Omagua and Yurimagua, once the most populous and advanced tribes on the Amazon, were dispersed and decimated. When the French scientist Charles de la Condamine descended the river in 1743 he reported that the Omagua lands were empty, with no Indians living on the 450 miles between Pebas and São Paulo de Olivença.

The early eighteenth century also saw the Portuguese pushing up the major tributaries of the middle Amazon. Jesuits found that their activities on the Madeira were impeded by the large and bellicose Tora tribe; but a powerful punitive expedition in 1719 'left them extinct'.[50] Other tribes of the lower Madeira agreed to descend to Jesuit missions near its mouth. The resulting vacuum was filled by the formidable Mura, a tribe that became implacable enemies of the whites after 400 of its people were enslaved while travelling peacefully towards a mission. The Mura learned to respect and avoid open combat against Portuguese firearms; but they were brilliant at ambushes and lightning attacks from

[50] José Gonçalves da Fonseca, 'Primeira exploração dos rios Madeira e Guaporé em 1749', in Cândido Mendes de Almeida, *Memórias para a história do extincto Estado do Maranhão* (Rio de Janeiro, 1860), II, 304.

the waterways of the lower Madeira. For many years during the mid eighteenth century the Mura prevented Portuguese settlement or movement on the rivers near their territory.

At this time, Carmelite missionaries were penetrating the Negro. Their advance was blocked by a 'rebellion' of the Manau under a paramount chief, Ajuricaba, in 1723. The Manau lived on the middle Negro, hundreds of miles upstream of the modern city that bears their name. During their war against the Portuguese they were in contact with the Dutch of Guiana, who supplied them with firearms, and for a time Ajuricaba flew a Dutch flag on his canoe. A large punitive expedition, based on the new mission of Mariuá (Barcelos), finally defeated the Manau and captured Ajuricaba in 1728. The great chief was brought in chains to slavery at Belém, but as he approached the city he and some fellow Manau tried to overpower their captors and then jumped into the river, still chained, preferring death to captivity.

In his monumental history of the Jesuits in Brazil, Serafim Leite lists no less than 160 expeditions made by the Fathers, most of them on the rivers of the Amazon basin during the century after 1650. There was also a steady succession of annual official and unofficial slaving expeditions. Through these activities the Portuguese penetrated far up all the Amazon's main tributaries, even if they tended to depopulate rather than to settle the areas they visited. There were also some longer explorations: in 1723 Francisco de Mello Palheta led a flotilla of canoes up the Madeira to Santa Cruz de la Sierra and back; in 1746 João de Sousa Azevedo made the first descent of the Arinos and Tapajós; others ascended the Negro to the Casiquaire canal, first discovered in 1744 by the Spanish Jesuit Manuel Román. These activities gave Portugal a physical presence in the Amazon basin, but at a terrible cost to the Indians. There were frequent epidemics of smallpox, influenza, and measles that destroyed the missions as fast as the missionaries could restock them with fresh converts. Father João Daniel reckoned that the Portuguese had descended or killed three million Indians from the Negro basin alone. He wrote that these rivers, once 'peopled with... Indians as numerous as swarms of mosquitoes, settlements without number, and a diversity of tribes and languages beyond count',[51] were reduced by 1750 to a thousandth part of their original population.

[51] João Daniel, 'Thesouro descoberto no maximo rio Amazonas', pt 2, ch. 15, *RIHGB*, 3 (1841), 50.

Travellers reported that hundreds of miles of the banks of the Amazon were 'destitute of inhabitants of either sex or any age'[52] and entire mission aldeias were abandoned.

It was Portuguese activity on the northern and southern extremities of Brazil -- into the upper Paraná and Paraguay to the goldfields of Mato Grosso, and up the Amazon – that paved the way for the Treaty of Madrid, signed on 13 January 1750. This was a diplomatic triumph for the negotiators of Dom João V, for it recognized *de facto* occupation and thus awarded almost half South America to the Portuguese. The treaty sensibly sought to follow geographical features in fixing the boundary. It thus followed parts of the Uruguay, Iguaçu, Paraná, Paraguay, Guaporé, Madeira, and Javari rivers and, north of the Amazon, ran from the middle Negro to the watershed between the Amazon and Orinoco basins and along the Guiana watershed to the Atlantic.

The quarter-century after the Treaty of Madrid, the years of Dom José I and Pombal (1750–77), had a profound effect on the Indians of Brazil. Pombal's own half-brother, Francisco Xavier de Mendonça Furtado, was sent as governor of Maranhão-Pará and remained there from 1751 to 1759. He was shocked by the colonists' ignorance and abuse of Indians; but he was even more critical of the wealth, moral laxity, insubordination, and mistreatment of Indians by the missionary orders. In his letters to his brother he wrote that the various orders had some 12,000 Indians in 63 missions in Amazonia. On the island of Marajó, the Mercedarians had between 60,000 and 100,000 head of cattle on their ranches, the Jesuits 25,000–30,000, and the Carmelites 8,000–10,000. Although the Jesuits ran only nineteen missions, and although the governor approved of the fact that they alone kept Indian women decently clothed, it was the Fathers of the Society who most infuriated Mendonça Furtado. When he took a great fleet of canoes up the river in 1754 to supervise the frontier demarcations, he compared Jesuits' lack of co-operation unfavourably with the warm welcome he was given by the Carmelites on the Rio Negro.

The Jesuits appeared to be equally obstructive at the other extremity of Brazil. By following the Uruguay river, the new frontier established in 1750 isolated the seven prosperous and long-established Spanish Jesuit missions of Guaraní on what was to become Portuguese territory,

[52] Gonçalves de Fonseca, 'Primeira exploração...', 274.

and they were expected to move to new locations east of the Uruguay. But they refused, declaring that they had always occupied the lands of their villages and that these contained their consecrated churches and the burials of their ancestors. After the failure of various attempts at persuasion, a joint Portuguese–Spanish army determined to evict the Guaraní by force. On 10 February 1756 matters came to a head with the battle of Caibaté, in which in a few minutes European artillery and cavalry slaughtered 1,400 Christian Indians who were pathetically holding aloft their banners, crucifixes and holy images. This was the fate of the group of Brazilian Indians who had accepted Christianity most fervently during two centuries of conquest launched on the pretext of converting Brazil's heathen.

Those two centuries of missionary control of Brazilian Indians came to an end with two laws that Pombal persuaded the king to issue in 1755. An edict of 4 April 1755 theoretically ended all racial discrimination, declaring that half-castes 'will be fit and capable of any employment, honour or dignity'.[53] Then on 6 June came the Law of Liberties, which freed the 'persons, goods and commerce' of the Indians of Pará and Maranhão. Indians were declared to be free citizens, enjoying all the rights and privileges that went with citizenship. They were to be integrated into Portuguese society. Aldeias were to receive Portuguese names and would henceforth become ordinary towns. Anyone could trade with Indians and these could – in theory – work for whomever they chose, but at rates of pay to be fixed by the governor and officials. Indians themselves were to control their villages, and there were special punishments for any who invaded Indian land or tried to exploit Indian simplicity. In a ringing declaration of Indian freedom, the Law admitted that 'many thousands of Indians have been "descended", but they are being extinguished and the number of villages and their inhabitants is very small; and these few live in great misery'.[54] On the following day, Dom José issued an edict stripping missionaries of all temporal control of aldeias and limiting them to evangelical work among uncontacted tribes. To anticipate any outcry from the settlers, a decree on that same day created the Companhia Geral do Comércio do Grão-Pará e Maranhão, which would import black slaves to the region in order to develop its exports – tasks that it achieved with considerable success for a few decades.

[53] Alvará of 4 Apr. 1735, *Ley sobre os casamentos com as índias.*
[54] *Ley porque V. Magestade ha por bem restituir aos indios do Grão-Pará e Maranhão a liberdade das suas pessoas, e bens, e commercio,* 6 June 1755, in Perdigão Malheiro, *Escravidão,* II, 99.

The liberation of the Indians that was proclaimed so eloquently in the legislation of 1755 never took place. Pombal and his half-brother immediately began to worry in their correspondence that the Indians would revert to their primitive 'laziness' – they would concern themselves with feeding their own families instead of working for the Portuguese state or for the colonists. Governor Mendonça Furtado waited until 1757 before publishing the new law, and he then introduced on his own initiative a white 'director' into each native village. He pretended that these directors would be altruistic paragons concerned with teaching the Indians civilized ways and encouraging their commerce, so that they would become rich and civilized Christian citizens. This new system, known as the *Diretório de Indios*, was introduced to all former mission villages on 3 May 1757. In return for supposedly teaching the Indians the Portuguese language, European methods of farming and trade, and domestic skills, the directors were to handle all the commercial transactions of their charges and were to receive 17 per cent of any gross income from the sale of produce, to which the government added a further tax of 10 per cent. In addition to these heavy levies (which were on turnover rather than profit), all Indian males aged between thirteen and 60 were still required to work on 'public works' and to spend half of each year working for the colonists. Their chiefs and the new directors were to enforce this 'even to the detriment of the best interests of the Indians themselves'![55]

Observers in Brazil immediately warned that such appalling legislation would lead to disaster. There was ample precedent to show that laymen in control of Indians abused their charges atrociously. Bento da Fonseca warned that settlers would capture wild Indians 'without the slightest impediment, and [would rule] Indians of the aldeias, using them all as if they were their slaves, without paying them for their labour'. He also knew that the introduction of Portuguese soldiers to enforce the new Indian 'freedom' was no answer: 'If a religious order could scarcely maintain the defence of the Indians, it is certain that army captains could not – even if they had any inclination to do so.'[56] Despite these warnings, the directorate system was introduced throughout Brazil in August 1758. A year later the Jesuits were expelled from Brazil.[57] When in 1798, after almost universal condemnation by all

[55] *Diretório regimento*, 3 May 1757, in Perdigão Malheiro, *Escravidão*, 11, 110.
[56] Capistrano de Abreu, *Capítulos*, 185.
[57] For further treatment of the expulsion of the Jesuits, see Alden, *CHLA* 11, ch. 15.

experts on Indian affairs, the directorate system was finally abolished, the mission villages, particularly in the former Jesuit heartland in the south and also throughout the Amazon, were in complete disarray and abandon.

During the three centuries since the Portuguese first landed in Brazil the native American population of at least two and a half million had been reduced by probably three-quarters. At the end of the colonial period the few Indians living under Portuguese rule were pathetic creatures at the bottom of society, half acculturated, stripped of most of their tribal traditions and pride, but entirely failing to adapt to European ways or to grasp any of the finer points of European civilization. Those tribes which had managed to retreat deeper into the interior before the advancing Portuguese, to avoid destruction or absorption into Portuguese Brazil, were no more than a vague threat on a distant frontier. Poets such as José de Alvarenga Peixoto or José de Santa Rita Durão could afford to glorify and romanticize Indians, but in a style that bore no relation to reality. Apart from a handful of indifferent sixteenth-century chronicles, the Portuguese totally failed to record anything of anthropological interest about the tribes they destroyed. On the contrary, seventeenth- and eighteenth-century literature, whether by missionaries, officials or adventurers, is striking for its almost total lack of interest in or information about native societies.

5

THE GOLD CYCLE, *c.* 1690–1750

DISCOVERY

For almost three centuries following the discovery of Brazil in 1500 the Portuguese court was flooded with reports of fabulous gold strikes in Brazil. These had often lacked foundation and had been a blend of misguided trust placed in native American legends, over-optimistic accounts by explorers, and the apparently undeniable logic that a continent which had rewarded the Spaniards with gold, emeralds, and silver must also possess precious metals in that part allocated to the Portuguese by the Treaty of Tordesillas (1494).

Not all these reports had been totally devoid of truth. Gold had indeed been found in São Vicente in the 1560s, and by the 1570s Paulistas had discovered alluvial gold in Paranaguá. There had been reports of gold strikes in the interior of the captaincy of Bahia by João Coelho de Sousa; his brother Gabriel Soares de Sousa had received official authorization (1584) to launch an expedition to confirm these findings. In the seventeenth century as the bandeirantes penetrated deep into the interior of Brazil in their search for Indian slaves and precious metals, reports from Paranaguá, Curitiba, São Vicente, Espírito Santo, and Pernambuco convinced the crown of the potential mineral wealth of Portuguese America. But only at the end of the seventeenth and during the first half of the eighteenth centuries did Brazil yield up her riches.

Around 1695 the governor of Rio de Janeiro received substantiated reports of major gold strikes within his jurisdiction, at Rio das Velhas in the region referred to in official correspondence initially as the 'mines of São Paulo'. There soon followed reports from the captaincy of Bahia of strikes in Jacobina, and in 1702 the governor-general notified the king of further strikes in Serro do Frio, Itocambiras, and in the sertão. Later strikes were confirmed in Rio das Contas. Concurrently, from the neighbouring captaincy of Espírito Santo there were reports of gold being found in 1701–2. In Bahia there was to be further successful exploration between 1726 and 1734 in Rio das Contas, Rio Pardo, and Rio Verde as well as in Araçuahi, Fanado, and Aguasuja in the sertão. In 1739 came reports of gold being found in the Serra da Baituração in Ilhéus, but this area was not exploited. These discoveries paled into insignificance beside events taking place within the area now known as 'general mines'. The discoveries in Rio das Velhas had triggered off widespread exploration and speculation. By 1720, when Minas Gerais was declared an independent captaincy, there was no part of it which was not being exploited profitably. Moreover, Minas Gerais was to serve as a base and stimulus for further exploration towards the west. The first result of such exploration was the discovery in 1718 or 1719 of gold on the river Coxipó and on the river Cuiabá, both in Mato Grosso. To the north further strikes were made about 1734 on the river Guaporé in the north-west of Mato Grosso. These were followed in about 1745 by a flurry of exploratory activity on the river Arinos, a tributary of the Tapajós, in the central northern area of Mato Grosso. In Goiás by 1725 discoveries in the area of Rio Vermelho in the central southern region augured well. By 1750 such major discoveries of gold as were to be made in Brazil had already been made, but this did not dampen further exploration. In the early 1750s mines in Trahiras and São Felix in Goiás were productive, as too were the mines of Kararis Novos in Pernambuco. Gold was discovered in the mid-century in the foothills of the Serra de Itabaiana in Sergipe, and in Espírito Santo in the Castelo mines. Bandeirante activity in the opening up of the sertão and exploration in a variety of regions continued throughout the century, but future developments merely served to confirm the royal designation (1754) of 'mining areas' as referring to São Paulo, Minas Gerais, Cuiabá, Mato Grosso, Goiás, and the judicial districts (*comarcas*) of Jacobina, Rio das Contas, and Minas Novas de Araçuahi in Bahia.

These discoveries of gold gave rise to two developments as unforeseen as they were confusing to the crown. The first was that during the first half of the century the crown received numerous requests for financial aid, concession of honorary titles, permission to use Amerindian labour as porters for expeditions, and the supply of mining equipment, powder, shot, and firearms. For the most part such claims were spurious or grossly inflated. Some were fraudulent. Petitioners had no intention of leaving coastal enclaves to undertake the promised expeditions, or else were trying to recoup financial losses incurred as the result of profitless speculation by claiming promising finds when the reality had been the reverse. Now that the potential of some regions had indeed been realized, the crown found it increasingly difficult to assess the validity of such requests. There are well-documented examples of the crown simply being duped. In contrast, deserving cases went unrecognized and unrewarded, and lack of royal support reduced the incentive for future exploration or exploitation of potentially productive areas which only later proved profitable. A second outcome was that the hope of royal favours led discoverers of anything remotely resembling precious or semi-precious stones or metals to submit their finds to the mints in Salvador, Rio de Janeiro, or Minas Gerais. The colonial mints often sent such samples to the Lisbon mint for expert evaluation. For the most part they proved to be valueless or low-value emerald, amethyst, garnet, and zircon.

More positively, the successful discovery of gold led to a careful scrutiny of old routes into the interior (*roteiros paulistas*), in some cases dating back to the sixteenth century, and intensified exploration which resulted in the discovery of mineral resources other than gold. During the viceroyalty of the Conde de Sabugosá (1720–35) numerous expeditions or *entradas* officially sponsored and led by Pedro Barbosa Leal, João Peixoto Viegas, António Velho Veloso, Pedro Leolino Mariz, and others, resulted in a gamut of mineral discoveries of varying significance, including lead, iron, copper, mercury, emery, and, above all, diamonds. The histories of saltpetre and silver offer two examples of mixed fortunes. As a prime ingredient in the manufacture of gunpowder, saltpetre was of critical interest to a crown in whose realms there were no natural deposits. In the 1690s deposits had been found near Jacobina but were exhausted within a decade. Experiments in Pernambuco proved unsuccessful. Finds in the Serra dos Montes Altos near the river São Francisco in the mid 1750s proved productive and were exploited in commercial quantities. In the governor-generalship of Dom João de Lancastre (1694–1702), and again during the viceroyalty of the Conde de Sabugosa, silver strikes were reported but the reality remained that as long as there was alluvial gold which afforded greater returns for less investment in time, effort, and cost, there was little incentive to engage in the more laborious and costly process of extracting silver ore.

COMARCA
DE
PARACATÚ

R. São Francisco

R. Jequitinhonha

R. Araçuahi

Bom Sucesso

R. do Fanado

COMARCA

Tijuco
DIAMOND
DISTRICT

DO

Vila do Príncipe

SERRA DE S. ANTONIO

SERRO FRIO

R. das Velhas

COMARCA DO

R. Paraopeba

R. Doce

SERRA DA LAPA

S e r r a

RIO DAS VELHAS

Pitangui

R. São Francisco

Vila Nova da Rainha

Sabará

SERRA DO CARAÇO

Catas Altas

d o

Vila Rica do
Ouro Preto

COMARCA DO

SERRA DO ITACOLOMI

Mariana

E s p i n h a ç o

OURO PRETO

Congonhas
do Campo

SERRA DA MANTIQUEIRA

COMARCA DO
RIO DAS MORTES

R. Grande

R. Grande

S. José
del Rei

BRAZIL

Salvador

S. João
del Rei

0   km   100

0   50 miles

Rio de Janeiro

Minas Gerais in the early eighteenth century

The discovery and subsequent exploitation of gold were to have immediate and far-reaching repercussions not only on the society and economy of Brazil but also on the mother country and her political and economic position within Europe. The crown did not wish to discourage mining activities, but at the same time acted to protect those sectors of colonial society and economy which might otherwise be adversely affected by unrestrained gold fever. Despite initial optimism, it appears

that the crown could not believe its good fortune and, even in the case
of the 'general mines', did not expect the results to be long-lasting.
Optimism was also tempered by concern that once other European
nations heard of the discoveries in Brazil they might invade Portuguese
America. In 1703 the king ordered the governor-general to stop mining
in Jacobina, Itocambiras, and Serro do Frio until their vulnerability to
foreign invasion could be assessed. This prohibition also applied to new
strikes in Espírito Santo. However, these orders either failed to arrive
or were ignored. The governor-general lacked the military strength to
enforce such orders in the hinterland, especially when confronted with
the reality that in each area there was increasing gold production, a
growing population, and, in the case of Jacobina, the important
subsidiary economic development of cattle and horse raising. But for
the next fifteen years the crown persisted in reiterating bans on mining
in these areas. Only in 1720, the royal appetite whetted by gold returns
and reassurances, did Dom João V authorize mining in Jacobina and
shortly afterwards in Rio das Contas and other areas of the sertão. In
1729 the king was again to seek reassurance that Araçuahi and Fanado
were not vulnerable to invasion from the sea, and in the 1750s
development of mines at Itabaiana in Sergipe and at Castelo in Espírito
Santo was refused because of their proximity to the coast.

The royal ban on development of mines in Bahia had been prompted
by the strategic consideration that they would induce people to desert
the city of Salvador and the Recôncavo. The king feared that there
would then be an inadequate pool of manpower to defend the city
against attack by foreigners or, once they saw the declining numbers
of whites, by insurgent blacks or Indians. These fears were groundless,
but the economic and demographic impact of the new discoveries did
represent a serious threat to the coastal areas of the north-east and
demanded strong measures. The city council of Salvador even petitioned
the crown for a ban on all mining activities, a request which was
ignored. Throughout the first half of the eighteenth century town and
city councils in coastal areas attributed all their misfortunes to mining.
A major complaint was that the lure of the mines siphoned off from
the coastal areas whites and freedmen of colour who would otherwise
have been involved in the cultivation of sugar, tobacco, or manioc.
While some farmers may have deserted their fields for the mining areas,
this was less prevalent than might be thought. Rather, the problem lay
in the fact that farmers, no less than miners, needed slaves for working

their fields. But miners had two advantages: first, they could afford higher prices for their slaves; second, instead of purchasing on credit and offering the yield of the next crop as security, they paid in cash. The result was that farmers in the coastal areas could not afford slaves of the best category (*primeiro lote*) and, even if they were interested, could not match prices offered by miners for slaves of the second category (*segundo lote*). The purchase of even inferior slaves stretched farmers' financial resources to the utmost. Many sold their holdings, or consolidated those few resources they had preserved intact, or were the victims of foreclosure for debt. Allied to increasing labour costs was the economic reality that export agricultural products were in any case (for more general, structural reasons) not as profitable to the producer in the first half of the eighteenth century as had been the case earlier.

Traditional lines of supply and demand for foodstuffs were also disrupted by the sudden increase in demand from the mining areas. When the town of São Cristóvão in Sergipe wanted to exploit the Itabaiana mines in 1750, one ground for the royal refusal to grant permission was that Sergipe was the cellar for Bahia: exploitation of the mines would disrupt and even paralyse the supply of foodstuffs to Salvador. Competition from mining areas severely disrupted the supply of meat to the coastal enclaves from the interior of Bahia, Pernambuco, Ceará, Piauí, and Maranhão. At the outset Minas Gerais was totally dependent on meat imports and, even with the development of its own industry, remained unable to support itself. Disruption of the supply and demand network was not limited to commodities produced in Brazil. Not only luxury items but such basic imports as salt underwent price increases and, in view of the inability of people in the coastal areas to meet these increased costs, were dispatched to the more profitable markets in the interior. In 1717 the viceroy reported that prices for basic commodities had skyrocketed. Breadwinners who had formerly supported a family could no longer do so and faced starvation or migration to the mining areas to try their luck. The result of these financial pressures was that many people from the coastal enclaves went into mining not so much because of the lure of ready wealth as because of impending starvation and poverty. Viceroy Sabugosa commented ironically in 1729 that the true golden age of Brazil had been before the discovery of gold; with the discovery of gold Brazil was experiencing an iron age.

The crown enacted a series of measures aimed at protecting agriculture while at the same time being careful not to discourage mining initiatives. In 1701 the king prohibited communication or transportation of cattle or foodstuffs from Bahia to the 'mines of São Paulo', or commerce in the opposite direction. Insufficient numbers of enforcement officers, coupled with the virtual impossibility of patrolling the vast areas of the hinterland, limited the effectiveness of such orders. In 1704 the crown forbade the re-export from Bahia to the mines of commodities imported from Portugal. Such restrictions were equally ineffectual; the lure of higher profits from sales in the mining areas was inducement enough to lead cattle drovers and merchants to evade controls and even to engage in hand-to-hand fighting with enforcement patrols rather than renounce their trading practices. The crown also forbade the opening of new roads to the mines. The king was moved in part by the desire to increase the effectiveness of patrols, but also by the more pressing need to exert some degree of control over the opening of new mining areas and the taxing of gold extracted from those already in operation. The vastness of the sertão, inadequately staffed patrols, and high returns on contraband – be it in gold, cattle, slaves, or other commodities – made the clandestine opening of paths and roads inevitable.

More pressing was the need, first, to guarantee that Bahia and the north-east received their fair share of slaves from West Africa, and second, to ensure that once these had arrived in the ports of the north-east they were not immediately siphoned off to Rio de Janeiro or the mining areas. On the first issue, in order not to put the captaincies of the north-east at a disadvantage, in 1703 the king restricted ships trading directly from Rio de Janeiro or Santos to Angola and the Costa da Mina. But threats of exile and confiscation of ship and cargo failed to halt the trade. The king also prohibited slave exports to Minas Gerais from the ports of Brazil by land or by sea, i.e., by re-export from the north-east to Rio de Janeiro. A royal *alvará* forbade the sale to Paulistas of slaves arriving in Bahia. Such restrictions were to be modified. From an outright ban the king moved in 1701 to a quota of 200 slaves annually to be exported from Rio de Janeiro to Minas Gerais, and then went to the point of removing all restrictions on trade from Rio de Janeiro in favour of free trade to the mines. Challenged by other captaincies that this concession granted to Rio de Janeiro an unfair monopoly, the king resolved (10 November 1710) that there be no further restrictions on taking slaves to Minas Gerais from Rio de Janeiro or anywhere else. Free trade was conditional: evidence had to be furnished that slaves had not been taken from plantations, or, if they had, that they had been replaced by an equal number of slaves. Such crown measures were misdirected; rather than concentrating on exports or re-exports of slaves to the mining areas, the crown should have focused its attention on ensuring that slaves were available to farmers at prices they could afford. The result of this misplaced emphasis was a shortage of first-quality slaves for the plantations of Brazil in the first half of the eighteenth century.

The crown also acted to protect the society and economy of Portugal from the potentially disastrous results of an uncontrolled gold rush. Restrictions were placed on the numbers and types of people whom captains were permitted to transport to the New World. By 1709 the impact on Portugal's population, especially in the northern provinces, forced the king to reiterate earlier orders that potential travellers must have passports, obtainable from the secretary of state in Lisbon or, in the case of travellers from Oporto or Viana do Castelo, from the respective governors. Foreigners were only permitted to travel to Brazil if they could furnish evidence that their business was legitimate and posted bond before leaving Portugal to guarantee their return on the same fleet. Later this bond had to be increased because experience showed that windfall profits in the mining areas led many to forfeit their bond rather than return. Similarly, although clerics and friars were forbidden to travel to Brazil without the prior consent of their superiors or prelates, some signed on as ships' chaplains, while others obtained the requisite authorization for a temporary visit to Brazil for the collection of alms and simply failed to return. Despite severe penalties (1709) imposed on ships' captains found guilty of carrying prostitutes, many made their way to Brazil. There was always a way to gain passage, even if it were as a cabin boy or sailor, on payment of ten or fifteen gold coins. Measures were not strictly enforced at ports of departure. Oporto was notorious for the laxness of its authorities. In 1733 three ships from Oporto arrived in Bahia carrying over 700 passengers without permission. In 1742 the viceroy, the Conde das Galvêas, noted the large numbers of migrants to Brazil from Portugal and the Atlantic islands. Their destinations were Bahia, Pernambuco, Maranhão, and especially Rio de Janeiro as affording quickest access to the mining areas. He estimated that some 1,500 to 1,600 persons left Portugal annually for Brazil and that the majority went to the mines. Because so few returned to Portugal, he sounded a warning note on the prejudicial effects such migration could have on the mother country.

For prospective searchers after Brazilian gold there was no easy route to the interior of Brazil. High mountain ranges, densely wooded valleys, and swift-flowing rivers proved substantial barriers. The coastal plain, the sertão, and the central highland area afforded extremes of cold and heat, humidity and dryness, and alternate periods of drought and torrential rain. Wild animals, poisonous insects, snakes, and flora harmful to man (and, for the most part, unknown to Europeans) abounded. Hostile Indians were a constant threat and, although their presence may have decreased on some routes, they were nevertheless a force to be reckoned with throughout the hinterland of Brazil in the eighteenth century. Should the traveller survive these natural hazards, he still faced the dangers which arose from personal inadequacies. Many were totally unprepared either physically or psychologically for such journeys. Few appreciated the enormous distances they would have to cover even to reach the mines of Bahia, let alone those of Mato Grosso or Goiás. The logistics of ensuring adequate supplies of food and water, not to speak of protection against the elements, were complicated, and few of those arriving in Rio de Janeiro, Salvador, or Pernambuco had any previous experience to help them cope with these problems.

Two main networks of routes to Minas Gerais had been developed. The first served the needs of those seeking access to the 'general mines' from São Paulo and from the coastal areas of Rio de Janeiro and Santos and the intervening smaller ports such as Angra dos Reis and Paratí. From the coastal areas of the captaincy of Rio de Janeiro there were three principal routes. The Caminho Velho started at Paratí, climbed the Serra do Facão, and passed the town of Taubaté where the road divided to cross the Serra da Mantiqueira; from here one route ran to the mining townships of Rio das Mortes and Vila Rica and another to Rio das Velhas. Another route started at Santos, ascended to São Paulo and led thence to Taubaté, joining the first route at Guaratinguetá. The journey from the coast to the mining communities took about one month. The difficulties of this route led the governor of Rio de Janeiro Artur de Sá e Meneses at the end of the seventeenth century to commission Garcia Rodrigues Paes to hack out a more direct route to Minas Gerais. This he did by going overland to Irajá, following the rivers Iguaçú, Paraíba, and Paraibuna, and thence to the mining areas. This route was known as the Caminho Novo. Writing in 1717, Dom Pedro de Almeida (later Conde de Assumar), who had himself travelled to his new appointment as governor from São Paulo, noted that all three routes were very rough going, full of outcrops, narrow ravines, high mountains, dense undergrowth, and heavily wooded terrain. During the rainy season there was loss of life and load by beasts and people alike. By 1725 a variant to the Caminho Novo started at Praia dos Mineiros, followed the river Inhomirim, and provided access via the river Piabanha to the river Paraíba. About the same time work was in progress on a road linking São Paulo directly to Rio de Janeiro.

A second network of routes was focused on the river São Francisco, which rises in Rio das Mortes in Minas Gerais and meanders north- and north-eastward before entering the Atlantic between Alagoas and Sergipe. Although it was navigable on its upper and lower reaches, the cataracts at Paulo Afonso were an obstacle to river transport over its whole length. Travellers from Salvador travelled by boat to the mouth of the river and thence from Penedo to Jacaré just below the cataracts, or by land or water through the Recôncavo to Cachoeira and thence started the long haul overland to the Arraial de Mathias Cardoso on the river. This was the converging point for travellers to Minas Gerais from Pernambuco, Ceará, Piauí, and Maranhão. Following the right bank of the São Francisco to the confluence with the Rio das Velhas, travellers could choose between a series of routes into central Minas Gerais or the isolated Serro do Frio. This route, known as the Caminho do Sertão or Caminho da Bahia, was over comparatively easy terrain, and had a ready supply of water, and the early establishment of cattle ranches guaranteed provisions. On the other hand the region of the São Francisco was unhealthy at certain times of the year and the greater distance meant a longer period of travel. Furthermore, even in the 1730s those Tupinambá who had been forced out of the Recôncavo during the governor-generalship of Afonso Furtado de Castro do Rio de Mendonça (1671–75) were still making lightning attacks on convoys en route to Minas Gerais, prompting the king to approve an outright war against these Indians in 1733. By the 1730s Jacobina was the centre for a series of routes from northern captaincies to the river São Francisco, as well as to Rio das Contas, and provided good access to

Salvador. From Salvador there was a route via São Pedro de Muritiba to Rio das Contas, crossing the treacherous river Una, and thence to Minas Novas de Araçuahi and finally to northern Minas Gerais.

Whereas travellers to the 'general mines' may have used river routes for part of their journeys, by and large overland travel predominated. Discoveries in Mato Grosso entailed a break with this tradition, at least in the early years. Furthermore, whereas the geographical position of Minas Gerais had made it equally accessible to Bahian and Paulista, circumstances favoured access to Mato Grosso by Paulistas and travellers from the coastal areas of Rio de Janeiro. These travellers exploited the network of rivers from Pôrto Feliz outside the town of São Paulo which all led to the river Cuiabá: those were the rivers Tieté, Paraná, Pardo, Anhandui, Aquidauna, and Paraguay. This route was to be modified and a portage developed from the river Pardo to the Coxim-Taquarí and thence by the river Taquarí to the river Paraguay.

Known as 'monsoons', voyages from São Paulo to Cuiabá took from five to seven months outwards and two returning because of lighter loads. Those leaving São Paulo between March and June caught the rivers in flood, which made shooting the more than 100 rapids between Pôrto Feliz and Cuiabá easier, although this was offset by exposure to malaria and other fevers at this season. Physical hardships were enormous and loss of life and stores from overturned canoes commonplace events. Perhaps the greatest danger was from hostile Indians on the upper Paraguay. The Paiaguá were river people and the Guaicurú were renowned horsemen. Together and separately, these two peoples killed many Portuguese. In two spectacular massacres the Paiaguá killed 600 in one single convoy in 1725, and 400 more in a fight lasting five hours in 1730. Before their virtual extinction in 1795, the Guaicurú were said to have accounted for 4,000 Portuguese. Physical hardship, distance, fear of Indians and the need for skilled canoe pilots forced prospective miners to travel in convoy as their best hope of survival. These convoys demanded organization, leadership, discipline and the subordination of the individual to the collective will. One of the largest, in 1726, was made up of some 3,000 passengers in 305 canoes and included the governor of São Paulo himself.

The route of Goiás, however, followed the more anarchic tradition characteristic of the rush to Minas Gerais. By the 1740s routes had been found from Rio das Velhas, from the north-east, and from Mato Grosso to Vila Boa de Goiás. The distance from Goiás to Salvador was estimated at 400 leagues (1,200 miles), but when Dom Marcos de Noronha was promoted from the governorship of Goiás to be viceroy in Salvador, he made the journey overland in eleven weeks to take up his new appointment in 1755.

Except in very general terms little is known of how many or what kind of people took part in the gold rushes which followed each new strike. The rush to Minas Gerais was by far the most important. It appears that migrants came from every walk of life, from the most diverse social backgrounds, and from all sorts of places: the coastal areas of Brazil, the Atlantic islands of Madeira and the Azores, and Portugal itself. There were a few English, Irish, Dutch, and French adventurers, especially in the early years before royal controls tightened; friars left monasteries in Salvador, Rio de Janeiro, and Maranhão, as well as Portugal; soldiers deserted from the garrisons of Brazilian port cities and Colônia do Sacramento; merchants, former planters, and people with claims to nobility were all infected with gold fever; freedmen of colour saw opportunity in the mining areas denied to them in the coastal enclaves; slaves abandoned their owners, or were dispatched under a factor to investigate the potential of mining; Paulistas, accompanied by their Indian slaves, were prominent both as discoverers and in subsequent gold rushes. Only one group appears to have been remarkable for its absence: women were, in the case of whites, virtually never present, and even among slaves were under-represented.

The rush to Mato Grosso was just as frenetic but the numbers were less. The reasons for this were various: the hardship of the journey was in itself a deterrent; second, even at this early date there were indications that disillusionment and failure in Minas Gerais had led some prospectors to have second thoughts; third, the dramatic rise in the price of slaves and the cost of provisions with no guarantee of return may have dissuaded potential prospectors. Finally, despite the discoveries at Cuiabá, there was not quite the same scattershot reporting of simultaneous discoveries which had characterized the early years in Minas Gerais. Many of these factors also held good for Goiás. The result was that participation by migrants from Portugal was smaller than had been the case in Minas Gerais.

The spectacular nature of the major rushes to Minas Gerais, Mato Grosso, and Goiás has diverted attention from the fact that gold fever did not die with the establishment of mining communities in the major regions of the interior. Throughout the first half of the eighteenth century there were lesser gold rushes in many parts of the interior. Secondary and even tertiary rushes from earlier strikes followed reports of newly productive areas. Discoveries in Rio das Contas in the early 1720s persuaded many miners to leave Minas Gerais in the hope of easier pickings. By the end of the decade new discoveries in Minas Novas de Araçuahi and Fanado and in the sertão of Bahia led the viceroy to report (1729) that Rio das Contas and Jacobina were virtually deserted. Much the same occurred in many areas of Minas Gerais. Discoveries in Goiás caused widespread desertion from Minas Novas and from Minas Gerais in 1736–7. Finally, there was the impact on gold miners of competing sources of wealth. The most famous were diamonds. Their discovery led gold miners from Bahia and Minas Gerais to desert their workings for Serro do Frio in the early 1730s. New strikes, and more especially rumours of potential riches, frequently disrupted the social and economic stability of the mining areas.

For a chosen few, there were indeed riches beyond their wildest dreams. But they were rare and hard-won. Although the Paulistas had the necessary skills for survival in the hinterland – as one enthusiastic governor said later, they could eke out an existence on bark and wild plants and by snaring animals and catching fish – they were in this regard unique among the first wave of miners. For most, already debilitated after long marches or perilous river journeys, arrival could only bring further physical deprivation. Especially in the early months of any mining encampment, before crops had been planted and harvested, food was in short supply and then only available at outrageous prices. Cats and dogs were as much sought after for food in Minas Gerais as they were in the early days in Cuiabá. Protection from rain and cold on the plateau was minimal – a wattle-and-daub hut with a straw roof, as likely to be destroyed by the elements as by fire. In the early years in Minas Gerais and, to a lesser degree elsewhere, the authorities imposed few restraints. Two visits to Minas Gerais by the governor of Rio de Janeiro in 1700–2 were little more than reconnaissance trips. Those few measures which were taken largely ignored the pressing social and economic needs peculiar to mining encampments and were directed instead at ensuring some return to the royal exchequer by setting up a system for allocating mining concessions and collecting the royal fifth, or *quinto*, on gold extracted. For many, poverty and an unmarked grave were the only rewards for their labours.

ADMINISTRATION

During the early eighteenth century the Portuguese crown introduced a series of administrative measures intended to curb the anarchy which characterized the mining areas and to establish a degree of stability. These measures had three main purposes: to provide effective government at the local and regional level; to administer justice and enforce the law; and to fulfil royal obligations as defender of the faith.

The prime instrument of this policy was the township or *vila*. In Portugal the *município* represented stability, the upholding of justice, a degree of self-determination at the local level, and – by virtue of its royal charter – a crown presence. All these aspects were also present in *vilas* overseas, where the last aspect took on especial importance. A royal order of 1693 had permitted the governor-general to establish *vilas* in the hinterland of Brazil, if these would assist in the introduction of law and order. In 1711 one of the first administrative acts of António de Albuquerque Coelho de Carvalho as governor of Minas Gerais and São Paulo was to raise three major mining encampments to the status of *vila*: Vila do Ribeirão do Carmo, Vila Rica do Ouro Prêto, and Vila da Nossa Senhora da Conceição do Sabará. São João del Rei (1713), Vila Nova da Rainha de Caeté (1714), Pitanguí (1715), São José del Rei (1718), and the more distant Vila do Príncipe (1714) completed the major administrative nuclei of Minas Gerais. In 1745 Vila do Carmo was the first *vila* of Minas Gerais to be accorded city status and was named Mariana. Perhaps the most spectacular example of the success of this policy came from Bahia. Between 1710 and 1721 532 firearm deaths occurred in Jacobina; once it was raised to a *vila* in 1721, in the succeeding four years there were only two violent deaths, one by a knife and one by a sword. The *vila* of Nossa Senhora do Livramento was raised in Rio das Contas in 1724, and in 1730 in Minas Novas de Araçuahi the town of Nossa Senhora do Bom Sucesso was established. In Mato Grosso and Goiás fewer towns were established. The most prominent were Vila Real do Senhor Bom Jesus de Cuiabá (1727) and Vila Bela da Santíssima Trindade (1752) in the former; in the latter Vila Boa de Goiás was officially installed in 1739. The order of priorities leading to the raising of these towns varied from region to region and from period to period. Before granting final approval for the establishment of a *vila* the king received reports on the following factors: the anticipated cost to the royal treasury and the extent to which it could be offset by increased revenues; current population and anticipated increase; the town's potential economic and military importance. In mining areas two questions were paramount. Would society be more stable and law and order more effective? Would revenues from the collection of the fifths (payment to the crown of a fifth part of any gold extracted) be enhanced? By offering various inducements such as land grants to new settlers and privileges and exemptions to members of town councils, and by providing new towns with sources of income in the form of lands to rent or fees on cattle, slaves, and other goods entering municipal territory, the crown not only encouraged the settlement of the interior but also provided a source of civic pride. Such towns served as points of departure for further exploration, and also became commercial and administrative centres for vast regions of their immediate hinterlands. The characteristic settlement pattern in the mining areas was of isolated nuclei at a considerable distance from each other; but, at least in Minas Gerais, the presence of concentric spheres of administrative influence helped to diminish such isolation and enhance administrative effectiveness. In the more sparsely populated regions of Mato Grosso and Goiás, the smaller number of towns sharply curtailed effective administrative control.

The move to the west and the rapidly growing importance of the Brazilian highlands and plateau also compelled the crown to create new captaincies, each with its own governor. These were carved out of the sprawling and undefined territories which fell under the jurisdiction of the governor of Rio de Janeiro. In 1709 the crown created a new captaincy, to be known as São Paulo e Minas do Ouro. By 1720 the importance of Minas Gerais and the impossibility of a single governor's effectively maintaining control over the territories of São Paulo and Minas Gerais led to the incorporation of Minas Gerais as a separate captaincy. The more westerly regions were slower in gaining administrative autonomy. Only in 1744 and 1748 respectively were the captaincies of Goiás and Mato Grosso carved out of the vast and largely undefined captaincy of São Paulo. The most dramatic indication of the transfer of strategic, demographic, economic, and political importance from the north-east littoral to the highlands of Brazil was the royal decision to move the viceregal capital from Salvador to Rio de Janeiro in 1763. This was the final step in a process which had started with the first gold strikes in Rio das Velhas some 70 years earlier and was to have profound effects on Brazil's future regional development.

In its attempt to bring justice to the backlands, the crown had to contend with the potent combination of distance from traditional seats of magisterial power coupled with the high inducements to corruption afforded to magistrates. The king attacked the first issue by creating judicial districts (*comarcas*) in new and existing captaincies where sudden shifts of population as the result of mining made a readily visible judicial presence desirable. In Minas Gerais, *comarcas* were initially created for Rio das Mortes, Rio das Velhas, and Vila Rica. Later, because of the territorial extent of Rio das Velhas and its prominence as a mining region as well as a pivotal route for commerce to and from the mining areas in legally sanctioned goods as well as contraband gold, a fourth *comarca* was established in Serro do Frio. Some *comarcas* were also established in Mato Grosso and Goiás. Perhaps the most telling example of the difficulties facing the crown and of the need to be responsive to a changing situation is provided by the saga of the *comarca* of Bahia do Sul. In 1714 the sertão of Bahia captaincy, which embraced the mining communities of Jacobina and Rio das Contas, as well as the much-travelled area of the river São Francisco, was described in an official document as a 'den of thieves'. After two decades of indecision coupled with long-winded discussion over the cost, a royal resolution of 10 December 1734 established a new judicial district to be known as the Comarca da Bahia da Parte do Sul.

The second manner in which the crown attempted to bring more effective justice to the mining areas was by authorizing judicial *juntas*. These had already functioned in the seventeenth century in more distant regions of Pernambuco and other captaincies, but it was in the eighteenth century in the predominantly mining areas where they were to be most common. Such *juntas* comprised the governor, the senior official of the royal treasury in the captaincy, and the senior crown judge of each *comarca*. The jurisdiction of the *junta* extended to passing sentence of death for crimes committed by blacks, mulattos, and Indians and there was no further recourse for appeal. In the case of whites the jurisdiction of such tribunals was prescribed by the social class of the accused. No records of the deliberations of these tribunals appear to have survived. Indeed, if the evidence from Minas Gerais is any indication, governors faced the continual problem of securing a quorum because crown judges were reluctant to travel considerable distances to a central meeting place for this purpose.

Within the institutional arena, the third recourse adopted by the crown to improve the effectiveness of the legal system in the mining areas was to create a second high court of appeals (*Relação*) in Rio de Janeiro. This started work on 15 July 1752 and represented the culmination of 30 years of lobbying by individuals and town councils in the mining areas. The grounds of their appeals were many: first, that judges handed down sentences arbitrarily, confident that the victim would lack legal expertise, money, and time to appeal to the only high court of appeals in the colony at Salvador; second, that even if such cases were appealed documents often were lost in the long overland journey by the Caminho dos Curraes, or ran the risk of the vessel carrying them being taken by pirates should they be sent by sea from Minas Gerais to Salvador, via Rio de Janeiro; third, that magistrates were so removed from traditional centres of justice that they were rarely held to account for their actions. First authorized by a royal resolution of 1734, the new tribunal found its final opening delayed by second thoughts over costs. When it did eventually become functional the new high court was composed of the same number of magistrates as its counterpart in Salvador and with the same authority. The new *Relação* became the appellate court for Rio de Janeiro and the captaincies to the south, but it was expected that its main area of effectiveness would lie in the mining captaincies of Minas Gerais, São Paulo, Mato Grosso, and Goiás.

Another problem concerned the quality and numbers of magistrates. There is no reason to believe that crown judges (*ouvidores*) of the mining areas were either more venal, or more virtuous than their counterparts elsewhere in Portugal or overseas. Indeed, before gaining such appointments they were expected to meet rigorous standards born of extensive training in the legal and administrative aspects of royal government and in many ways were viewed by the crown as a collective right arm. This royal trust resulted in the king imposing on his magistrates a range of responsibilities which were not primarily judicial. This was especially the case in the mining areas. In Minas Gerais crown judges took charge of the royal treasury in their respective regions until such time as the king saw fit to establish a royal exchequer headed by a *provedor mór*. Thus the crown judge became involved in the time-consuming task of supervising the fifths from the initial levying of the appropriate fees through to the final collection. Nor was it unusual for decisions over the granting of mining concessions, and the solving of unavoidable disputes, to be charged to the crown judge, although there were other officials with specific responsibilities for these areas. Many crown judges concurrently held the post of *provedor* of the dead and absent (*dos defuntos e ausentes*), which involved settlement of estates. Furthermore, it was to his crown judges that the king turned for additional information on the general state of their captaincies on the one hand or closer scrutiny of the conduct of an individual on the other. Inevitably the quality of justice deteriorated because of these many non-judicial demands.

But this was only part of the problem. Although crown judges were forbidden from engaging in commercial transactions or contracting marriages with local women without royal permission, neither constraint prevented them from making lucrative personal connections in their areas of jurisdiction. It was alleged that judges were more concerned about leaving at the end of their customary three years terms as wealthy men than in the administration of impartial justice. This may have been true in some cases, but ignores the many excellent magistrates of the highest integrity who served in the mining areas.

The crown also faced the difficulty of assessing what was a reasonable salary for magistrates in mining areas, and the extent to which they should be permitted *ajudas de custo* or expense allowances. This issue had a direct and negative impact on judges' effectiveness, especially when it came to administering justice away from their places of residence. In 1716 magistrates and other legal officials in Minas Gerais received authorization to set fees three times higher than their counterparts in Rio de Janeiro and the coastal captaincies, where the cost of living was lower. As the cost of living decreased with more extensive planting of crops in Minas Gerais, so accordingly were salaries reduced and in 1718 annual salaries of *ouvidores* were cut from 600$000 to 500$000 reis. Salaries regulated by Dom Lourenço de Almeida in 1721 were so clearly outmoded by 1754 that the king ordered a re-evaluation of salary scales for all judicial officers in the mining areas. The new rates of fees promulgated that year for the mining areas ranged between 50 and 300 per cent more than those for the coastal areas. Although on the whole such salaries remained higher than elsewhere in Brazil, so too were the costs of slaves, horses, living, and transportation. Moreover, in order to fulfil the obligation of making an annual 'visit of correction' (*correição*) to every part of a judicial district, *ouvidores* had to meet heavy expenses not only for transportation but also for replacing clothing and equipment spoilt during several weeks' travel on rough paths through the hinterland. Reluctance to meet such costs, coupled with the physical hardships of such judicial visits, resulted in crown judges' frequent failure to discharge this responsibility.

The crown was compelled to recognize that in the mining areas there was a chronic shortage of skilled lawyers, especially in the early years of settlement, and that governors had totally inadequate manpower at their disposal to enforce the law or bring criminals to justice. The appointment of additional judges known as *juízes de fora* was an administrative rather than a judicial expedient. In response to complaints about the absence of public notaries in rural areas which led to people dying intestate or without wills being witnessed, and to remedy the refusal of law enforcement officers to travel to outlying areas without substantial remuneration, the crown authorized town councils to appoint judges of the twentieth (*juízes da vintena*) in every parish more than one league distant from the nearest seat of municipal government. Such appointees were responsible for drawing up wills, deciding minor civil cases, levying fines, and arresting criminals. They lacked formal legal training and were unsalaried, their sole remuneration being fees derived from their services.

In enforcing laws and preserving the peace governors faced the problem of inadequate forces to patrol vast expanses of largely unmapped territory. There were no garrisons to which governors of Minas Gerais, Goiás, or Mato Grosso could turn in case of need. Unlike the coastal enclaves, such forces were rarely required for military duties. Rather their assignments reflected the social and economic priorities and pressures peculiar to mining areas: enforcing settlement of mining disputes; escorting bullion; curbing evasion of payment of the fifths; stopping illegal traffic in gold and other commodities; suppressing revolts and disturbances; enforcing curfews on slaves, shops, and taverns; arresting criminals; and holding in rein the 'powerful men of the backlands' (*poderosos do sertão*). Most effective were the two companies of professionally trained dragoons which arrived in Minas Gerais from Portugal in 1719. Under officers who had seen service in European and North African campaigns, they were immediately pressed into service to suppress a revolt in Pitanguí. They were to prove invaluable in maintaining law and order in Minas Gerais and were dispatched to Goiás when the need arose. Their example led Viceroy Sabugosa to establish a troop of dragoons in Minas Novas in 1729. Although lacking professional training, militia companies multiplied throughout the mining areas. Convoked in times of emergency and disbanded again, they proved to be valuable arms of the law. Militia companies were established on a regional or parochial basis, largely depending on the population density in a given area, but usually several companies were loosely regimented to form a *terço*. Such *terços* were composed mainly of companies of whites, but annexed to the regiments were companies of free blacks and free mulattos under their own commanders. Each numbering some 60 strong, these companies represented a cross-section of the free coloured population. Companies of free mulattos and half-castes (*pardos e bastardos fôrros*) were the most common in eighteenth-century Minas Gerais, followed by companies of free blacks and mulattos (*prêtos e pardos fôrros*), of free blacks and free mixed-bloods (*prêtos e mestiços fôrros*), and even of Indians and half-castes (*índios e bastardos*). Ethnic composition depended on the region. But official efforts were made, probably for reasons of security, to compose coloured companies of a mixture of blacks, Indians, and mulattos. Finally, reference should be made to the 'bush captain' (*capitão do mato*). Mining areas were characterized by a predominance of slaves and considerable laxity in supervising their activities as speculators. These factors, coupled with geographical isolation and inadequate policing, resulted in a high incidence of runaways. The responsibility for capturing such runaways and attacking smaller *quilombos* (groups of runaway slaves) lay with 'bush captains' – for the most part mulattos – who formed their own troops and worked on a commission basis.

Those factors – distance, accountability, corruption, and avarice – which hindered the effective enforcement of justice in the mining areas, contributed equally to difficulties confronting the Catholic Church in the hinterland, for which the crown had special responsibility because of the *Padroado Real*. As had been the case in conceding royal approval for new legal institutions, so too in the ecclesiastical area was the crown extraordinarily dilatory. The bishop of Rio de Janeiro was responsible for the newly populated areas of Minas Gerais, Mato Grosso, and Goiás as well as São Paulo during the period of their greatest economic and demographic expansion in the first half of the eighteenth century. Only in 1745 were bishoprics established at São Paulo and Mariana and prelacies in Cuiabá and Goiás. This dearth of ecclesiastical authority at the higher levels in the mining areas would in itself have been extremely prejudicial, but the degree of spiritual guidance available in these regions was further diminished by the royal ruling – inspired by fears that friars were traffickers in contraband gold – at the opening of the century forbidding the religious orders and the Society of Jesus from establishing themselves in Minas Gerais.

The religious and social repercussions were the subject of extensive correspondence between governors of Minas Gerais and the king. Governors complained that priests took concubines, worshipped the 'Mineral Church' (*Igreja Mineral*), raised families, engaged in mining, opposed efforts to collect the fifths, sowed dissent among the populace, and extorted outrageous fees for services performed at baptisms, marriages, and funerals as well as levying fees for communion. Little or no effort was made to catechize slaves arriving in Minas Gerais. In view of the great distances, there was little likelihood that wayward clerics would be reprimanded by their superiors. For his part, the bishop of Rio de Janeiro largely neglected complaints made by governors of Minas Gerais and either refused or was reluctant to collaborate with civil authorities in bringing the worst offenders to heel. The Conde de Assumar and his successors suggested numerous reforms including declaring Minas Gerais a mission area, making knowledge of an African language a prerequisite for appointment to a parish in Minas Gerais, and even using the tithes (*dízimos*) for their intended purpose rather than as yet another source of royal revenue. The crown issued decrees intended to curb some of the excesses, for example, that friars and priests without regular employment in the mining areas be expelled. Enactment of this single resolution ran into the practical problems of locating such churchmen, gaining the collaboration of vicars general, who were notoriously reluctant to co-operate with the civil authorities and not infrequently issued notices of excommunication against civil officers trying to perform their duties, as well as separating illegal clerics and friars from those to whom the crown had granted licences to come to the mining areas and collect alms for monasteries and churches in Portugal and the Atlantic islands.

As had been the case with the magistracy, the crown was in the final analysis reluctant to divest itself of any of its revenues, either by building new churches or by appointing more and better qualified priests. The former lack was partly offset by the initiative shown by the faithful who, both individually and corporatively, built and furnished churches in great profusion throughout the mining areas. As to the latter the king took two steps. The first was to terminate the situation whereby a parish priest was totally dependent on his flock for his income. In 1718 Dom João V ordered that parish priests in Minas Gerais be paid 200$000 reis annually from the royal exchequer. This measure, designed to improve the quality of clerics and reduce extortion, failed in practice. Nor did the introduction of permanent, salaried parochial appointments prove more effective. The second was to impose regulations concerning the fees priests could levy. As with judicial fees, these were modified in accordance with prevailing economic conditions. Although these regulations may have curbed some excesses, they were a palliative rather than a solution.

Administrative measures taken by the crown to cope with developments in the mining areas of Brazil in the first half of the eighteenth century also produced conflict and bitterness among the officials who had to implement them. In creating the new captaincies and making appointments, the crown failed to establish boundary lines for the new captaincies, *comarcas*, and different ecclesiastical jurisdictions. The peripheries of many of the newly designated captaincies were unexplored and at the time when the first migrations to Minas Gerais took place there was no qualified mapmaker in the colony. The crown failed to send any trained cartographers from Lisbon despite pleas from governors and viceroys, who were reduced to commissioning army engineers, marine pilots, and Jesuit mathematicians to determine the extent of their captaincies. Because his captaincy bordered on Bahia, Rio de Janeiro, Espírito Santo, Pernambuco, São Paulo, and Goiás the governor of Minas Gerais was constantly involved in disputes of this kind. In 1720, acting on royal orders, the Conde de Assumar had established boundary lines between Minas Gerais, Bahia, and Pernambuco. This resulted in a decade of challenges from the viceroy concerning the appropriateness of the bar of the Rio das Velhas as a point of division. The issue was critical because it would decide whether ecclesiastical appointments should be made by the archbishop of Bahia or the bishop of Rio de Janeiro, whether tithes and the fifths should be collected by appointees of the viceroy or the governor, and whether the crown judge of Rio das Velhas would have jurisdiction over that region. The dispute was finally resolved in favour of Minas Gerais. With the development of Minas Novas the question as to whether or not the area was in Bahia or Minas Gerais also produced conflict. According to the division made by Assumar, they were in Bahia, but his successor Dom Lourenço de Almeida challenged this. In 1729 the king ruled that Araçuahi and Fanado fell in Bahian territory, but that the crown judge of Serro do Frio (Minas Gerais) would have jurisdiction there. This did not end the matter. With the creation of the Comarca da Bahia da Parte do Sul, the king ruled that Araçuahi and Fanado would form part of the new judicial district, but in 1757 – faced with the fact that Fanado, although rich in diamonds, lay beyond the *Distrito Diamantino* – the king reversed his decision and ordered that Araçuahi and Fanado should henceforth be part of Minas Gerais. No aspect of colonial life in the new captaincies was untouched by the irritants of ill-defined boundaries and changes of the royal mind. The results were heated debates over a variety of issues such as the placing of registers, ecclesiastical appointments, collection of the tithes, contracts on road and river passages, creation of militia companies, the administration of justice, and the varying forms of imposing the royal fifth on the extraction of precious metals and stones.

Another problem the crown failed adequately to face up to was the impact on existing chains of command of newly created bureaucratic entities and the need for areas of jurisdiction to be clearly defined. Viceroy Sabugosa repeatedly complained that governors of Minas Gerais failed to keep him informed of events in the mining areas and did not accord him due respect. Dom João V ruled in favour of his viceroy, but this did not alter the fact that the transfer of the economic epicentre of the colony from the north-east to the highlands had been accompanied by a change in the traditional chain of command between king, the Overseas Council, viceroy, and governor. Greater distances and difficulties in communication between mining areas and even Brazilian coastal cities meant that by the time instructions were requested through normal channels, they might well no longer be applicable. Governors in the mining areas lived in highly volatile communities, where 'but a single spark could ignite a bonfire'. Such a spark could be an unpopular decision on the collection of the fifths, a slave uprising, a shortage of foodstuffs, or heavy-handed action by an over-zealous or arrogant crown judge. In the event of civil disorder, speedy decisions were essential. If time permitted or the matter was highly sensitive, governors bypassed the viceroy and the Overseas Council and wrote directly to the secretary of state in Lisbon, who had the royal ear. Should events break so fast that communication was impracticable, the governor, as the man on the spot, had to take a unilateral decision or attempt to reach a negotiated settlement in consultation with elected representatives of the people. Inevitably such decisions did not always meet with crown approval, and governors were accustomed to having their decisions overturned or being objects of royal anger. Nevertheless, there had been a fundamental change in the traditional method of decision-making in Portuguese America.

A governor's task was made more difficult in the mining areas because his areas of jurisdiction were ill defined. If the assertions of the Conde de Assumar were correct, he had apparently not been given any *regimento* establishing his own special responsibilities and setting guidelines for his relations with other organs of government. On at least one occasion his own views were overruled by crown judges whom he had convoked to implement crown policy. His relations with the mining bureaucracy were also ill defined. Although responsible for the stability of the mining areas, once Assumar started to appoint *guarda-móres* in isolated areas, he was immediately accused of abusing his powers. In dealing with renegade clerics and friars, governors were charged with usurping the jurisdiction of the ecclesiastical authorities. As if such conflicts of jurisdiction were not enough, the governor had to contend with a plethora of privileged groups, each jealously clinging to its own prerogatives. One such group were the minters; the *provedor* of the mint insisted that he was exempt from the governor's authority. Such conflicts of jurisdiction were not limited to the governor, but were shared by fiscal, judicial, and ecclesiastical officials especially in the early years of the establishment of royal government in Minas Gerais, Mato Grosso, and Goiás.

SOCIETY

The most evident characteristic of the emerging society of Minas Gerais, Mato Grosso, and Goiás was its 'instant' quality. In 1695 the population of the highland region of Brazil comprised assorted groups of bandeirantes, occasional cattle ranchers, a handful of missionaries, some speculators, and the Indians. Within less than two decades complete townships had been established and the bureaucratic machinery of government had begun to function. In human terms (and those figures which are available are as scarce as they are selective) in Minas Gerais the number of black slaves alone increased from zero to about 30,000 in the same period. The pattern was repeated elsewhere. By 1726 the population of Cuiabá was 7,000. Within three years of the first strikes in Minas Novas, the estimated population was 40,000, including whites and enormous numbers of black slaves. Within four years of being accorded municipal status, Bom Sucesso in Araçuahi had a permanent population of 1,000.

Inevitably, in the earlier years in Minas Gerais – and with each move to a major discovery or a minor strike in Mato Grosso or Goiás the process was to be repeated – there were popular 'revolts' against crown control. On the one side was the crown, following an essentially exploitative policy under the increasingly absolutist aspirations of João V, whose reign (1706–50) coincided with the development of the mining areas. On the other side were the settlers, notoriously independent, whose livelihood was at best unpredictable, and who felt bureaucratic and fiscal pressures increasing to the point of threatening their existence. The combination was explosive. Widespread evasion of authority took the forms of avoiding payment of the fifth, tithes, and other taxes, working new discoveries without reporting them, mining in forbidden areas, failing to license shops or taverns, and transporting slaves and other commodities through the mining areas without registration. Outright resistance was invariably due to changes in the method of collecting the fifth. By 1721 there had already been three revolts in Pitanguí. There were numerous reports of disturbances in the townships and outlying areas of the judicial district of Rio das Velhas, a region notorious for its population's resistance to any official measure. In the 1730s there were to be further disturbances in the sertão. All too frequently such revolts owed less to popular unrest than to the presence of *poderosos do sertão*, such as Manuel Nunes Viana or Manuel Rodrigues Soares, defending their authority and their profits.

By far the most serious popular uprising anywhere in Minas Gerais, Mato Grosso, and Goiás during the first half of the eighteenth century occurred in Vila Rica late on the night of 28 June 1720. It was directed against the local crown judge and new regulations (February 1719) for the collection of the fifths. Governor Assumar had little difficulty in restoring calm, with the help of the loyal populace of Vila do Carmo. He and his successors exploited the guilt of Vila Rica to induce the town council to contribute to the cost of building barracks, a mint, and a governor's residence by way of atonement. Furthermore, the lesson of evident differences between townships of Minas Gerais was not lost on governors, who adopted a policy of 'divide and rule' in their discussions with representatives of town councils and on the whole were successful in enacting royal policy.

The nature of settlement also made the mining region unusually susceptible to conflict between rival groups. The most famous is the so-called 'War of the Emboabas' in Minas Gerais in 1708–9. Briefly put, this was a series of clashes between Paulistas, who had made the discoveries, and Emboabas, or outsiders who flooded into the mining areas to profit from the strikes. A series of skirmishes in late 1708 in Rio das Velhas spread to the central mining area of Minas Gerais in the following year. The results were little, if any, loss of life, and a victory for the Emboabas. The Paulistas' hatred was not appeased by their (justified) impression that the authorities favoured the Emboaba cause. The *Guerra dos Emboabas* and later serious clashes between the two factions in Goiás in 1736 epitomized the divisions within the population of the mining areas. On the one hand were the Paulistas, of mixed blood with a strong Indian element, bilingual in Portuguese and Tupí-Guaraní, nomadic, consummate backwoodsmen, successful gold discoverers, with a well developed entrepreneurial streak, and distrustful of authority. On the other were the Emboabas – the term designated anybody not a Paulista – unversed in mining, with little interest in exploration, static, Portuguese-speaking, with no knowledge of the flora and fauna of Brazil, inexperienced once away from urban centres, and heavily dependent on others for their skills as well as for survival. Successive governors of Minas Gerais in the first half of the eighteenth century tried to integrate both factions by ensuring equal Paulista and Emboaba representation on town councils in newly developing areas such as Pitanguí.

The very nature of gold mining constituted a further threat to stability. Mining demanded speculation and speculation demanded mobility. The result was a constant ebb and flow of prospectors to new or highly touted discoveries. So sudden were these movements that there was no time to provide any infrastructure. Food shortages were a chronic problem. By 1726 the populace in Minas Gerais was so great that its fledgling cattle industry could not meet the demand. From the peripheral regions came a constant litany of complaint that people were kept away from promising discoveries by food shortages, droughts, floods, and sickness. Even where foodstuffs were available, miners' returns from panning the alluvial deposits were not always enough to permit them to buy much-needed supplies. This happened in Minas Novas in 1729: travellers bringing in food for sale did so at a financial loss because not enough gold was being extracted to permit the miners to pay for the goods. More frequently than has been appreciated, miners felt that the odds against success were too long. They sold their mining equipment and began to migrate back to the coastal regions.

Even for successful miners, the nature of gold mining exerted the kind of pressure unknown to the sugar planters of the north-east, for gold deposits were a wasting asset. Furthermore, higher immediate returns were more likely to be achieved with greater investment in machinery and labour. But higher fixed costs forced miners to keep producing if they wanted any profits. Even if these conditions were met, income was less certain for the miner than for the planter. Drought or flooding could halt mining operations. Collapse of a shaft or discovery of an unexpected rock face could mean loss of investment in time, labour, and machinery. Nor was there any guarantee that a given area actually held rich enough gold deposits to justify mining it. All these factors were characteristic of the mining areas of colonial Brazil. Risk notwithstanding, the lure of high profits resulted in a common tendency to over-invest and over-extend financial resources. The effective working of mines demanded a higher ratio of skilled to unskilled labour than was needed on a plantation. Slave carpenters, masons, or smiths were as expensive as they were essential to the miner seeking high yields from more sophisticated mining operations. The purchasing medium was the product – gold. Unlike the planter, who could in part offset higher costs by demanding more for his product, the miner was powerless to alter the price of gold: the selling price was set by the crown. The universal practice was to buy slaves and other commodities on credit. This could extend over three or four years at monthly interest rates of as much as 10 per cent. Collateral took the form of gold dust. Even successful miners lived in debt to Rio de Janeiro merchants for the purchase of slaves. In view of all these risks, failure was commonplace and could only contribute to the uncertainty and instability of mining communities.

The threat to stability did not reside solely in unrealized hopes of new finds, physical calamities, improvident provisioning, and acts of God. All too often the crown exacerbated an already insecure situation by policies whose intended objective was to increase royal revenues but whose unforeseen impact was the disruption of communities and individuals. One set of such measures placed restrictions on certain sections of the population that were held to constitute a potential threat to effective fiscal control or to security. Two examples will illustrate the impact of such measures on stable, settled families. Inevitably, because of their trade, goldsmiths fell under suspicion whenever there was discussion of contraband. In 1730 the king ordered the viceroy to forbid any goldsmith or foundryman to enter Minas Gerais, and announced that those already there should be expelled. This draconian order was enforced in Jacobina, Rio das Contas, Itocambiras, and Minas Novas; but when its enforcement was ordered in Minas Gerais the governor pointed out to the king that this would uproot not only goldsmiths who were currently plying their trade but also those who had ceased to practise and had families. A second ruling permitted those no longer practising to stay, provided that they signed an affidavit confirming renunciation of their trade. Others, regardless of family and home, had to sell up and leave the mining areas. The second example comes from Serro do Frio in northern Minas Gerais, which embraced the Diamond District. Suspicious of the presence there of free blacks and free mulattos, and in part to impress on the people that all mineral-bearing areas were crown property, in January 1732 the governor of Minas Gerais ordered the expulsion of all free blacks and mulattos from the *comarca* of Serro do Frio, famous not only for its diamond but also for its gold deposits. All pleas were rejected, as were testimonials by the town council as to the stability of the free blacks and mulattos and their valuable contributions to the tax base of the community. In September 1732 the Conde das Galvêas replaced Dom Lourenço de Almeida as governor and free blacks and free mulattos were permitted to stay.

Unrest and insecurity in the mining areas were increased by the crown's policy of revenue collecting. Virtually from the outset, the king realized that the thrust to the west, the dislocation of large numbers of people, their need for basic supplies, and their possession of gold, could be turned to the royal advantage in two ways. One was by restricting access to the mining areas and by controlling all entry points through which goods might be imported to the mining regions. No less than other colonists, inhabitants of the mining areas were affected by the crown monopoly of certain sectors of the import economy, such as salt, wine, and olive oil; but miners had to bear the additional burden of paying dues on imports into the mining areas. The crown followed a policy of tax-farming, and contracts usually for three years were auctioned off to the highest bidder. The contractor was at libery to establish registers on major routes to the mining areas. In addition to registers on land routes, similar contracts were auctioned off on river passages. To cover the costs of such contracts, fees were high and were sometimes collected ruthlessly. Tariffs were calculated on weight or volume rather than value, which bore particularly heavily on miners because, as a result of crown prohibition on manufacturing in the colony, tools, pickaxes, iron, and gunpowder all had to be imported. These fees had a dramatic inflationary impact on all sectors of the import economy, but nowhere more than on slaves – the *sine qua non* of mining. Taxes on slaves, gratuities to officials, fees – usually two *oitavas* of gold (1 *oitava* = 3.6 g) – payable at registers, and actual transportation costs, raised prices in the mining areas for slaves by as much as 200 per cent over the coastal costs. By 1735 the price of a male slave had soared to 400$000 reis in Minas Gerais and special skills could force the price even higher. Although in the long run such high prices reflected the miners' ability to pay, in the short term they spelt ruin for many.

Secondly, people in the mining areas had to pay all the usual taxes of tithes, etc., but were expected in addition to make extraordinary contributions to the building of barracks, a governor's residence, salaries for officials of the mint, wages for the dragoons, the rebuilding of Lisbon after the earthquake of 1755, the building of the royal palace at Mafra, dowries for royal marriages, and a so-called 'literary subsidy'. It was the responsibility of town councils to impose levies (*fintas*) fairly among the populace. In addition, town councils in mining areas faced higher costs than their coastal counterparts in building roads, bridges, gaols, municipal offices, water conduits, and fountains. The combination of higher costs for labour and materials, coupled with a higher incidence of need for replacements, imposed financial restraints on town councils which they tried to offset by heavy licensing fees for taverns, slaughter-houses, stores, and pedlars. Not only did such fees contribute to the inflationary spiral, but they encouraged active black-marketeering, hoarding of foodstuffs, and manipulation of the supply of foodstuffs to provide windfall profits for producers and middlemen.

The demographic pattern of the mining areas during the first half of the eighteenth century was fundamentally the same as that of the coastal enclaves of the north-east: a white minority in which males predominated; a black majority in which slaves predominated and males outnumbered females; a gradual growth in the number of manumitted slaves; a gradual increase in the number of mulattos. But there was a great difference in the relative numbers of each sector which dramatically affected their relationship and thus was sufficient to create an entirely distinctive society. Because the demographic data are culled primarily from capitation records, there is little information about the white population, but at least for the first half of the eighteenth century gubernatorial correspondence suggests that there was an overwhelming predominance of males, the majority of them unmarried. Few families migrated to the mining areas, especially in the formative period of each mining community when hardships were the greatest. Migration to the mining areas by whites was predominantly by bachelors, or bread-winners who had left wife and family in the security of Portugal or a Brazilian coastal city while they went in search of fortune. Some may have rejoined their families, but the records abound with pleas by daughters and wives for the authorities to trace missing fathers and spouses. Desertion or widowhood were often the lot of those left behind. The resulting dearth of white women of marriageable age was exacerbated by the practice of dispatching a daughter to Portugal rather than have her make a disadvantageous local marriage. In response to complaints by governors of Minas Gerais, the king finally (1732) laid down stringent conditions which had to be met before females could leave the colony. The results of this sexual imbalance among the white population were concubinage and a low marriage rate within the captaincy. Concubinage was a way of life in the mining regions and, although the sexual imbalance among whites was to be redressed somewhat in the course of the eighteenth century, many white males continued to prefer black or mulatto concubines even when white women were available. Recent research has suggested that the incidence of marriage overall in the mining areas was low, not only among white partners but also among blacks, and that 'marriage at the doors of the church' was related to the financial means of the prospective bride and groom.

The black and mulatto population in the mining areas also had distinctive characteristics. Based on evidence from Minas Gerais in the eighteenth century, certain generalizations are permissible. Most evident is the overwhelming black majority. This factor alone, coupled with the further characteristics, peculiar to mining regions, of excessively heavy concentrations of slaves in limited areas and considerable mobility permitted to slave speculators, was enough to keep the authorities in constant fear of a black revolt and constitute a threat to the preservation of law and order. Secondly, in the overall population of African descent males predominated, this again being largely attributable to the special labour needs of mining. This predominance was especially noticeable among slaves. In the course of the eighteenth century, two developments resulted in changing sexual ratios. The first was a dramatic increase in the numbers of manumissions. Whereas in the years 1735–49 *fôrros* accounted for less than 1.4 per cent of the population of African descent, by 1786 they accounted for 41.4 per cent of such persons and 34 per cent of the total population. More mulattos than blacks gained their freedom, and among mulattos females predominated. Secondly, there was an increase in the number of mulattos, both slave and free. These two factors had a startling impact on sexual ratios among people of African descent. By 1786, with the single exception of the category of black slaves (*prêtos*), there was a female majority among persons of African descent, be they slaves, free mulattos, or free blacks. In that year in Minas Gerais free female mulattos comprised the largest segment (22 per cent) of the free population of the captaincy.

ECONOMY

Despite physical hardships and royal fiscal and regulatory policies which placed a burden on every person in the mining communities, the increase of population alone is testimony enough to the very real opportunities which existed in Minas Gerais, Mato Grosso, Goiás, and the other mining regions of Brazil. In the course of half a century the economy of Minas Gerais developed from one based on a single commodity, gold, to one with a much broader base. From an initial function of directly servicing the miners, many commercial enterprises diversified markets and supply networks to embrace the community as a whole. In this way they became less dependent on the ebb and flow of mining fortunes and better able to survive the eventual collapse of the mining industry. The supply of foodstuffs to the mining regions and the growth of a construction industry afford two examples of this process.

The mining areas depended heavily on beef for food. Before the discovery of gold, cattle ranching had developed in the north-east with the cities of the coastal areas as the traditional markets not only for cattle on the hoof but also for jerked beef, the production of which was made possible by the presence of natural salt deposits. This industry received an enormous impetus from the development of Minas Gerais, Mato Grosso, and Goiás and expanded accordingly. In fact, such was the dependence of Minas Gerais on cattle imports that it offered an obvious point of exploitation for the *poderosos do sertão* such as Manuel Nunes Viana, who in the first two decades of the century threatened the stability of central Minas Gerais by his control of cattle moving from the upper São Francisco region around the bar of the Rio das Velhas into the towns of central Minas Gerais. Partly as a reaction to this dependence, cattle ranching developed within the mining regions themselves, although these could never be self-sufficient.

From the beginning of the eighteenth century *sesmarias* were granted by the crown within Minas Gerais, and especially along the routes to the mining areas, to people who wished to raise cattle. The same applied to the raising of pigs, the cultivation of manioc, and small poultry farms, which prospered alongside the mining industry. There were regional variations, and even within Minas Gerais Rio das Velhas was famed for its agriculture and smallholdings. The only restriction concerned the cultivation of sugar, in part because the crown feared that it would divert labour from mining.

The demands of an expanding industry and the needs of a growing population in the mining areas created a ready market for those with skills or trades. Mining areas attracted artisans in the building trades – stonemasons, carpenters, and blacksmiths – whose skills were needed to meet the surge in demand for civil and ecclesiastical building, as well as the requirements of mining enterprises. There were handsome profits for those willing to make modest investments in tile manufacture. Subsidiary industries developed: soap boiling, or the manufacture of pans essential to mining. In some instances these smaller industries conflicted with mining interests. Access to supplies of wood and water was hotly disputed by miners, soapmakers, and manufacturers of lime. Waxmakers, coppersmiths, cutlers, tinsmiths, saddlers, coopers, wood turners, and braziers, all found a ready demand for their skills, as did tailors, hatmakers, and hairdressers.

An interesting aspect of the relationship between economic growth and opportunities for artisans was the development of the decorative arts. Gold was not only a means of payment but also a medium of expression and there were many ways of working the precious metal for secular and religious decoration. Goldsmiths, gilders, and gold-beaters were much in demand. Brotherhoods of laymen and women commissioned painters, plasterers, cabinetmakers, woodcarvers, and sculptors to embellish the exteriors and interiors of the churches built in every parish. Even the fine arts benefited and musicians – instrumentalists, vocalists, and even composers – were sought after for religious services, municipal celebrations, or lavish welcomes for visiting functionaries. A musical tradition was born in Minas Gerais which was largely in the hands of mulatto performers.

Gold had been the reason for the migratory thrust towards the west. The obsessive and exclusive fascination it exerted in their early years brought individual mining settlements, and almost the entire region, to the verge of self-destruction. But the development of alternative outlets for entrepreneurial initiative and the possibility of social and geographical mobility provided the necessary safety valves. In the long run this permitted the waves of opportunist and speculative migrants differing in race, status, and origin to be moulded into a balanced and increasingly stable society. For a short span of time in the eighteenth century, Vila Rica do Ouro Prêto was to be the most dazzling town of the Portuguese overseas empire.

MINING

Gold was the basis of the economy and society of Minas Gerais, Mato Grosso, and Goiás during the first half of the eighteenth century. But there were in fact many types of gold, as surviving place-names – *ouro prêto, ouro podre, ouro branco* – reveal. The three essential criteria for assessing gold were form, colour, and touch. The most highly esteemed forms of gold were flakes and grains, which ideally would be smooth and devoid of roughness or splinters. As to colour, which ranged from bright yellow to black, a slight tendency towards darkness was preferable. The touch could only be determined by assaying and this was performed in mints or smelting houses. The best-quality gold needed little mercury to 'sweeten' it; consequently there was less wastage (*quebra*) in the foundry process. Gold of 23 carats was considered exceptionally good; 21 and 22 were the norm. It was important that there should be a uniform standard of gold from any region, even though it might have been extracted in different mines at different periods. Skilled assayers and technicians could establish the place of origin of gold samples, a skill which was especially valuable in determining whether the sample had originated in a particular area or had been brought there to avoid payment of the fifths. In the 1740s there were persistent reports that gold dust from Paracatú with a low touch was being imported into Minas Novas, renowned for the high touch of its gold. The unfortunate recipient of such gold was doubly defrauded because he himself would have to pay taxes in gold of the higher touch. In Minas Gerais there was a wide range of colour, form, and touch: the gold of Vila Rica, Vila do Carmo, and Sabará reached and could exceed 22 carats, whereas that of Rio das Mortes and Serro was lower and that of Borda do Campo never reached more than nineteen carats. In 1731 a report prepared in the mint of Salvador singled out the mines of Araçuahi and Fanado as giving gold which was superior in form, colour, and touch.

Gold deposits fell into two prime categories: gold found in veins, and gold found in rivers. The most widespread source of gold was placer mines. Prospectors (*faiscadores*) panned watercourses, using a wooden or metal pan (*bateia*). When the pan was oscillated gold particles sank because of their higher density and siliceous material was washed over the shallow sides. The same technique was used in more elaborate workings known as *taboleiros*, when a whole river bed was worked, or in *grupiaras*, which were workings in the banks of rivers or adjacent hillsides. Openings into hillsides were known as *catas*. Quartz and gravel were dug out and carried to the nearest water source to be worked by *bateias*, or else water was brought to the *cata* where the gravel beds could be worked by hydraulic pressure. The resulting sludge passed through a series of sluice boxes, each of which retained gold particles, to a trough where slaves panned the residue. Such enterprises were known as *lavras* and although they offered the highest yield they also demanded high initial investment. Lode or vein mining was rare in Minas Gerais but was the more common method in Jacobina. Regardless of the technique employed, the fact remained that water was critical to success. Too much could be as detrimental as too little.

Throughout the colonial period, mining technology remained rudimentary. Although the king had reportedly sent mining engineers to Brazil in the sixteenth century, requests in the eighteenth century for mining technologists from Hungary or Saxony went unanswered. As a result technical innovation was limited to the development of hydraulic machines to increase the availability of water for mining or to remove water from *catas*. Slaves of West African origin may have been more familiar with mining and metallurgy in general than their white owners and indeed were specifically selected for these skills. A writer at the beginning of the nineteenth century was to comment that the most ignorant miner of Minas Gerais was better informed than the best of Goiás, and the most ignorant miner of Goiás was infinitely more skilled than the best of Mato Grosso. Although in some regions Indian labour may have been used in mining, by and large the labour force was made up of African slaves. Among these, slaves from the Bight of Benin – the so-called 'Costa da Mina' – predominated. Miners' demands stimulated the slave trade to the Costa da Mina to the point that, during the first three decades of the eighteenth century, imports of Minas into Brazil exceeded those of Angolans. Minas were held to be better workers, more resistant to disease, and stronger than their Angolan counterparts. Gold mining made severe physical demands. Panning demanded immersion up to the waist in cold streams while the upper body was exposed to the heat of the sun. Sun poisoning, acute dysentery, pleurisy, pneumonia, intermittent fevers, and malaria were commonplace. Slaves in subterranean galleries were the victims of pulmonary infections resulting from inadequate ventilation, and death caused by fall-ins. Physical deterioration from overwork was rapid and slave mortality high. Estimates as to the useful working life of a slave in mining ranged from seven to twelve years.

Slavery in the mining areas provided points of contrast to plantation slavery. Prime among these was underproductivity. Estimates of the weekly takings (*jornaes*) of slaves varied from region to region. A report from Minas Gerais in 1721 recognized that a *jornal* of $\frac{1}{2}$ dram (*oitava*) was good. It was generally acknowledged that *jornaes* in Goiás were equal to or lower than Minas Gerais. In 1736 *jornaes* of half a *pataca* were reported from Goiás. *Jornaes* of half a *pataca*, twelve *vintéis*, a dram, and even $1\frac{1}{2}$ drams were reported from Rio das Contas in 1736 and there had been one fantastic *jornal* of 6 drams. Writing at a time of decline, in 1780 Teixeira Coelho suggested an average yield per slave of 20 drams in the course of a year. This productivity depended only in part on the slave's diligence and good health. Mining was often halted because of legal disputes, bureaucratic intervention, and seasonal changes. Owners prescient enough to engage in agriculture offset their losses by employing their labour force in the fields. For the owner engaged exclusively in mining the only way of cutting costs lay in a contractual arrangement with a slave which relieved the owner of the burden of providing sustenance by allowing the slave to prospect at will. The only condition was that at the end of the week he would return to his owner with the *jornaes*. Such an arrangement applied only to *faiscadores*; slaves on *lavras* remained under close supervision. This licence had two immediate repercussions. The first was the presence in the mining areas of both male and female slaves over whom there was no direct control and who posed a constant challenge to law and order. The second was that the potential for abuse was self-evident and the mining areas became infested with *quilombos* of runaway slaves. However, for those who remained within the law, there was a very real possibility of acquiring enough gold dust to buy their freedom.

Technical limitations, exhaustion of the most readily available gold deposits, and underproductivity were not the only factors contributing to the failure to realize maximum extractive potential. All too often it was the result of a combination of factors not directly related to the availability of gold. For instance, it was alleged that declining productivity was attributable to lack of incentives for discoverers. Although a discoverer was accorded two mining concessions (*datas*), many felt that the bureaucratic hassle was simply not worth the effort. Repeatedly, governors recommended to the crown that greater incentives be instituted, with the direct object of enticing the Paulistas, who virtually monopolized actual discoveries, to continue their endeavours. Disease and Indian attacks also took their toll, but a powerful disincentive was heavy taxation. The most oppressive tax was that on the fifth part of all gold extracted. Of the variety of forms which were experimented with (and which will be discussed later) most made little or no allowance for the setbacks which beset the industry. The combination of excessive taxation, maladministration, disillusionment, lack of technical knowledge, and the gradual move to agriculture all contributed to the decline in gold production. To these factors should be added the failure of the crown to co-ordinate mining activities. The result was uncontrolled exploitation in a series of regions isolated from one another and for each of which a supporting economy was only built up at the cost of financial and physical hardship. The chronic individualism characteristic of mining meant that too little capital was available in an industry where there was a well-established relationship between capital investment and productivity. For instance, potentially productive regions were not exploited because there was not enough capital to build an aqueduct to bring water to the mining area. By failing to stimulate collaborative efforts until late in the century, the crown contributed to the decline in production.

This failure becomes understandable when seen against overall policy towards the mining area, which was characterized by an obsession with regulatory controls and taxation, especially the fifths. The first *Regimento das terras mineraes* dates from 1603, and this was amplified by a second set of regulations in 1618. Formulated before the major discoveries, these regulations proved inadequate to deal with the new American reality. A more detailed set of mining codes was issued by the governor of Rio de Janeiro in 1700 and approved by the crown in 1702. Taken in conjunction with royal orders of 1703 amplifying some areas and clarifying doubts, these regulations were to constitute the definitive mining code for the colony. A superintendent of mines, possessed of legal and administrative rather than mining skills, was to be appointed. To assist him in more technical matters he could appoint a *guarda-mór*, who could, if distance warranted it, appoint *guarda-menores*. The *guarda-mór* was responsible for the allocation of mining concessions. The discoverer received two *datas*, one as a reward for discovery and a second in his role as a miner. A third *data* was reserved for the crown, but was auctioned off to the highest bidder. All concessions were of 30 square *braças* (1 *braça* = 6 feet). Distribution of the remainder of the discovery was by lots and depended on the number of slaves a miner could put to work, i.e. a miner with twelve slaves received an entire *data* whereas a miner with fewer slaves received proportionately less. There was widespread abuse. One reason was that crown judges could also be superintendents. Thus, on being informed of a discovery, an *ouvidor* could intervene personally to make divisions, ignoring the rights of the discoverer to the first two *datas*, which he usurped for himself. But the major source of abuse was the 1703 ruling that superintendents and *guarda-mores* were themselves permitted to mine, thereby giving rise to conflict of interest. In the 1740s the crown judge of Cuiabá was also the superintendent of mining lands; in lieu of extra salary for the work involved in collecting the fifths, he received a preferential mining concession. In other cases, powerful local figures seized water supplies with impunity. Although all mining disputes should be referred to the *guarda-mór* in the first instance and, depending on the severity, to the *ouvidor* as superintendent, in 1733 the *juiz de fora* of Vila do Carmo tried to usurp this prerogative for himself. Further complaints were that *ouvidores* charged excessively for making visits to the mineral areas and that *guarda-mores* nominated totally unsuitable people as *guarda-menores* in return for financial favours. Although the *guarda-mór* could make recommendations it was the governor's duty to give the final stamp of approval and they were instructed to scrutinize more carefully all such nominations.

THE FIFTHS

If mining legislation remained comparatively unaltered in Portuguese America, the same cannot be said of the diversity of methods used by the crown in its attempts to collect, in the least inefficient manner, the *quintos*, or fifths, the tribute due to the crown of the fifth part of all gold extracted. During the colonial period at least a dozen different forms of collection were tried, only to be rejected or modified after costly experience. These fell into two general categories: collection by a form of capitation tax or collection in foundry houses. Capitation varied, ranging from a levy imposed on each *bateia* in operation to a more general tax imposed not only on slaves regardless of occupation but on shops, stores, taverns, slaughterhouses, and smallholdings for the cultivation of manioc, and even including taxes on those engaged in the mechanical trades and in business. A foundry house for the collection of the fifths had existed in São Paulo in the 1630s or 1640s, but it was in the eighteenth century that foundry houses were established throughout all major mining areas. Miners brought their gold to these buildings, where, after a fifth part had been removed for the crown, the remainder was cast into gold bars, stamped with the royal coat of arms, a sphere, and marked to identify the place of foundry. At various times mints played a similar function, returning a miner's share to him in coin.

Neither method of collecting the fifths met with the full favour of sovereign or subject. The crown claimed – wholly justifiably – that both methods afforded exceptional opportunities for evasion of payment and smuggling of untaxed gold. In the space of 30 years the search for the perfect method led the crown in Minas Gerais to go from a quota based on a form of capitation to a foundry house (1725), to capitation (1735) and back to foundry houses (1751). Evidence of royal frustration was the proposal floated in 1730 and again in 1752 to examine tax farming as an alternative to direct collection by the crown, but this was never adopted. The advantage of foundry houses (from the crown's perspective) was ease and speed of collection, whereas collection by capitation could result in delays of two or three years. As for the colonists, they were as adamant as they were inconsistent in their public opposition to one or the other method. Colonists in Minas Gerais who had openly challenged and physically resisted implementation of the royal law of 11 February 1719 concerning a foundry house, when confronted with a capitation tax, were to recall in the early 1740s the period of the foundry houses as being 'a time of joy'. When Viceroy Sabugosa established a foundry house in Minas Novas in 1730 he encountered no opposition; a decade earlier in Vila Rica this had defeated the best efforts of the Conde de Assumar. The major grievance against the capitation tax was that it failed to take into account the unpredictability of the industry's fortunes, not to mention death, sickness, or flight by slaves. It was also claimed that capitation imposed a heavy burden precisely on those whose potential productivity was highest – the owners of *lavras* who had invested heavily in the hope of higher returns. Miners argued with less justification that they should not have to shoulder the entire tax burden of their respective captaincies, especially when their expenses were the heaviest and the high prices they paid for slaves and essential tools were attributable to middlemen seeking to offset customs dues and other fees. Not surprisingly, this brought the rejoinder from other sectors of the community that legally the fifth was a tax imposed on the extractive industries, and that its imposition hit hard those not directly engaged in mining. Farmers were liable not only for the fifth but also for the tenth on their produce. A particularly sore point was that the clergy and public officials were exempt from the capitation tax on a stipulated number of slaves supposedly used in domestic service but in fact often used in placer mining. All agreed, however, that the method of collection resulted in extortion by over-zealous officials: collections were supposed to be twice a year, but officials advanced the collection date, thereby imposing an additional burden on miners and others. Furthermore, the heavy penalties for failure to pay did not discriminate between those who wilfully failed to register slaves and those who had complied with royal orders but had simply not been able to pay on time. As to the foundry houses, once the psychological hurdle had been overcome, it was generally agreed that this form of taxation at source was more equitable. But miners were wont to complain that in taking gold to the foundry houses they lost income while away from their workings, were exposed to robbery en route, and suffered delays through official harassment and dilatory processing of their gold.

The strength of popular sentiment on the issue of the fifths was shown on several occasions when the royal will was thwarted or implementation of an order delayed. Although in 1711 António de Albuquerque Coelho de Carvalho had with royal approval signed an agreement with the miners of São Paulo for collection on *bateias*, this was rejected two years later by miners of Minas Gerais. Despite royal anger and gubernatorial insistence, for over a decade the miners rejected all royal proposals and agreed only to a quota ranging from 25 to 37 *arrobas* annually. The royal law ordering the establishment of foundry houses was implemented only in 1725, following the revolt in Vila Rica in 1720 and scattered uprisings, especially in the district of Rio das Velhas, where discontent was fanned by powerful landowners. Such uprisings were as local in appeal as they were short-lived, but all opposed any change in the status quo, and claimed that the fiscal system did not allow for fewer discoveries or any decline in mining fortunes. So urgent was the need to return to full mining production that governors invariably pardoned the insurgents.

Indecision or inability to impose the royal will had adverse repercussions not only on the mining industry but on commerce in general. The crown's most serious failure was that it did not develop a single, uniform system. This was partly because the industry changed so rapidly: bureaucratic responses inevitably lagged behind new and unpredictable developments. Furthermore, the different types of mining could make one method of collection more advantageous to the crown than another and governors in different areas, sensitive to royal concern over revenue, authorized the locally more productive tax, unaware of the damage to the overall fiscal structure. In 1726, for example, the foundry house of Vila Rica was in full operation, but in Bahia the form of collection was by *bateias* and in São Paulo no systematic form of collection had been instituted. The result was a flourishing trade in gold exported illegally from Minas Gerais to Bahia, where it was claimed that it had been extracted locally and was thus not liable for taxation because the fifths had already been collected on the *bateias*, and to São Paulo, where it was alleged to have originated in the new discoveries in Cuiabá. The extent of this illicit trade was revealed by the diminished income in the foundry house of Minas Gerais. Similarly, the decision by Dom Lourenço de Almeida in 1730 to reduce the tax in Minas Gerais from 20 per cent to 12 per cent in the hope of stimulating internal productivity had the unforeseen effect of providing the incentive for illegal exporting of gold from Bahia to Minas Gerais, where it was used to buy coin, which was in turn clandestinely taken back to Bahia for the purchase of more gold. The result was a dramatic fall in gold entering foundry houses in Araçuahi and Jacobina because the Bahian miners hoped that the viceroy would issue a similar order. A royal order of 1732 ordered restoration of the 20 per cent tax in Minas Gerais. Bureaucratic inefficiency also played into the hands of smugglers: stoppages in gold smelting forced by exhaustion of supplies of mercury *ipso facto* encouraged people to seek alternative outlets for their gold dust rather than comply with royal orders for its dispatch to the mints of Salvador and Rio de Janeiro, where it would be smelted.

Inconsistency and frequent changes in policy could not fail to have an unsettling effect on commerce generally. Merchants struggled with greater controls on their movements, additional fees, and demands that they maintain strict records of imports, sales, and income. New methods of collecting the fifth were accompanied by additional regulations defining areas in which gold dust could circulate legally as the medium of trade, or where its circulation was forbidden and trade had to be conducted in bars or coin. Changes in the price of gold also had far-reaching repercussions on commerce to and from the mining regions. The periods immediately preceding the establishment of foundry houses were full of uncertainty: creditors harassed debtors to make their payments before the foundry houses came into operation, after which all gold would have to be smelted with the corresponding loss of a fifth. The result was insolvency and flight to the sertão by debtors unable to meet the sudden demands. Crown officials, priests, and merchants took advantage of this atmosphere of uncertainty to increase payments by a fifth, although the original services had been performed or contracts had been signed at a time when capitation was in effect.

The imposition of new systems proved extremely costly to the crown through bureaucratic confusion and because of loss of revenue through delays. Depending on the time and place, the actual task of collecting the fifths was divided between the public and private sectors. Town councils, *provedores* of the fifths, prominent citizens, and militia captains were all authorized to collect the fifths. The fiscal bureaucracy established by the crown to administer the industry participated to varying degrees. Most closely involved were the superintendents of foundry houses or intendants of the capitation; slightly removed were superintendents of royal mints, whose prime purpose was the minting of coin but who were called in to reduce dust to coin; further removed, but also with administrative oversight for some of the foundry houses, were the intendants of gold established in the port cities in 1751, whose direct responsibility was the reduction of contraband. Finally, there were treasury officials, crown judges, and governors and viceroy, who were held responsible in the final analysis not only for the collection of the fifths but for their safe passage to the coastal ports and thence to Lisbon. It was inevitable that conflicts of jurisdiction would reduce even further the effective collection of the fifths. There were two telling incidents in 1751: on one occasion the *provedor* of the royal treasury in Bahia refused to release funds for the purchase of materials for the smelting house at Jacobina; on the other the king had to intervene to decide a dispute as to whether the *provedor* of the mint or the intendant general in Salvador was the senior official (he ruled in favour of the latter).

Delay accompanied every change. Foundry houses had to be built, sometimes of stone (as in Vila Rica) and sometimes of wattle and daub (as in Minas Novas), but always there was a delay after the royal order was issued. Furthermore, all dies and equipment came from Portugal or, later, after the mints were established, from Rio de Janeiro and Salvador, and had to be carried over mountainous terrain often by Indian porters. Breakages, desertion by porters, or bad weather washing out roads and bridges, postponed the opening of foundry houses. All technical personnel – assayers and foundrymen – came from Portugal. When a smelting house was established at Vila Rica, the new *provedor* Eugenio Freire de Andrade, who had been *provedor* of the mint at Salvador, delayed his arrival; meanwhile, the technical staff had nothing to do but collect their salaries. Even when he did arrive, the equipment had not, and the governor employed the *provedor* in drawing up statutes for the royal treasury in the captaincy. Another source of delay was the grace periods during which people were permitted to make the adjustments necessary to comply with the new law, for instance by bringing gold dust to be smelted before the transition to foundry houses. In short, the administrative infrastructure was quite inadequate to cope with the logistic demands of changes in the method of collection. Even afterwards, foundry houses were sometimes brought to a standstill because promised shipments of mercury and other essential items such as printed tickets for the twice-yearly capitation *matrículas* either failed to arrive or arrived in over-generous quantities.

CONTRABAND

The very nature of gold, administrative inadequacies, the terrain, human greed, and the lure of high profits combined to make contraband rampant. Although generally short-lived, false mints and foundry houses existed in the colony. The former dedicated themselves to counterfeiting gold coins, especially the highly valued *dobrões* of 24$000 and 12$000 réis; the latter smelted bars from untaxed gold. These operations could usually count on the presence of a former employee of a royal mint or foundry house and the use of false dies, or dies which the authorities had failed to destroy. On a less organized level was the debasement of gold dust by the introduction of tin or other metals, a skill in which slaves were supposed to have reached a high level of sophistication. Gold dust was artificially coloured to raise its value from eight or ten *tostões* per *oitava* to twelve. Clipping and emptying of coins was common enough to force the crown to order a periodic recall to the mints when owners would be compensated on the basis of the intrinsic value of the coin. All these activities flourished, but the real profits to be made from contraband lay in smuggling gold on which the fifth had not been paid from the mining areas to the port cities. While the royal conviction that friars and lay priests were active in this trade was well grounded, the prime carriers of contraband gold were in fact cattle drovers and traders whose knowledge of back roads, sites of registers, and frequency of patrols made their services highly sought after. In order to evade the 1719 law that no gold should leave Minas Gerais unless it had first been smelted, subterfuges resorted to by individuals included fashioning gold dust, on which the fifths had not been paid, into rough and unpolished domestic utensils, chains and bracelets, or religious objects. It has already been noted that the vagaries in the collection of the fifth contributed to smuggling. In addition, official failure to close the loophole afforded by permitting the circulation of dust and coin concurrently in Minas Gerais meant that in the early 1730s merchants from Rio de Janeiro and Salvador could go to the mining areas, buy all available gold dust with coins minted in Rio de Janeiro and Salvador, and then clandestinely export the dust to the coast, where it could be worked into objects by goldsmiths or simply be sold. The authorities often claimed that miners had safe deposit boxes hidden in the convents of Bahia and Rio de Janeiro. Certainly there is evidence of the ease with which illegal gold could be transported. In his report of 1729 Dom Lourenço de Almeida estimated that over 200 arrobas of gold on which no taxes had been paid were being sold openly on the streets of Rio de Janeiro.

The crown did its best to curb this trade. Customs houses and registers were established on roads and rivers to the mining areas, especially in the Recôncavo of Bahia. Patrols were increased, especially on the Serra da Mantiqueira, and in the 1750s Indian soldiers were used to patrol Rio das Contas and the new road to Montes Altos. With the re-introduction of foundry houses, additional registers were created to cope with the growing population centres in outlying areas. On the judicial front special enquiries (*devassas*) were opened on counterfeiting and the debasement of gold. These measures produced few successes – the discovery of a false mint in Paraopeba in 1731 (after four years of successful clandestine operations) and the public burning in 1732 in Salvador of two counterfeiters. Investigations of this kind were made by local crown judges in the captaincies of the interior and, in the cities of Salvador and Rio de Janeiro, by the chief magistrate and crown judge for criminal affairs and the *juiz do crime*. In 1755 the king ruled that all such enquiries be carried out by the newly established intendant general of gold. Legislation was passed on 8 February 1730 reinforcing the law of 19 March 1720 forbidding the circulation of dust in Minas Gerais, as the presence of a mint there could no longer justify official toleration of those breaking the earlier law. Miners were permitted to have up to 500 *oitavas* in their possession but, with this exception, only coin and bar were to be the media for commerce. A law of 28 January 1735 made the crime of debasing gold punishable by death or exile and confiscation of property. The crown sought to meet the challenge of counterfeiting by a law of 29 November 1732 which ordered that the minting of coins exceeding 6$400 réis should cease; that a uniform die be introduced for all minters, the only variation being in the date and place; and that the collar (often illegally removed) be replaced by a milled edge, as this had proved successful in the minting of silver coins. The responsibilities of mints were extended to include verification of the origin of gold brought to them for making into coin, and in 1734 there was a ruling that mints should collect the fifth on all roughly fashioned gold utensils and chains submitted for coining. Goldsmiths had their purchases of gold placed under closer supervision. In 1752 the Conde de Atouguia received royal support for his proposal that the goldsmiths of the colony's capital be required to follow their profession in specially designated streets.

The second stage in the contraband cycle lay beyond the shores of Brazil, in Portugal, Africa, and northern Europe. Homeward-bound Indiamen put into Salvador or Rio de Janeiro, where officers and crew became carriers of contraband gold. This also applied to crews of vessels leaving Brazilian ports for Portugal, where the gold was distributed illegally. In 1729 it was alleged that officers carrying such gold illegally received a 3 per cent commission and that those of royal warships were preferred because they were less likely to fall prey to pirates. Passengers, soldiers, and sailors hid gold in firearms, barrels of molasses, hollowed-out wooden saints, and in concealed places in ships' hulls. The crown enacted legislation for the inspection of ships before leaving Brazil and on arrival in Lisbon. Laws of 1720 and 1734 required that all remittances of gold should be manifested before leaving Brazil and that payment of 1 per cent be made to the Junta da Companhia Geral do Comércio do Brasil. Captains were ordered to make manifests on board and submit these on arrival in Lisbon. Vessels from Brazil putting into the Tagus were visited by the crown magistrate for criminal affairs and gold and manifests were sent to the mint in Lisbon where the 1 per cent was collected and where the carrier or the consignee received his gold. But these laws were only partially effective, mainly because those on whom they depended – ships' captains and officers – themselves participated in the illegal trade. The crown's creation in 1751 of the intendancies general of gold was meant to control evasion, but the officials failed to live up to royal expectations.

Whereas Rio de Janeiro's contraband trade was directed primarily towards Portugal, that of Salvador was oriented towards West Africa. Despite royal orders that no gold should be exported to West Africa, the telling combination of demand for labour in the mines plus the ability to pay in gold rather than in officially sanctioned third-grade tobacco made this a profitable trade. In the 1720s ships from Bahia carried silver coins in addition to substantial amounts of gold, and it was opined that illegal exports of gold were increasing. In 1721 the viceroy estimated that 500,000 cruzados (1 cruzado = 480 réis) annually left Salvador illegally for the Costa da Mina; the following year unofficial estimates placed the figure at 90 arrobas. After the establishment of the factory at Whydah, intended originally to be a potential control on the trade in contraband gold, the factor regaled the viceroy with reports of Bahian ships arriving laden with gold. Sabugosa's draconian solution – the death penalty for anyone found taking gold from Salvador, Pernambuco, or Paraíba to West Africa – was overruled by the crown. In 1730 the viceroy claimed to have arrested the traffic by other means, but any success was short-lived. In the eyes of the crown the evil was twofold: first, loss of revenue; secondly, Brazilian gold falling into the hands of foreigners, notably the Dutch, who maintained a very lucrative trade with the Portuguese from their stronghold at El Mina. The result was that ships returned to Brazil from West Africa loaded with European merchandise simply because the purchase of the slave cargo alone could not provide an outlet for the large amounts of gold exported from Brazil. Five agencies were responsible for searching ships and it was only in 1756 that the king ordered this to be a major responsibility of the intendant general of gold.

Northern Europe also provided an attractive alternative for contraband. Between 1709 and 1761 the crown issued at least two dozen laws or decrees forbidding Portuguese subjects to trade with foreigners and ruling against the entry into Brazilian ports of foreign vessels except under extraordinary circumstances. Viceroys and governors were charged with implementing these decrees. One exception was for French and Spanish vessels homeward bound from the Río de la Plata, where a certain tolerance was exercised in the light of the viceroy's report of 1714 that their ability to pay in silver for provisions and services made such vessels welcome in Salvador. However, heavy penalties did not deter trade with foreigners, some of whom put into Brazilian ports alleging the need of emergency repairs or claiming to be engaged in whaling activities, while in fact carrying little or no whaling equipment but cotton, cloth, and powder instead. Others cruised off shore in order to make contact with agents who would arrange for light craft to bring out gold to the vessels. The problem facing the authorities was threefold. First, the extent of the Brazilian coastline made the task of patrolling it impossible. Secondly, the variety of ports included the smaller ports of Santa Catarina or Paratí as well as Rio de Janeiro, Salvador, and Pernambuco. In 1718 it was recommended that a fort be established at Paratí to curb the flood of foreign merchandise being unloaded there. Thirdly, such was the intensity of the foreign onslaught that any crown measures could only have been of limited effect. There were reports that companies had been established in London and Liverpool specifically to engage in this clandestine trade. Because foreign goods entering Brazil illegally paid no customs dues their vendors were able to undercut the sales price of identical merchandise from Lisbon. The result was very damaging to Portuguese merchants as well as those merchants who depended for their livelihood on the trade from Rio de Janeiro to Minas Gerais. The ineffectiveness of a century of royal measures was demonstrated in a report of 1799 giving the enormous amounts of gold in dust and bar as well as precious stones arriving in the ports of the United Kingdom.

A BALANCE SHEET

The vagaries and deficiencies in the collection of the fifths is doubly unfortunate. In the absence of production figures, fiscal records are our main source for assessments of gold production in the colony. Whereas the fifths collected in the foundry houses provide an indication as to levels below which production did not fall, during the periods when this tax was based on capitation our estimates have to be based on further calculations of the annual productivity of the slave population involved in mining. Both processes have obvious limitations. For a century and a half scholars from a variety of disciplines and nationalities have proposed wildly varying estimates. The results of the most recent research are contained in table 1, but further research in European and Brazilian archives and greater knowledge of production processes in Mato Grosso, Goiás, and Bahia (especially the latter) will doubtless result in further modifications. It appears that overall gold production in the colony increased almost fivefold within the first two decades of the eighteenth century, and progressively, but at a more leisurely pace, over the period 1720–35. The years 1735–50 witnessed another dramatic increase in productivity, reaching a climax in the mid-century. The second half of the century saw a steady decline. Overall figures conceal significant differences between rates of growth and decline in different mining regions, and even within different areas of the same captaincy. Minas Gerais remained pre-eminent throughout, but maximum levels of production were reached within three decades of the first significant discoveries. All major strikes had been made by 1720. In contrast, Bahia and Mato Grosso enjoyed two cycles of discovery: Jacobina and Cuiabá initially and, later, strikes in Minas Novas and the region around Vila Bela. Furthermore, less intensive exploitation coupled with smaller

Table 1 *Production of Brazilian gold in the eighteenth century (kg)*

	Minas Gerais	Goiás	Mato Grosso	Total
1700–1705	1,470			1,470
1706–1710	4,410			4,410
1711–1715	6,500			6,500
1716–1720	6,500			6,500
1721–1725	7,000		600	7,600
1726–1729	7,500		1,000	8,500
1730–1734	7,500	1,000	500	9,000
1735–1739	10,637	2,000	1,500	14,137
1740–1744	10,047	3,000	1,100	14,147
1745–1749	9,712	4,000	1,100	14,812
1750–1754	8,780	5,880	1,100	15,760
1755–1759	8,016	3,500	1,100	12,616
1760–1764	7,399	2,500	600	10,499
1765–1769	6,659	2,500	600	9,759
1770–1774	6,179	2,000	600	8,779
1775–1779	5,518	2,000	600	8,118
1780–1784	4,884	1,000	400	6,284
1785–1789	3,511	1,000	400	4,911
1790–1794	3,360	750	400	4,510
1795–1799	3,249	750	400	4,399

Source: Virgílio Noya Pinto, *O ouro brasileiro e o comércio anglo-português* (São Paulo, 1979), 114.

populations resulted in a more protracted but less dramatic level of production than in Minas Gerais. In both cases the new discoveries offset the decline of gold production in the areas of initial discovery. In contrast, Goiás was characterized by transformation from rags to riches to rags again in the short span of four decades.

Overall production figures, based as they are on official fiscal records which indicate a decline in the amounts of gold reaching Lisbon only in the 1760s, tend to conceal the harsh reality that, although colonists may have contributed lavishly to the royal exchequer, even during their apparently most productive years mining communities were far from enjoying the benefits of a golden age. In 1730 the provedor of the royal treasury in Salvador lamented the decline of placer mining in the captaincy and two years later the mines of Cuiabá were described as 'offering no more than a shadow of former riches'. In Minas Gerais as early as 1732 ecclesiastical fees were modified in view of 'the wretched circumstances of these peoples because of the dearth of gold being extracted'. By 1741 the town council of Vila Rica referred to 'greatest poverty' occasioned by the absence of further discoveries and the alleged exhaustion of present deposits. Such was the plight of Brazil's richest captaincy that in the 1740s the governor reformed fee structures for a variety of services ranging from baptisms to medicines and even rewards for bush-whacking captains on the grounds that the original statutes had been made 'in another era when there was an abundance of gold'. This was no longer the case. Although miners, no less than sugar planters, were notorious Jeremiahs and such complaints should be taken with a grain of salt, everything indicates that the majority of the population in the mining regions enjoyed only fleetingly the benefits of their own production.

For over half a century the Portuguese crown derived enormous revenues not only from the fifths but from monopoly contracts, tithes, and a full range of duties on every aspect of colonial commerce. In addition, the crown turned to the mining areas in particular when seeking 'voluntary donations' for a variety of undertakings which included dowries for royal weddings, the building of Mafra, or the rebuilding of Lisbon after the earthquake of 1755. The fifths received by the crown represented not only revenues derived as the result of collection in the foundry houses or by capitation, but also included revenue from confiscations and proceeds from the sale of mining concessions. On the deficit side, deductions were made from the fifths for a variety of purposes. These included the twentieth due to the queen by virtue of a royal decree of 1720. The expenses of each intendancy were met from its own revenues; salaries of officials in the foundry houses were paid from revenue derived by these establishments. Gold derived from the first year of capitation in Minas Novas (1 September 1735–6) was directed to the building of an Indiaman for which the timber alone cost 60,000 cruzados. Against the fabulous revenues should be set the no less fantastic costs to the crown of the administration of the mining areas and the collection of the fifths: freight charges for materials for mints and foundry houses; salaries for officials and dragoons, which could exceed by four times those current in Portugal; costs of building mints in Rio de Janeiro (1702), Salvador (1714), and Vila Rica (1724), and foundry houses, of which eight had been authorized by 1755. Despite the contrary advice of governors and viceroys the crown persisted in the construction, maintenance, and overstaffing of these expensive undertakings. In 1721 and again in 1730 the governor of Minas Gerais tried in vain to curb royal enthusiasm for the building of foundry houses in the captaincy on the grounds that they could only be losing propositions and were thus against the royal interest. Both Dom Lourenço de Almeida and his successor as governor of Minas Gerais, the Conde das Galvêas, recommended that the mint of Vila Rica be abolished. In Bahia the building of foundry houses in Jacobina and Rio das Contas meant that the Salvador mint showed a deficit; in the 1730s and 1740s its staff was largely idle from lack of work. Revenue from seigniorage and brassage was inadequate to meet the expenditure on salaries. By 1789, the position of the mint in Salvador was so critical that a loan had to be sought from the royal treasury to meet payroll costs. The costs of collecting the fifths had led the crown to consider tax farming in 1752 but with this exception the Portuguese crown blithely ignored all advice to cut back on unnecessary expenditures. Even when the writing was on the wall the crown continued to follow a policy which oppressed the mining communities instead of stimulating growth and further discovery by the removal of all restrictions. By the time the crown had started slowly to move in this direction it was already too late.

The discovery and exploitation of gold had a major impact not only on the social and economic fortunes of the colony, but on the mother country, the south Atlantic economy, and the relationship of the Luso-Brazilian world with other European nations in the eighteenth century. In social and demographic terms a major impact was the sudden stimulus to migration – of freemen from Portugal and the Atlantic islands and of slaves from West Africa – to the New World, in a manner previously unparalleled in Brazilian history. The transatlantic phase was followed by a second phase which witnessed the dislocation of blacks and whites alike from coastal enclaves to the interior of Brazil. In contrast to the stability and permanence of settlements in agricultural areas on the coast, mining communities were characterized initially by their temporary nature and the fragility of their economic bases. Each area went through the experience of sudden population growth and intensive exploitation. Although the leading mining towns and cities could not rival their coastal counterparts in size, it was mining which stimulated urbanization in Brazil, something which agriculture had failed to do in the preceding two centuries.

The society of the mining areas shared many of the broad characteristics of the littoral regions, but the combination of special demands made on society by mining itself, the nature of settlement, and even the topography exaggerated and distorted them to such a degree as to result in a society which reflected only distantly that of the patriarchal plantation areas of the north-east or even of the port cities of Salvador or Rio de Janeiro. The sudden demographic growth made the mining areas true 'melting pots' for persons of widely divergent national, social, economic, racial, religious, and linguistic backgrounds. Never totally absent from the mining regions were tensions born of social differences, a highly competitive industry, both social and financial opportunism, and the distrust miners had of the crown and its representatives. The potential for social and financial self-advancement – be it represented by increased rates of manumission or the emergence of a comparatively prosperous middle class of miners, artisans, and smallholders in Minas Gerais particularly – was so unlimited and genuinely democratic in the focus of its aspirations as to constitute in itself a threat to stability.

From the crown's perspective the move to the west, the opening of new lands, and the development of extractive industries stretched Portuguese administrative resources to breaking point. Crown policy was characterized overall by restraint, caution, and restriction. The crown resorted to the narrowly legalistic expedient of issuing laws, edicts, and regulatory measures when the situation demanded imagina-tive policy dedicated to stimulating social and economic growth by fostering stability and a programme of incentives. Colonialist policies which had proved effective for the coastal areas and for agriculture were totally unsuited to the mining areas. The result was that large sectors of the population lived beyond the effective control of the crown. Popular challenges to royal authority were symptomatic of a society which was well aware of the fragility of crown authority and tested it to the full in a spirit of evasion, reticent co-operation, or outright revolt. The Portuguese crown may have secured new territories by the move to the west, but they proved an administrative liability.

The discovery of gold came at a time of recession in Brazilian agriculture attributable to the falling off in sugar and tobacco prices. Remittances to Portugal were therefore made in coin with a resulting severe shortage in the colony. Gold precipitated the dislocation of the economic epicentre of the colony from the north-east to the Brazilian highlands and plateau and from agriculture to mining. Thanks largely to the vociferous and repeated complaints by the city council of

Salvador in particular, alleging the disastrous impact on plantation economies of the north-east wrought by higher prices and the shortage of labour, the negative aspects of the impact of mining on agriculture have received undue attention. Certainly, the development of new markets represented a challenge which Salvador and Recife were initially unable to meet, resulting in shortages of foodstuffs and imports. But within a comparatively short space of time tobacco and sugar planters were taking advantage of the new markets for their products offered by the presence of mining communities, increased demand, and higher prices. In this respect the mining areas acted as stimuli not only for the agriculture of Bahia but also of Rio de Janeiro and São Paulo. The cattle industry of Bahia, Piauí, Ceará, Pernambuco, and Maranhão responded to increased demand in Minas Gerais, Goiás, and Mato Grosso by increasing production. Ranchers southwards from Curitiba to São Pedro do Rio Grande supplied cattle to the mining areas, using Paulista intermediaries. Gold therefore created new centres of production and consumption while stimulating the productivity of the more traditional regions of supply.

Higher prices in Minas Gerais had inflationary repercussions throughout the colonial economy, but the more prejudicial aspects were offset to some degree by greater flexibility in commercial transactions afforded by gold as a medium of exchange. Shortages of coin occurred frequently throughout the first half of the eighteenth century, but supplies from the colonial mints opened up new markets, increased competition, and moved certain parts of Brazil away from commodity exchanges and towards a monetary economy. The impact was readily apparent in the dramatic growth of commercial sectors in Salvador and Rio de Janeiro, which responded to increasing demands from Minas Gerais, Goiás, and Mato Grosso by acting as intermediaries for imports from Europe and Africa. The fortunes of merchants in these port cities were tied to the prosperity of gold. When production declined, so too did the demand and the acquisitive power, leading to retrenchment especially for Rio de Janeiro.

For Portugal, news of the discovery of gold came at a time of severe economic recession and balance of payments problems resulting from the Methuen Treaty (1703) with England. While in the short term Portugal was to be saved economically by imports of gold from Brazil, the long-term benefits to the nation's economy were limited because of the failure to develop any systematic agricultural or industrial policy.

The nature of the colonial pact was to be irremediably altered. That the colony had become wealthier than the mother country was self-evident. A universally recognized commodity of exchange – gold – placed Brazil vis à vis Portugal in a position of greater economic autonomy. Miners were in a better position than the Brazilian planters had been to dictate demands rather than being subservient to the Lisbon commercial establishment or to prices set in European markets. The demand came from the irresistible combination of growing population, urbanization, and the enhanced purchasing power of all sectors of the free community, which sought not only cloths and metal utensils, but luxuries such as spices, porcelain, silks, and velvets from Europe and Asia. Increased demand, which had proved so beneficial to the commercial growth of the port cities of Brazil, was no less so for Lisbon. But in the broader perspective the result was to reduce Portugal to the status of an entrepot, on the one hand for imports from England and northern Europe that Brazilians demanded but Portugal herself was unable to supply, and on the other for remittances of Brazilian gold which arrived in the Tagus only to be dispatched to London in payment for these imports. It was the presence of middlemen in this train of supply and demand which made contraband so attractive. As noted above, this could take the form of trade directly from Brazil to England or the illicit trade carried on by packet boats, vessels of the British navy, and merchantmen, whose ubiquitous presence in the Tagus at the time of the arrival of the Brazil fleets was a constant irritant to the Portuguese authorities. Brazilian gold, legal or contraband, stimulated English trade and exports to Portugal increased throughout the first half of the eighteenth century. (Brazilian gold may have laid the foundations for the future industrial revolution in England.) The decline in gold production, decreasing purchasing power, and reduced demand by the colonists were to be reflected in a decline in British exports to Portugal starting in the late 1750s. Truly prophetic had been the observation made in 1716 by the secretary of state in Lisbon to the Marquês de Angeja in Brazil: 'despite the floods of gold arriving from America, never was Portugal so poor because at the time of our greatest fortune the foreigners carry away everything from us'.

   Brazilian gold had less measurable repercussions. In the political arena Dom João V was encouraged to emulate the despotism and the absolutist aspirations of Louis XIV. At no time did the king or his successors feel the need to convoke the Côrtes. Whether truly or falsely,

Dom João V enjoyed the enviable reputation of being the wealthiest sovereign of Europe. While much gold was squandered in both the mother country and the colony, enough remained to finance public works, royal academies and libraries, and social philanthropy. In the private sector remittances were made to Portugal for dependants, heirs, and charity. In Brazil, the increase in the mining areas in the number of brotherhoods of laymen and women devoted to the assistance of the less fortunate was a characteristic of eighteenth-century Minas Gerais. Such brotherhoods cut across differences of race, civil status, and ethnic heritage to include whites, free and slave mulattos, and blacks. Hospitals, foundling homes, and hostels for the destitute were the product of this charitable sentiment. Social philanthropy was paralleled by an increase in the building of convents and churches in the mining areas and in the coastal cities of Brazil. Although Brazil may have siphoned off skilled artisans from Portugal, there is every indication that it was in the mining areas that schools of native talent emerged whose best-known figure is the mulatto sculptor in wood and stone popularly known as Aleijadinho. Indeed, it is the interiors of the churches of Minas Gerais with their painted ceilings, carved pulpits, and altars and chapels laden with gold leaf which are the most enduring and the most visible legacy of the golden age of Brazil.

6

IMPERIAL RE-ORGANIZATION, 1750–1808

Around 1738 the Portuguese ambassador to Paris, Dom Luís da Cunha, wrote that 'in order to preserve Portugal, the king needs the wealth of Brazil more than that of Portugal itself'.[1] Despite the abundance and diversity of its natural resources and manufactures, its large population and its military and naval strength, Portugal could not have survived if it had been reduced to its European territory alone. For two and a half centuries the Portuguese crown and a large part of the population had derived their main income from the commercial exploitation of the resources of their overseas territories. By the middle of the eighteenth century Brazil was by far the most important. A brief survey of the Portuguese empire will show how accurate Luís da Cunha's statement remained at the accession of Dom José I in 1750, and will help to explain the policy adopted with regard to Brazil during the second half of the eighteenth century.

To the east of the Cape of Good Hope, the *Estado da India*, which comprised all the Portuguese possessions from the east coast of Africa to Macao and Timor and which was controlled from Goa on the west coast of India, had been suffering from local rebellions and wars as well as the incursions of other European colonial powers. The Portuguese had long since lost their trading and shipping monopoly in the East and the Portuguese presence there was restricted to a few ports and trading posts. The *Estado da India* was thus weakened territorially – and also economically. It faced severe competition from England, Holland and France in importing goods from the East (spices, silks, cotton

* Translated from the French by Mrs Susan Burke; translation revised by Cynthia Postan; chapter reduced in length and in part reorganized by the Editor.
[1] *Instruções inéditas de D. Luís da Cunha a Marco António de Azevedo Coutinho* (ed. Pedro de Azevedo and António Baião, Academia das Sciencias de Lisboa, Coïmbra, 1930), 218.

goods, porcelain, furniture and diamonds) and it had practically abandoned imports from Mozambique (ivory, slaves, gold) to Indian traders from Surat, with the result that the Portuguese crown had for some time been earning less than it was spending on the maintenance and defence of those conquests which in this part of the world were all that remained from a glorious past.

Various Portuguese settlements along the west coast of Africa had been either repeatedly attacked by foreigners or else the scene of local riots, notably in the Cape Verde islands and in Angola. Brazil had suffered two civil wars (the War of the *Emboabas* in the gold mines of the Rio das Mortes, 1708–9, and the War of the *Mascates* at Recife, 1710–11) and two attacks by the Spanish on the outpost of Colônia do Sacramento at the mouth of the Río de la Plata (1706 and 1736). However, this western part of the empire, especially Angola and Brazil, had made, and was continuing to make, considerable territorial gains.

Moreover, on the economic side, while Angola and the territories in the Gulf of Guinea were treated more and more as reservoirs of slave labour, from Minas Gerais, Mato Grosso and Goiás came gold, and from the Serro do Frio diamonds; from Grão Pará e Maranhão came some coffee and cacao, which were added to Brazil's traditional exports of sugar, tobacco, brazilwood, timber, drugs and spices, whale oil and whalebone. Every year the *frotas* (fleets) of Bahia, Pernambuco, Rio de Janeiro and Maranhão unloaded cargoes of sugar and tobacco at Lisbon, through which all the empire's trade had to pass. Only a very small proportion of this was destined for the market of the metropolis: the rest formed the major part of Portugal's exports, along with wines from Oporto and olive oil, to the great markets of Europe, where they were exchanged for manufactured goods and grain which then returned to Brazil via Lisbon, where only essential supplies for the metropolis and for the rest of the empire were unloaded. Increasing quantities of gold from Brazil also went to centres of foreign trade, especially London, as an official means of balancing the trade deficit, but also as a result of the smuggling and fraud which was common in Brazil, the Río de la Plata and even the port of Lisbon itself. Thanks to its products and its trade, Brazil had thus become, by the middle of the eighteenth century, not only an important element in the wealth of the metropolis but also one of the chief sources of government income. This was accomplished through a complex fiscal system involving taxes on production, consumption, internal circulation, imports and exports in addition to special temporary duties. It is, however, impossible to estimate with any degree of accuracy exactly what proportion of Portugal's total income at mid-century came from Brazil.

During the second half of the eighteenth century and the early years of the nineteenth century – the reigns of Dom José I (1750–77), Dona Maria I (1777–92) and the Prince Regent Dom João (1792–1816) – Portuguese colonial policy was largely in the hands of three remarkable men: Sebastião José de Carvalho e Melo, better known as the Marquis of Pombal (1699–1782), a representative of the lesser nobility who had been envoy extraordinary in London and then Vienna (1738–49) before entering the service of Dom José I as Secretary of State for Foreign Affairs and War and later Secretary for Internal Affairs and President of the *Erário Régio* – in effect a prime minister in charge of the most important affairs of the empire from 1750 to 1777; Martinho de Mello e Castro (1716–95), son of a governor of Mozambique and grandson of the Count of Galveas, viceroy of Brazil, who was Portuguese envoy at The Hague and London (1751–70) and then Secretary of State for the Navy and the Overseas Territories (1770–95); Dom Rodrigo de Souza Coutinho (1755–1812), son of a governor of Angola and ambassador to Madrid, who was Portuguese envoy at Turin (1778–96) and then Secretary of State for the Navy and the Overseas Territories (1796–1801), president of the *Erário Régio*, the Royal Treasury (1801–3) and, finally, Secretary of State for War and Foreign Affairs (1808–12). All three were *estrangeirados*, that is to say, men who had acquired great experience in the more advanced courts of Europe, and who were fired with a burning desire to pass on to their country the benefits of their experiences abroad in order to raise it to the level of those nations which were currently the most intellectually and economically developed. All three were of noble birth, though coming from different strata of the aristocracy; they all belonged to families with past or present connections with the colonial administration; they had all received a legal training at the University of Coimbra; and their policies were based on a firm belief in the absolute power of the king, supported by an 'enlightened' government. As far as colonial policy was concerned their aims were identical: they believed that Brazil was vitally important to the very survival of the metropolis, and so they wanted to extend its territory as far as possible, to strengthen its administrative, judicial and military structures by reinforcing the absolute power of the monarchy, and to ensure that the Brazilian economy developed strictly within the framework of the colonial pact, in other words, to the exclusive benefit of the metropolis. Their intention was to preserve the internal unity of the enormous territory of Brazil and, above all, the unity of the empire as a whole, which was achieved, with the establishment of the Portuguese court at Rio de Janeiro in 1808.

TERRITORIAL CHANGES IN BRAZIL

The last great act of Dom João V's reign had been the Treaty of Madrid (1750) which, superseding all previous treaties from Tordesillas in 1494 to Utrecht in 1713, had attempted to delimit the frontiers of Spanish and Portuguese possessions in America, Africa and Asia on the basis of actual occupation. There was one exception: Portugal renounced all claim to Colônia do Sacramento, while in exchange Spain ceded an area on the east bank of the Uruguay river occupied by Jesuits and Indians grouped into *aldeias* – the so-called Territory of the Seven Missions – which Spain undertook to evacuate as soon as possible. Although agreement on frontiers had to be reached, the exchange of territories was openly criticized by many, in both Madrid and Lisbon as well as in South America. Pombal – Dom José I's Secretary of State for War and Foreign Affairs – had to implement a treaty that he had neither negotiated nor approved. He doubted whether the Territory of the Seven Missions would actually be ceded and he resolved not to hand over Colônia until the Seven Missions had been completely evacuated. In return, the Spanish had strong grounds for suspecting that the Portuguese would not in fact give up their claim to Colônia, a centre for silver smuggling and strategically important for control of the Río de la Plata. The negotiations over the implementation of the treaty, therefore, took place in an atmosphere of mutual distrust, and so did the work of two mixed commissions of engineers, mathematicians, cosmographers, cartographers and other experts which were supposed to conduct a geographical survey of the interior of Brazil to mark the frontiers. In fact, the northern commission never got off the ground. And the southern commission experienced endless delays and disputes. Meanwhile, in the Territory of the Seven Missions the Spanish Jesuits and the Guaraní Indians refused to obey the order to evacuate and in 1754 openly rebelled against His Catholic Majesty's troops. The War of the Guaranís ended in 1756 with the crushing of organized resistance, though peace did not come to the region. Mutual suspicion deepened,

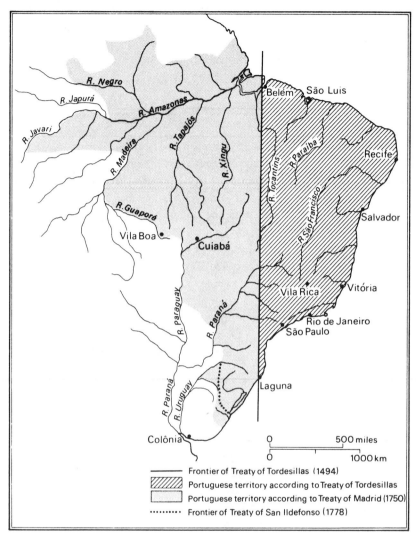

R. Negro

R. Japurá

R. Javari

R. Amazonas

R. Madeira

R. Tapajós

R. Xingu

R. Guaporé

Vila Boa

Cuiabá

R. Paraguay

R. Paraná

R. Tocantins

R. Paraíba

R. São Francisco

Belém   São Luis

Recife

Salvador

Vila Rica   Vitória

Rio de Janeiro
São Paulo

Laguna

R. Paraná

R. Uruguay

Colônia

0   500 miles
0   1000 km

——— Frontier of Treaty of Tordesillas (1494)
////   Portuguese territory according to Treaty of Tordesillas
        Portuguese territory according to Treaty of Madrid (1750)
·······   Frontier of Treaty of San Ildefonso (1778)

Brazil before and after the Treaty of Madrid, 1750

the discussions became increasingly hostile and it was clear that the
Treaty of Madrid was unenforceable. On 12 February 1761, in a treaty
signed at the Pardo, it was nullified.

Territorial disputes between Portugal and Spain continued for a
further sixteen years before a new compromise was reached. The Treaty
of San Ildefonso (1 October 1777) was less favourable to Portugal than

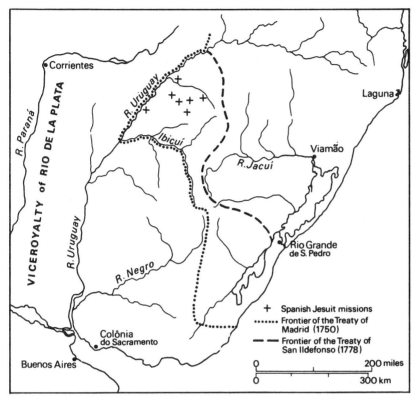

The territories exchanged: the Seven Missions and Colônia do Sacramento

the previous two treaties, since her only advantage was to retain her sovereignty over the Rio Grande de São Pedro and the island of Santa Catarina, losing Colônia do Sacramento as well as the Seven Missions territory. The treaty was followed by further attempts at fixing the frontiers, both north and south, but progress was slow because both governments still secretly hoped to expand. The news that Portugal had been invaded by Spain in 1801 led to another flare-up of war in southern South America between their Catholic and Most Faithful Majesties, when the Spaniards tried unsuccessfully to establish themselves to the south of the Mato Grosso and the Portuguese invaded the Territory of the Seven Missions, making a successful conquest which the silence of the Treaty of Badajoz (1801) later confirmed.

While military operations continued in the southern part of Brazil throughout the whole of Dom José I's reign, Pombal, following the policy initiated by his predecessor, Marco António de Azevedo Coutinho, exploited Portugal's advantages in the key areas of the north and west, vast regions not yet fully explored: the Estado do Maranhão, bordering the French, Dutch and Spanish colonies to the north of the Amazon, and the captaincy of Mato Grosso, created in 1748 and considered to be 'the key and the rampart' of the interior of Brazil on the Peruvian side.[2] Before the Portuguese-Spanish mixed commissions began work on the frontiers it was clearly necessary to collect as much geographic information as possible, to encourage new discoveries, even to take possession of territories which had not yet been occupied by the other powers – in other words, the sovereignty of the Portuguese crown had to be asserted over as large an area as possible. To do so, the Portuguese strengthened their defences by adding to the network of fortresses along the Amazon river and its main tributaries and by encouraging the occupation of areas which were still deserted or where the population had been decimated by epidemics. This was done mainly by installing Portuguese settlers from areas with a surplus of labour – the famous *casais* of the Azores and Madeira. They were given material assistance and were expected to work without the help of slave labour. In this way the fortresses of Gurupá, Macapá, São José de Rio Negro, São Joaquim, São Gabriel, São José de Marabitanas, Tabatinga, Braganza and Principe da Beira were restored or created, as well as the new capital of Mato Grosso, Vila Bela, on the east bank of the Guaporé river.

However, these relatively simple measures did not provide an adequate solution to the problem of how to colonize such vast regions. This was particularly true in the Amazon basin where a small population of Portuguese extraction, mostly poor, lived amongst a large Indian population, part of which was still at liberty outside the influence of the colonizing power while the rest led a miserable existence either in the aldeias of the Jesuits and other missionaries or in slavery – in defiance of the law – in the service of individual settlers. Pombal, helped

---

[2] See the royal instructions given in 1749 to the governor of Mato Grosso, and in 1751 to the governor of the Estado do Grão Pará e Maranhão, in Marcos Carneiro de Mendonça, *A Amazônia na era pombalina*, 3 vols. (Instituto Histórico e Geográfico Brasileiro, Rio de Janeiro, 1963), I, 15–24 and 26–38.

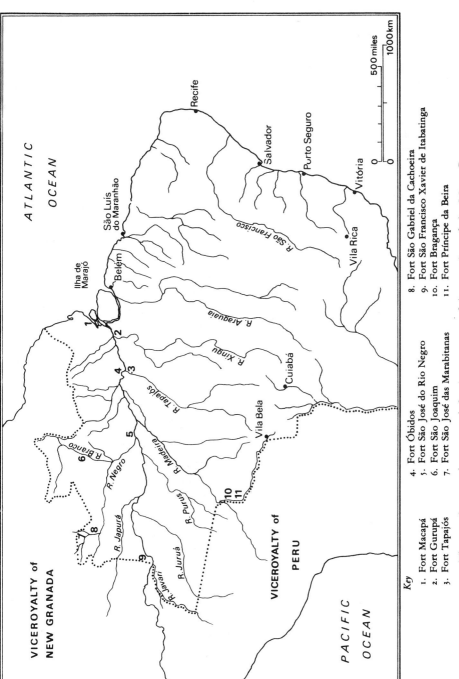

VICEROYALTY of
NEW GRANADA

ATLANTIC
OCEAN

Ilha de
Marajó

São Luis
do Maranhão

Belém

Recife

Salvador

Porto Seguro

Vitória

R. Araguaia

R. Xingu

R. Tapajós

R. São Francisco

Vila Rica

Cuiabá

Vila Bela

R. Madeira

R. Negro

R. Branco

R. Japurá

R. Purus

R. Juruá

R. Javari

VICEROYALTY of
PERU

PACIFIC
OCEAN

500 miles

1000 km

Key

1. Fort Macapá
2. Fort Gurupá
3. Fort Tapajós

4. Fort Óbidos
5. Fort São José do Rio Negro
6. Fort São Joaquim
7. Fort São José das Marabitanas

8. Fort São Gabriel da Cachoeira
9. Fort São Francisco Xavier de Itabatinga
10. Fort Bragança
11. Fort Príncipe da Beira

The northern and western defensive systems of Amazonia and the Mato Grosso

by his half-brother, Francisco Xavier de Mendonça Furtado, governor
and captain-general of the Estado do Grão Pará e Maranhão, drew up a
set of measures concerning the Indians. According to Pombal, 'the only
way to dominate a barbarous nation is to civilize it and establish a bond
between conquered and conquerors, who will live in society under the
same laws, as one people without any distinctions; if we conduct
ourselves there (in Brazil) in relation to these wretched Indians as the
Romans conducted themselves here (in Portugal), in no time at all in
Pará there will be as many Portuguese as there are at present natives
living in the forests – just as we ourselves have lived at certain periods'.[3]
Mendonça Furtado himself wished to introduce *casais* from the Azores
into the villages of Xingú and Tapajós Indians in order to encourage
active relations between the two groups – which was forbidden under
the constitution of the Jesuit missions – and he did not hesitate to
suggest that marriages between white men and Indian girls, far from
being regarded as shameful, should become a source of honour and
privilege, since this was the only way to 'populate this vast Estado and
to make the local people realize that we honour and esteem them, and
most suitable to change into genuine love the hatred that they quite
naturally feel for us as a result of the poor treatment and the scorn we
have meted out to them, and to give us a common purpose. Without
this', he concluded, 'it is not possible for this vast country to survive
and prosper.'[4] The interests of the state are transparently obvious in
these statements, as well as the underlying hostility of the Portuguese
government towards the Jesuits and their mission to convert and
educate the Indians. However, we should not doubt the sincerity of
'enlightened' men anxious to save their brothers from 'the darkness
of barbarism' and to establish a new relationship with them, nor deny
the significance and consistency of the legislation promulgated between
1755 and 1758 intended to give dignity to the Indians, to liberate and
educate them and integrate them into Portuguese society. The aldeias
were converted into parishes (*paróquias*) under the jurisdiction of the
secular clergy. The largest of them were elevated to the status of *vilas*,
with their own local administration and a Portuguese instead of a Tupi
name: over 70 vilas were created in this way, with names like Alenquer,

[3] Pombal to Mendonça Furtado, Lisbon, 15 May 1753, in Carneiro de Mendonça, *A Amazônia
na era pombalina*, I, 390–1.
[4] Mendonça Furtado to Pombal, Pará, 11 October 1753, in Carneiro de Mendonça, *A Amazônia
na era pombalina*, I, 414.

Barcelos, Borba, Chaves, etc., reminiscent of Portuguese provincial towns.

In the southern half of the country there were similar attempts to forestall foreign invaders by means of a settlement programme, though these took different forms. The defences of Río Grande de São Pedro and the island of Santa Catarina were strengthened, and *casais* from the Azores and emigrants from other parts of Brazil were actively encouraged to settle there. In the captaincy of São Paulo Pombal sought to maintain Portuguese sovereignty over the western territories by establishing settlements every ten leagues, by civilizing the Indians and by teaching them to work – in other words, by setting up 'colonies of vilas and aldeias complete with judges, aldermen and municipal authorities (*câmaras*), modelled on those founded by Francisco Xavier de Mendonça Furtado in Pará'.[5]

Finally, Pombal completed the administrative reorganization of Brazil which had been begun during the reign of Dom João V. The aim was to provide a political and administrative structure to serve the geographical and strategic needs arising from the Treaty of Madrid and the new economic realities and problems of communications arising from the continuing exploration and settlement of the interior of Brazil. Essentially, the measures were of two kinds: first, new captaincies were carved out of territories which were too vast and too difficult to administer directly, and secondly, the last remaining small captaincies, nominally in private hands but often abandoned by their donataries, were taken back by the crown.

The vicissitudes of the Estado do Maranhão provide a good example of the kind of reorganization which took place. The Estado was made up of three crown captaincies (Pará, Maranhão and Piauí) and six small private captaincies (Cabo do Norte, Ilha Grande or Marajó, Xingú, Cametá, Caeté and Cumá on the periphery of the Amazon delta) but after 1751 its structure was radically altered when it received the title Estado do Grão Pará e Maranhão. This officially recognized the strategic importance and superior economic strength of Pará. The Estado was split into two 'governments', with a governor and captain-general residing permanently in Belém do Pará, the capital since

---

[5] Pombal to Dom Luís António de Souza, governor of São Paulo, 22 July 1766 (MS of the Arquivo Histórico Ultramarino, Lisbon, *Conselho Ultramino*, Códice 423 (São Paulo), 'Estado Político nº 7').

1737, and a 'deputy' governor living in the old capital, São Luís do Maranhão. Between 1752 and 1754 the six small captaincies were taken away from their donataries and incorporated into the Estado, while in 1755 the western part of the enormous captaincy of Pará was hived off to form a new subordinate captaincy, São José do Rio Negro, like Maranhão's subordinate captaincy of Piauí.

The Estado do Brasil was similarly reorganized, beginning in 1752. The last small private captaincies were taken back from their owners and incorporated into the nearest crown captaincies: Itamaricá into Pernambuco; Itaparica, Paraguaçu, Ilhéus and Porto Seguro into Bahia; Campos dos Goitacazes into Rio de Janeiro and Itanhaém into São Paulo. The captaincy of São Paulo, which was subordinate to that of Rio de Janeiro, was restored to its former status as a captaincy-general (1765). Finally, the seat of government was moved in 1763 from Bahia (where it had been established since 1549) to Rio de Janeiro. This was a logical consequence of the displacement of the economic, political and strategic centres of gravity in the Estado do Brasil, which had been taking place since the end of the seventeenth century, from the north-east (Bahia and Pernambuco) towards the centre (Minas Gerais, São Paulo and Rio de Janeiro) and the south (island of Santa Catarina, Rio Grande de São Pedro and Colônia do Sacramento). Lastly, the Lisbon government's desire to unify all its South American territories outweighed any consideration of the peculiarities of the immense area of the Amazon basin. The Estado do Grão Pará e Maranhão was dissolved in 1774. Its captaincies were then transformed into captaincies-general (Pará and Maranhão) and subordinate captaincies (São José do Rio Negro and Piauí) and integrated into an enlarged Estado do Brasil.

ADMINISTRATIVE REORGANIZATION

The process of simplifying the administrative divisions of Brazil was not accompanied by a parallel simplification of the administrative machinery of government either in the metropolis or in the colony. Nor were any concessions made to local autonomy. Throughout the second half of the eighteenth century, as the economic dependence of the metropolis on its richest colony grew, the administration of the empire became increasingly complex and political authority was further centralized and strengthened.

In Portugal the new government of José I, soon dominated by

Pombal, reacted against the weakening of royal authority during the last years of João V and took various measures which were intended to re-establish respect for the authority of the state and to discourage disputes which hampered the smooth functioning of government as well as to stifle criticism of the king and his ministers. Individuals, factions and institutions who were accused or merely suspected, rightly or wrongly, of criticizing the power of the state were eliminated. The *Mesa do Bem Comun dos Mercadores* (the corporation of Lisbon merchants) which dared to protest against the creation of a trading company for Grão Pará e Maranhão was abolished at a stroke in 1755; aristocratic families were accused of plots against the king and were tortured or imprisoned for life (for example, the trial of the Távoras and the Duke of Aveiro in 1759); other noblemen, higher civil servants, magistrates, priests and clergy who were suspected or accused of either plotting, criticizing, maladministration or corruption were imprisoned or exiled; and the Jesuits who were accused of betraying the principles and basic aims of their mission, accumulating excessive wealth, establishing a state within a state, obstructing the implementation of the Treaty of Madrid, disloyalty, even treason, were expelled in 1759 from Brazil and the whole of the Portuguese empire.[6]

Throughout the reigns of Dom José I, Dona Maria I and the Prince Regent Dom João there was a long campaign, not entirely successful, to strengthen and rationalize the machinery of government affecting Brazil. As early as 1736 the creation of three secretaries of state (Home Affairs; Navy and Overseas Territories; and War and Foreign Affairs) had been a move in this direction, but it was Pombal who was largely responsible for making the system work, and for giving the ministry of the Navy and Overseas Territories effective control over the other metropolitan bodies which shared responsibility for colonial affairs. This higher body, placed under the direct control of the king, nominated the principal officials of the administration in the colonies (the viceroy, the governors of the captaincies, the financial and judicial officials, and the highest ranks in the army and the church). It also supervised general policy and issued orders about the economy and the administration of justice, as well as about the affairs of the missions. However, some specialized matters continued to go through the

---

[6] For further discussion of the expulsion of the Jesuits from Brazil, see ch. 7 below.

traditional channels of existing councils and organizations (such as the *Conselho Ultramarino*, the *Mesa da Consciência e Ordens*, the *Conselho da Fazenda*, the *Junta do Tabaco*). Therefore the intricate web of authority and overlapping functions so characteristic of the old regime did not disappear. It was even compounded by the creation of new administrative bodies set up to resolve the various problems which, in one way or another, arose concerning colonial affairs. The following were amongst the most important of the new bodies. The *Junta do Comércio* (Board of Trade), 1755, had as its original purpose the encouragement and regulation of commerce and everything to do with trade and navigation, including the organization of fleets bound for Brazil and the prevention of smuggling (see below p. 489). This committee was essential to Pombal's policy for the industrial development of the metropolis (see below p. 491). It was a symbol of the close alliance between the great merchants involved in the tobacco monopoly and the central government, and it acquired increasingly wide powers until in 1788 it was elevated to the status of a royal tribunal under the title of *Real Junta do Comércio, Agricultura, Fábricas e Navegações destes Reino e seus Domínios* (Royal Committee for Trade, Agriculture, Factories and Navigation). The Royal Treasury (*Erário Régio*), 1761, had overall control of all the financial transactions of the metropolis and its colonies, and Pombal himself was its first president. It took over all the functions of the ancient *Casa dos Contos*, destroyed in the earthquake of 1 November 1755. The Royal Treasury broke with tradition in two ways: in its centralizing function – important from the political angle – and in the introduction of techniques not yet common in public accounting, such as double-entry book-keeping and the systematic treatment of the various kinds of income and expenditure. The Treasury was divided into four departments (*Contadorias*), each responsible for part of the empire; administration of the finances of Brazil was thus divided between two Contadorias, based on the two major judicial divisions (Bahia and Rio de Janeiro). The Council for Finance (*Conselho da Fazenda*), was reformed in 1761, when the Erário Régio was created. Its function was to deal with disputes over the collection of crown revenues, and it continued to control the *Armazéns da Guiné e India*, its associated shipyards and the *Casa da India*, whose function had been reduced to that of a customs office. In 1790 the Conselho da Fazenda was taken over by the Erário Régio. The jurisdiction of the Ministry of Financial Affairs (*Secretaria de Estado dos Negócios da Fazenda*), 1788, covered all economic aspects of the empire, and the fact that the secretary of state in charge was *de jure* president of the Erário Régio ensured that these two bodies worked closely together. The Council for the Admiralty (*Conselho do Almirantado*), 1795, was responsible for the navy, and hence for organizing convoys for the merchant fleet and a permanent squadron to protect the Brazilian coast.

Within Brazil, following the transfer of the seat of government from Bahia to Rio de Janeiro in 1763, it became customary for the governor-general (viceroy) to receive letters-patent designating him the *Vice-Rei e Capitão General do Mar e Terra do Estado do Brasil.* The holder of this office was given such wide powers that the absolute power of the sovereign, with authority over all the captaincies, appeared to be delegated to him. In practice, his only real authority, as before, was over the captaincy in which he lived – previously Bahia, now Rio de Janeiro. Only the governors of the subordinate captaincies of Rio de Janeiro were under his control: all the governors of captaincies-general were directly dependent on the Ministry for the Navy and Overseas Territories in Lisbon, to which they were answerable and from which they took their orders. Only in an emergency could the viceroy request direct military aid from them.

The municipalities represented an important sector of the Brazilian-born population and were a potential source of conflict with Lisbon. However, the system was now so highly centralized that the Câmaras in the capitals of captaincies were even deprived of one of their essential powers: in the absence of the viceroy or the governor, the town council (*Senado da Câmara*) had originally been responsible for the interim administration of public affairs, but in 1770 Pombal withdrew this prerogative in favour of a provisional government of three members: the bishop or dean; the *Chanceler* of the *Relação* (High Court of Appeal); and the highest-ranking officer in the army – the *Ouvidor* (crown judge) of the Câmara being able to replace the bishop or the *Chanceler* only if either of these were not available.

The creation of the Erário Régio in Lisbon produced an important reform affecting the powers of the *provedores da fazenda*, the principal local financial administrators. From 1767 the finances of each main captaincy were to be administered by a *Junta de Fazenda*, a collegiate body of five or six members, including the *provedor*, with the governor as its president. These juntas, which were independent from one another, were responsible for collecting and distributing royal income and they were accountable only to the inspector-general of the Erário Régio in Lisbon, as the office of *Provedor-mor da Fazenda* was abolished in 1770. The creation of these Juntas da Fazenda was thus the means by which reforms attempted in Portugal were to be extended to Brazil. The provedores also lost some of their powers through the creation of specialized bodies; for example, checking the quality of sugar and tobacco which was taken over in 1751 in Bahia, Recife, Rio de Janeiro and São Luís do Maranhão by *Mesas de Inspecção de Açúcar e Tabaco*, and the management of ammunition stores and shipyards which was handed over to a naval intendant (*Intendente da Marinha e Armazéns Reais*), in Bahia, Rio de Janeiro and Recife. A campaign to raise the standard of administration and to stamp out bribery and extortion should also be mentioned: the rights and duties of the various offices were defined and fixed salaries were introduced, thus putting an end to the traditional system of bonuses paid in cash or kind. However, as local magnates and business men were closely involved with the administration of finance, either because they were tax farmers (*contratadores*), owned certain offices, or else exercised certain functions, such as serving on a Junta da Fazenda, this reform was largely ineffective.

The first of the judicial measures taken by the new government of José I was to establish in 1751 a second *Relação* (High Court) in Rio de Janeiro, with the purpose of giving speedier justice to the people who lived in the south, far away from the Relação in Bahia. It was made up of ten *desembargadores* (high court judges), including the *ouvidor do cível* and the *ouvidor do crime* and was presided over by the governor. The Relação in Rio de Janeiro had jurisdiction over the thirteen districts (*comarcas*) covered by the captaincies of the south and the interior, and like the Relação at Bahia, it possessed both judicial and administrative powers. The attempts to speed up judicial procedures were backed up by the introduction first in Pará and Pernambuco (1758), then throughout Brazil (1765) of committees of justice (*Juntas de justiça*) composed of one or two ouvidores, the *juiz de fora* (district crown judge) and the governor of the captaincy. Pombal also introduced legislation designed to reduce corruption in the judicial system. By fixing the stipends of magistrates and officers of justice in the various comarcas of Brazil, together with those of the magistrates in the Relações of Bahia and Rio de Janeiro (1754), the oppression suffered by plaintiffs and prisoners was alleviated. Another important innovation was that

Roman law was abandoned in favour of natural and international law, and secular magistrates were no longer allowed to base their decisions on canon law. Henceforward 'in the temporal matters within their jurisdiction', they could only follow 'the laws of our country and subsidiary laws, together with praiseworthy customs and legitimately established practices' (*Lei da Boa Razão*, 1769). This modernization of judicial concepts might be compared with other decisions taken during Pombal's ministry, such as the freedom granted to the Indians in Brazil (1755 and 1759), abolition of African slavery in Portugal (1761 and 1773), abolition of discrimination between 'old Christians' and 'new Christians' (1768 and 1773), turning the Inquisition into a tribunal dependent on the government (1769), and even reforming the University of Coimbra (1772). These reforms should be regarded as an attempt to free Portugal from 'obscurantism' and to place her amongst the most 'enlightened' nations of Europe.

The Treaty of Madrid focused attention on the need to defend Brazil's frontiers and led as we have seen to the construction and repair of fortresses in the north and south. Dom José I's government was also concerned with the problems of military organization in general, starting with the recruitment of regular troops in metropolitan Portugal (*tropas de linha, tropas regulares*, or *tropas pagas*). Ever since the beginning of the period of overseas expansion, Portugal had, in fact, adopted the habit of sending to the colonies regiments largely composed of delinquents, vagrants and other elements deemed undesirable at home. These regiments were then made up to strength by the more or less compulsory enlistment of local personnel, often of similar quality. As a result, there were problems arising not only from the lack of discipline within the regiments but from the trouble they frequently caused in the community, which provoked numerous complaints from the governors.

The main efforts to reform the army took place during the 1760s, as a result of serious military defeats which were sustained more or less simultaneously in various parts of the Portuguese empire. During the Seven Years' War, not only did Spanish troops invade north-west Portugal but from Buenos Aires the Spanish seized Colônia do Sacramento (October 1762) and launched a successful attack on the captaincy of Rio Grande de São Pedro (April 1763). These defeats were particularly serious because of the almost total lack of resistance by

Portuguese troops, their lack of discipline and the excessive number of desertions. To remedy this situation, Pombal called on his traditional ally, England, which immediately sent reinforcements to Portugal under the command of one of the most prestigious officers of the time, the Count of Schaumburg-Lippe. It was he, together with the English and German officers who accompanied him, who took in hand the Portuguese troops, who were poorly organized, poorly trained, poorly equipped and poorly paid. His reforms, which only affected Portugal itself, encompassed the whole organization of the army, from recruitment and equipment to tactics. This work was to be rounded off some years later when the reforms in the education system which Pombal had promoted began to bear fruit; in other words, when young Portuguese nobles educated at the Royal College of Nobles at Lisbon (inaugurated in 1766) and then at the University of Coimbra (reformed in 1772) had acquired the intellectual baggage of mathematics, physics and military arts considered indispensable for the training of officers. However, there were never enough trained Portuguese personnel, as we can see from the permanent presence of foreign officers – German, English, French and others – in the Portuguese regiments and squadrons, in the metropolis as well as in the colonies, from the reign of José I to that of João VI.

In Brazil, Pombal was most concerned with the protection of the threatened captaincies of the south and in 1767 he sent to Rio de Janeiro three of the best (and recently reformed) Portuguese regiments, as well as two military specialists, the Austrian general, J. H. Böhm (who had been the adjutant of the Count of Lippe in Portugal and to whom was given the title of inspector general of the troops of Brazil), and the Swedish general, J. Funk (who had come to Portugal from England in 1764), who had the job of reinforcing the fortifications of Rio. General Böhm, who was used to dealing with European troops in European conditions, did not take sufficient account of the social and even the climatic conditions of Brazil and his rigid methods sometimes had dire results which were severely condemned by the Marquis of Lavradio, viceroy of Brazil, under whom he served (1769–79). One of the most serious faults with which he was reproached was that of not having understood the exceptional importance of locally enlisted troops, the only ones capable of solving the Portuguese problem of defending an empire infinitely greater than herself and scattered all over the world. A force of this kind had been planned from the beginning of the first

governor-generalship (*regimento* of Tomé de Souza, 1548), being divided
into two types: first, the permanent militia (*tropas auxiliares* or, from
1796, *milícias*) who were recruited by unpaid conscription and with
officers of the same type who were sometimes instructed by officers of
the Portuguese regiments, and, secondly, reserve troops, known as
ordenanças, who included the rest of the available male population and
whose activity in peace time was restricted to occasional exercises. The
milícias were frequently called upon to defend their territory whereas
the corpos de ordenanças were more important in maintaining order,
by supporting the action of the civil administration. Since their officers
were chosen by the governors of the captaincies from lists drawn up
by the Senados das Câmaras according to social hierarchy criteria, they
did, in fact, reinforce this social hierarchy, based as it was on wealth
and ownership of land.

Throughout the second half of the eighteenth century, the various
ministers in charge of colonial policy urged the governors of the
Brazilian captaincies to reduce the number of exemptions and privileges
which a large section of the male population could invoke to avoid
military service, as well as to organize and train the troops needed to
supplement the Portuguese regiments of the *tropa paga*. In addition, the
captaincies had to be ready to help one another in the event of an attack
from outside, and from 1757 this was one of the essential points in
Pombal's directives. These instructions, which sprang directly from the
effects of the Treaty of Madrid, became incorporated into what, some
years later, was to be called 'the fundamental system which today
governs the political, military and civil administration of the whole of
Portuguese America, adapted to each captaincy of this continent,
according to its situation and circumstances' and which was constantly
evoked through the last decades of the eighteenth century.[7]

REORGANIZATION OF THE ECONOMY

A balance sheet of the Portuguese economy in mid-eighteenth century
reveals the disastrous situation into which, paradoxically, Brazilian gold

---

[7] See, for example, the instructions to the governors of the captaincies of Mato Grosso (13 August
1771), Goiás (1 October 1771), São Paulo (20 November 1772 and 24 January 1775), Minas
Gerais (24 January 1775), quoted by Marcos Carneiro de Mendonça, 'O Pensamento da
metropole portuguesa em relação ao Brasil', *Revista do Instituto Histórico e Geográfico Brasileiro*,
257 (1962), 52–5, as well as instructions to the governor of Minas Gerais (29 January 1788)
(MS of the Biblioteca Nacional, Lisbon, *Coleção Pombalina*, Códice 643, f. 168).

and diamonds had led the empire during the previous 50 years. A prisoner of clauses of the famous Methuen Treaty of 1703, Portugal had gradually relinquished her developing manufactures in favour of a return to viticulture and the export of wine and olive oil. She found herself increasingly dependent on the outside world and, above all, on England, her principal trading partner and major supplier of manufactured goods, and time-honoured guarantor of her political independence. Had they been invested in a more general effort at development, Brazilian gold and diamonds could have stimulated a better exploitation of Portugal's natural resources, agriculture and mining and, even more, the manufactures needed to satisfy the increased demand in Brazil arising from population growth and greater wealth. Instead, they were used for ostentatious expenditure and, above all, as an easy method of financing a steadily worsening deficit in the balance of payments. At the same time, Brazilian gold, clandestine as well as legal, was one of the factors in England's own industrial and commercial growth. Towards the end of Dom João V's reign the easygoing climate and false euphoria of a long period of peace was already beginning to evaporate and signs of a crisis were increasingly apparent, and during the reign of José I the crisis deepened. Lisbon was destroyed by an earthquake and fire on 1 November 1755 and the rebuilding was to prove immensely costly. Two expensive wars with Spain over the southern borderlands of Brazil during the third quarter of the century put a further great strain on Portugal's resources. And at the same time, the crown's income from Brazil declined sharply from the 1750s to the 1770s, largely because of a 50 per cent drop in the yield from gold and diamond mining.[8]

Economic policy under Pombal

Pombal, who had been brought up on the ideas of English mercantilist thinkers of the first half of the eighteenth century and was impressed by the wealth and power of England which he had observed closely for several years, was without doubt the politician of his age who had most understanding of the serious imbalance in the Portuguese economy and of its causes. All Pombal's policies sprang from two main concerns: to increase crown revenue by encouraging trade, especially with Brazil,

---

[8] For gold and diamond mining in eighteenth-century Brazil, see ch. 5 above.

and, at all costs, to reduce the deficit in the overall balance of trade, and hence to reduce Portugal's economic dependence on England. Pombal, a pragmatist, found his weapons in the traditional arsenal of mercantilist ideas and policies, but made them more wide-ranging and effective, adapting them to changes in economic conditions and trends.

Because sugar, tobacco, gold and diamonds, Brazil's main products, played a crucial role in Portugal's overall balance of trade and in crown revenue, Pombal first turned his attention to them when he attempted to stimulate the economy by introducing fiscal measures controlling production, prices and transport costs. With regard to gold, Pombal abandoned the capitation tax which had been in force since 1734 and returned to the system of taking 20 per cent of the gold dust compulsorily smelted in the *Intendências do Ouro* and the *Casas de Fundição* (*alvará* of 3 December 1750 and *regimento* of 4 March 1751). He simultaneously banned the use of gold as currency, as well as its removal from the mining zone. These measures had three aims: they were to spread the tax burden more fairly, to make the repression of smuggling more effective and to increase production to meet the obligation to provide the Royal Treasury with an annual quota (100 arrobas of gold, about 1,400 kg). As for diamonds, so many had been produced that prices had fallen on the European market and, despite severe penalties, diamond smuggling was almost out of control. Since duties were payable to the crown in the form of a capitation tax levied on each slave employed, according to a system (*contrato*) in force since 1739, the administration of the contrato was changed in 1753 in order to maintain prices and stabilize the market. Henceforth, the mining of, and trading in, diamonds were separated into two contratos under the strict control of the crown. The initial success of this new arrangement proved ephemeral and the government actually lost revenue. Therefore, in 1771 Pombal ended the contrato system by setting up a general inspectorate for diamonds. This was dependent solely on the Erário Régio and its function was to administer directly the royal monopoly for the mining and sale of diamonds.

As sugar and tobacco were taxed so heavily that they ceased to be competitive with sugar and tobacco produced in the English, French and Dutch colonies, steps were taken to lighten export duties and reduce freight charges (*regimento da Alfândega do Tabaco* of 16 January 1751 and *decreto* of 27 January 1751). Inspection offices were set up in Bahia, Recife, Rio de Janeiro and São Luís do Maranhão to control the quality and price of these two commodities (the *Mesas de Inspecção do Açúcar e Tabaco*, set up by *alvará* of 1 April 1751). Efforts were also made to develop cultivation of these products in new areas (e.g. tobacco around Rio de Janeiro and sugar in the Amazon basin). Pombal paid special attention to tobacco, a particularly valuable foreign export, as is clear from a later regulation aimed at improving the cultivation, processing and storage of tobacco (alvará of 15 July 1775).

It was obvious that if all these industries were to be stimulated there had to be more slave labour and various attempts were made to channel the slave trade towards Brazil alone: the export of African slaves outside the Portuguese colonies was totally prohibited in 1751, in 1761 slaves sent to Portugal itself were given their liberty, and these two measures were followed, logically, in 1773, by the total abolition of slavery in Portugal.

Finally, the desire to profit from all Brazil's products and to make a stand against smuggling (which had reached vast proportions during the reign of Dom João V) led to a strengthening of the fleet system in which fleets sailing between Portuguese and Brazilian ports left on fixed dates (alvarás of 28 November 1753 and 25 January 1755). The *comissários volantes*, small-scale itinerant merchants trading between Portugal and Brazil, whose activities were hard to control, were banned (alvará of 6 December 1755).

The suppression of the *comissários volantes* fitted in with Pombal's policy of creating a highly structured commercial sector, in which small middlemen were to be deliberately squeezed out to the advantage of owners of large amounts of capital, and monopoly trading companies modelled on those of England (especially the British East India Company), Holland and Spain were to be encouraged. One company had been formed in 1753 to increase trade with China and with the Indian coast. This was the *Companhia de Comércio do Oriente*, whose principal shareholder was Feliciano Velho Oldemberg, one of the most important merchants in Lisbon, and well known as a tobacco farmer and as the man who introduced emigrants from the Azores into Brazil. In 1755 the *Mesa do Bem Comun dos Mercadores* (the corporation of Lisbon merchants) was abolished (decreto of 30 September 1755) (see p. 480) and the *Junta do Comércio* (Board of Trade) set up (decreto of 30 September 1755 and statutes of 12 December 1755) (see p. 481). During the same decade several trading companies – for Brazil, for metropolitan Portugal and for Mozambique – were established.

That Pombal wanted to attract men who disposed of large amounts of capital is clear from the constitution of the great companies. Important social privileges were granted to the shareholders: nobles were offered guarantees that they would not lose their status; commoners – government officials, metropolitan and colonial merchants, colonial landowners – who applied for a certain number of shares were given access to the military orders and opportunities for ennoblement; and foreigners received an assurance that they could participate on the same terms as nationals. The new companies had much wider objectives than previous trading companies. They were to promote shipbuilding as well as navigation and to develop vast areas of Brazil by improving traditional methods of production and by introducing new crops. Pombal also hoped that, through these companies, he would be able to control all economic activity, avoid over-production, fix prices in the light of the international competition on the European markets, guarantee the quality of the products and, finally, achieve a better balance between imports of manufactures and the means to pay for them.

Three monopoly trading companies were created for Brazil: the *Companhia Geral do Comércio do Grão Pará e Maranhão* (1755–78) was set up, (a) as the means by which African slaves could be introduced into the Amazon basin to take over from the local labour force after Indian slavery was abolished (1755–8), (b) to contribute to the agricultural development of a potentially rich region through the purchase and transportation of colonial staples, traditional and new and, later (c), to control and regulate imports of manufactures from metropolitan Portugal, through a monopoly of trade and navigation. Its role was of great importance in the development of the cultivation of rice and cotton, in an increased production of timber and dyestuffs, as well as in the production of meat (cured and salted) and hides. The *Companhia Geral do Comércio de Pernambuco e Paraíba* (1759–79) was closely modelled on that for Grão Pará and Maranhão. It was to help remedy the shortage of agricultural labour by importing large numbers of African slaves and to contribute to a revival in the production and export of sugar. It was also hoped to increase exports of leather, tobacco and new commodities such as cacao. Like the Maranhão company, it was later expected to develop the colonial market for Portuguese manufactures. Finally, the *Companhia de Pesca da Baleia das Costas do Brasil* (1765–1801) took the place of the farmed-out royal monopoly. It increased the quantity and quality of whaling and of the extraction of oil and whalebone, thanks to a heavy investment of capital in slave labour and in equipment (boats and tools) for the new fishing grounds. It also encouraged sperm whale fishing hitherto untried in Brazil.

During the period 1753–65 colonial trade had been considerably reorganized: shipping controlled, capital concentrated, monopolies reinforced. The greater part of the Brazilian colonial trade in the ports of Belém do Pará, São Luís do Maranhão and Pernambuco was henceforward monopolized by the fleets of the companies of Grão Pará and Maranhão, and of Pernambuco and Paraíba. The maintenance of the *frotas* – which in practice now served only Bahia and Rio de Janeiro – was not so important. In any case, more than ten years' experience had once again made clear the inconveniences of this rigid and always controversial system: the failure to establish proper shipping schedules in Portugal and in Brazil, the deterioration of perishable goods like sugar and tobacco as a result of being kept too long, the consequent problem of disposing of them at a profit and the long delays in getting payments, extensive contraband. All efforts by the Junta do Comércio to reform the fleet system failed. So, in 1765, in a move which illustrates Pombal's pragmatism, the frotas were abolished. Licensed vessels were free to sail to and from the ports of Bahia, Rio de Janeiro and all other ports where the companies did not have exclusive rights. The following year the ban on coastal trade between the Brazilian ports was also lifted.

Historians usually date the beginnings of Pombal's 'industrial' policies to the years 1769–70, thereby giving the impression that up till then the minister had neglected manufacturing. In fact, Pombal's observations even before he joined the government of José I in 1750 reveal that he understood clearly that a large number of prosperous small-scale workshops needed to be encouraged just as much as the large-scale manufactures, such as the famous Lisbon silk manufactory (*Real Fábrica das Sedas*). Pombal's 'industrial' policy rested on two fundamental elements: (1) obtaining raw materials within Portugal itself and the colonies, and (2) maintaining and developing small manufacturing units whose output could be integrated into the working of larger concerns which undertook the finishing processes. The organization charged with promoting industrial development by recruiting foreign master craftsmen, creating workshops, factories and the larger productive units and granting privileges of manufacture and sale was the *Junta do Comércio*. Set up in 1755, it was given responsibility for the Real Fábrica das Sedas in Lisbon, then in financial difficulties. This indicates clearly the destination for which at least some of its output was intended, since, as well as representatives of the junta itself, there were on the board representatives of the Grão Pará and Maranhão company, and, some years later, of the Pernambuco and Paraíba company. During the 1760s a series of shocks – the costs of war in Europe and southern Brazil, the continuing decline of sugar exports from Brazil, the beginning of the decline in Brazilian gold production, the consequent decline in revenue from tithes, the fifth and other taxes and dues – profoundly altered the basis of the economic structure of the Portuguese empire. It now became more essential than ever to reduce the deficit in the trade balance, especially by stimulating production of Portuguese manufactured goods to compete with English and French goods in Portugal, Brazil and other colonies. The Junta do Comércio set in motion by means of loans the policy of import substitution which Pombal had planned through the creation of factories and workshops. In the years 1765–6, but continuing into the early nineteenth century, factories producing cotton, linen, wool and silk goods, hats, leather goods, hardware, glassware, tapestries, clocks and watches, buttons, metal buckles, ivory combs and many other luxury items were set up, in large part due to *private* initiative. The years 1769–70 did not, as is generally accepted, represent the point of departure for Pombal's 'industrial' policy, but saw the culmination of an *official* initiative which provided assistance to a very few large factories, either reorganized or newly formed, and imposed various protectionist measures. The Portuguese manufacturers had close ties with the Brazilian trading companies, who supplied them with the raw materials, for example for dyeing and weaving, and subsequently conveyed the finished products to Brazil.

In Brazil the great trading companies of the north and north-east helped to improve the production and export of traditional staples (cacao in Pará, sugar in Pernambuco) and to introduce new export crops (cotton in Maranhão, rice and coffee in Maranhão and Pará).[9] The authorities in the central and southern captaincies also tried with some success to stimulate traditional agriculture (sugar and tobacco). They were also encouraged by Pombal, especially after 1765, to diversify agriculture and adapt new products which were likely to find a market in the metropolis and further the policy of import substitution. And

---

[9] For a full discussion of the agricultural renaissance in Brazil in the second half of the eighteenth century, see ch. 7 below.

the extremely energetic viceroy, the second Marquis of Lavradio (1769–79) gave his active support. Planters were provided with seeds and cuttings brought from the metropolis or selected locally, and profitable sales were guaranteed, the crown itself sometimes being the main purchaser. Though good in intention and principle, the policy did not always work out in practice because private enterprise was feeble and royal finance lacking: there were both successes and failures. Tobacco was a commercial failure. The inferior quality produced in the captaincies of Rio de Janeiro and São Paulo could only be marketed locally or in Africa. Cotton and silk were also failures, and only insignificant quantities were produced. Hemp, greatly in demand for ships' ropes and for which Portugal depended entirely on foreign imports, also failed as a crop. There were repeated attempts to cultivate it in the captaincy of Rio Grande de São Pedro, but to no avail, even though the climate appeared to be favourable. Cochineal, a dyestuff for which New Spain was the main source of supply to Europe, was partially successful in Rio Grande de São Pedro and on the island of Santa Catarina. On the other hand, there were several very significant successes. There was, for example, a great expansion in sugar production in the Campos de Goitacazes region, to the north-east of Rio de Janeiro. Between 1769 and 1778, the number of *engenhos* (mills) doubled, the production of sugar increased by 235 per cent and that of *cachaça* (rum) by 100 per cent. Wheat, already grown in the captaincy of São Paulo, was introduced without difficulty into Rio Grande de São Pedro, and early success in the decade 1770–80 was the prelude to the profitable development of this cereal. Finally, under the Marquis of Lavradio's government, rice and indigo, already since the 1750s reasonably successful in the captaincy of Rio de Janeiro, were protected to give planters and merchants an incentive to take up production. Export of these products to the metropolis then began in ever greater quantity.

There is still insufficient information from Portuguese sources to make an overall evaluation of the economic policies pursued in Pombal's time, especially as the available statistics are distorted by smuggling. But British statistics (see Table 1 on p. 494) reveal a favourable trend in Portugal's balance of trade with England.

Portugal's deficit at the start of the period appears unusually large, but we can see that 25 years later it had been reduced by about 70 per cent, exports having increased by just over 34 per cent and imports decreased by just over 44 per cent. The sharp decline in the import of

Table 1 *Portugal's Balance of Trade with England: 1751–75*
(average annual value in £1,000s)

Years	Exports Portugal–England	Imports England–Portugal	Balance
1751–55	272	1,098	−826
1756–60	257	1,301	−1,044
1761–65	312	964	−652
1766–70	356	595	−239
1771–75	365	613	−248
Total	1,562	4,571	

Source: Elizabeth Boody Schumpeter, *English Overseas Trade Statistics (1697–1808)* (Oxford, 1960), 17–18.

manufactured goods, most noticeable after 1765, illustrates the success of Portugal's joint policies of manufacturing import substitution and great colonial companies. For example, 78 per cent of manufactures imported into Brazil by the Companhia Geral do Comércio de Pernambuco e Paraíba between 1760 and 1777 were produced by the Real Fábrica das Sedas in Lisbon which administered several units producing widely differing goods (silks and various textiles, buttons, hats, combs, clocks, etc.).[10]

Economic policy after Pombal

The death of Dom José I in 1777 brought some important political changes. Dona Maria I's accession was followed immediately by the fall of Pombal (who actually resigned of his own accord), precipitated by a powerful reaction – known as the *Viradeira* – to 27 years of tyranny: political prisoners were liberated and rehabilitated, political exiles were allowed to return to Portugal – a breath of freedom swept through the country. However, most of the men who had held government office in Pombal's time remained in power. Martinho de Mello e Castro, for example, had been Secretary of State for the Navy and the Overseas Territories and remained so until his death in 1795. Economic policy followed the same broad lines. There were very few measures which

[10] Percentage calculated from Kenneth R. Maxwell, *Conflicts and conspiracies: Brazil and Portugal 1750–1808* (Cambridge, 1973), 261, table 3. On the Real Fábrica das Sedas, see J. Borges de Macedo, *Problemas de história de indústria portuguesa no século XVIII* (Lisbon, 1963), 152–3.

ran directly counter to Pombal's policies and these largely affected the
two companies trading with Brazil. Ever since these had been set up
they had become ever more unpopular with merchants in Portugal and
Brazil and with colonial landowners who were critical of their pricing
policies, especially with respect to slaves, and their limited achievements
after two decades. The Companhia Geral do Comércio of Grão Pará and
Maranhão was abolished in 1778 and that of Pernambuco and Paraíba
in 1779. Free trade between Portugal and northern Brazil was established. In 1777 the control of factories in Portugal was transferred from
the Junta do Comércio to a specially-created body, the *Junta de
Administração das Fábricas do Reino*, but ten years later (1788) there was
a return to Pombal's formula, with a single *Real Junta do Comércio,
Agricultura, Fábricas e Navegações* (see above p. 481). Otherwise, not only
was the policy of import substitution and expansion of trade pursued
with remarkable continuity throughout the reign of Dona Maria I and
the *de facto* regency of her son, Dom João, after 1792, but the principle
of the colonial pact was also reaffirmed on several occasions, by
Martinho de Mello e Castro as well as by his successor Dom Rodrigo
de Souza Coutinho.

In metropolitan Portugal preference was always given to private
enterprise, so new factories were set up and the management of the
woollen mills at Fundão, Covilhã and Portalegre was granted to
individuals (1788). The efforts of the state itself concentrated particularly
on stimulating silk manufacture. Finally, new protectionist tariffs
favoured the entry into the colonies of goods manufactured in the
metropolis (1794 and 1797).

In Brazil the development and production of traditional and new
staples continued to be encouraged, and the economic policies begun
under Pombal benefited from two important geopolitical changes. The
first came after 1777 when the North American War of Independence
forced England to look for new sources of raw materials for her rapidly
developing cotton industry, especially cotton itself and dyestuffs, and
the second came after 1789, when the French Revolution and Napoleon's
rise to power led to revolution in Saint-Domingue (and the destruction
of the world's leading sugar industry) and war on the European
continent. As a result Portugal found other profitable outlets on the
international market for her colonial products like sugar (from Pernambuco, Bahia and, increasingly, Rio de Janeiro), cotton (from Maranhão
but now also Pernambuco, Bahia and Rio de Janeiro), tobacco, indigo,

cochineal and cacao, and, naturally, demand pushed up prices. More-over, rice production was expanding rapidly in Rio de Janeiro as well as in Pará and Maranhão, and the metropolis was soon self-sufficient. Rice, like indigo, was the object of very important protectionist measures between 1777 and 1783. Coffee cultivation, grown largely for local consumption, spread throughout Brazil during the eighteenth century. Its production was now concentrated in the captaincies of Rio de Janeiro, São Paulo, Espírito Santo and Minas Gerais, where climatic conditions were nearly perfect, and, towards the end of the century, exports to the metropolis and other European markets, especially from Rio de Janeiro, became increasingly significant.

Meanwhile the various illicit forms of trade (gold smuggling inside and outside Brazil, illegal exports of colonial products and imports of foreign manufactures) were undermining Portugal's whole economic policy during the difficult years of recovery, but they were not the only problems posed by Brazil to a government more than ever anxious to preserve its prerogatives. There was concern that small workshops producing all kinds of luxury cloths and gold and silver embroidery were proliferating. This local production was not only competing with similar industries in the metropolis, but was in the long run threatening to engender in the richest of Portugal's colonies a desire for economic and political independence. The existence of these problems led Martinho de Mello e Castro to publish simultaneously in 1785 two *alvarás*, one of which was intended to strengthen the measures against all forms of fraud and smuggling, while the other ordered all workshops and factories in Brazil producing cloth other than the coarse cotton intended as clothing for slaves or as packing material for exported goods to close. In fact, the second of these alvarás may not have had the impact some historians have assumed. But it is true, all the same, that the 'Pombaline' policy adopted by Mello e Castro reaffirmed Brazil's political and economic dependence on the metropolis, in accordance with the principles of the mercantilist colonial system. Until the court of the Braganzas was transferred to Rio de Janeiro in 1808, the colonial pact was never called into question by the government which, even after the independence of the United States of America and Saint-Domingue, or after the two attempted revolts in Brazil in 1789 and 1798, never admitted the possibility of relaxing its hold. However, the growth of a more liberal spirit can be detected, particularly in the attitude of Mello e Castro's successor, Dom Rodrigo de Souza Coutinho, who put forward somewhat different arguments for maintaining the links between Portugal and Brazil. These arguments were no longer based on the authority of classic mercantilist principles, but were inspired by 'mercantilism influenced by enlightenment, enlightened mercantilism'[11] and by a new vision of the Portuguese empire.

The first attempts to reform the Portuguese education system had been undertaken at Pombal's instigation and they continued during the reign of Dona Maria I. They quickly produced a generation of men with a new philosophical, scientific or technical outlook, who joined forces with an older generation of 'enlightened' men in an attempt to introduce reform and progress into Portugal. Besides traditional institutions such as the University of Coimbra, which was reformed in 1772, various other bodies made a powerful contribution to this movement. Curiously enough, it was in Brazil that the first scientific academy in the Portuguese empire was created in 1772. This was the *Academia Científica* of Rio de Janeiro which was founded to stimulate the study of natural sciences, physics, chemistry and agriculture, and hence to develop or improve Brazil's economy. Like another institution which followed it a few years later (the *Sociedade Literária*, 1786–94), the Academia Científica did not survive for long (1772–9) but it helped promote the diffusion of new staples for export. In Lisbon, the *Academia Real das Sciencias*, founded in 1779, played an important role by arousing public interest in the study of subjects connected with the economy and industry. The first three volumes of the famous *Memorias Economicas da Academia Real das Sciencias de Lisboa para o adiantamento da Agricultura, das Artes e da Industria em Portugal e suas Conquistas* were published as a series of articles between 1789 and 1791. They included various studies relating to Brazil which illustrate the persistence of colonial mercantilism, combined with a desire for improvement. There were monographs on whaling, cotton, sugar prices, raw materials still needing to be exploited and sectors of the economy needing development. A 'physical and economic' description of the Ilhéus region of Bahia even contained a detailed development plan. The Academy of Science applied itself to the stimulation of agriculture, but as part of

[11] The expression is Fernando Novais's in *Portugal e Brasil na crise do antigo sistema colonial (1777–1808)* (São Paulo, 1979), 230

a general trend which emphasized agrarian development rather than as a result of genuine physiocratic influence.[12] However, it also took an interest in metallurgy, notably by enabling two young Brazilians trained at the University of Coimbra to make the long journey to Europe to study the most important metallurgical establishments and to inform themselves about current scientific theories. As a scientific body, the Academy could not intervene directly in economic policy, so it was at the most no more than what we would today call a pressure group. On the other hand, some of its members later held important office in the government or in the administration and had a hand in policy-making. For example, the specialists in mineralogy and metallurgy sent to Europe by the Academy rose to highly responsible and influential positions, one as inspector general of Brazil's gold and diamond mines (Manuel Ferreira da Câmara) and the other as inspector general of Portugal's mines (José Bonifácio de Andrada e Silva).

But clearly it was at government level itself that 'enlightened' men were to be found, capable of formulating overall policies, of influencing the decisions of the sovereign and of shaping the destiny of the nation. The most important of these men, especially for Brazil, was undoubtedly Martinho de Mello e Castro's successor, Dom Rodrigo de Souza Coutinho. While Secretary of State for the Navy and for the Overseas Territories (1796–1801), and later, while president of the *Erário Régio* (1801–3), Dom Rodrigo de Souza Coutinho corresponded almost daily with the prince regent. These letters, and those he wrote to the viceroys, governors and other officials in Brazil, religious and secular, offer ample evidence of the wide scope of his projects and, in particular, of his persistent efforts to consolidate Brazil's pre-eminent position in the Portuguese empire. He was tireless in seeking to promote progress in every aspect of Brazilian life, especially in the economic sector. Some of his projects were a continuation of the work of his predecessors (e.g. the attempts to introduce crops, such as hemp, and to develop others, such as cinnamon, pepper, cochineal, etc.). But some projects were extremely original; for example, he wanted to make a cadastral survey

---

[12] The question is a contraversial one: see especially Magalhães Godinho, *Prix et monnaies*, 284, and Albert Silbert, *Le Problème agraire portugais au temps des premières Cortès libérales 1821–1823* (Paris, 1968), 22. Here I accept the conclusions of Abílio Carlos d'Ascensão Diniz Silva, 'La Formulation d'une politique de développement économique au Portugal à la fin du XVIIIe siècle', Mémoire for the diploma in Sciences Économiques, University of Paris-I, 1969, 44–5 and 56–7, whose views depend on the analysis of the *Memorias Economicas* and on the observations of Joseph A. Schumpeter, *History of economic analysis* (6th edn., London, 1967), 157–8.

of the territory; he also wished to introduce the ox-drawn plough and to popularize 'scientific' agriculture among Brazilian landowners by distributing free pamphlets on agronomy printed in Lisbon and specially written in, or translated into, Portuguese by the learned Brazilian, Frei Mariano da Conceição Veloso. Some of Dom Rodrigo de Souza Coutinho's other projects sought to extend the use of cleaning and shelling machinery for cotton and coffee and of new technology in sugar production; to protect the forests by strictly controlling felling; to encourage the search for saltpetre; to improve the productivity of the iron mines in the captaincy of São Paulo, to develop the nascent iron and steel industry there and to extend these efforts to the captaincies of Rio de Janeiro and Minas Gerais; to promote the establishment of banks offering credit and discounts to agriculture and trade, as well as insurance companies; to promote freedom of circulation of goods in the Brazilian interior; and to establish regular packet-boats sailing between metropolitan Portugal and Brazil. His most important ideas are set out in a long report on 'the improvement of His Majesty's domains in America' which he put before the government and the Council of State in 1798, two years after he had been appointed Colonial Secretary.[13]

Leaving aside for the moment the political aspects of this important document, let us consider the economic proposition based on the minister's own ideas and on the various reports from his advisers. At the risk of encroaching on a domain reserved in theory for the president of the *Erário Régio*, who had sole responsibility for the administration of finance throughout the empire, Souza Coutinho considered it part of his duty to suggest ways of remedying the lamentable state of royal finances. Not only did he propose ways of reforming their administration, but also of modifying fiscal policy itself. He suggested that in every captaincy the junta de fazenda should administer all taxes directly. In other words, the 'pernicious' system of tax farming (contratos) would be abolished, an experiment which had already been carried out successfully in Minas Gerais. Book-keeping would be improved, estimates and accounts would be drawn up annually; and a plan to replace the tithe by a land tax proportional to the net income of the land would be studied. Next, local currency and the circulation of gold dust would be abolished and replaced by paper money. Coins of the

[13] Published by Marcos Carneiro de Mendonça, *O Intendente Câmara, Manuel Ferreira da Camara Bethencourt e Sá, Intendente Geral das Minas e Diamantes 1764–1835* (Rio de Janeiro, 1933), 268–90.

same value as those in circulation in metropolitan Portugal, however, could continue to be used. One or two mints were to be established in the captaincies of Minas Gerais and Goiás, while those in Rio de Janeiro and Bahia would be abolished. The *districtos diamantinos* were to be opened up and their deposits freely exploited. However, the diamonds were still to be sold to authorized representatives of the crown alone. The 20 per cent tax on gold would be reduced to 10 per cent; the tax on salt would be abolished altogether; all duties on imports and exports would be reduced to 4 per cent and a preferential system would be introduced for goods from the metropolis: 2 per cent on manufactured goods and a complete exemption for iron, steel, wines and olive oil. Duties payable on black slaves would be abolished throughout Brazil, except in ports, where they would be reduced. The special import duties (*entradas*) on black slaves and on various products (iron, steel, copper, gold dust, olive oil and wines) would be abolished in the captaincy of Minas Gerais. To compensate for the loss of revenue resulting from all these changes it would be necessary to introduce a stamp duty, already in force in the metropolis, together with moderate taxes on houses in the coastal towns and on all shops, inns and drinking establishments. There would also be a reduced capitation tax on all slaves. A postal service would be introduced throughout the Brazilian interior, the profit going to the Fazenda Real; and finally, lotteries would be set up, as in the metropolis.

For Souza Coutinho, influenced as he was by Adam Smith, the wealth of nations depended on 'the products of the land, the wages of agricultural workers and craftsmen, and on the income from accumulated capital which was used either to improve the land and make it productive or to increase the work force, and only in our time had this indisputable truth been concealed by the subtleties of the sect of Economists' – in other words, the physiocrats. So it was from within the framework of a pre-liberal economy that Souza Coutinho made his first attempts to reform the fiscal system in a way which was to affect not only Brazil but the whole empire: by relieving fiscal pressure he hoped to stimulate economic activity in Brazil, certainly, but also in Portugal since any increase in production in the colonies should improve her trade. In fact, the prosperity of the whole empire was at stake, since any increase in state revenue was essentially derived from the increased income of private citizens.

As is well known, the government of the Prince Regent Dom João was never distinguished for making speedy decisions; in addition, there was considerable opposition to a daring programme which was likely to disrupt cumbersome administrative machinery and the entrenched interests of a powerful financial oligarchy. We should not, therefore, be surprised that many of the measures put forward by Dom Rodrigo de Souza Coutinho in his report of 1798 were only slowly realized, and that many more were indefinitely postponed. Nevertheless, the minister did manage to abolish the farming of the salt tax in 1801. The farm of the tax on whale fishing was partially abolished in May 1798 and dropped completely in 1801. The planned reduction in tariffs and the introduction of new taxes were modified to suit local needs and the requirements of the Treasury.

Souza Coutinho was particularly concerned about the decline in gold production. We know that the regulations governing the various stages of production and the levying of the *quinto* (fifth) had not changed since Pombal's time, in spite of the social upheaval provoked by the unfair compensatory tax (the *derrama*), notably in Minas Gerais in 1789 where the Inconfidência Mineira was an unsuccessful plot for independence.[14] At last, in 1803 efforts were made to revive this basic industry along the lines suggested by the minister and his advisers: exchange bureaux for gold dust were to be set up in each of the captaincies involved; the Rio de Janeiro mint was to be transferred to Minas Gerais and the Bahia mint to Goiás; and a junta was to be set up to administer the mines and the minting of money. This junta was to be composed mainly of mineralogists (mine-owners with experience or trained technicians), and the presence of such experts working alongside the civil servants shows that there was a new spirit, which was also reflected in the plan to set up local schools of mineralogy and metallurgy modelled on German schools. It was hoped that technological progress would in this way jolt gold production out of the rut it had been in since 1765. To encourage the efforts of the mine-owners the quinto was reduced to a tax of 10 per cent. As for diamonds, the oppressive system of totally isolating areas containing diamond deposits was abandoned: the Districto Diamantino was opened up again, gold prospecting was authorized there and a new method of sharing out and working the concessions was adopted. Miners were advised to form societies or companies in order to increase their profits. The sale of diamonds, however, was still the exclusive prerogative of the crown:

[14] For the further discussion of the Inconfidência Mineira, see ch. 7 below.

the stones were either inspected and bought in the main diamond centre (Arraial do Tijuco) by a junta de fazenda specially created for the purpose, or else, in areas too far from this centre, in the exchange bureaux which had been set up to deal with gold dust.

No doubt the delay in deciding to put these measures into practice often reduced their impact. The reforms came too late. However, they were necessary and helped prepare the way for the upheavals which were to shake the empire after 1808.

A fair idea of the success of the economic policy of Pombal's successors can be gained from examining Portugal's trade with England, as was done for Pombal's period, using as a basis the English data which run in a continuous series up to the year 1800. However, it is worth checking the result against Portuguese sources on the balance of trade for which we also have a continuous series from 1796.[15] This series is particularly interesting because it covers the whole of Portugal's export trade, not only with foreign countries but also with each of her colonies. The figures enable us to evaluate the internal structure of the economy of the Portuguese empire and to assess the efforts made to reorganize it. We shall, therefore, draw on English data for the period 1776–95, and on Portuguese data for the period 1796–1807.

Table 2 on p. 503 shows that between 1776 and 1795 there was the same continuous trend in Anglo-Portuguese trade already observed in Pombal's period (see above, Table 1 on p. 494).

Between 1776 and 1795, Portugal's exports to England increased by 90 per cent, while imports from England only increased by 13 per cent. During the period 1791–5 this led to the first spectacular reversal of the balance of trade in favour of Portugal: the balance which had previously been negative now showed a large surplus. Benefiting from the international trends which worked in favour of her trade, Portugal had clearly succeeded in expanding her trade by promoting her colonial products. Brazilian cotton, for example, was playing an increasingly important role in Portuguese exports: between 1781 and 1792 the total

[15] Pointed out and used for the first time by Adrien Balbi in his famous *Essai statistique sur le royaume de Portugal et d'Algarve*, 2 vols. (Paris, 1822), i, 401–45, these trade figures have been used more recently and partially by a number of historians, notably Magalhães Godinho, Borges de Macedo, Silbert and, above all, by Fernando Novais, *Portugal e Brasil*, 285–96 and 306–91 (graphics and figures), as well as by José Jobson de A. Arruda, *O Brasil no comércio colonial* (São Paulo, 1980).

Table 2 *Balance of Trade with England: 1776–95*
(average annual value in £1,000s)

Years	Exports Portugal–England	Imports England–Portugal	Balance
1776–80	381	525	− 144
1781–85	340	622	− 282
1786–90	597	622	− 25
1791–95	724	594	+ 130
Total	2,042	2,363	

Source: Elizabeth Boody Schumpeter, *English Overseas Trade Statistics (1697–1808)*, 17–18.

weight of Brazilian cotton exported annually from Portugal to England rose from 300,000 lbs to 7,700,000 lbs, while during the same period France also imported about 1,376,000 lbs of cotton per annum.[16]

For the period 1776–95, Portuguese sources can only provide two complete sets of trade figures, one for 1776 and one for 1777 (see Table 3). These indicate that a radical change in the economic structure of the Portuguese empire was taking place, an observation which is confirmed by later data (from 1796).

Table 3 *Portugal's Balance of Trade: 1776–7*
(value in milréis)

Years	Portugal–Colonies	Portugal–Foreign Countries
1776	+ 1,177,159	− 1,795,390
1777	+ 545,329	− 1,492,427

Source: Fernando A. Novais, *Portugal e Brasil na crise do antigo sistema colonial (1777–1808)*, p. 289.

Table 3 shows us the beginnings of the change since the deficit in Portugal's trade with other countries was reduced by nearly 17 per cent, while the balance favouring the metropolis in its trade with its colonies decreased by nearly 54 per cent. The latter figure is particularly

---

[16] For English data, see Maxwell, *Conflicts and conspiracies*, 255, and for French data, Magalhães Godinho, *Prix et monnaies*, 361.

important as it shows clearly that the colonies were tending to improve their economic position as against the metropolis, and we shall see later that Brazil's dominant position – for which we have precise data after 1796 – was preparing the way for the colony's economic and political independence.

It is no exaggeration to say that the period 1796–1807 appears to have been a new Golden Age for Portuguese trade. In her dealings with foreign countries Portugal enjoyed a constant surplus in her balance of trade, except in 1797 and 1799. The average annual value of exports increased by nearly 4 per cent and imports by only 2.6 per cent, as Table 4 shows.

Table 4 *Portugal's Balance of Trade with all Foreign Countries: 1796–1807*
(value in milréis)

Years	Exports Portugal–Foreign Countries	Imports Foreign Countries– Portugal	Balance
1796	16,013,356	12,652,771	+ 3,360,585
1797	11,822,970	14,498,399	− 2,675,429
1798	15,053,960	14,729,238	+ 324,722
1799	17,688,107	19,755,284	− 2,067,177
1800	20,684,802	20,031,347	+ 653,455
1801	25,103,785	19,337,425	+ 5,766,360
1802	21,405,349	17,942,240	+ 3,463,109
1803	21,528,379	15,068,304	+ 6,460,075
1804	21,060,962	17,841,034	+ 3,219,928
1805	22,654,204	19,656,685	+ 2,997,519
1806	23,255,505	16,440,921	+ 6,814,584
1807	20,999,506	13,896,318	+ 7,103,188
Total	237,270,885	201,869,966	

Source: Novais, *Portugal e Brasil*, 320 and 322.

After 1798 Portugal's trade with England always showed a balance in Portugal's favour, and from 1800 there were even some significant improvements, as can be seen in Table 5 on p. 505.

If we compare Tables 4 and 5, we can see that Portugal's imports from England represented 34 per cent of the total value of her imports from all foreign countries, and that Portugal's exports to England represented 39 per cent of the total value of all her exports to foreign countries. This shows clearly that, while England remained one of

Table 5 *Portugal's Balance of Trade with England: 1796–1807*
(value in milréis)

Years	Exports Portugal–England	Imports England–Portugal	Balance
1796	4,887,076	4,951,737	−64,661
1797	3,979,976	4,627,613	−647,637
1798	6,828,261	6,661,419	+166,842
1799	9,058,217	8,835,649	+222,568
1800	6,702,836	2,911,061	+3,791,775
1801	9,651,014	4,879,357	+4,771,657
1802	8,472,170	6,693,774	+1,778,396
1803	10,514,250	5,587,493	+4,926,757
1804	7,462,492	5,764,885	+1,697,607
1805	8,865,210	5,837,705	+3,027,505
1806	6,587,150	8,201,116	+1,613,966
1807	7,971,196	5,422,272	+2,548,924
Total	92,593,814	68,760,115	

Source: Novais, *Portugal e Brasil*, 356 and 358.

Portugal's main trading partners, she was no longer the almost exclusive partner that she had been for so long. Portugal maintained regular trading relations with about fifteen countries, and the volume of business conducted annually with Hamburg, Russia, Spain and France, for example, is evidence of an interesting diversification.[17]

An analysis of Portugal's trade figures from 1796 to 1807 also yields much detailed information about the economic structure of the Portuguese empire – both within itself as well as in relation to foreign countries.

If we look at the overall picture of Portugal's trading relations with its colonies, Portugal showed a deficit in the balance of trade in most years, as we can see from Table 6 on p. 506.

Imports from the colonies, then, increased annually by an average of 10 per cent. On the other hand, the growth rate of exports from Portugal to the colonies, which had averaged over 17 per cent per annum until the end of 1799, fell after this year to just below 3 per cent per annum – an indication of the growing importance of the contraband trade in English manufactures. At the end of the period the balance of trade showed an overall surplus of 10.6 per cent in favour of the

[17] Balbi, *Essai statistique*, I, 431–42.

Table 6 *Portugal's Balance of Trade with all her Colonies: 1796–1807*
(value in milréis)

Years	Exports Portugal–Colonies	Imports Colonies–Portugal	Balance
1796	7,527,648	13,413,265	−5,885,617
1797	9,651,734	5,519,870	+4,131,864
1798	12,418,654	12,802,090	−383,436
1799	20,458,608	15,169,305	+5,289,303
1800	13,521,110	14,850,936	−1,329,826
1801	13,133,542	17,527,723	−4,394,181
1802	12,800,313	12,966,553	−116,340
1803	12,741,308	14,193,353	−1,452,045
1804	14,905,960	13,579,874	+1,326,086
1805	12,245,019	15,843,481	−3,598,462
1806	11,313,313	16,103,966	−4,789,653
1807	10,348,602	16,968,810	−6,620,208
Total	151,065,811	168,939,226	

Source: Novais, *Portugal e Brasil*, 310 and 312.

colonies. This amply confirms the trend noticeable from the figures for 1776 and 1777, when the surplus in favour of the metropolis had begun to decline.

These trade figures also enable us to assess the exact place Brazil occupied in the total volume of Portugal's trade: Brazil alone accounted for over 83 per cent of the total value of goods imported by Portugal from her colonies, and for 78.5 per cent of Portugal's exports to her colonies.[18] Even more striking are the respective percentages from each part of the Portuguese empire within the total value of Portuguese exports to foreign countries (100 per cent): products from the metropolis, 27.43 per cent; products from Brazil, 60.76 per cent; products from other colonies, 2.95 per cent; re-exports, 8.86 per cent.[19]

Thus, despite a certain revival of Portuguese commerce with those of her colonies in Asia which had in earlier times been her principal source of wealth, the overwhelming preponderance of Brazil is clear,

---

[18] Novais, *Portugal e Brasil*, 290. See also ch. 7 below, table 11, 'Brazilian exports to Portugal 1796 and 1806', and table 13, 'Balance of Trade between Portugal and leading Brazilian captaincies, 1796–1806'.

[19] Novais, *Portugal e Brasil*, 292–3. See also ch. 7 below, table 12, 'Origins of exports from Portugal to Europe, Barbary and United States, 1789, 1796, 1806'.

whether we look at the internal or the external structure of Portugal's economy. Portugal's international trade owed its positive balance to the exports of Brazilian staples.

At the end of the eighteenth century, when Britain and France's union with several of their American colonies had already been severed, the question of Brazil's dependence on Portugal was raised. In the preamble to the report 'on the improvement of His Majesty's domains in America', the economic aspects of which have been examined above, Dom Rodrigo de Souza Coutinho (in charge of colonial affairs since 1796) expounded his ideas on the political system which he considered would enable Portugal to keep its overseas empire. Assuming *a priori* that 'the happy position of Portugal' as middleman between northern and southern Europe made the union of the Portuguese colonies with the metropolis 'as natural as the union of the other colonies, which have declared their independence of the motherland, was unnatural', the minister defended 'the inviolable and sacrosanct principle of unity, the basis of the monarchy, which must be jealously maintained so that Portuguese, wherever they are born, may consider themselves uniquely Portuguese'. He then went on to state its corollary: it was important to reinforce commercial links between the metropolis and its colonies, above all Brazil, 'the chief of all the possessions that Europeans have established outside their continent, not because of what it is at present, but because of what it can become if we can develop all the advantages offered by its size, situation and fertility'. To ensure the defence of Brazil from its neighbours Dom Rodrigo recommended that it should again be divided into two great regions, each depending on a military centre, Belém do Pará in the north and Rio de Janeiro in the south, according to a geopolitical plan which would allow Portugal 'gradually and imperceptibly' to 'expand to the true natural frontier of our possessions in South America, in other words, the northern bank of the Río de la Plata' – the old expansionist dream which none of the three frontier treaties signed with Spain since 1750 had been able to dissipate.[20]

A few years later, another ancient dream was revived by certain statesmen anxious to preserve the integrity of the Portuguese empire and the independence of its rulers from increasing French pressure. This was an idea of the old diplomat, Dom Luís da Cunha, who, in 1738, had foreseen that the king of Portugal would transfer his court to Brazil

[20] Memorandum of Dom Rodrigo de Souza Coutinho, see note 13.

and assume one day the title of Emperor of the West.[21] Soon after the breakdown of the Peace of Amiens (1802), Dom Rodrigo de Souza Coutinho and other counsellors, weighing up 'the new risks and imminent dangers' which threatened the Portuguese monarchy, decided that in the last resort the prince regent must move to Brazil.[22] However, the dream did not become a reality until France invaded Portugal. On 28 November 1807, under the protection of an English squadron, the royal family and part of the court left Portugal for Brazil.

Thus, the reorganization of the empire, which had been in progress ever since 1750, was brought to its logical conclusion by pressure of outside forces. Already the most important economic unit in the world-wide Portuguese empire, Brazil now became its political centre. The step taken in 1807 was a decisive one, but not in the way Souza Coutinho imagined it would be. Far from serving as a base for the 'complete reintegration of the monarchy' Brazil, following the return of Dom João VI to Lisbon in 1821, initiated the disintegration of the Portuguese empire by proclaiming its independence in 1822.[23]

[21] *Instruções inéditas de D. Luis da Cunha a Marco António de Azevedo Coutinho*, 211.
[22] Dom Rodrigo de Souza Coutinho to the Prince Regent Dom João, 16 August 1803, in Angelo Pereira, *D. João VI Príncipe e Rei*, 4 vols. (Lisbon, 1953–7), I, 127–36. Totally rejected at the time by the Portuguese government, this hypothesis was analysed in all its consequences a year later by the British Admiral Donald Campbell in an important report to the Foreign Office: see Andrée Mansuy, 'L'Impérialisme britannique et les relations coloniales entre le Portugal et le Brésil: un rapport de l'Amiral Campbell au *Foreign Office* (14 août 1804)'. *Cahiers des Amériques Latines*, 9–10 (1974), 138, 147–8, 152 and 186–9; also Maxwell, *Conflicts and conspiracies*, 233–9.
[23] On the period from the arrival of the Portuguese court in Rio de Janeiro in March 1808 to the return of Dom João VI to Lisbon in April 1821, and on the background to Brazil's declaration of its independence from Portugal in September 1822, see Bethell, *CHLA*, III, ch. 4.

7

LATE COLONIAL BRAZIL, 1750–1808

If the years 1808–22, following the dramatic arrival of the Portuguese court at Rio de Janeiro, are considered for Brazil a period of transition from colony to independent empire, then the years 1750–1808 may be regarded as the last phase of Brazil's colonial experience. The era began as the mining boom was reaching its zenith; then, quite unexpectedly, the boom was over and an extended depression ensued. But Brazilians readjusted to the decline of the mineral sector by returning to agriculture, their traditional source of wealth. The result for coastal Brazil (but not the interior) was several decades of renewed prosperity based, in part, upon an expansion in the production of traditional staples, particularly sugar and tobacco, but also upon the development of new exports, especially cotton and rice, as well as cacao, coffee, and indigo. That recovery was accomplished without any fundamental improvements in technology or alterations in the patterns of land tenure, but through the growth of old and new markets and an intensified reliance upon slave labour. During this period Brazil accepted without protest the crown's decision to expel her most respected missionary order (the Jesuits) and to restrict the role of the remaining religious bodies. Portugal fought and lost two wars to secure Brazil's southern boundaries, but a third conflict (1801) gained Brazil rich agricultural and pastoral lands in the temperate south. Colonial Brazil had reached her territorial limits.[1] Though she virtually ignored the first American Revolution, Brazil became far more aware of the French Revolution. Not only did Europe's subsequent maritime wars open up new markets for Brazilian products but the Revolution's ideological underpinnings and its successes inspired the first serious

---

[1] See D. Alden, *Royal government in colonial Brazil* (Berkeley and Los Angeles, 1968), pt. 2; also ch. 6 above.

separatist conspiracies in several parts of the colony. Even though those movements were rigorously repressed, the call for reforms of the so-called colonial pact binding Brazil to Portugal became more insistent. The urgency for change became irresistible in 1807–8, when the Portuguese government found itself unable to withstand competing Anglo-French pressures and fled to the security offered by its richest and most populous colony.

By the 1770s it becomes possible for the first time to obtain sufficient information to estimate the size and distribution of Brazil's population. In 1776 the colonial minister directed secular and ecclesiastical authorities throughout the colony to join together to provide complete counts of their inhabitants according to age and sex, but not, unfortunately, race. The crown's motives were obviously the traditional ones, those of determining the number of men capable of bearing arms and evaluating the number of potential taxpayers. In pursuance of that order, local officials (militia commanders and parish priests) compiled data from the *lista de desobrigas*, the parish register of persons receiving communion at Easter. Since that register excluded children under seven, their number was determined by actual count or (more likely) by estimate. The parish counts (*mapas particulares*) were forwarded to district officers; they sent condensed reports to their superiors, who remitted consolidated tabulations to the crown.

Such reports were supposed to be submitted to Lisbon annually, but with the exception of the captaincy of São Paulo they were seldom prepared so regularly. Many of the reports have been lost; others remain in the archives awaiting scholarly analysis. But a sufficient number have been gathered to permit estimates to be made of late colonial Brazil's population at two points in time. One clustering ranges from 1772 to 1782 and centres on 1776; the other spans the years 1797–1810, though most of the data reported for the latter year were compiled somewhat earlier, so that 1800 becomes a reasonable benchmark. The distribution of Brazil's enumerated inhabitants *c.* 1776 and *c.* 1800 is indicated in tables 1 and 2.

Several observations arise from these tables and the sources from which they are derived. First, it is evident that the census-takers substantially underestimated the number of children below the age of

Table 1 *Distribution of the population of Brazil, c. 1776*

Captaincy	Number of inhabitants	Percentage
Rio Negro	10,386	0.6
Pará	55,315	3.5
Maranhão	47,410	3.0
Piauí	26,410	1.7
Pernambuco	239,713	15.4
Paraíba	52,468	3.4
Rio Grande do Norte	23,812	1.5
Ceará	61,408	3.9
Bahia	288,848	18.5
Rio de Janeiro	215,678	13.8
Santa Catarina	10,000	0.6
Rio Grande do Sul	20,309	1.3
São Paulo	116,975	7.5
Minas Gerais	319,769	20.5
Goiás	55,514	3.5
Mato Grosso	20,966	1.3
Totals	1,555,200	100.0

Source: D. Alden, 'The population of Brazil in the late eighteenth century: a preliminary survey', *Hispanic American Historical Review* [HAHR], 43/2 (May 1963), 173–205.

fifteen. More will be said later about the consequences of such under-enumeration. Second, many Indians (estimated by one contemporary at 250,000) who were beyond the pale of Portuguese authority, especially within the Amazon basin, Goiás, Piauí, and Mato Grosso, were not counted; nor does it seem possible to provide any reliable approximation of their numbers. Third, in spite of repeated land 'rushes' to the mineral and pastoral lands of the interior west and south, during the eighteenth century, most of the enumerated population (78.8 per cent in 1776 and 73.4 per cent *c.* 1800) was still concentrated around the principal ports and hinterlands of the coastal captaincies, especially in the traditional staple export centres of Paraíba, Pernambuco, Bahia, and Rio de Janeiro, which contained more than half (51.1 per cent) of Brazil's recorded inhabitants in 1776 and 46.8 per cent *c.* 1800. Fourth, with minor exceptions, the general pattern of the distribution of Brazil's population did not change significantly during the last decades of the colonial period: the rank order of the captaincies was about the same in 1800 as it had been a quarter-century earlier. Fifth, while the urban

Table 2 *Distribution of the population of Brazil, c. 1800*

Captaincy	Date of report	Number of inhabitants	% of total population	Source
Rio Negro/Pará	1801	80,000	3.8	A
Maranhão	1798	78,860	3.8	A
Piauí	1799	51,721	2.5	B
Pernambuco	1810	391,986	19.0	C
Paraíba	1810	79,424	3.8	C
Rio Grande do Norte	1810	49,391	2.4	C
Ceará	1808	125,764	6.1	D
Bahia	1799	247,000	11.9	E
Rio de Janeiro	1803/1810	249,883	12.1	F
Santa Catarina	1797	23,865	1.2	G
Rio Grande do Sul	1802	38,418	1.8	H
São Paulo	1797	158,450	7.5	I
Minas Gerais	1805	407,004	19.7	J
Goiás	1804	52,076	2.5	K
Mato Grosso	1800	27,690	1.3	L
Totals		2,061,657	99.4	

Sources: **A**: Colin M. MacLachlan, 'African slave trade and economic development in Amazonia, 1700–1800', in R. B. Toplin (ed.), *Slavery and race relations in Latin America* (Westport, 1974), 136. **B**: F. A. Pereira da Costa, *Chronológia histórica do estado do Piauhy desde os seus primitivos tempos até...1889* ([Recife]), 1909), 109. **C**: Enclosure in Lord Strangford to Marquis of Wellesley, Rio de Janeiro, 20 May 1810, PRO, FO 63/84/ERD/2255 (copy courtesy of Dr F. W. O. Morton). **D**: Luiz Barba Alardo de Menezes, 'Memória sôbre a capitania do Ceará', [1808], *Revista do Instituto Histórico e Geográfico Brasileiro* [*RIHGB*], 34 (1871), 276, table 3. **E**: Luiz dos Santos Vilhena, *Recopilação de notícias soteropolitanas e brasílicas...em XX cartas*, ed. Braz do Amaral (3 vols., Bahia, 1921), II, 481. **F**: The data for the city of Rio de Janeiro is based on an 1803 census in Strangford to Wellesley, **C** above. Also included is the subordinate captaincy of Espiritu Santo, but I have deducted data for Santa Catarina. **G**: João Alberto de Miranda Ribeira, 'Dados estatísticos sôbre...Santa Catarina, 1797', Biblioteca Nacional do Rio de Janeiro [BNRJ], II–35, 30, 3. The census of 1810 (**C**) gives 31,911. **H**: 'Mappa de todos os habitantes da capitania do Rio Grande de São Pedro do Sul...1802', Arquivo Histórico Ultramarino (Lisbon), papéis avulsos (miscellaneous papers) [AHU/PA], Rio Grande do Sul, caixa 1. I have added to the existing total the uncounted 1,697 infants under one year. **I**: 'Mappa geral dos habitantes da capitania de S. Paulo no anno de 1797', Arquivo do Estado de São Paulo, *Publicação oficial de documentos interesantes para a história e costumes de São Paulo* [*DI*], 31 (1901), 151–5, 157. **J**: A. J. R. Russell-Wood, 'Colonial Brazil', in David W. Cohen and Jack P. Greene (eds.), *Neither Slave nor Free* (Baltimore, 1972), 97. **K**: Luis Antonio da Silva e Sousa, 'Memoria...de Goiás' [1812], *RIHGB*, 12 (2nd edn, 1874), 482–94. **L**: Caetano Pinto de Miranda Monte Negro to Visconde de Anadia, 17 April 1802, *RIHGB*, 28/1 (1865), 125–7.

Table 3 *Estimates and counts of principal Brazilian cities, 1749–1810*

City	Date	Number of inhabitants
Belém, Pará	1749	6,574
	1788	10,620
	1801	12,500
São Luís, Maranhão	1757	7,162
	1810	20,500
Recife, Pernambuco	1750	7,000
	1776	18,207
	1782	17,934
	1810	25,000
Salvador, Bahia	1757	35,922
	1775	36,393
	1780	39,209
	1807	51,000
Rio de Janeiro	1760	30,000
	1780	38,707
	1799	43,376
	1803	46,944
São Paulo	1765	20,873
	1798	21,304
	1803	24,311
Porte Alegre, Rio Grande do Sul	1808	6,035
Oeiras, Piauí	1762	1,120
	1810	2,000
Vila Boa, Goiás	1804	9,477
Vila Bela, Mato Grosso	1782	7,000
Ouro Preto, Minas Gerais	1740s	20,000
	1804	7,000

Sources: **Belém**: J. R. do Amaral Lapa, *Livro da visitação do santo ofício da inquisição ao estado do Grão Pará* (Petrópolis, 1978), 38. **São Luís**: AHU/PA/Maranhão, caixa 37; *RIHGB*, 17 (1854), 64. **Recife**: *Anais da Biblioteca Nacional do Rio de Janeiro* [*ABNRJ*], 28 (1908), 407; José Ribeiro Júnior, 'Subsídios para o estudo da geografia e demografia histórica do nordeste brasileiro', *Anais de História* (Marília, 1970), vol. II, 156–7; *ABNRJ*, 40 (1918), 102. **Salvador**: Thales de Azevedo, *Povoamento da cidade do Salvador* (2nd edn, São Paulo, 1955), 192; Vilhena, *Cartas*, II, map facing 480; Russell-Wood, 'Colonial Brazil', 97. **Rio de Janeiro**: Eulalia Maria Lahmeyer Lobo, *História do Rio de Janeiro*, I (Rio de Janeiro, 1978), 55; *RIHGB*, 47/1 (1884), 27; *ibid.*, 21 (1858), table facing 176; PRO, FO 63/84/ERD/2255, Strangford to Wellesley, 20 May 1810. **São Paulo**: Maria Luiza Marcílio, *La ville de São Paulo* (Paris, 1968), 119. **Porto Alegre**: *RIHGB*, 30/1 (1867), 69. **Oeiras**: Domingos Barreira de Macedo, 'Cenço das casas proprias e de aluguer q. occupa os moradores da cidade de Oeiras...', Sept. 1762, Arquivo Nacional da Torre do Tombo (Lisbon) [ANTT], Ministério do Reino, maço 601; *RIHGB*, 17 (1854), 56. **Vila Boa**: *RIHGB*, 12 (2nd edn, 1874), 482f. **Vila Bela**: José Roberto do Amaral Lapa, 'Ciclo vital de um polo urbano: Vila Bela (1751–1820)', *Anais do VII simpósio nacional dos professores universitários de história* (São Paulo, 1974), 315. **Ouro Preto**: Donald Ramos, 'Vila Rica: profile of a colonial Brazilian urban center', *The Americas*, 35 (April 1979), 495–526.

history of late colonial Brazil remains to be written, it is evident that the processes of urbanization were much more advanced in some parts of Brazil than in others. In the captaincy of Bahia, for example, 170,489 out of an estimated 193,598 persons in 1780 lived in the capital city, its immediate suburbs, and eight towns around the Bay of All Saints. By contrast, the average size of 36 municipalities in the captaincy of Rio de Janeiro (excluding the capital) was only 1,625 in the late 1770s. One further example: the 1782 census of Pernambuco reported that there were 169,043 persons living in 25 municipalities of the district (*comarca*) that included the captaincy's capital (Olinda) and its chief port (Recife), an average of 6,761 persons per community; but in the captaincy's other *comarca*, where there were twenty communities, the average fell by more than half, to 3,035.

Table 3 summarizes various contemporary counts and estimates of the size of Brazil's principal cities and towns during the last decades of colonial rule. All are low, in most instances excluding small children (0–7 years) and in some cases slaves as well. It is evident that throughout these years Salvador, the colonial capital until 1763, still retained a lead over its rival and successor, Rio de Janeiro, but that lead was to disappear during the years 1808–22, when Rio's population doubled. But whereas Salvador and its satellite communities claimed a large share of the captaincy of Bahia's inhabitants, that was untrue of other cities such as São Paulo. The city of São Paulo grew surprisingly little between 1765 and 1803. Moreover, while one in every four persons in the captaincy of São Paulo lived in its capital city in 1765, that proportion fell to one in eight by 1803, reflecting the growth of towns of intermediate size during the economic growth of the last colonial decades. While evidence is sparse, the seaports seem to have continued to increase more rapidly than did interior towns, the most notable of which, Ouro Preto, suffered a loss of more than half of its population after the mid-century because of the decline of the mining industry. Although colonial Brazil has generally been depicted as a distinctly rural colony, its leading cities were impressive for their size, if not for their beauty, cleanliness, or safety. By the mid 1770s Salvador was larger than every city in English colonial America save Philadelphia (pop. 40,000 in 1775) and possessed a larger population than did Bristol, Liverpool, Birmingham, or Manchester. Recife, only the fourth ranking city in Brazil, was then larger than Boston (25,000 in 1775), the third largest in English America, and very likely Rio de Janeiro was larger than

Table 4 *Racial composition of Brazil at the end of the colonial period*

Place	Whites	Mulattos and blacks Free	Slaves	Indians	Total
Pará[a]			23	20	80,000
Maranhão[b]	31	17.3	46	5	78,860
Piauí	21.8	18.4	36.2	23.6	58,962
Goiás	12.5	36.2	46.2	5.2	55,422
Mato Grosso[c]	15.8			3.8	26,836
Pernambuco	28.5	42	26.2	3.2	391,986
Bahia	19.8	31.6	47	1.5	359,437
Rio de Janeiro[d]	33.6	18.4	45.9	2	229,582
Minas Gerais	23.6	33.7	40.9	1.8	494,759
São Paulo	56	25	16	3	208,807
Rio Grande do Sul[e]	40.4	21	5.5	34	66,420
Average for eight jurisdiction[f]	28.0	27.8	38.1	5.7	

Source: PRO, FO 63/84/ERD/2255, Strangford to Wellesley, 20 May 1810.

[a] Not included in source. See MacLachlan, 'African slave trade', 136, where it is reported that 57% consisted of free persons. [b] Not included in source. I have substituted data derived from the census of 1801 cited in *ibid.* [c] Not included in source. I have used the census of 1800 (*RIHGB*, 28/1 (1865), 125–7), which gives 53.2% as *prêtos* and 27.2% as mulattos, but does not distinguish between slaves and free persons. [d] Based on the 1803 census for the city and later counts for the captaincy. Espíritu Santo and Santa Catarina excluded. [e] Data defective. See text. [f] Except Mato Grosso, Pará, Rio Grande do Sul.

pre-revolutionary New York (25,000 in 1775). At the turn of the century Rio was growing at the impressive rate of 9.2 per cent per year.[2]

When the crown began to require regular census counts in 1776, it did not stipulate that racial distinctions be included. However, some governors, especially those who administered captaincies where there were large numbers of slaves, did ask for such information themselves. Some of the resulting tabulations distinguished Brazil's four primary

[2] See Carl Bridenbaugh, *Cities in revolt. Urban life in America 1743–1776* (reprint., New York, 1964), 216 and 217 n. 4, and Jacob M. Price, 'Economic function and growth of American port towns in the eighteenth century', *Perspectives in American History*, 7 (Cambridge, Mass., 1974), 176–7. Cf. Gary B. Nash, *The urban crucible: social change, political consciousness, and the origins of the American revolution* (Cambridge, Mass., 1979), 407–9. Nash provides substantially lower estimates than Bridenbaugh or Price and makes the contrast between the largest English and Portuguese colonial cities appear even greater. For the 1799 census of the city of Rio de Janeiro, see *RIHGB*, 21 (1858), table facing 176; that of 1803 is cited in table 2, source C.

racial strains: whites, i.e., persons socially accepted as Caucasians; *pardos*, or mulattos; *prêtos*, or blacks; and Indians within effective Portuguese control. But other reports only differentiated between freemen and slaves. Since Indian slavery was officially (though not always in practice) abolished in the 1750s, it is evident that all slaves enumerated were persons of African origin, whether or not Brazilian-born, but what proportion of the slaves were black or brown is hard to say. Though we possess one or more censuses that do identify racial elements in one or another part of Brazil during the late eighteenth century, we do not have sufficient reports with comparable classifications for any decade to be able to generalize about the racial composition of Brazil as a whole.

Fortunately, soon after the arrival of the Portuguese court, the ministry of the interior did compile a census in which racial distinctions were included for major Brazilian captaincies. The results, as reported by Lord Strangford, the British minister at Rio de Janeiro, to his government in 1810, are summarized in table 4, which also includes somewhat earlier counts for captaincies missing in the Strangford dispatch. As table 4 demonstrates, nearly two-thirds of Brazil's population at that time was of African origin (blacks and mulattos), and there appear to have been more free persons of colour than whites in the colony. Regrettably, the ministerial census did not distinguish between mulatto and black freemen, but what we know from other studies suggests that six or seven out of every ten free persons of colour were mulattos, making them probably the most rapidly growing racial element in Brazil.

It is interesting to compare the racial data reported by Strangford with that derived from some of the censuses of the 1770s. In the far north the percentage of free persons (described as 'whites, mulattos, and other mixtures as well as...blacks') in Pará increased during the last three decades of the eighteenth century from 44.8 to 57, but in neighbouring Maranhão the percentage of free persons fell slightly (from 32.4 to 31). The racial composition of two of the most important sugar captaincies, Pernambuco and Bahia, is lacking in the earlier censuses, but the ministerial report shows a striking contrast: in Pernambuco there were substantially more free persons of colour than slaves; while the reverse was true in Bahia. As for the third-ranking sugar captaincy, Rio de Janeiro, in 1780 the percentage of free persons was almost equal to that of slaves (50.7 to 49.3), but the 1799 census reveals that the percentage of free persons had grown to 65.5. São Paulo was one of two captaincies where whites appear to have predominated numerically, though their percentage fell from 56.4 in the 1770s to 50.8 c. 1810. The racial data Strangford reported for Rio Grande do Sul does not accord with that contained in the censuses of 1798 and 1802, and the discrepancy must be due to clerical error. Those more detailed censuses indicate that whites comprised between 57.7 and 55 per cent of the population, compared with free persons of colour (5.5–6 per cent), slaves (34.5–35.5 per cent) and Indians (2.3–3.4 per cent). As might be expected, the interior captaincies were the least attractive to whites; coloured majorities predominated everywhere.

Since the censuses of the late colonial period are deficient by modern standards, it is not surprising that scholars differ as to the actual size of Brazil's population during these years. The evidence summarized here suggests that by about 1800 Brazil possessed more than two but less than three million inhabitants. Such a conclusion suggests several additional observations. First, by the turn of the nineteenth century Brazil held nearly as many people as did Portugal, whose population in 1798 stood at between three and three and a half million;[3] by contrast, Spanish America's population then outnumbered that of Spain by about 50 per cent. Second, it appears that during the course of the eighteenth century Brazil's population had grown between 2.5 and four times; however, what percentage of that growth was due to natural increase as opposed to immigration from Portugal or from Africa is impossible to say, though for the late colonial decades we do have far more abundant data concerning the volume of the slave trade than for earlier periods.

Brazil received its slaves from a number of African sources. Guiné, a major supplier during the sixteenth century, was only a minor source in the eighteenth, except for the Pará and Maranhão markets, which obtained nearly 70 per cent of their slaves from the ports of Bissau and Cacheu during the years 1757–77. Both the northerners and Mineiro gold miners preferred Guiné or Mina slaves over Angolan because they were considered more capable of withstanding hard labour. Bahians also favoured slaves from the Mina coast, i.e., four ports along the Dahomey littoral. They were able to exchange Bahian tobacco, sugar brandy (*cachaça*) and – illicitly – gold for slaves. After the Mina coast trade declined in the mid 1770s, the Bahian demand shifted mainly to the Bight of Benin. Rio de Janeiro drew the bulk of its slaves from the ports of

---

[3] *A população de Portugal em 1798. O censo de Pina Manique* (Paris, 1970), introd. Joaquim Veríssimo Serrão.

Luanda and Benguela in Angola, which is believed to have been the source of 70 per cent of the slaves sent to eighteenth-century Brazil.

Contemporary estimates of the number of slaves entering Brazil exceed those of modern scholars. Writing in 1781, the Bahian economic thinker, José da Silva Lisboa, advised his former mentor, Dr Domingos Vandelli, head of the royal botanical gardens in Lisbon, that Brazil imported more than 25,000 slaves a year. A decade later a Spanish agent of the British government stated that 19,800 slaves annually entered the three major Brazilian ports – Recife, Salvador, and Rio de Janeiro.[4] Neither informant provided sources to support his estimate and because of fraud, contraband, clerical errors, the frequent practice of counting several slaves as portions of a prime slave (a male in good health aged fifteen to 25), and scholarly differences over numerical proximates for slave tax records, as well as incomplete or missing documents, it is impossible to be certain how many slaves really did reach Brazilian ports during this period. Table 5 summarizes the best information that we possess concerning the volume and fluctuations in the slave trade.

Neither the figures offered here nor those of the well-known demographer of the slave trade, Philip D. Curtin, in his *The Atlantic slave trade: a census* (Madison, 1969), are complete. Curtin relies mainly on Mauricio Goulart, a Brazilian scholar who ignored northern Brazil and was sketchy on Pernambuco's imports. Both Curtin and Goulart ignore shipments from Guiné and Benin. But there are lacunae in our estimates as well. No reliable data have yet been found for Belém or São Luís at the beginning of the period, nor for Bahia or Rio de Janeiro in the late 1770s, nor for Pernambuco during the last fifteen years of the eighteenth century. Except for the years 1801–5, the estimates proposed here are lower than Curtin's, though they are based upon a wider array of sources. Still, the same general trends are observable: slave imports fell during the 1760s and continued to do so during the 1770s, reflecting the economic crisis of these decades; then came a revival in the 1780s, mirroring the growth of staple exports, which continued to expand, as did the slave trade, for the rest of this period.

If our knowledge of the number of slaves brought to late colonial Brazil remains incomplete, it is even more deficient with respect to the

---

[4] Lisboa to Vandelli, 18 October 1781, *ABNRJ*, 32 (1914), 505; 'Copia del papel que de a D^n Josef de Siqueira y Palma en respuesta de las preguntas que me hiso...', Madrid, 12 December 1791, British Library, Add. MS 13985, fo. 248r.

Table 5 *Estimates of annual slave imports into Brazil, by port of entry,*
1750–1805 ('000)

Inclusive dates	Belém do Pará	São Luís do Maranhão	Recife de Pernambuco	Bahia de Todos os Santos	Rio de Janeiro	Total	Curtin's estimates
1750–55	n.a.	n.a.	1.7	9.1	5.5	16.3 +⎫	
1756–60	0.7	0.5	2.7	3.6	6.4	13.9 ⎭	16.0
1761–65	0.7	0.5	2.4	3.3	8.6	15.5 ⎫	
1766–70	0.7	0.5	2.4	2.6	7.8	14.0 ⎭	16.5
1771–75	0.7	0.5	2.4	2.3	6.7?	12.6 ⎫	
1776–79	0.6	0.5	2.4	4.0?	6.0?	13.5 ⎭	16.1
1780–85	0.6	1.2	1.0	2.4	9.2	14.4 ⎫	
1786–90	0.6	1.8	n.a.	2.4	8.9	13.7 +⎭	17.8
1791–94	0.3	1.6	n.a.	3.4	8.9	14.2 +⎫	
1795–1800	0.5	1.7	n.a.	4.4	10.0	16.6 +⎭	22.2
1801–05	1.6	1.7	2.5	5.3	10.5	21.6	20.6

Sources: **Pará**: 'Recapitulação dos dois mapas dos escravos introduzidos pela companhia geral do Grão Pará e Maranhão... 1757 até 1777', AHU/PA/Pará, caixa 39; MacLachlan, 'African slave trade', 137; Joseph C. Miller, 'Legal Portuguese slaving from Angola. Some preliminary indications of volume and direction, 1760–1830', *Revue Française d'Histoire d'Outre-Mer*, 62 (1975), 171. **Maranhão**: 'Recapitulação dos dois mappas...'; MacLachlan, 139; Miller, 171. **Pernambuco**: 'Parallelo dos escravos que ficaram em Pernambuco de 10 annos antes do estabelecimento da companhia, com os 10 annos primeiros da mesma companhia...', Arquivo Histórico Ultramarino (Lisbon), codex series [AHU/CU/cod.] 1821, n. 13; António Carreira, *As companhias pombalinas de navegação, comercio e tráfico de escravos entre a costa africana e o nordeste brasileiro* (Bissau, 1969), 261; Miller, 171. **Bahia**: 'Relação dos escravos vindos da costa da Mina, desde o 1º de janeiro de 1750 thé o último de dezembro de 1755', Arquivo Público da Bahia, ordens régias (royal dispatches) [APB/OR], 54/83; P. Verger, *Flux et reflux de la traite des nègres entre le golfe de Bénin et Bahia do Todos os Santos du XVIIᵉ au XIXᵉ siècle* (Paris, 1968), 664; K. David Patterson, 'A note on slave exports from the costa da Mina, 1760–1770', *Bulletin de l'Institut Français d'Afrique Noire*, 33/2 (1971), 252; Carreira, 280–1; Biblioteca Nacional, Lisbon [BNL], cod. 6936; Miller, 170; Mauricio Goulart, *Escravidão africana no Brasil* (3rd edn, São Paulo, 1975), 212–15. **Rio de Janeiro**: Corcino Medieros dos Santos, 'Relações de Angola com o Rio de Janeiro (1736–1808)', *Estudos Históricos*, 12 (Marília, 1973), 19–20; Herbert S. Klein, *The Middle Passage: comparative studies in the Atlantic slave trade* (Princeton, 1978), 28 and 55; Miller, 169.

internal slave trade, i.e. the numbers of slaves admitted to one port and later transhipped to destinations elsewhere. During the first half of the eighteenth century the *câmaras* (municipal councils) of the north-eastern sugar captaincies constantly complained of shortages of slaves because of the re-export of new arrivals to the mining zones. Such complaints continued during the later decades. In 1754, for example, the câmara of Salvador protested that dealers in Rio de Janeiro and Salvador sold the best slaves to the premium markets of the interior, leaving only the refuse for local buyers. During the years 1750–9, 61.2 per cent (13,385) of the slaves brought to Pernambuco were subsequently forwarded to Rio de Janeiro for sale in the mines. But of the 21,299 slaves landed at Pernambuco between 1761 and 1770, only 1,653 (7.7 per cent) were reshipped to Rio, reflecting an upswing in the plantation economy of Pernambuco as well as a decline in the mining districts. Rio de Janeiro was the entrepot not only for slaves sold to buyers in that captaincy but also for those sent to São Paulo, Mato Grosso, and especially Minas Gerais. In 1756, for example, 3,456 slaves (37.5 per cent of those arriving at Rio that year) passed the Paraibuna checkpoint en route to Minas Gerais; in 1780 a well-informed magistrate reported that about 4,000 slaves a year, presumably including those smuggled, entered Minas from Rio. At the beginning of the nineteenth century Rio Grande do Sul, by then a prosperous agricultural and stock-raising captaincy, received 452 slaves from Rio de Janeiro and another 66 from Bahia; a few years later it took 515 from Rio de Janeiro, 28 from Bahia, and two from Pernambuco.[5] Though there is much more to be learned about slavery and the slave trade in colonial Brazil, it seems unlikely that the upswing in the trade at the end of our period significantly altered the magnitude of the population estimates offered here.

THE EXPULSION OF THE JESUITS

The expulsion of the Jesuits in 1759 constituted the first serious crisis to beset Brazil during the late colonial period. Since the first members of the Society of Jesus had entered Brazil with the founders of royal government in 1549, the Jesuits had become the premier missionary order in the colony. Their missions extended from Paraná in the south to the upper Amazon in the north, from the Atlantic coast to the Goiás plateau, though, along with other orders, they were excluded from Minas Gerais. Every major city and some interior towns like Belém de Cachoeira (Bahia) boasted Jesuit facilities: schools, seminaries, distinc-

---

[5] Câmara to viceroy, 6 February 1754, Arquivo Público do Estado da Bahia, ordens régias (royal dispatches) [APB/OR], 49/1051; 'Parallelo dos escravos que ficaram em Pernambuco...' (see table 5, Pernambuco); 'Lista dos escravos e cargoes que passarao neste registro da Parahibuna no anno de 1756 para o continente das minas', AHU/PA/Rio de Janeiro, 1º catalogo, caixa 40, no. 19,818; AHU/PA/Rio Grande do Sul, caixas 2–3.

tive, often sumptuous churches, religious retreats. In support of these facilities the Jesuits had become Brazil's largest landowner and greatest slave-master. Every sugar-producing captaincy possessed one or more Jesuit plantation; Bahia alone had five. From the Amazonian island of Marajó to the backlands of Piauí the Jesuits possessed extensive cattle and horse ranches. In the Amazon their annual canoe flotillas brought to Belém envied quantities of cacao, cloves, cinnamon, and sarsaparilla, harvested along the great river's major tributaries. Besides flotillas of small craft that linked producing centres with operational headquarters, the Society maintained its own frigate to facilitate communications within its far-flung network. The Jesuits were renowned as courageous pathfinders and evangelists, as pre-eminent scholars, sterling orators, as confessors of the high and mighty, and as tenacious defenders of their rights and privileges, which included licences from the crown to possess vast holdings of both urban and rural property and complete exemption of their goods from all customs duties in Portugal and in Brazil.

The Jesuits were also Brazil's most controversial religious body. From the outset they posed as champions of Indian freedom, untroubled by the fact that they themselves held thousands of blacks in slavery. They served as contentious intermediaries between Indian free workers and colonial planters and farmers. They were accused of providing asylum for legitimately ransomed Indians who had fled from merciless masters. Their economic competitors resented their special privileges and accused the Jesuits (and other religious orders) of monopolizing the spice trade of the Amazon, of engrossing lands belonging to their neighbours and tenants, and of engaging in forbidden commercial activities by means of retail sales conducted within their colleges. Such criticism was voiced by angry câmaras, which on several occasions expelled the Fathers from their captaincies during the seventeenth century, by court lobbyists, by rival churchmen, and by hostile royal officials. But the Jesuits always successfully defended themselves and, despite minor reverses, appeared to be as firmly rooted in mid-eighteenth-century Brazil as they had ever been.

The downfall of the Jesuits may be traced back to 1750, for that was the year of the ratification of the Treaty of Madrid, establishing a new boundary between Brazil and Spanish America, and of the appointment of Sebastião José de Carvalho e Melo (best known by his later title as the marquis of Pombal), a one-time Jesuit protégé, as one of the king's three ministers. He soon came to dominate the other ministers, as well as the sovereign himself (José I, 1750–77). Viewed by some writers as one of the most progressive, enlightened statesmen of the century and by others as a nepotistic, merciless, over-rated paranoiac, he was undoubtedly a proud, dynamic figure who found in the dogma of regalism the opportunities to modernize Portugal by means that had eluded his predecessors. Though Pombal became the arch-opponent of the Jesuits for two decades, the origins of his intense, uncompromising hatred for them remains unknown. The first indication that he was preparing for a fight came in 1751 in the instructions that he prepared in the king's name for his brother, Francisco Xavier de Mendonça Furtado, newly designated governor of the state of Grão-Pará and Maranhão and chief Portuguese boundary commissioner in the north. One of the instruction's secret articles warned that if the Jesuits offered opposition to the crown's policies in the Amazon, they should be informed that José I expected them to be the first to obey his orders, particularly 'because the estates which they possess are [held] entirely or for the most part contrary to the laws of the realm...'

Throughout the 1750s Mendonça Furtado, hard-driving, violent-tempered, gullible and suspicious, and the bishop of Pará, Dom Miguel de Bulhões e Sousa, a greedy, self-serving Dominican long known for his hostility towards the Jesuits and a zealous collaborator of Pombal and his brother, filled their dispatches to Lisbon with an endless stream of supposed Jesuit misdeeds. They repeated long-standing, unverified and, in fact, often discredited settlers' allegations concerning the Fathers' tyrannical mistreatment of the Indians, their monopoly of the spice trade, their reputedly enormous wealth, including that supposedly derived from hidden mines, and, on the basis of the discovery of a single cannon which the crown had authorized a generation earlier so that an exposed Jesuit mission could frighten off hostile Indian raiders, contended that the Jesuits had become an armed menace against the state and were even engaging in treasonable relations with Spaniards. (It was the Spanish Jesuits, of course, who were at the time organizing Guaraní resistance to the implementation of the Treaty of Madrid in southern Brazil.)

The voluminous dispatches that the governor and the bishop filed, those sent by Gomes Freire de Andrada, governor of Minas Gerais, Rio de Janeiro and southern Brazil, and a barrage of reports from remote Piauí concerning a bitter land dispute between the Jesuits and other landowners and a reforming royal magistrate, convinced Pombal that the Jesuits were the hidden hand behind every adversity that Portugal sustained. True, he did not blame them for the Lisbon earthquake of 1 November 1755, but he was incensed when a Jesuit orator dared to suggest that that calamity was a manifestation of God's judgement against the king's impious subjects. And he was even more indignant when another padre ill-advisedly warned that those who invested in one of Pombal's pet schemes – the Companhia do Grão-Pará e Maranhão – 'would not be members of the Company of Christ'.

Both Jesuit statements led to the arrest, imprisonment or exile of individual padres who joined others, notably foreign-born Jesuits, whom Mendonça Furtado had expelled for various alleged offences. In 1757, following a popular uprising in Oporto known as the Taverners Revolt, the Jesuits were accused of fomenting the tumult, though no proof of their involvement was ever found. Nevertheless, the charge served as the pretext for the banishment of the Jesuits from the royal palace and for the government's refusal to permit the Jesuits to continue preaching in Lisbon's cathedral. In his explanation of these measures to the papal nuncio, Pombal assured him that he possessed irrefutable proof that the Jesuits were guilty of the most heinous crimes and that if they were not immediately disciplined, within a decade they would become so powerful that all the armies of Europe would be unable to oust them from the heartland of South America, where they kept hundreds of thousands of Indians as slaves working on fortifications prepared by European engineers disguised as Jesuits. Such charges were further elaborated in a white paper prepared under Pombal's personal direction. Entitled 'Brief Account of the Republic founded by the Jesuits in the Overseas Territories of Spain and Portugal', it cited evidence purporting to demonstrate that the Jesuits constituted a state within a state, threatening Brazil's very security. Then, under Pombal's relentless prodding, the pope reluctantly designated a cardinal, a kinsman of Pombal and much beholden to him for past favours, to verify the government's charges, especially those concerning the Society's illicit commercial activities. Though he submitted no evidence and persistently refused to discuss the case with the papal nuncio, with whom he was obliged to consult, the cardinal quickly announced that all the charges were true, that every Jesuit facility was guilty of engaging in forbidden commercial and banking ventures. Two days after that report was issued, the patriarch of Lisbon, the highest ranking ecclesiastical dignitary of the realm, suspended all Jesuits within Portugal from preaching or hearing confessions.

Further humiliations followed. After an unsuccessful attack on José I in September 1758 (which may have been staged) several Jesuits were formally charged with being instigators of the regicide attempt, and in January 1759 the king ordered the arrest of all Jesuits in Portugal and the seizure of the Society's properties in the kingdom. On 3 September 1759, José I became the first Europen monarch to expel the Jesuits from all his domains and confiscate their properties.

When the top-secret instructions to arrest the Fathers and occupy their holdings were received in Brazil in late 1759, high magistrates accompanied by well-armed troops swiftly surrounded every Jesuit facility, arresting the occupants and ransacking their domiciles in the expectation of finding bullion and jewels – which, in fact, were not discovered. Closely guarded, the Fathers – approximately 670 of them – were returned to Portugal on the first available warships several months later. Although the crown had feared the possibility of popular uprisings in support of the Jesuits, none occurred, in part because of the military precision with which the detentions were accomplished and in part because the public response was conditioned by government-dictated anti-Jesuit pastoral letters distributed by co-operating bishops. As soon as former Jesuit properties were inventoried, those of a perishable nature, including crops, barnyard animals, and some (but not all) slaves, were auctioned off; in at least one captaincy, Rio Grande do Norte, they were actually distributed gratis to local inhabitants, particularly militia officers. Most of the urban properties, including blocks of rented shops, houses, and wharves, were quickly sold, but for a time the crown considered maintaining the large agricultural and stock-raising estates for their income; however, after it became obvious that such properties were constantly losing value because of mis-management and looting, they, too, were put on the auction block. Though the crown possessed a unique opportunity to diversify ownership of developed Jesuit lands by dividing them among small-holders, it refrained from doing so and sold the bulk of them to syndicates of wealthy landowners and merchants. Not all estates immediately found buyers. Some of the largest remained royal properties for as long as two decades; others, including more than 30 former Jesuit cattle ranches in Piauí and the great polycultural estate of Santa Cruz in Rio de Janeiro, remained state properties well into the twentieth century. The major Jesuit churches passed to the eager bishops and became their cathedrals, while most of the colleges were transformed into governors' palaces or military hospitals. The once impressive Jesuit libraries were pillaged and allowed to deteriorate until they became worthless.

It would, of course, be simplistic to conclude that the removal of the Jesuits and the dispersal of their assets were merely consequences of the paranoia of Pombal and his claque. The end of the Jesuits came about because of various other factors as well. Though not one of the criticisms uttered against them during the 1750s was fundamentally new, the uncompromising response of the Pombaline regime certainly did break with the tradition of church–state relationships in Portugal. The Pombaline regalists insisted that every element of society, particularly the religious, must be wholly subservient to the dictates of the king as interpreted by his ministers. The medieval concept of the two (and equal) swords was replaced by that of a single weapon ruthlessly and enthusiastically wielded by the king's ministers and their minions. Resistance, passive or active, could be interpreted only as a sign of disloyalty or treason. Certainly the reputedly enormous wealth of the Jesuits was tempting to a traditionally impecunious government, especially after it was beset by the hugely destructive Lisbon disaster. And for some years the windfall derived from the disposal of Jesuit properties lightened the crown's financial burdens, even if it failed to contribute to the development of the Brazilian infrastructure. Then, too, the physiocratic notion of the useful man was very much on the minds of the Portuguese elite, both at home and abroad. They were inclined to ridicule reclusive, contemplative monks or dedicated but impractical missionaries and to extol the virtues of the truly productive members of society, i.e., tax-paying heads of families who produced agricultural or industrial goods and who fathered sons. To men like the well-travelled diplomat Dom Luis da Cunha, Ribeiro Sanches, the peripatetic physician and self-proclaimed Jew, or the duke of Silva-Tarouca, long-time adviser to Maria Theresa of Austria, as well as Pombal himself and those who served under him, the day of the religious had passed. The modernizing state required other partners in its quest for advancement. Since the Jesuits were the largest, most influential, and most outspoken of the religious orders in the Portuguese dominions, they must be the first to be struck down.

The expulsion of the Jesuits had important but often overlooked consequences. One, especially noticeable in the 1760s, was a government campaign against former Jesuits, ex-Jesuit students and friends of Jesuits, many of whom were carefully watched and arrested on the slightest pretext and confined to gaols in Brazil or Portugal. That campaign was inspired by fears that ousted Jesuits were conspiring with the enemies of Portugal to infiltrate Brazil for seditious purposes, but it was also the product of a determined government policy to enforce religious orthodoxy in Brazil, and the episcopate of Brazil was expected to play a decisive role in the implementation of that policy through appropriate pastoral letters and close surveillance of the priesthood.

The most bizarre manifestation of that campaign was the dispatch of Giraldo José de Abranches, archdeacon of Mariana, Minas Gerais, to Belém do Pará in 1763. Abranches' mission was to conduct a special investigation for the Holy Office. Brazilians have taken pride in the fact that, unlike Spanish America or Portuguese India, colonial Brazil never had a branch of the Inquisition established there. While that is true, on several occasions during the late sixteenth and early seventeenth centuries special teams of inquisitors travelled from Portugal to Brazil to conduct lengthy inquiries. But the Abranches inquiry of 1763–9 was the first in a century and a half. Precisely why the commissioner was sent to Pará at that time remains obscure.[6]

Although the Visitor's authority extended throughout northern Brazil, he conducted hearings only in the ex-Jesuit college in Belém, and most of the 485 persons who appeared before him as confessants or denunciants seem to have come from that city and its environs. In spite of the tribunal's protracted duration, only 45 persons were identified as having committed serious offences, ranging from sorcery (21), blasphemy (6), and quackery (9) to sodomy (4), bigamy (5), heresy (2), and excessive corporal punishment of slaves (1). Nearly all were members of the lowest strata of society – Indians, black slaves, or free persons of colour – and only one was a (presumably white) sugar-mill proprietor.

The Abranches inquiry was an exceptional exercise of ecclesiastical authority in Brazil at this time, for it was more common for the bishops to be charged with responsibility for the suppression of deviance and

---

[6] The very existence of this mission remained unknown until 1963, when the manuscript of the tribunal was discovered in the National Library in Lisbon. See J. R. do Amaral Lapa, *Livro da visitação do santo ofício da inquisição do estado do Grão Pará* (Petropólis, 1978), which included the text of the official findings and a lengthy introduction.

the maintenance of ecclesiastical discipline. During the Pombaline era prelates were selected on the basis of evidence of severe piety, militant anti-Jesuitism, and abject subserviency to ranking secular authorities. Some of them conducted lengthy investigations during the early 1760s into alleged Jesuit misdeeds, enquiries which produced lurid if dubious testimony. After the expulsion, the episcopate was given complete authority over the religious orders and, once the Jesuits were no longer around to organize their defence, the others were powerless to resist. For a time the orders were prohibited from admitting any novices, and even after that right was restored special licences were required from the crown before new members could be admitted. Such consent was grudgingly given and by the end of the century many monasteries were half empty and most of their inmates advanced in years.[7]

Well might the heads of other orders shudder when the Jesuits were rounded up, for they knew that their turn would come. And it did. In the mid-1760s the most affluent of the remaining orders in the lower Amazon, the Mercedarians, were peremptorily recalled to the kingdom and their properties, consisting of vast cattle ranches on the island of Marajó, were seized by the crown. At the end of the same decade the crown imposed forced loans upon the wealthier religious orders which declined to surrender their properties voluntarily in exchange for government bonds. As a result of these and other measures, the religious orders in Brazil were weakened to such an extent that they never fully recovered. But the diocesan branch of the church was not much better off, and throughout the late colonial period its leaders were constantly appealing for funds to establish seminaries and augment the number of priests in non-urban areas. With rare exceptions, the crown turned a deaf ear to such requests. The enfeeblement of the Catholic church in Brazil in the nineteenth century can be traced back to the Pombaline era and to the generation that followed.[8]

[7] King to archbishop elect of Bahia, 30 June 1764, AHU/PA/Bahia, 1º catálogo, annex to no. 6554; *alvará* of 30 July 1792, Antonio Delgado da Silva (ed.), *Collecção da legislação portuguesa de 1750 a [1820]*, (9 vols., Lisbon, 1830–47), *1791–1801*, 152–3; colonial minister, circular to archbishop of Bahia, bishops of Rio de Janeiro, Funchal, and Angra, 30 January 1764, AHU/CU/cod. 603, no. 222; same to same and to bishop of Pernambuco, 19 August 1768, *ibid.*, cod. 604, no. 154; D. Antonio de Salles e Noronha, governor, to Martinho de Melo e Castro, 21 May 1781, AHU/PA/Maranhão, caixa 48; Fr Manoel de Santa Rosa Henriques to queen, *c.* 1793, AHU/PA/Pará, maço 3.

[8] George C. A. Boehrer, 'The Church in the second reign, 1840–1889', in Henry H. Keith and S. F. Edwards (eds.), *Conflict and continuity in Brazilian society* (Columbia, S.C., 1969), 114. The foregoing relies upon Manoel Barata, *Formação histórica do Pará* (Belém, 1973), 44, 78, 92–3; AHU/PA/Bahia, 1º catálogo, nos. 19,765–6, 19,687–9, and 22,826; for contemporary

ECONOMIC CRISIS AND REMEDIES

The prolonged economic malaise that afflicted Portugal and Brazil during the 1760s and 1770s constituted a deeper and more enduring crisis than that presented by the conflict between the state and the Jesuits, and remedies were less easily found. The economic crisis was preceded by the destruction of Lisbon, the imperial city and one of the leading cities of Europe, larger than Rome or Vienna, by earthquake and fire on Sunday morning, 1 November 1755 and the enormous cost of rebuilding it.[9] The crisis coincided with, and was partly caused by, two exceedingly expensive wars with Spain for control of the vast borderlands extending from São Paulo to the north bank of the Río de la Plata. The main cause of the crisis, however, was the precipitous fall in income, both public and private, from Brazil beginning in the early 1760s. There had, in fact, been warnings that the Brazilian milch cow was running dry even before the earthquake, particularly the repeated postponements in the departures of the great fleets from both peninsular and Brazilian ports during the early fifties, but such delays had occurred so often in the past that no one seemed unduly alarmed. The principal cause of the severe curtailment of the crown's income from Brazil was the declining yield of the gold and diamond mines of the interior. While the three leading bullion-producing captaincies reached peak levels of production at slightly different times, the maximum yield from the

comments on the decline of the Orders, see [Luiz Antonio Oliveira Mendes], 'Discurso preliminar...da Bahia' (*c.* 1789), *ABNRJ*, 27 (1905), 286, and Vilhena, *Cartas*, II, 464–5.

[9] The loss of life in the Lisbon earthquake of 1755 has been conservatively estimated at 10,000, but other guesses run much higher. The physical destruction, especially along the Tagus and in the eastern quarter of the city, was enormous. The great wooden royal palace that had graced the city's principal maritime square since the late sixteenth century, 33 noble palaces, 54 convents, all six of the city's hospitals, the newly finished patriarchal residence, the opera house, several foreign embassies, and most of the port's warehouses, filled with the cargoes of fleets recently arrived from Brazil, with shipments intended for the next outbound fleets, and with the year's wine harvest, all were gone. Out of 20,000 homes, 17,000 were in ruins. Additional damage occurred in other cities, especially Sintra, Santarém and even Coimbra. Estimates of total damage to property range up to 20,000 contos, three or four times more than the annual public revenues. The conto (1,000 milreis or 2,500 cruzados) was quoted on the London market at about £280 (1760–5 average); John J. McCusker, *Money and exchange in Europe and America, 1600–1775. A handbook* (Chapel Hill, 1978), 114. Inevitably Portugal's most important colony was expected to come to her rescue, and Brazilian cities responded generously. Salvador alone pledged to contribute 1,200 contos over the next three decades towards the rebuilding of Lisbon. Conde D. Marcos de Noronha, viceroy, to crown, 20 July 1759, C. R. Boxer manuscript collection; see also Ignácio Accioli de Cerqueira e Silva, *Memórias históricas e políticas da província da Bahia*, ed. Braz do Amaral [*MHB*] (6 vols., Bahia, 1919–40), II, 182–90. The most useful accounts of the earthquake are T. D. Kendrick, *The Lisbon earthquake* (London, 1956) and José-Augusto França, *Lisboa pombalina e o iluminismo* (Lisbon, 1976).

mining sector occurred during the latter half of the 1750s and between 1755–9 and 1775–9 there was a drop in output of 51.5 per cent. It was also during the late 1750s that the diamond mines of Minas Gerais began to give out, resulting in bankruptcy for several contractors and in an eventual royal takeover (1771), which, however, failed to reverse the steady fall in productivity of the mines. At the same time, the two major agricultural export crops of Brazil, cane sugar and tobacco, from Pernambuco, Bahia, and Rio de Janeiro, were in something of a slump, the former because of low European prices, the latter owing to difficulties with Mina coast slave suppliers. And exports of cacao from the Amazon had become irregular because of a scarcity of Indian collectors, a shortage of shipping, and a decline in prices.

One of the crown's leading sources of revenue had long been the fifths or *quintos* from Minas Gerais. During the years 1752–62 they generated an average of 108 arrobas (32 lb or 14.5 kg each) of gold a year, but that yield fell to 83.2 arrobas in the course of the next decade and to 70.8 between 1772 and 1777. Similarly, the fifths in Goiás declined by 33.6 per cent from 1752–62 to 1762–72, and by the years 1782–92 were only 29.5 per cent of the 1752–62 level.[10] One of the most lucrative customs houses in Brazil during the Age of Gold had been that of Rio de Janeiro, but between the mid-1760s and the mid-1770s its yield fell by 25 per cent. While the total value of public and private remittances sent from Rio de Janeiro to Lisbon dropped by 39 per cent between 1749 and the mid-1770s, the crown's share shrank even more alarmingly, diminishing by 73.8 per cent. Because the Rio de Janeiro branch of the royal exchequer was unable to pay its bills, its debt load increased to over 1,272 contos by 1780. But what concerned the colonial minister even more was that by that date the crown was owed over 4,000 contos from insolvent tax contractors and tax payers in ten Brazilian captaincies. Between 1752–6 and 1769 emissions by the royal mint in Lisbon declined by more than 38 per cent.[11]

Obviously this extended crisis affected many different interest groups – Brazilian planters, merchant factors, tax contractors, royal officials; Portuguese merchants, shippers, and government officials. For the

---

[10] 'Goiases, Rendim.to dos q.tos ...', BNRJ, II–30, 34, 21, no. 1.

[11] Jorge Borges de Madeco, *A situação económica no tempo de Pombal* ... (Lisbon, 1951), ch. 4; Antônio de Sousa Pedroso Carnaxide, *O Brasil na administração pombalina* ... (Rio de Janeiro, 1940), 76–82; Alden, *Royal government*, 317–18, 328, 330 n. 68, 349–50, and 507–8; Corcino Medeiro dos Santos, *Relações comerciais do Rio de Janeiro com Lisboa (1763–1808)* (Rio de Janeiro, 1980), 60–2.

Portuguese government which had come to rely on the gold and diamonds of Brazil to finance the deficit in Portugal's balance of trade with the rest of the world, especially England, it was urgently necessary to find effective solutions to the problems besetting the Brazilian economy. Steps were taken to halt the decline in gold and diamond production – and to reduce smuggling – but without success. In order to improve the competitiveness of Brazilian sugars and tobaccos, the government, with rather more success, strengthened the powers of local boards of inspection (*mesas de inspecção*) previously established (1751) in major colonial ports. Presided over by high magistrates assisted by locally chosen deputies, the boards were responsible for setting quality standards for the export of both commodities, and later also of cotton; the determination of a just price between sellers and buyers; and the resolution of disputes between colonial shippers and European importers. More dramatic was the creation of two monopoly trading companies to promote the economic development of the backward north and the stagnant north-east.

The marquis of Pombal had become convinced that what Brazil and Portugal needed was a series of well-financed monopoly trading companies. Accordingly, in 1755 he persuaded a group of wealthy government officials and Lisbon merchants to invest in the Companhia do Grão-Pará e Maranhão. Its initial mission was to supply black slaves to the north, to offer attractive prices for colonial staples, existing (cinnamon, cloves, sarsaparilla, and especially cacao) and new (cotton and rice), and to transport these commodities to Portugal via its own armed convoys. By the early 1770s, however, the company began to perform other functions too. It served as a conduit through which the government conveyed large sums to maintain an expanded military presence and an augmented bureaucracy in the Amazon. It was also expected to cultivate a lucrative illicit trade with Spanish Quito via the Amazon and Mato Grosso,[12] and it was asked to develop a colonial market for the products of newly established factories in Portugal. Four years after the creation of the first company, its sister, the Companhia Geral de Pernambuco e Paraíba, was created to revive the faltering agrarian economy of the north-east. Each company was initially chartered for twenty years, the Maranhão company being nominally capitalized at 480 contos, that of Pernambuco at 1,360 contos. Shares were available to both domestic and foreign subscribers. Prominent

[12] 'Instrucção secretissima…para João Pereira Caldas', 2 September 1772, AHU/CU/cod. 599.

government officials, led by Pombal himself, were expected to invest
heavily, and many did. Pressure was applied to other members of the
nobility, lesser government functionaries, convents and other religious
bodies, and affluent colonial merchants and planters to subscribe too.
Those who purchased a minimum of ten shares were promised habits
in the Order of Christ, a prestigious order of chivalry in Portugal, and
exemption from certain taxes and from military call-ups. Much as they
coveted those privileges and honours, colonial magnates did not rush
to contribute: 90 per cent of the capital that financed the Maranhão
company came from investors in the kingdom, as did 85 per cent of
that behind the Pernambuco company. Of the two, the Maranhão
company proved to be the better investment, yielding dividends
averaging 8.4 per cent (1768–74) compared with under 6 per cent for
the Pernambuco company (1760–79).

Neither company long survived the fall of the marquis of Pombal
in March 1777, following the death of José I. Although Manuel Nunes
Dias, the most indefatigable analyst of the Maranhão company
(1755–78) confidently concludes that it was 'a great achievement (*êxito*)
of enlightened Pombaline mercantilism', his own student and the author
of a complementary study of the Pernambuco company (1759–79)
regards that company mainly as a successful vehicle for exploitative
European, especially British, capital. While both authors may be
correct, it is not easy to determine how much the companies achieved
for Brazil. Both obviously increased the levels of slave imports so
essential for agricultural development (see table 5 above). Both provided
a more dependable shipping service than had existed in the past;
however, the Maranhão company did not lessen the Amazon's dependence upon cacao nor increase the volume of its exports, but it
contributed to the beginnings of two new exports that would play
important roles in the regional economy of the north in later decades
– cotton and rice, discussed below. During the years 1760–80 the
volume of both sugar and hide exports from the north-east increased
significantly, though the Pernambuco company was unsuccessful in
stimulating exports of new commodities in appreciable volumes. Both
companies distributed to colonial markets impressive quantities of
goods ranging from cotton and woollen cloth to hats, ribbons, china,
silks, and hardwares manufactured in newly founded Portuguese
factories, most of them opened since 1770. Lastly, both companies
surrendered their monopolies but continued for many years to try to

collect large sums owed them by colonial debtors, a source of continuing irritation to such planters and merchants.

Although there had been proposals to extend the system of monopoly companies to Bahia and Rio de Janeiro, they had proved stillborn, apparently because of a lack of available investment capital as well as strong British opposition. Instead, the government had moved in the opposite direction by terminating the convoyed fleet (*frota*) system that had been in effect since 1649. In spite of repeated efforts by the crown and the great Lisbon merchants to establish satisfactory shipping schedules at both ends of the vital Luso-Brazilian trade and to prohibit contraband, delays in Lisbon and in the colonial ports had become both costly and endemic and contraband rampant. After the Lisbon earthquake the number of sailings to Brazil had declined precipitously, from 262 departures in 1754–8 to only 191 in 1758–63. The Junta do Comércio (the board of trade) tried without success to reform the fleet system in order to safeguard the interests of Portuguese merchants and speed up payments to both the crown and merchants. In the end the crown decided in 1765 that the best way to accomplish that was to abolish the fleet system.[13]

The last fleets sailed together in 1766. Thereafter, with exception of wartime periods in the 1770s and in the late 1790s, properly licensed ships were free to sail whenever they pleased to Salvador and Rio de Janeiro and, after the termination of the monopoly companies, to other Brazilian ports as well. In addition, the crown also encouraged intra-Brazilian trade (*cabotagem*). Though some merchants attributed the declining volume of trade in the 1760s and 1770s to the cessation of the *frotas*, Jacome Ratton, a well-informed French businessman in Pombaline and post-Pombaline Portugal, was convinced that the establishment of free trade greatly accelerated Luso-Brazilian commerce, shortening the length of time peninsular merchants had to await their payments from the colony and making it possible for ships to make two voyages to Brazil in less than a year, whereas in the past they could expect to complete only two round trips in three years.[14]

Several other economic measures intended to stimulate trade may be briefly noted. The first was the creation of a centralized royal treasury in Portugal in 1761. One of the responsibilities of its colonial branches

---

[13] On the *frota* system and the monopoly trading companies, see also Mansuy-Diniz Silva, *CHLA* I, ch. 13.

[14] *Recordaçõens sobre occurrencias do seu tempo em Portugal,...1747 a...1810* (London, 1813), 96–7.

was to offer subsidies and price guarantees to colonial producers of crops in which the crown was particularly interested (e.g., dyestuffs and fibres). Second, it was also in 1761 that the crown abolished the slave trade to Portugal, a measure undertaken not for humanitarian reasons, as some writers have contended, but to ensure an adequate supply of slaves for Brazil, where the Pombaline ministers believed they were most needed. Thirdly, in order to lessen Portugal's dependence upon foreign, especially English, manufactured goods, the government, for the first time since the reign of Pedro II (1683–1706), actively fostered the industrial sector of the kingdom. Brazil became a prime market for the output of the new factories, the source of 40 per cent or more of their earnings. It is not surprising, therefore, that in the mid-1780s, when the superintendent of contraband and thefts in Lisbon learned of the existence of small weaving shops capable of producing luxury cloths in Brazil, especially in Minas Gerais, he became seriously concerned. As a result, in 1785 the colonial minister ordered that all such shops be closed, their looms dismantled and shipped back to Portugal. Only coarse cottons intended for slaves were exempted from the well-known draconian decree of 1785, which symbolized Portugal's determination to keep Brazil exclusively an agricultural, ranching, extractive colony and to restrict most manufacturing activities to the mother country.[15]

But the crown did adopt other measures that were, in part, designed to benefit the Brazil trade. In 1797–8 it belatedly instituted a system of semi-monthly packets between the kingdom and major colonial ports to carry priority freight and mail, an innovation introduced long before in the British and Spanish empires. Then, in 1801, came a reform that had been under discussion for some years and one that must have been greeted in Brazil as a mixed blessing. The salt monopoly, in existence since 1631 and long viewed as oppressive to ranching, agricultural, and urban interests, was abolished. However, it was replaced by a system of taxes on salt extracted along the Brazilian littoral and at some points in the interior, by a new stamp tax, and by government monopolies on saltpetre and gunpowder.

Conspicuously missing from these efforts to stimulate trade was any step by the crown to facilitate transportation within Brazil, even though a programme of internal improvements might have paid large dividends in expediting the movement of goods from the interior to seaports. Not

---

[15] For further discussion of Portuguese economic policy in the late eighteenth century, see ch. 6 above.

untypical of the attitude of the government was the case of a proposed canal in Maranhão. In 1742 the câmara of São Luís called attention to the need for a canal between the Cachorro and Bocanga rivers to facilitate canoe traffic from the sertão. Submitting a plan drafted by a military engineer, it argued that such a project would also benefit the commerce on the larger Itapicurú and Mearim rivers, especially during winter months. In 1750 the crown directed the governor to contact important people in the captaincy to determine the proposal's fiscal feasibility, but they concluded that Maranhão was too poor to pay for such an undertaking. Again in 1756 the governor was directed to get the canal started and to find ways of raising local revenues to pay for it, but nothing came of that order either, because the level of exports, the only perceived taxable possibility, seemed too low. From time to time during the next two decades the câmara expressed the need for the canal, but nothing came of its appeals until 1776, when a special impost was levied upon cotton exports. Work then began on the canal but, for reasons not evident, was soon stopped. The cotton impost was still being collected in the early 1790s, even though no progress had been made on the canal for more than a decade.[16]

Land transportation remained extremely backward in late colonial Brazil. One must agree with Caio Prado Júnior that 'colonial roads were...almost without exception beneath criticism; they were no more passable even by travellers on foot and animals in the dry season, and in the wet season they became muddy quagmires, often defeating all hope of passage'.[17] What progress was made in this period came as a result of the efforts of energetic colonial governors and the co-operation, often coerced, of local communities. The most noteworthy example is the reconstruction of the *caminho do mar* between the plateau city of São Paulo and its chief port, Santos. Long in disuse because of the lack of maintenance, it was reconstructed between 1780 and 1792, thanks to the efforts of determined governors, the financial contributions of municipalities, merchants, mule-team owners, and exporters, and the labour of militia companies. The result was one of colonial Brazil's rare paved roads, one sufficiently wide so that 'two mule-teams meeting... could pass each other without stopping', and a vital avenue for opening up the agricultural possibilities of the rich plateau lands.[18] Another road

[16] Martinho de Melo e Castro, 'Instrução para o governador...do Maranhão, D. Fernando Antonio de Noronha', 14 July 1792, AHU/CU/cod. 598, fols. 107r-110r.
[17] *The colonial background of modern Brazil*, trans. Suzette Macedo (Berkeley, 1967), 298.
[18] Elizabeth Anne Kuznesof, 'The role of merchants in the economic development of São Paulo 1765-c.1850', *HAHR*, 60 (November, 1980), 571-92.

that was improved in the late eighteenth century was the famed mule trail between Rio Grande do Sul and São Paulo. Further north, modest roads were built at the beginning of the nineteenth century in the manioc-producing regions of southern Bahia, and what was probably no more than a trail was opened up connecting the sertão with Parnaíba, Maranhão.[19] But there is not much progress to report elsewhere. It is significant that the first among the proposals suggested by a memorialist advocating the alleviation of the stagnant condition of Minas Gerais was the opening up of river routes from the coast to the interior and the construction of a series of internal highways.[20]

THE AGRICULTURAL RENAISSANCE

In the midst of the general Luso-Brazilian depression coastal Brazil began to make an economic recovery, but the depression lingered on in the interior. Given the imperfect quality of the statistics we possess, it is not possible to date the recovery precisely, but it could be said to have occurred by the early 1780s, when the agricultural renaissance of the coastal captaincies was already well established. Despite occasional downturns, that revival persisted for the remainder of the colonial period. In varying degrees the upsurge in the agrarian sector was a response to several factors: the measures adopted by the government of Pombal and his successors; the development of new industrial technology, principally in England and France (for example, in the cotton industry); the virtual disappearance of a major sugar supplier, the formerly flourishing French colony of Saint-Domingue, largely destroyed by a series of bloody upheavals beginning in 1791; and the deteriorating international situation, especially the resumption of Anglo-French hostilities beginning in 1793.

Sugar

Brazil's two leading agricultural exports, sugar and tobacco, both recovered and achieved new export levels during the late colonial

[19] For the Ilhéus road see Eulália Maria Lahmeyer Lobo, *História político-administrativa da agricultura brasileira 1808–1889* (Brazília, 1980), 26; the opening of the 'new road' beyond Parnaíba by João Paulo Diniz is mentioned by an anonymous writer in his 'Roteiro do Maranhão e Goiaz pela capitania do Piauí', *RIHGB*, 62/1 (1900), 64.

[20] Joze Eloi Ottoni, 'Memoria sobre o estado actual da capitnᵃ de Minas Gerais' (1798), *ABNRJ*, 30 (1912), 307.

period. The sugar industry, the mainstay of Brazil's exports during the seventeenth century but depressed for much of the eighteenth because of low market prices and high costs, especially of slaves, emerged from its slump. Spurred by more favourable prices, particularly at the end of the 1770s and in the 1790s, it significantly increased the volume and value of its exports. Although sugar was grown in many captaincies, the major export centres remained Pernambuco (plus Paraíba), Bahia (and the subordinate captaincy of Sergipe), and Rio de Janeiro; but at the end of the period sugar was also becoming a major crop in São Paulo. The industry had remained stagnant for decades prior to the establishment of the north-eastern monopoly company. In 1761 there were 268 engenhos in Pernambuco and Paraíba, not many more than had existed 40 years earlier. Furthermore, 40 of those mills were inoperative (*fogos mortos*) because of soil exhaustion, the disappearance of fuel supplies, the dispersal of slave gangs, and lack of maintenance. By the end of 1777, however, the number of mills in both captaincies had increased to 390 and exports had doubled.[21] We cannot trace the development of the industry in the north-east after 1777 until further research has been done.

From the data presented in table 6 below, it would appear that during the 1760s and 1770s Pernambuco regained the lead it had lost to Bahia in the middle of the seventeenth century as Brazil's principal producer, but that advantage may have been only temporary, for the industry also underwent expansion in Bahia. From 1759 until the late 1790s the number of mills in Bahia increased from just over 170 to 260, and by the latter date the sugar zone extended some 50 miles (sixteen leagues) north and north-west of the port of Salvador. By the end of the century there were also 140 engenhos in neighbouring Sergipe. Between the late 1750s and the late 1790s the level of exports, despite numerous fluctuations, increased from about 10,000 to about 11,500 crates (*caixas*); however, that figure is not as meaningful as it might seem, since the weight of the *caixa* tended to increase over time. In 1759 one contemporary wrote of crates varying from 26 to 45 arrobas while in 1781 another writer, also living in Bahia, spoke of crates of 40–60

[21] 'Relação do n° de engenhos moentes e de fogo morto que ha nas cap^nias de Pernambuco e Parahyba...', 1 February 1761, AHU/PA/Pernambuco, caixa 50; 'Mapa dos engenhos que existem nas capitanias de Pernambuco e Paraiba...ate 31 de dezembro de 1777', AHU/CU/cod. 1821, no. 9.

arrobas. Still, the conversions generally employed in the tables of exports periodically reported to Lisbon are of crates of 40 arrobas, and that is the basis of the calculations summarized in this table. Between 1757 and 1798 the level of exports of Bahian sugars rose by 54.6 per cent and advanced another 9.3 per cent during the next decade. Since about 10 per cent of the sugar produced in Bahia was locally consumed, it appears that yearly production rose from nearly 360,000 arrobas in 1759 to about 880,000 *c.* 1807, or a gain of 69 per cent.

Dramatic changes in sugar production in this period also occurred in the captaincies of Rio de Janeiro and São Paulo. The most rapid growth in Rio de Janeiro was in the six northern parishes around the town of São Salvador dos Campos, the famous Campos de Goitacazes district, still an important source of cane sugar today. There, between 1769 and 1778, the number of engenhos nearly doubled (from 56 to 104) and production went up by 235 per cent. By 1798–9 there were 378 mills in the Goitacazes, more than half of the 616 engenhos in the captaincy.[22] Table 6 provides some idea of export levels in Rio de Janeiro from the 1770s until the end of the period. Most of the data is based on a carefully researched, recently published dissertation whose author probably understates the actual figures; at least his estimates are at considerable variance with those derived from other coeval sources.

Attractive prices and the construction of the *caminho do mar* stimulated the beginnings of an important sugar industry in São Paulo in the 1780s and 1790s. The two major areas of cultivation were along the coast north of Santos and the so-called quadrilateral defined by the townships of Sorocaba, Piracicaba, Mogi Guaçú, and Jundiaí, all situated within ten leagues of the city of São Paulo. By 1797 the plateau plantations were milling 83,435 arrobas for export. Sugar was destined to remain São Paulo's principal export crop until it was overtaken by coffee in 1850–1.

Considering the amount of scholarly attention devoted in recent decades to the Brazilian sugar industry, it seems surprising that the statistical base we possess for the late colonial period remains so incomplete. As is evident from table 6, we have estimates for the major growing areas – Pernambuco, Bahia, and Rio de Janeiro – for only two

[22] Santos, 49–51, 174; 'Mapa da população, fabricas e escravaturas do que se compoem as…freguezias da villa de…Campos…no anno de mil setecentos noventa e nove', *RIHGB*, 65/1 (1902), 295. Albergo Lamego, 'Os engenhos de açucar nos recôncavos do Rio de Janeiro, em fins do século xvii[i]', *Brasil Açucareiro* (March 1965), 18–25.

Table 6 *Estimated sugar exports from principal Brazilian regions, 1757–1807 (arrobas)*

Year	Pernambuco	Bahia	Rio de Janeiro	Totals
1757		407,824		
1758				
1759		321,584		
1760	8,000	200,000		
1761	69,720	226,000		
1762	359,080	226,000		
1763	165,320	226,000		
1764	495,640	200,000		
1765	178,400	160,000		
1766	282,160	160,000		
1767	263,120			
1768	284,160			
1769	332,160			
1770	278,160			
1771				
1772			131,515	
1773	377,760		80,184	
1774	405,480		156,515	
1775	404,640		23,779	
1776	313,200		106,773	
1777	271,000		103,926	
1778		480,000	634,349	
1779		480,000	127,741	
1780		480,000	154,944	
1781		480,000	146,082	
1782		480,000	144,200	
1783		480,000	91,750	
1784		480,000	180,141	
1785		480,000	101,141	
1786		480,000	84,053	
1787		480,000	117,140	
1788		480,000	104,646	
1789		480,000	110,027	
1790	275,000	400,000	115,615–200,000	790,643–875,000
1791			144,045–232,184	
1792			221,765	
1793			140,916–378,410	
1794			222,032	
1795			102,165	
1796			384,077	
1797		468,220	174,425	
1798		746,645	257,885–714,783	

Table 6 (*cont.*)

Year	Pernambuco	Bahia	Rio de Janeiro	Totals
1799			400,282	
1800			487,225	
1801			535,209	
1802			329,247	
1803			178,697	
1804			171,263	
1805			226,095	
1806			312,372	
1807	560,000	800,000	250,201–360,000	1,610,201–1,720,000

Sources: **Pernambuco**: 1760–77, Ribeiro Júnior, *Colonização*, 137; 1790, British Library, Add. MS 13,985, fol. 248v; 1807, Francisco Adolfo de Varnhagen, *História geral do Brasil*, v (5th edn, São Paulo, 1956), 61. **Bahia**: 1757 and 1759, João Antonio Caldas, 'Noticia geral de toda esta capitania de Bahia...desde o seu descobrimento até...1759' (fasc. ed., Salvador, 1951), fols. 438 and 442; 1760–6 and 1778–89, [Luiz Antonio Oliveira Mendes], 'Discurso preliminar...da Bahia' [*c.* 1789], *ABNRJ*, 27 (1905), 306, 315; 1790 and 1807, as for Pernambuco; 1797 and 1798, *MHB*, III, table facing 160 and 204–5. **Rio de Janeiro**: 1772–1807, Santos, *Relações comerciais*, 165; 1790 and 1807, as for Pernambuco; 1791 and 1793, 'Almanaque[s] da cidade do Rio de Janeiro... 1792...1794', *ABNRJ*, 59 (1937), 284 and 350 (from which 10% has been deducted for local consumption); 1798, Antonio Duarte Nunes, 'Almanac historico...do Rio de Janeiro' [1799], *RIHGB*, 21 (1858), 172.

years, 1790 and *c.* 1807. The former was provided by an apparently knowledgeable Spanish informant of the British government, the latter appears in the standard history of colonial Brazil and seems to be derived from contemporary sources. Those estimates suggest that Brazil's sugar exports in 1790 were about 11,500–12,700 metric tons and that by 1807 they had doubled to somewhere between 23,400 and 25,000 metric tons.

Tobacco

While several captaincies shared in the export of sugar, Bahia continued to be the dominant producer and supplier of tobacco in this period, as it had been since the inception of the industry. It was, of course, cultivated elsewhere – in Maranhão, Pernambuco, and Alagoas, for example. One of the tasks assigned to the boards of inspection in 1751 was the promotion of tobacco cultivation in areas where it did not exist or languished, but those efforts, for instance in Rio de Janeiro, were

Table 7 *Tobacco exports from Bahia to Portugal and the Mina coast,
1750–1800, and re-exports from Portugal to foreign markets, 1764–1803
(arrobas)*

	Shipments from Bahia			Re-exports by Portugal
Year	Portugal	Mina Coast	Total	
1750	161,423	150,094	311,517	
1751	(197,454)	179,367	(376,821)	
1752	254,089	(239,813)	(484,902)	
1753				
1754	201,148	(182,722)	(383,870)	
1755	199,339	97,674	297,073	
1756	186,866	75,922	262,788	
1757	247,832	124,377	372,209	
1758	80,765	139,165	219,930	
1759	173,237	146,094	319,331	
1760	125,341	118,884	244,225	
1761	151,638	127,208	278,846	
1762	56,547	179,364	235,911	
1763	292,560	(265,760)	(558,320)	
1764	33,460	(30,395)	(63,855)	102,267
1765	69,914	237,448	307,362	86,121
1766	184,942	(168,001)	(352,943)	54,452
1767				191,121
1768				100,873
1769				112,432
1770				123,850
1771				83,888
1772				97,711
1773				109,971.
1774				97,161
1775				110,950
1776				175,641
1777				232,330
1778				266,410
1779				196,827
1780				122,944
1781				168,451
1782	272,296	(247,353)	(519,649)	195,406
1783	332,416	(401,976)	(634,382)	197,407
1784	374,676	(340,354)	(715,030)	286,205
1785	362,783	(329,551)	(692,334)	233,165?
1786	265,328	(241,023)	(506,351)	196,830
1787				180,175
1788				242,037
1789				224,048
1790				136,611

Table 7 (*cont.*)

Year	Shipments from Bahia			Re-exports by Portugal
	Portugal	Mina Coast	Total	
1791				174,799
1792				215,499
1793				187,996
1794				137,557
1795				171,947
1796				122,048?
1797	265,065	153,457	418,522	130,381
1798	371,607	(127,874)	499,481	130,168
1799	(253,155)	(229,965)	483,120	155,598
1800	209,734	190,403	405,859	176,178?
1801				177,535
1802				220,001
1803				233,539

Sources: **Shipments from Bahia:** 1750–66, Junta do Tabaco, Arquivo Nacional da Torre do Tombo (Lisbon) [ANTT], maços 96–106, courtesy of Prof. J. H. Galloway, Department of Geography, University of Toronto; 1782–6, 1799–1800, C. Lugar, 'The Portuguese tobacco trade and tobacco growers of Bahia in the late colonial period', in D. Alden and Warren Dean, *Essay concerning the socioeconomic history of Brazil and Portuguese India* (Gainesville, 1977), 48–9; 1797, annex to report of 1798, *MHB*, III, 204–5; 1798, 'Mapa da exportação dos produtos da capitania da Bahia para o reino e outros portos do Brazil e Africa... 1798', APB, letters sent to the king, 139, no. 334. **Re-exports:** Lugar, 47.

Note: Blanks have been left when data for that year are missing. Data in parentheses have been reconstructed, based on assumption that on the average 52.4% of Bahian tobacco went to Portugal and that 47.6% went to Mina, the average for the complete years.

unsuccessful. Bahia remained the source of upwards of 90 per cent of the Brazilian tobacco that entered commerce. Though tobacco was grown in several parts of the periphery of the Bay of All Saints and in the Sergipe district, the prime centre of its cultivation, in terms of both the quantity and quality produced, was around the town of Cachoeira fourteen leagues north-west of Salvador, still a source of good cigars. Contemporaries reckoned that there were more than 1,500 tobacco farms in the Bahian region in this period and rated their annual production at about 35,000 rolls. During the eighteenth century the weight of rolls sent to Europe, as with that of cases of sugar, steadily increased from eight arrobas at the beginning of the century to between fifteen and twenty at its end, though tobacco rolls sent to Africa seem to have remained constant at about three arrobas. About a third of the annual Bahian crop was consumed within Brazil. Slightly more than half of the exports, the better qualities, were reserved for the European market (Portugal and her chief customers, the Italian ports, northern Germany, Spain, and sometimes France), while the rest, the so-called refuse, was dispatched along with sugar brandy and gold to Africa to purchase slaves.

Table 7 summarizes what is known about the volume of Bahian tobacco trade in this period and exposes several problems. First, there are the obvious lacunae which, where possible, I have tried to remedy (see note to table 7). Second, there was a market not included in the table, Angola. We know that Bahian tobacco was an important article of the slave trade there, as well as along the Mina coast. Between 1762 and 1775, for example, the Pernambucan company purchased 11,500 arrobas a year of Bahian tobacco to facilitate its Angolan slave purchases. Slaves sent to Rio de Janeiro from Angola were also procured by means of tobacco, but how much came from Bahia we do not know.

These lacunae make the generalizations that follow tentative at best. Yearly exports of Bahian tobacco appear to have averaged about 320,000 arrobas during 1750–66 and to have nearly doubled by the 1780s to almost 615,000. It has been suggested that the peak of eighteenth-century Bahian production came in the 1790s, but evidence is contradictory. Certainly prices were higher then than at any other time during the period, averaging nearly twice the level officially set in the early 1750s, and the number of ships that passed from Bahia to the Mina coast during the 1790s increased from about eleven a year (the average of the 1750s through the 1780s) to fifteen, though the number would nearly double during the first years of the nineteenth century.[23] But the known or estimated level of exports in the late 90s was markedly lower (averaging 452,000 arrobas) than during the 1780s. Furthermore, re-exports of Brazilian (mainly Bahian) tobacco by Portugal, which had increased from 108,000 arrobas a year during the 1760s to nearly 150,000 in the 70s, seem to have peaked at just under 205,000 in the 1780s, and then to have fallen to about 177,000 in the 1790s, before reaching a new plateau of close to 200,000 in the early 1800s. There is much that we still need to learn about the tobacco industry, but three conclusions seem

[23] Verger, *Flux et reflux*, 654.

firm. First, the industry was vitally important to Bahia not only because of its European earnings but especially because of the slave trade. Secondly, the industry was still expanding at the end of the colonial era, but that phase would abruptly stop in 1815, when Great Britain moved to restrict the slave trade. Thirdly, by the late eighteenth century tobacco was vastly overshadowed as a Brazilian export not only by sugar but also by an entirely new commodity, cotton.

Cotton

Though native to Brazil, cotton was not grown for commercial purposes until 1760, when the Maranhão company began making modest purchases. Its cultivation, initially confined to the delta formed by the Mearim and Itapicurú rivers, spread rapidly throughout the length of the Itapicurú until, by the 1790s, production came to centre around the town of Caxias, 184 miles south-east of São Luis.[24] Long before, cotton raising had leapt beyond the confines of Maranhão, to Pará by the early 1770s and to the littoral extending from Ceará to Pernambuco by the latter part of that decade. By the 1780s the cotton frontier was moving from the coastlands to the drier interior, where rains were less severe and the soils were sandy (e.g., the intermediate *agreste* zone of Pernambuco) and advancing into the hinterlands of Bahia, Piauí, Goiás, and Minas Gerais. Effectively those were the limits of successful cotton cultivation in this period, for efforts to spur production in Rio de Janeiro and São Paulo were unfruitful.

As table 8 indicates, Maranhão remained the leading cotton-producing captaincy for four decades. Cotton was then to Maranhão what cacao was to Pará and sugar to Bahia, Rio de Janeiro, and São Paulo, a dominant staple that justified dispatching considerable numbers of ships on a regular basis to colonial ports to load such staples and less important commodities. As Ralph Davis has reminded us, 'what really mattered to the shipowner [in the seventeenth and eighteenth centuries] was weight and volume, not value. What created demand for shipping was mass, not price.'[25] But by the early 1800s mass was shifting to the north-east – to Ceará, Rio Grande do Norte, Paraíba, and especially

[24] A sense of how rapidly cotton developed in Maranhão is given by Joaquim de Melo e Povoas, governor, to Mendonça Furtado, colonial secretary, 17 June 1767, ANTT, Ministerio do Reino, maço 601 (orig.).
[25] Ralph Davis, *The rise of the English shipping industry in the seventeenth and eighteenth centuries* (London, 1962), 176.

Table 8 *Brazilian cotton exports to Portugal, 1760–1807 (arrobas)*

Year	Pará	Maran-hão	Ceará	Pernam-buco	Paraíba	Bahia	Rio de Janeiro	São Paulo
1760		6,510						
1761		5,197						
1762		3,396						
1763		3,659						
1764		6,476						
1765		7,521						
1766		11,217						
1767		12,705						
1768		23,810						
1769		25,470						
1770		15,542						
1771		12,015						
1773		37,236					115	
1774	60	40,813					176	
1775	12	25,886						
1776	879	25,521				89	245	
1777	2,053	40,553	80			54		
1778	3,386	38,051	241					
1779	5,155	40,386					635	
1780	4,912	42,159					2,975	
1781	8,572	54,421					1,780	
1782	7,315	57,697					255	
1783	7,188	49,756					1,515	
1784	6,608	54,090					2,330	
1785	4,908	46,724					1,380	
1786	3,795	66,750					330	
1787	4,212	73,496			451		620	
1788	5,718	63,510		37,000	5,529		70	
1789	4,743	68,016			7,292		155	
1790		62,756			3,163		895	
1791		63,675			8,883		1,110	
1792		74,365	30,937	100,905	15,879		2,795	
1793		67,565		100,905			800	
1794	7,832	99,600		100,905	7,397		5,583	
1795		105,935		100,905	6,440		1,050	
1796	12,666	123,400		100,905	15,320		590	
1797	7,974	94,410		100,905		13,831	72	
1798	8,341	91,215		83,311		31,223	10,013	4,686
1799	11,569	152,485					880	
1800	15,930	203,256					1,630	
1801	10,931	145,410		107,905			2,000	160
1802	14,040	216,595		235,000			2,000	
1803		226,560		183,114			5,552	13

Table 8 (*cont.*)

Year	Pará	Maran-hão	Ceará	Pernam-buco	Paraíba	Bahia	Rio de Janeiro	São Paulo
1804	15,236	228,412	3,047	164,934		55,533	4,529	10
1805	14,710	168,693	6,248	278,329		73,955	2,608	44
1806	11,098	177,009		245,254			3,449	20
1807		206,449		334,914			1,792	

Sources: **Pará**: Except for 1804–6, Manoel Barata, *A antiga producção e exportação do Pará*... (Belém, 1915), 3–7; the remaining years from 'Balanças gerais do comércio' series, cited in Alden, 'The significance of cacao production in the Amazon in the late colonial period', American Philosophical Society, *Proceedings* (April 1976), 120/2, 134–5. **Maranhão**: 1760–78, Dias, *Companhia geral*, 353; 1783, 1788 and 1805–7, Gaioso, *Compêndio*, tables 2–3, facing 210; 1782–90 from AHU/CU/cod. 598, fols. 127 and 119; 1791–7, 1799, and 1801–3, Luiz Amaral, *História geral da agricultura brasileira* (1940 edn), II, 210–11, as quoted in Santos, *Relações comerciais*, 172–3. Amaral's figures are substantially lower than other sources used here. **Ceará**: Amaral (1956 edn), II, 30 and 'Balanças gerais' series. **Paraíba**: von Spix and von Martius, *Viagem*, II, 439. **Pernambuco**: 1788 and 1802, Frédéric Mauro, *Le Brésil du xvi* à la fin du xviii* siècle (Paris, 1977), 171; 1792–99, derived from data in source in n. 27; the remainder from the 'Balanças gerais' series. **Bahia**: *MHB*, III, 204–5, and 'Balanças gerais' series. **Rio de Janeiro**: Except for 1798, 1802, 1804–6, which are taken from the 'Balanças gerais' series, based on Santos, 172–3. **São Paulo**: von Spix and von Martius, I, 226–7, and 'Balanças gerais' series.

Pernambuco – whose product was esteemed as finer and cleaner than that of Maranhão.[26] The importance of cotton to Pernambuco amazed the bishop of Olinda, who wrote that its rapid progress had been so 'extraordinary' that by the turn of the century it 'almost equals [in value] sugar and all other products combined'.[27]

Several factors account for the rapid growth of Brazilian cotton. One was the ease of its cultivation and processing and another was the prospect of handsome earnings. Cotton was a far less complicated crop

[26] For near-contemporary assessments, see Henry Koster, *Travels in Brazil*, ed. C. Harvey Gardiner (Carbondale, Ill., 1966), 80, 170; L. F. de Tollenare, *Notas dominicais tomadas durante uma viagem em Portugal e no Brasil em 1816, 1817 e 1818* (Bahia, 1956), 113f; and J. B. von Spix and C. F. P. von Martius, *Viagem pelo Brasil*, translated from the German by Lucia Furquim Lahmeyer (3 vols., Rio de Janeiro, 1938), II, 455–7. The classic description and defence of the superiority of Maranhense cotton is Raimundo José de Sousa Gaioso, *Compêndio histórico-político dos princípios da lavoura do Maranhão* (1818; reprinted Rio de Janeiro, c. 1970); see especially pp. 178–81, 263–5.

[27] D. Jose Joaquim Nabuco de Araujo to D. Rodrigo de Souza Coutinho, colonial secretary, Recife, 16 November 1799, AHU/PA/Pernambuco, maço 21.

to produce than sugar and required no expensive equipment. The ground was prepared by the immemorial practice of slash-and-burn, which in Maranhão began after the first rains in January. A dozen seeds were then dropped into small holes three to four inches deep and spaced at intervals of five to six feet. In the north-east a variable number of seeds, depending on whether the land was situated in a humid or a dry zone, were carefully placed in furrows and covered over. Corn, beans, or manioc were sometimes interplanted with cotton, although one contemporary complained that, as with sugar cultivation, planters too often neglected to grow food crops. In Maranhão harvests began in October and November, while they started in May in Pernambuco. The processing consisted of picking the balls from the bushes and, as Whitney's gin was unknown, separating out the lint by primitive techniques. This was then baled and sacked. The sacks (weighing up to 200 lb in Maranhão and about 140 in Pernambuco) were transported to seaport warehouses by mules or river boats.

It was reckoned that a single slave could produce only 20 arrobas of cotton lint a year, half the amount expected of a slave in the sugar industry,[28] but the cotton-grower's potential profits were higher. Apart from the purchase of slaves, the owner's major expenses included their maintenance and clothing, the cost of sacking, freight, and the tithe. Even when warehouse charges, commissions, and insurance fees were added, one informant, Raimundo Gaioso, calculated that a planter's profits might come close to 50 per cent of his costs. Significantly, he had in mind a typical Maranhão planter who possessed about 50 slaves, a large and expensive gang, larger, in fact, than the slave force of many sugar planters elsewhere in Brazil. It should not be forgotten that there were risks, some peculiar to cotton-growing. Epidemics might wipe out the workforce, who were becoming increasingly expensive to replace throughout this period. And the crop might be ravaged by a plague of caterpillars, grubs, or other vermin, or rotted by excessive rains.

What made the risk worth taking was favourable prices and a constantly rising demand. In 1772 the Maranhão company was offering twice as much for an arroba of cotton as the Pernambuco company was paying for sugar. And prices continued to soar – from 3,200 réis an arroba in the 1770s to 4,500 réis in the early 1790s and to 5,900 réis by the late 1790s and early 1800s.[29] The principal reasons why prices

[28] See ch. 3 above, table 3.
[29] Melo e Castro, 'Instrução para...Noronha', fol. 96r; von Spix and von Martius, II, 502 n. 1.

continued to rise were the rapid expansion of the cotton textile industry, especially in England and France, made possible by a technological revolution, and the demand for high quality fibres for the manufacture of fine fabrics. Though much Brazilian cotton ran to coarser grades, some of that produced in Pernambuco and Paraíba was considered by Portugal's major customers as among the best available from any world source.[30]

For twelve of the years between 1776 and 1807 – 1776, 1777, 1789, 1796, and 1800–7 – we have adequate data to measure Brazilian cotton exports to Portugal and re-exports from it. During those years 5,433,087 arrobas were shipped to the kingdom, of which more than three-quarters (76.1 per cent) was sent to foreign markets, chiefly England (55.4 per cent) and France (31.2 per cent). Between 1781 and 1792 Brazil's share of the English market for raw cotton increased from 5.8 to over 30 per cent. By 1800 cotton represented 28 per cent by value of Portugal's re-exports from Brazil, compared with 57 per cent for sugar and only 4 per cent for tobacco.[31]

For another two decades cotton was to flourish in Brazil, then wither away in the face of competition from the more technologically advanced United States. Why Brazilian cotton could not successfully match that competition, who its leading producers and brokers had been, and whether, as seems likely, life on a Brazilian cotton plantation was even less bearable for slaves than it was on a sugar plantation, are among the important questions that scholars need to explore.

Rice

During the late colonial period Brazil also became a source of two important cereals, rice and wheat. Rice had long been an article of general consumption in Portugal, but it was dependent upon foreign sources of supply, especially northern Italy down to the beginning of the 1730s and from that decade onwards the new English colony of South Carolina. Carolina rice was also exported to Brazil, though a less attractive type, called *arroz da terra* or *arroz vermelha*, was apparently indigenous to Brazil. The processing of this rice was handicapped by

---

[30] Edward Baines, *History of cotton manufacture in Great Britain* (2nd edn, New York, 1966), 304–6; Michael M. Edwards, *The growth of the British cotton trade, 1780–1815* (New York, 1967), 83–4, 103.

[31] Jorge Borges de Macedo, *O bloqueio continental. Economia e guerra peninsular* (Lisbon, 1962), 44, table 5; Lugar, 'Portuguese tobacco trade', 46.

Table 9 *Brazilian rice exports to Portugal, 1767–1807 (arrobas)*

Year	Pará	Maranhão	Rio de Janeiro	São Paulo
1767		225		
1768		273		
1769		555		
1770		627		
1771		8,133		
1772		30,217	1,782	
1773	935	57,465	68	
1774	7,163	50,920	3,550	
1775	19,480	109,599	1,418	
1776	27,872	75,154	725	
1777	40,346	144,845	5,161	
1778	29,473	129,032	4,130	
1779	89,236	96,748	79,000	
1780	107,252	194,930	37,350	
1781	96,791	171,564	56,475	
1782	114,895		21,573	
1783	73,116	164,520	21,276	
1784	118,604		23,841	
1785	84,681		36,792	
1786	83,849		27,324	
1787	136,022		28,575	
1788	85,521	313,434	7,425	
1789	96,140		9,014	
1790		199,699	18,684	
1791			64,620	
1792			12,816	
1793			24,854	
1794	103,503		3,600	
1795			25,065	
1796	46,880		176,000	
1797	90,171		14,994	
1798	59,618		97,096	
1799	46,417			
1800	90,836	294,950	19,940	
1801	39,172		15,363	135
1802	65,467		9,310	891
1803			38,534	265
1804			11,088	
1805		235,243	33,961	21,472
1806		374,331	29,889	52,695
1807		321,595	135,078	62,525

Sources: **Pará**: Barata, *Antiga producção*, 3–7. **Maranhão**: 1767–78, Dias, *Companhia geral*, 353; 1779–81, 'Mapa dos effeitos exportados da cidade do Maranhão para Lisboa no anno de 1779…1780…1781', BNL, no. 7194; 1783, 1788, 1805–7, Gaioso, *Compêndio*,

the absence of husking and polishing mills. The first rice mill was built two leagues from the city of Rio de Janeiro in 1756, its owner being given the customary monopoly on the polishing of all rice produced in the captaincy. The initial rice shipments from Rio de Janeiro to the kingdom began about 1760, but the enterprise did not prosper.

That venture, however, alerted Lisbon authorities to the possibility of stimulating rice culture elsewhere. In 1766 the local administrator of the Maranhão company was directed to distribute Carolina rice seed to farmers in Maranhão. Though exports from that captaincy began by the latter part of the decade (see table 9), their level was disappointingly low, partly because growers preferred to cultivate local rice, which was heavier and larger grained, and also because of a shortage of processing mills. The governor and company officials exerted pressure upon growers to switch to Carolina rice, and new mills, modelled in part after one built by a wealthy local planter and slaver, an Irishman known as Lourenço Belfort, were constructed. Rice culture became firmly established in Maranhão by the early 1770s. Its success there prompted the crown to instruct the governor of neighbouring Pará to introduce Carolina rice there too, and with the aid of a French-born engineer, Theodosio Constantino Chermont, rice cultivation began in Pará in 1772. By 1781 Portugal was receiving sufficient rice from Brazil to be able to bar further entry of all foreign rice.

The sketchy statistics available concerning the levels of Brazilian rice exports in this period are summarized in table 9. It is evident that Maranhão, where rice was cultivated primarily in the lower Itapicurú river and where it became the second most important crop after cotton, continued to be the major source of supply. In Pará, where the rice bowl was around the town of Macapá, north-west of Belém, rice followed cacao as the captaincy's leading export, but after the 1780s exports became increasingly irregular, for reasons that remain to be determined. In Rio de Janeiro rice continued to be grown in low-lying areas north of the capital, but much of that captaincy's harvest was locally

tables 2–3, facing 210. 'Resumo da exportação...1805 a 1812', 220. **Rio de Janeiro**: Except for 1779, 1796, and 1807, based on Santos, *Relações comerciais*, 165 (where the data is expressed in sacks, which I have assumed corresponded to the legal definition of 2.25 arrobas, though I suspect that they may have weighed more); for the sources for 1779 and 1796, see Alden, 'Manoel Luis Vieira: an entrepreneur in Rio de Janeiro during Brazil's...agricultural renaissance', *HAHR*, 39 (Nov. 1959), 536–7; 1807, 'Balança geral...1807', BNL, no. 9198. **São Paulo**: von Spix and von Martius, I, 224.

consumed. There were occasional shipments from Bahia and shortly after 1800 São Paulo, a dominant supplier in modern times, began to export rice, apparently from plantations north of the port of Santos.[32]

Wheat

The south, specifically Rio Grande do Sul, also became a wheat exporter of consequence in this period – an especially welcome development from the crown's point of view, since Portugal had long suffered from chronic wheat deficits, the yields of peninsular crops being supplemented in the eighteenth century by imports from northern Italy, the Low Countries, England, and the Azores. During the Pombaline years 15–18 per cent of the grains consumed in the kingdom came from abroad. Wheat, together with codfish, olive oil, and wine, was one of the principal cargoes brought to Brazilian ports by the annual fleets, and when supplies were short governors and câmaras strove frantically to control supplies of the major alternative, manioc flour, which, though widely produced throughout tropical Brazil, was commonly disdained by the elites as fit only for slaves and other common folk.

Wheat growing in Rio Grande do Sul began about 1770 but, as with the cultivation of rice, its production was initially restricted by the absence of grist mills or of a knowledge of how to make them. In 1773 the crown dispatched a master carpenter and a master miller from Lisbon to remedy that problem, and three years later they returned from Rio Grande do Sul having apparently accomplished their mission. By 1780 wheat was being sown at the northern and southern extremities of the Lagoa dos Patos, around the towns of Porto Alegre and Rio Grande, the first centres of wheat farming in the captaincy, and in exceptional years yields as high as 70:1 were attained. Grain shipments to other parts of Brazil began in the early 1790s, averaging nearly 94,000 *alqueires* (75,200 bushels)[33] a year, and by the turn of the century the annual harvest reached nearly 160,000 bushels. Half of the crop was sent to Rio de Janeiro, Bahia, and Pernambuco, and wheat joined processed beef and hides as one of Rio Grande do Sul's most conspicuous exports. The availability of a local grain source within Brazil meant that Portugal was able to reduce wheat shipments to Brazil and apparently to lessen her dependence on foreign sources.

[32] D. Alden, 'Manoel Luis Vieira', 521–37.
[33] The local *alqueire* was approximately twice the volume of that of the kingdom.

Cacao

One Brazilian export for which Portugal had only limited use was cacao. The Maranhão company had been set up in part to stimulate and stabilize cacao exports from the Amazon, which had been irregular since the 1740s. By the time the company's charter lapsed, cacao was also being produced in two other captaincies, Maranhão and Bahia; by 1800 Rio de Janeiro would also become an exporter. But Pará remained the dominant supplier. Between 1777 and 1807 its share of Brazilian cacao exports never fell below 87 per cent and was usually much higher. Pará's export levels (ranging from 1.6 to 1.9 million lb a year) remained about the same throughout the late 1770s and 1780s, at a time when European prices were generally low. Although prices rose rapidly during the 1790s, when the long cycle of maritime wars began, Pará did not immediately respond by increasing its exports, perhaps because insufficient shipping was available. However, the continued shortage of cacao derived from other New World sources, especially from Venezuela, during the first years of the nineteenth century did stimulate a spectacular increase in shipments from the Amazon which averaged 5.5 million lb (171,875 arrobas) a year (1800–7), much the highest level attained in colonial times. By then Brazil had become the second- or third-ranking New World supplier. One-half to two-thirds of Brazilian cacao was re-exported by Portugal to seven European lands, led by France and the north Italian ports.[34]

Coffee

Cacao was to remain the dominant export of the Amazon for another half-century. Long before then, however, it was to be superseded as Brazil's most important beverage source by its rival, coffee. The origins and early development of Brazilian coffee are still curiously murky. It seems surprising that coffee aroused so little interest in either Brazil or Portugal during the eighteenth century. It was the subject of few *memórias* or royal directives, and contemporaries who wrote about the state of the economy of Brazil rarely mentioned coffee, nor was it commented on by foreign visitors to Brazil. And while the archives are full of petitions framed by other interest groups, especially sugar

---

[34] Alden, 'Cacao production', 103–35.

Table 10 *Coffee exports from Brazil, 1750–1807 (arrobas)*

Year	Pará	Maranhão	Pernam-buco	Bahia	Rio de Janeiro	São Paulo
1750	4,944					
1751	5,483					
1752	1,429					
1753	9,944					
1754	256					
1755	7,214					
1756	3,590					
1757	3,641					
1758	852	740				
1759	4,344	4,035				
1760	8,470	2,295				
1761	5,919	7,440				
1762	3,833	6,775				
1763	2,639	1,695				
1764	4,292	2,390				
1765	6,270	4,735				
1766	5,104	5,300				
1767	6,422	5,418				
1768	4,052	6,017				
1769	189	4,639				
1770	3,088	2,021				
1771	7,393	4,284				
1772	4,815	5,202				
1773	4,273	2,646				
1774	141	2,547				
1775	4,468	4,005				
1776	5,792	7,000		33	3	
1777	3,542	3,600				
1778	6,579					
1779	4,513	101			10	
1780	3,122	68			60	
1781	2,838	81			10	
1782		14			810	
1783					120	
1784	1,796				70	
1785	1,683				25	
1786	1,282				445	
1787					345	
1788		30			560	
1789					625	
1790					470	
1791					609	
1792					2,752	
1793					180	

Table 10 (*cont.*)

Year	Pará	Maranhão	Pernam-buco	Bahia	Rio de Janeiro	São Paulo
1794	2,811				3,171	
1795	5,150				235	
1796	4,042	165		1,983	8,454	13
1797	3,576	23		758	5,231	107
1798	5,019	155		2,020	14,642	528
1799	3,224	97	20	4,917	17,147	
1800	4,903	304	137	5,193	41,582	
1801	2,562	208		4,872	20,678	132
1802	4,793			6,433	31,836	116
1803	6,255		584	6,927	53,191	675
1803						243
1805	2,623			4,267	61,868	954
1806	2,656	132	303	553	70,574	1,060
1807		257		4,979	103,102	2,184

Sources: **Pará**: 1750–5, 'Mappa dos differentes generos que...da cidade do Pará consta se exportarao do seu porto...1730...1755...', AHU/PA/Pará, caixa 38; 1755–72, Dias, *Companhia geral*, 291–2; 1773–1802, Barata, *Antiga producção*, 3–7; 1803, 1805–6, 'Balanças gerais do comércio' series, in Alden, 'Cacao production'. **Maranhão**: 1758–77, Dias, 293; 1779–81, BNL, no. 7194; 1782 and 1788, Gaioso, *Compêndio*, tables 2–3; 1796–9 and 1806–7, 'Balanças gerais' series. **Pernambuco and Bahia**: 'Balanças gerais' series. **Rio de Janeiro**: 1776–95, Santos, *Relações comerciais*, 165; remaining years from 'Balanças gerais' series. **São Paulo**: 1796–8, 'Balanças gerais' series; 1801–7, Afonso de Escragnolle Taunay, *Historia do café no Brasil*, II (Rio de Janeiro, 1939), 281.

planters and tobacco growers, coffee planters were as strangely silent as manioc farmers were.

Coffee has been so long identified with São Paulo that it may seem surprising to recall that its first Brazilian home was the Amazon. Seed, brought apparently from Cayenne, was planted in farms around Belém in the 1720s, and the first trial shipments to Lisbon were made in the early 1730s. In 1731 the crown, primarily interested in the development of Amazonian stocks of cinnamon, offered producers of cinnamon or coffee exemption from all customs duties for a dozen years. Thirteen years later, in response to a plea from the câmara of Belém, the crown prohibited foreign imports of coffee, even though between 1736 and 1741 only 1,354 arrobas had reached Lisbon from Pará, compared with 564 from India and 1,494 from other foreign sources.[35] By 1749, according to a regional historian, there were 17,000 coffee trees in Pará,

[35] Overseas council to king, 26 June 1742, AHU/PA/Pará, caixa 10.

yet exports remained below 2,500 arrobas, compared with nearly 58,000 for cacao. In fact, coffee never really flourished in Pará. At no time in the late colonial period did exports of it exceed 8,500 arrobas and the same was true of Maranhão, where coffee was first grown in the 1750s (see table 10).

Between the 1760s and 1790s coffee-growing spread from the north of Brazil to Pernambuco, Bahia, Rio de Janeiro, Minas Gerais, and São Paulo. In Rio de Janeiro, where the crop first attained significance, it was cultivated near the capital in such now fashionable sections as Lagoa de Rodrigo de Freitas, Gávea, and Tijuca. By the nineties, if not earlier, coffee-houses – prototypes of the ubiquitous *cafezinho* bars so characteristic of modern Brazilian cities – made their appearance in Rio de Janeiro, increasing from 26 to 40 during the last lustrum of the century.

By the 1790s, 70 years after its introduction, coffee was finally becoming a significant Brazilian export, at least from Rio de Janeiro. Between 1798 and 1807 its coffee exports grew sevenfold, attaining nearly 1.5 million kg by the latter year. By the early 1800s, in spite of its reputation for tasting bitter because of improper drying procedures, Brazilian coffee was to be found in markets all the way from Moscow to Venice, in Hamburg, Copenhagen, Amsterdam, Paris, Lisbon, and the ports of the Barbary coast.

Both traditional and new commodities thus contributed to the economic revival of late colonial Brazil. The dramatic increase in the volume of Brazilian exports in just over a decade at the very end of the period is depicted in table 11.[36] The table clearly indicates the declining importance of gold, now less than half the value of hides, for example, and the rise of Rio de Janeiro and its chief dependency, Rio Grande do Sul. Because of sugar, coffee, indigo, hides, and gold, Rio de Janeiro had become the economic centre of Brazil in this period and, like Pernambuco, had surpassed Bahia, long the economic mainstay of the colony. In spite of persistent high expectations and very considerable crown investment, Maranhão and, more particularly, Pará lagged far behind the rest of coastal Brazil.

It should be remembered that the economic gains registered during this period were achieved using backward forms and techniques. Despite the elimination of the Jesuits and the harassment of other

[36] See also ch. 6 above, table 7.

Table 11 *Principal Brazilian exports to Portugal, 1796 and 1806 (contos de réis)*

Place	Foodstuffs[a]		Chiefly tobacco[b]		Drugs[c]		Cotton		Hides		Gold		Totals	
	1796	1808	1796	1806	1796	1806	1796	1806	1796	1806	1796	1806	1796	1806
Rio de Janeiro[e]	1,457	2,109.6	53	97.7	139.4	189.7	28.5	26.9	233.5	1,393	1,790.5	853	3,702	4,670
Bahia	2,721	1,794.8	575.8	446.7	24.8	27.4	345.8	399.7	242.3	570	50	46	3,961	3,284.7
Pernambuco[d]	1,207	1,697	2.5	1.5	4.4	20.8	827	1,844.3	199.4	227	0.3	26	2,250	3,817.8
Paraíba	65				0.1		82.4		4.9				153	
Maranhão	171	316.6	7.3	19.4	1.1		845.9	1,148	28.6	32.5	0.8	8.8	1,055	1,527.7
Pará	186	614	0.8	0.6	8.8	78.1	71	71	22.6	16.4	8	5.6	297	785.9
São Paulo[e]	41.8				0.2		0.5		7.0		5.9		55	
Ceará		1.7				1.5		54		9.5	0.5			67.4
Totals	5,858.8	6,533.7	639.4	565.9	178.8	319.9	1,592.9	2,398.2	732	2,248.4	1,995.3	939.4	11,473	14,153.5

[a] Incl. rice, sugar, cacao, coffee. [b] Incl. wax (from Africa), snuff, etc. [c] Incl. indigo, quinine, sarsaparilla, brazilwood and hardwoods. [d] In 1796 included Ceará, Alagoas, and Rio Grande do Norte. In 1806 included Paraíba. [e] Incl. Santa Catarina, Rio Grande do Sul and (in 1806) São Paulo.

Source: Balbi, *Essai statistique sur le royaume de Portugal et d'Algarve...*, I (Paris, 1822), tables I and III, facing 430.

land-owning religious orders, no fundamental changes occurred in land tenure. The rise of cotton, the expansion of sugar, and the growth of livestock ranching, particularly in Rio Grande do Sul, merely accentuated existing patterns of latifundia. And the backbone of the plantation and ranch labour force remained, as it had been since the sixteenth century, black slaves. If the figures presented above in table 5 are reasonably accurate, it appears that slave imports increased by 66 per cent between 1780–5 and 1801–5, a direct consequence of the agrarian revival. But slave labour still meant hoe culture, for the plough was virtually unknown in Brazil at this time and, with the exception of tobacco growers, Brazilian planters still resisted the use of any form of fertilizer save wood ash.[37] Slash-and-burn practices, borrowed from the Indians, remained the customary method of land clearance and soil 'preparation'. Sugar planters continued with reckless abandon to destroy the forests to fuel their processing plants, further depleting an already scarce resource in many areas. Neither bagasse, the residue of crushed cane, nor the Jamaican train, both developed in the Caribbean sugar industry to economize on fuel, were extensively employed in Brazil. Though the need for agricultural innovations was certainly recognized, basic changes did not occur, and the agricultural improvement manuals that the government sent to Brazil, beginning in the 1790s, were expensive and, not surprisingly, often rotted in warehouses.[38]

Moreover, the benefits of the economic surge were largely confined to the littoral of Brazil, while the interior, which in minor ways contributed to the seaports' volume of exports, languished in decadence. Except for Minas Gerais, where gold mining continued on a reduced scale, and enlightened methods of stock raising accompanied subsistence agriculture, the interior became a largely barren land. Such was the case, for example, with Piauí, a region of extensive, mostly absentee-owned cattle ranches and little else. Once a major supplier of cattle to the gold

[37] The frustrating efforts of one enlightened governor to bring about agricultural improvements, including the use of fertilizer, may be seen in the correspondence of Dom Francisco Inocêncio de Sousa Coutinho, the governor of Pará, with his brother, Dom Rodrigo de Sousa Coutinho, the colonial minister, in Biblioteca e Arquivo Público do Pará. Belém [BAPP], cod. 683, nos. 5 and 99; cod. 685, no. 42 and annex; cod. 689, no. 200; and cod. 703, no. 34.

[38] For contemporary criticism of Brazilian agriculture, see Vilhena, *Cartas*, 1, 174–5, and Diogo Pereira Ribeiro de Vasconcelos, 'Breve descripção geographica, physica e politica da capitania de Minas Gerais', (1806), *Revista do Arquivo Público Mineiro*, 6 (1901), especially 837–8. On the failure to protect forests, F. W. O. Morton, 'The royal timber in late colonial Bahia', *HAHR*, 58 (February 1978), 41–61.

camps of Minas and the urban market of Salvador, it saw the Mineiro market decline in the 1760s with the falling off in gold production and the development of a more efficient kind of pastoralism in Minas itself. By about 1770 the number of *boiadas* (drives) sent annually from Piauense ranches via the banks of the São Francisco river to Minas had declined to 50 per cent of their 1750s level, and soon they disappeared altogether. Twenty years later the most devastating of a series of eighteenth-century droughts (*secas*) destroyed half the Piauense herd, a blow from which the economy did not recover for decades. The inability of Piauí to supply its other major market, Salvador, after the onset of the 'Great Drought' enabled a distant economic rival, Rio Grande do Sul, to capture the Bahian market for processed (salted or sun-dried) beef.

The 'Great Drought' also devastated parts of the interior of Maranhão and Ceará, but it was probably most seriously felt in Goiás. There the rapid exhaustion of gold placers in the 1760s left no money-making alternative, such as cotton or rice, to stock raising, since agriculture had never developed at a more than rudimentary level and the difficulties of transport made it impossible to dispose of surpluses to the more populous littoral. The *seca* of the 1790s was thus a serious blow to the local economy. Little wonder that while royal expenses were kept at an average of 62 contos a year (1762–1802), income fell steadily from 87 contos in 1765 to less than 33 in 1802.[39]

But Portugal had long operated marginal parts of the empire at a deficit: for example, her remaining enclaves along the west coast of India, which were sustained throughout most of the eighteenth century by subsidies from Lisbon; Mozambique; and (in the late colonial period) Mato Grosso and the upper Amazon, the sub-captaincy of São José do Rio Negro. It had long been Portuguese practice to compensate for fiscal losses produced in some parts of its empire with surpluses gathered elsewhere. In the sixteenth century India produced a large share of imperial income, but it is doubtful in spite of the royal monopoly on brazilwood, whether the crown netted much income from Brazil at all.[40] One of the earliest estimates of imperial income for the seventeenth century is that of a career fiscal officer, Luiz de Figueiredo Falcão, who indicates that at the opening of the century the state (*estado*) of India provided 45 per cent of crown income (760 out of 1,672 contos),

[39] Santos, *Relações comerciais*, 72–5.
[40] On this point see ch. 1 above.

compared with a mere 2.5 per cent (42 contos) from Brazil, scarcely more than the yield of the Azores.[41] If we may believe Fr Nicolao d'Oliveira, who published his *Livro das grandezas de Lisboa* in 1620, income from India fell precipitously during the intervening years (to 412.5 contos, or 23.6 per cent of total crown revenue), while that of Brazil increased to 54 contos (3 per cent of the total), but he notes that the entire yield from Brazil was spent within the colony.[42]

Without question Brazil's share of total royal income increased steadily during the seventeenth century and markedly during the eighteenth century, but by how much is hard to say. A calculation for 1716 indicates that out of a total royal income of 3,942 contos, 545 (13.8 per cent) came from Brazil. In 1777 the treasurer general reported to the queen that the crown's ordinary income amounted to 4,400 contos. But he showed only 636 contos as originating within the empire, of which 24.5 came from India and the rest from Brazil. However, 1777 was a singularly bad year for income from Portugal's leading colony because of the borderlands' conflict with Spain. Not recorded is a remittance of 297 contos from Rio de Janeiro and an additional 131.8 contos from various other captaincies, diverted to Rio de Janeiro to defray extraordinary expenditures of the viceregal exchequer. If we add both sums to the reported remittances, total royal income from Brazil would have been 1,195 contos, or 27.15 per cent of the crown's ordinary income that year.[43]

Unfortunately, from 1777 until 1805 we lack details concerning the levels of crown income. Balbi, the French geographer, reports that it peaked in 1805 at 11,200 contos, almost three times greater than receipts in 1777. Brazil's share of that total must have been very large, but it is not ascertainable since Balbi never received the promised income breakdown, nor has it subsequently come to light.[44]

There are, however, statistics that demonstrate the extent of Brazil's contribution to Portugal's foreign trade during the last years of this era. According to the Portuguese historian Jorge Borges de Macedo, between 1789 and 1807 the volume of that trade quadrupled. Table 12

[41] *Livro em que se contem toda a fazenda, & real patrimonio dos reynos de Portugal, India, ilhas adjacentes...& outras muitas particularidades* (1607) (Lisbon, 1859), 7f.

[42] Fr Nicolao d'Oliveira, *Livro das grandezas do Lisboa* (Lisbon, 1620), 173–185v.

[43] J[oão] Lúcio de Azevedo, *Épocas de Portugal económico...* (2nd edn., Lisbon, 1947), 463; 'Reflexõens ao resumo da receita e despeza do erario regio do anno de 1777', Biblioteca da Ajuda, Lisbon, 51–x–11, no. 57; Alden, *Royal government*, 328, 339, and 344.

[44] *Essai statistique*, I, 304.

Table 12. *Origins of exports from Portugal to Europe, Barbary, and the United States of America, 1789, 1796, 1806 (contos de réis)*

| | Place of origin | | | | | | Percentage |
Year	Portugal	Atlantic islands	Brazil	Asia	Other	Total	Brazilian
1789	3,251.1	0.6	3,965	702	20	7,534.5	52.6
1796	3,911.8	11.4	9,833	277	1,928	16,013	61.7
1806	6,080.2	34.0	14,506	624	2,010	23,255	62.4

Sources: 'Alfabeto das importaçoens e exportaçoens do reino de Portugal com as naçoens estrangeiras em...1789', Ministério das Obras Públicas, Arquivo Geral, fols. 31v–32r; Balbi, *Essai statistique*, I, 442.

demonstrates that during three of those years for which we have sufficient data Brazil supplied between one-half and two-thirds of the products that contributed to the expansion of the mother country's commerce. Thanks to Brazil's non-mineral exports, the balance of trade between Portugal and her principal trading partner, England, was completely altered at the end of the late colonial period. From the beginning of the century until 1791 that balance had always heavily favoured England, but from 1791 until 1810 it shifted substantially in Portugal's favour.[45] Of the products that Portugal sent to Britain during those two decades 35.7 per cent were of Brazilian origin. Similarly, the terms of trade between the kingdom and another important customer, France, also shifted in Portugal's favour in the early 1800s, mainly because of heavy purchases of Brazilian cacao, coffee, cotton, indigo, and sugar.[46]

Such statistics were naturally pleasing to Portuguese merchants and to high authorities, but there were others that caused concern. In spite of Portugal's favourable trade balances with her European markets, the value of Portuguese-made manufactured goods sent to the empire declined by 69 per cent between 1801 and 1807. Such a decline, which very likely began a decade earlier, was particularly alarming since nearly

[45] Excepting only 1797 and 1799. Balbi, I, 441. The Anglo-Portuguese trade balance from 1698 to 1775 is given in H. E. S. Fisher, *The Portugal trade 1700–1770* (London, 1971), 16; from 1776 to 1800 in Elizabeth Boody Schumpeter, *English overseas trade statistics 1697–1808* (Oxford, 1960), 17–18, tables 5–6; and from 1801 to 1810 in Macedo, *O bloqueio*, 41, where the data is expressed in contos, convertible at £ stg = 3,555.5 reis. See also ch. 6 above, tables 4, 6, and 7.
[46] Macedo, *O bloqueio*, 38, 42, 201–3.

Table 13 *Balance of trade between Portugal and leading Brazilian captaincies, 1796–1806 (contos de réis)*

Year	Rio de Janeiro[a]		Bahia		Pernambuco		Maranhão		Pará	
	Exp.	Imp.	Exp.	Imp.	Exp.	Imp.	Exp.	Imp.	Exp.	Imp.
1796	3,702	2,474	3,960	2,070	2,250	1,384	1,055	635	297	330
1797	916	3,721	1,661	2,734	850	1,270	352	462	256	226
1798										
1799	4,526	6,575	4,002	3,818	2,647	3,369	836	1,372	448	565
1800	4,840	4,080	2,640	2,306	2,270	1,733	1,956	1,819	628	418
1801	6,290	5,332	3,503	2,985	3,335	1,377	1,354	778	295	194
1802	3,643	3,579	2,620	2,506	2,295	2,362	1,378	1,143	417	538
1803	3,295	3,493	2,914	3,042	2,504	1,779	1,892	1,187	717	410
1804	3,245	3,959	2,700	2,858	2,914	2,880	1,807	978	512	645
1805	3,960	3,150	3,736	2,340	3,975	2,614	1,584	754	647	626
1806	4,670	3,056	3,385	2,110	3,818	1,789	1,528	832	786	653

[a] Includes São Paulo and Rio Grande do Sul.

Source: 'Balanças gerais', series, in Alden, 'Cacao production', 134–5.

four-fifths of such goods were supposed to find markets in Brazil, whose economy for the most part was flourishing.

The explanation for the lessening demand for Portuguese goods in Brazil is not hard to find. It lay in the growth of foreign, especially British, smuggling – 'a scandalous scourge', as the colonial minister bitterly declared, 'which extends to almost all the Brazilian captaincies'. If that minister's sources are to be trusted, by the mid-1780s a dozen English ships a year were boldly sailing direct from England to Brazilian ports in defiance of Portuguese laws to the contrary, and exchanging British manufactures for Brazilian raw materials.[47]

Smuggling had always been prevalent in Brazil, and to combat it the crown devised elaborate procedures to discourage unauthorized foreign ships from seeking admission to Brazilian ports under the pretext of being in distress but actually in order to engage in clandestine trade. Those procedures were often so rigorously enforced in the past that sea captains like James Cook charged zealous colonial officers with being despotic and inhumane. Nevertheless, they served to discourage all but three or four distressed vessels (*arribadas*) a year from entering, for

[47] Melo e Castro, 'Instrução', fols. 92v–98v.

example, Rio de Janeiro. But it is patent that by the 1780s and 1790s foreign ships were frequenting Brazilian ports in ever growing numbers, especially the premier port of Rio de Janeiro, where the number of British *arribadas* increased from eight to 30 a year between 1791 and 1800.[48]

As a consequence of the growth of the contraband trade in imported foreign manufactured goods and the increasing value of colonial exports because of an exceptionally strong European market, Portugal found herself in the undesirable – and from the perspective of crown officials absurd – position of having an adverse balance of payments with important parts of Brazil. The results are summarized in table 13.[49] Well might the colonial minister conclude that if the situation did not improve, 'within a few years this kingdom will be drained of money'. And, he might have added, the Brazilians might as well declare their independence.

SIGNS OF POLITICAL UNREST

The two decades before the transfer of the Portuguese court to Rio de Janeiro (1807–8) in fact witnessed several abortive conspiracies intended to free parts of Brazil from Portuguese rule. The first is the much-studied Mineiro conspiracy of 1788–9, organized in the city of Ouro Preto by a small group of Mineiro and Paulista intellectuals, some of whom were poets and admirers of the achievements of the first American revolution. Though Minas had obviously been in economic recession since the early 1760s, the immediate precipitant of the plot was the determination of the colonial secretary, Martinho de Melo e Castro, to collect large sums that he considered were due the crown. Melo e Castro (1716–95), an experienced diplomat and secretary of state for the navy and overseas territories since 1770, when he succeeded Pombal's late brother, Francisco Xavier de Mendonça Furtado, was the only person of his rank to survive in office after Pombal's dismissal. He shaped (or mis-shaped) Portugal's colonial policies for two and a half decades. Ignoring evidence to the contrary, he became convinced that the persistent shortfall in revenues from Minas was a consequence not of the exhaustion of the placers, but of the wilful negligence of public

---

[48] Santos, *Relações comerciais*, 119. Between 1791 and 1798, thirty-nine foreign ships were admitted to the port of Salvador under similar circumstances. Luis Henrique Dias Tavares, *História da sedição intentada na Bahia em 1798* ('*A conspiração dos alfaiates*') (São Paulo, 1975), 88.

[49] See also ch. 6 above, tables 5 and 8.

authorities in the captaincy and of the wholesale frauds perpetrated by mining entrepreneurs, tax contractors, and others. Brushing aside proposals to ameliorate the depression in Minas, he directed the newly designated governor, the Visconde de Barbacena, to undertake prompt efforts to collect the arrears, which in 1788 totalled 5,455 contos. Melo e Castro's 'root and branch' reform was bound to be painful to mine operators, tax contractors, ranchers, ecclesiastics, merchants, and even royal officials in the captaincy, yet, strangely, he saw no need to send troops from Rio de Janeiro to accompany the new (and untried) governor in enforcing such a draconian programme.

The conspirators, consisting of several ecclesiastics, a prominent landowner, two dragoon officers, one of whom was popularly called 'Tiradentes' (the tooth-puller), planned their uprising in December 1788. Associated with them was a larger, shadowy group including a local magistrate, several heavily indebted tax contractors, other landowners, and troop commanders. Their intent was to establish a Mineiro republic, where existing restrictions on diamond extraction, coinage, and manufacturing would no longer exist, and all debts to the Portuguese crown would be excused. They planned to establish a university (none existed in colonial Brazil) and various social services. The republic was to be democratically governed by municipal assemblies, a national parliament, and an annually elected head, whose title and functions remained undefined. Instead of a standing army, the republic would be defended by a citizen militia in which, presumably, Brazilian-born blacks and mulattos, to whom the revolutionaries promised freedom (without offering compensation to their former owners), would figure prominently. Precisely how such a republic might survive in the interior, surrounded by royalist-controlled captaincies, seems never to have been worked out, though it was apparently hoped that the Mineiro example would inspire similar uprisings in adjacent São Paulo and Rio de Janeiro.

There were about twenty conspirators. They intended to launch their revolt in mid-February 1789. That was when the governor was expected to announce his intention to collect an unpopular head-tax, the *derrama*, which was certain to provoke popular unrest. The rebels planned to fan that discontent until it became a full-fledged riot in the capital, Ouro Preto. During the tumult Tiradentes was to decapitate the governor and proclaim the establishment of the republic. However, the governor took the wind out of the conspirators' sails by suspending the *derrama*, and a few weeks later the plot was exposed. Following the arrest of the principal conspirators, three separate judicial inquiries were conducted, and in April 1792 sentences were handed down. Five of the conspirators were banished to Angola, but the sixth, Tiradentes, was sentenced to be hanged in a symbolic gesture of warning to others harbouring treasonable ideas. Shortly afterwards the sentences were carried out.

Rather more has been claimed for the significance of the Mineiro conspiracy than the evidence will support. According to its most recent interpreter, it represented a 'confrontation between a society growing in self-awareness and self-confidence within an economic environment that encouraged and stressed self-sufficiency, and a metropolis bent on the retention of dependent markets and the safeguarding of a vital producer of precious stones, gold, and revenue'.[50] Perhaps so, but it is not clear whether other towns and their elites in Minas, not to say the slaves, would have supported the revolutionaries, nor how many Mineiros were at the time really prepared to surrender their lives and their property – including their most important investment, their slaves – in an effort to secure their freedom by means of such an ill-conceived scheme.

Some of the participants in the Mineiro conspiracy possessed copies of books by some of the well-known French *philosophes*, but how much they were influenced by such works is hard to say. Familiarity with reformist French literature did inspire other plots or alleged plots in late colonial Brazil. One example of the latter is the so-called *conjuração* of Rio de Janeiro of 1794. There the viceroy, the Conde de Resende, prohibited all gatherings by intellectuals because of fear of revolutionary talk. When he was informed that nocturnal meetings were being held in the home of a regius professor of rhetoric, he immediately ordered the participants' arrest. Among those detailed were a woodcarver, a cabinetmaker, a shoemaker, a physician, a surgeon, a jeweller, and several businessmen. Though one of them possessed copies of works by Rousseau, Raynal, and the author of a religious treatise listed on the index of prohibited books, the 60 witnesses called before the enquiry panel had nothing more incriminating to report than the fact that the group discussed the current political situation in Europe, the incompetence of certain clerics, particularly Franciscans, and the probability that the Portuguese army could not stand up to French forces. No

---

[50] Kenneth R. Maxwell, *Conflicts and conspiracies: Brazil and Portugal 1750–1808* (Cambridge, 1973), 114.

conspiracy having been proven, the twelve were quietly released in 1797, after two and a half years' confinement in the dungeons of a local fortress.

A very different fate befell those who participated in the most fascinating conspiracy in Brazil during this period, the so-called 'Tailors' Conspiracy' of 1798 in Bahia. On 12 August of that year, handwritten manifestos were affixed to church walls and other prominent places throughout Salvador, addressed to the 'Republican Bahian people'. In the name of the 'supreme tribunal of Bahian democracy', the inhabitants were urged to support an armed movement claiming to include 676 persons – soldiers, ecclesiastics, merchants, even agents (*familiares*) of the Holy Office – whose purpose was to overthrow 'the detestable metropolitan yoke of Portugal' and to install a French-style republic. Although designating a shoeless Carmelite to head an independent church, the rebels issued dire warnings to clergymen who opposed the republic, in which 'all citizens, especially mulattos and blacks', would be equal, a regime based on 'freedom, equality and fraternity'. Slaves were promised freedom and soldiers pay rises; merchants, free trade with all nations, especially France; consumers, a rollback in prices, especially of manioc and beef, both of which had advanced 25 per cent in recent years.

The authorities, residing in a city where two out of three persons were black or brown and in a captaincy where whites were outnumbered five to one (see table 4 above), moved with alacrity to apprehend the culprits. Forty-nine suspects, including five women, were arrested. Most were free mulattos, including their leader, João de Deus do Nascimento, a penniless 27-year-old tailor, but eleven were slaves. In a society in which an estimated nine out of ten persons were illiterate, a surprisingly large number of the conspirators were able to read and, indeed, many possessed translations of incriminating French writings of the period. They ranged in age from sixteen to 38 but averaged just over 26. Although some historians insist in labelling the movement a mulatto plot to do away with whites, ten of the conspirators, including a schoolmaster whose greatest sin appears to have been his ability to read French, were white.

In spite of the apprehension of all but two of the suspects and the discovery of many suspicious documents, no revolutionary plan was ever discovered. Nor had any weapons been fired, although many of the conspirators were troops of the line or militiamen. Yet, upon the conclusion of a lengthy investigation, in November, 1799, João de Deus and three others were publicly hanged, their bodies being quartered and exhibited about the city; seven others were whipped and banished to other parts of the empire; others were confined for additional months in local dungeons; five were sent to Africa and abandoned in places not under Portuguese control.

This severe punishment of the Bahian 33 was carried out upon express orders from Lisbon. The clear objective was to convince persons of African origin of the futility of seeking to alter their status by radical means and to reassure the dominant white colonials that as long as they supported the existing regime, Brazil would not become another Saint-Domingue. Yet not all blacks were intimidated, nor were all whites reassured. In 1807 still another plot was uncovered in Bahia, this time involving plantation and urban slaves of Hausa origin. Though the plotters, armed with bows and arrows, pistols, and muskets, do not seem to have devised any political programme, their social goal was unmistakable: the massacre of all whites in the captaincy. Once again there were executions and whippings, but Bahian and other Brazilian whites must have wondered how long such measures would suffice.

Little wonder that few whites in Brazil favoured either an end to the slave trade or the elimination of slavery, both of which were so vital to their way of life and so intimately tied to the prosperity that coastal Brazil was then enjoying. It may be true that plots such as the Tailors' Conspiracy and the Hausa movement disposed the elites to accept compromises short of independence, but it is clear that while their spokesmen refrained from expressing the need for political reforms, they felt no reluctance about urging the crown to concede greater economic liberties that would benefit Brazil, or at least her dominant elites. One of the most influential of those spokesmen was José Joaquim da Cunha de Azeredo Coutinho (1742–1821). A member of the new rich sugar aristocracy of the Campos dos Goitacazes in Rio de Janeiro, Azeredo held many important ecclesiastical posts in Brazil and in Portugal and repeatedly prodded the government to undertake reforms that would benefit the economies of both the kingdom and her most vital colony. Thus, in 1791, he strongly opposed new price restrictions on sugar, arguing that higher prices would allow Brazilians to buy more goods from Portugal. Three years later he published a series of reform proposals in 'An economic essay on the commerce of Portugal and her colonies', in which he revived the century-old argument that the 'true mines' of Brazil were her agricultural resources, not the gold placers which had produced illusory gains. He urged the abolition of the salt monopoly (accomplished, as noted, in 1801), the elimination of restrictions upon the exploitation of Brazilian forests in order to promote the always disappointing shipbuilding industry, the development of a fishing industry based on Indian know-how; and the removal of restrictions on the manufacture of essentials. In a third essay on the state of the Brazilian mining sector (1804), the sometime bishop of Pernambuco reiterated a Mineiro appeal of a generation earlier, calling for a revival of gold mining through the introduction of the latest European knowledge and equipment.[51]

Although the bishop indicated general remedies that he believed would promote harmony, between Portugal and Brazil, a group of Bahian critics were far more specific. In 1807 the governor of Bahia wrote to the câmara of Salvador to inquire whether it felt that there were particular circumstances that inhibited the development of agriculture and commerce in the captaincy. The câmara, in turn, consulted leading figures throughout Bahia, several of whom responded at length. Judge João Rodrigues de Brito, a member of the high court of Salvador, clearly spoke for many proprietors when he candidly wrote,

In order for the farmers to achieve full liberty which the wellbeing of agriculture demands, it is necessary for them to have (1) the liberty to grow whatever crops they deem best; (2) the liberty to construct whatever works and factories they judge necessary to utilize fully their resources; (3) the liberty to sell in any place, by any means and through whatever agent they wish to choose, free of special fees or formalities; and (5) the liberty to sell their products at any time when it best suits their convenience. Unfortunately, the farmers of this captaincy enjoy none of these liberties at present.

The judge and several other respondents particularized many specific grievances of the agricultural interests of Bahia, including many restrictions imposed by the very câmaras controlled by the proprietary interests. But they also criticized the shortcomings of the religious, especially those living in monasteries, and the board of inspection, which they felt inhibited rather than facilitated sales of sugar, tobacco, cotton, and other crops; and they stressed the need for educational reforms and for freedom of the press.[52]

---

[51] Sergio Buarque de Holanda (ed.), *Obras económicas de J. J. da Cunha de Azeredo Coutinho* (*1794–1804*) (São Paulo, 1966).

[52] João Rodrigues de Brito *et al.*, *Cartas económico-políticas sôbre a agricultura e commércio da Bahia* (Lisbon, 1821; reprinted Salvador, 1924 and 1940). The quotation appears on p. 28 of the 1821 edition.

The articulation of such complaints, so similar to those voiced in Spanish America at that time, as well as the appearance of the first revolutionary plots in Brazil, testify to the extent of dissatisfaction that existed in late colonial Brazil. Not only sansculottes but men of substance and eminence, Portuguese- as well as Brazilian-born men, focused the crown's attention upon the need for fundamental improvements, without which revolutionary sentiment was bound to grow. And Portugal depended on Brazil far more than the colony needed the mother country.

At the conclusion of his 'Economic essay', Bishop Azeredo Coutinho had predicted:

If Portugal...preserves an adequate navy and merchant marine; if, satisfied with her vast dominions in the four quarters of the globe, she renounces further conquests; if she promotes by every [possible] means the development of the riches which her possessions have the capacity to produce; if she maintains her vassals in peace and tranquillity and assures their right to enjoy the fruits of their estates; if she establishes manufactures only of the most indispensable necessities, and abandons those of luxury to foreigners, in order to allow them an opportunity to purchase her superfluities...no enemy will molest her, or disturb her quiet...[53]

Unfortunately for the bishop and for the kingdom, the enemies of Portugal did molest her and profoundly upset her tranquillity. Portugal, which for years had profited from the succession of European conflicts, was finally a victim of those conflicts herself. In August 1807 Napoleon had demanded that Portugal close her ports to British ships and seize British subjects and their property. For a time the government sought to comply with those demands, but on 16 November a British fleet appeared off the Tagus and threatened to destroy elements of the Portuguese merchant marine and navy and possibly to bombard Lisbon as well. In addition, the British foreign secretary spoke darkly about the necessity of taking Brazil if Portugal failed to accept the assistance the British had proffered to facilitate the government's escape. While the lion was waving its tail angrily, the French tricolour appeared on Portuguese soil at the head of Marshal Junot's army of occupation (19 November). Squeezed by the Anglo-French nutcracker, the government implemented an emergency plan whose origins went back to 1640, and sought safety in its most important colony. On 29 November 1807 the

[53] *Obras*, 172.

government of the regent prince Dom João, *de facto* ruler of Portugal and the empire since his mother, Maria I, had become mentally incompetent in 1792, fled from Lisbon and sailed for Brazil under British naval escort, accompanied by thousands of courtiers, bureaucrats, soldiers, servants, and others. He arrived in Salvador in January 1808 and two months later was safely installed in Rio de Janeiro.

For Portugal, the economic euphoria of the past two decades, stemming in large part from profits earned on the resale of Brazilian agricultural and pastoral products, was over. It remained to be seen whether the regime of the prince regent (the future João VI) could accommodate the Brazilians by means that would satisfy their demands for change without at the same time seriously alienating the people whom it had just abandoned.[54]

---

[54] On the period from the arrival of the Portuguese court in Rio de Janeiro in March 1808 to the return of Dom João VI to Lisbon in April 1821, and on the background to Brazil's declaration of its independence from Portugal in September 1822, see Bethell, *CHLA*, III, ch. 4.

A NOTE ON LITERATURE AND
INTELLECTUAL LIFE

The first account of Brazil dates from Cabral's landfall on the coast of South America in 1500: the letter of Pero Vaz de Caminha to Dom Manuel I, 1 May 1500 (in William Brooks Greenlee (ed.), *The voyages of Pedro Álvares Cabral to Brazil and India from contemporary documents and narratives* (Hakluyt Society, London, 1937)). The three most important sixteenth-century chronicles are, first, Pero de Magalhães de Gandavo, *Tratado da terra do Brasil* and *Historia da Provincia da Santa Cruz* (Lisbon, 1576; Eng. trans., John B. Stetson, Junior, *The histories of Brazil* (2 vols., Cortes Society, New York, 1922)); secondly, Fernão Cardim S.J., *Do clima e terra do Brasil* and *Do principio e origem dos indios do Brasil* [*c.* 1584], published as 'A treatise of Brasil' in Samuel Purchas, *Hakluytus Posthumus, or Purchas His Pilgrimes* (4 vols., London, 1625; 20 vols., Glasgow, 1905–7), and *Tratados da terra e gente do Brasil*, ed. Capistrano de Abreu (Rio de Janeiro, 1925); thirdly, and most important of all, Gabriel Soares de Sousa, *Tratado descritivo do Brasil em 1587* (first published Rio de Janeiro, 1851; São Paulo, 1938). Especially interesting and valuable are the letters and reports of the Jesuits who arrived with the founders of royal government in 1549. Most notable are the writings of Manoel de Nóbrega (during the period 1549–70) and José de Anchieta (during the period 1554–94). There are a number of collections of Jesuit letters. See, in particular, Serafim Leite, *Monumenta Brasiliae* (4 vols., Rome, 1956–60). The Jesuits set up ten colleges, four seminaries and a novitiate, beginning with Santo Inácio (São Paulo) in 1554, Todos os Santos (Bahia) in 1556, Rio de Janeiro in 1567, and Olinda in 1576. The Jesuits dominated secondary education in colonial Brazil until their expulsion in 1759. Unlike colonial Spanish America, no university was ever established in colonial Brazil. There are numerous descriptions of Brazil in the sixteenth century by non-Portuguese: André Thévet, Jean de Léry, Ulrich Schmidel, Hans Staden, Anthony Knivet, Gaspar de Carvajal, and many others.

The foremost chronicle of the more complex society of seventeenth-century Brazil is Ambrosio Fernandes Brandão, *Os diálogos das grandezas do Brasil* (1618; ed. José António Gonsalves de Mello, Recife, 1962; 2nd edn, 1966). Also interesting is the satirical verse of the *bahiano* Grégorio de Matos (1633–90). The first history of Brazil, written by a Brazilian-born Franciscan (who drew heavily on Gabriel Soares de Sousa), is Vicente do Salvador's *Historia do Brasil* of 1627 (eds. Capistrano de Abreu and Rodolfo Garcia, 3rd edn, revised, São Paulo, 1931). The Dutch occupation of north-east Brazil (1630–54) produced important studies by Dutch scholars and scientists. The Jesuits continued to write about Brazil, especially about the interior: a notable contribution is Simão de Vasconcellos, *Chronica da Companhia de Jesus do Estado do Brasil* (Lisbon, 1663; 2nd edn, 2 vols., Lisbon, 1865), which deals largely with the second half of the sixteenth century. The exemplary literary figure of the seventeenth century is, however, the Jesuit António Vieira (1608–97); his sermons and writings, especially in defence of the Indians, represent one of the high points of Luso-Brazilian culture. See *Padre António Vieira: Obras escolhidas* (12 vols., Lisbon, 1951–4); *Padre António Vieira: Sermões* (14 vols., Lisbon, 1679–1710; 3 vols., Porto, 1908); *Cartas do António Vieira*, ed. J. L. de Azevedo (3 vols., Coimbra, 1925–8).

The most famous treatise on Brazil's natural resources and economy at the end of the seventeenth and beginning of the eighteenth centuries is *Cultura e opulência do Brasil por suas drogas e minas* by Giovanni Antonio Andreoni (João Antonio Andreoni) (1649–1716), an Italian Jesuit who wrote under the pseudonym Andre João Antonil. It was prepared over ten years beginning in 1693 and first published in Lisbon in 1711. There are various modern editions; by far the most scholarly is that edited by Andrée Mansuy (Paris, 1968). 1730 saw the publication in Lisbon of Sebastião da Rocha Pitta, *História da América Portuguesa* (3rd edn, Bahia, 1950), the first general history of Brazil by a Brazilian since that of Vicente do Salvador a century earlier.

Brazilians had to travel to Coimbra for a university education, but in the middle decades of the eighteenth century a number of attempts were made in both Bahia and Rio de Janeiro to set up scientific and literary academies and societies. The most notable were the Academia Cientifica (1771) and the Sociedade Literaria (1785) of Rio de Janeiro.

It was, however, in Vila Rica (Ouro Preto), Minas Gerais, in the 1780s that the literary and intellectual life of colonial Brazil reached its highest level. And outstanding were the *mineiro* poets: Claudio Manuel da Costa (*Vila Rica*), José Inácio de Alvarengo Peixoto, Manuel Inácio da Silva Alvarengo, José Basílio da Gama (*O Uraguay*), José de Santa Rita Durão (*Caramurú*) and Tomás Antonio Gonzaga (most famous for his satirical *Cartas chilenas*). Many of this brilliant generation of intellectuals and poets participated in the *Inconfidência mineira* (1788–9).

During the last decade of the eighteenth century and the first decade of the nineteenth, a number of important political and economic works were produced in Brazil, although, as always, published in Lisbon. (Until 1808 there was no printing press in Brazil.) Most worthy of note are José Joaquim da Cunha de Azeredo Coutinho, *Ensaio económico sobre o comércio de Portugal e suas colonias* (1794; in *Obras económicas*, ed. Sérgio Buarque de Holanda, São Paulo, 1966); Luis dos Santos Vilhena, *Recopilação de notícias soteropolitanas e brasílicas contidas em XX cartas* (1802; 3 vols., Bahia, 1921–2), the most important source on the economic, social, and political conditions of late colonial Brazil and especially Bahia, where the author lived from 1787 to *c*. 1804; and João Rodrigues de Brito, *Cartas económico-políticas sobre a agricultura e o comércio da Bahia* (1807; Lisbon, 1821; Bahia, 1924).

For more detailed information on these and other colonial texts (and their various editions), see Samuel Putnam, *Marvellous Journey. A survey of four centuries of Brazilian writing* (New York, 1948); Rubens Borba de Moraes, *Bibliographia Brasiliana. A bibliographical essay on rare books about Brazil published from 1504 to 1900 and works of Brazilian authors published abroad before the Independence of Brazil in 1822* (2 vols., Amsterdam, 1958; rev. and enlarged, 2 vols., Rio de Janeiro and Los Angeles, 1983); Rubens Borba de Moraes, *Bibliografia brasileira do período colonial* (São Paulo, 1969); and José Honório Rodrigues, *História da história do Brasil*, 1: *Historiografia colonial* (São Paulo, 1979).

BIBLIOGRAPHICAL ESSAYS

ABBREVIATIONS

ABNRJ	*Anais da Biblioteca Nacional do Rio de Janeiro*
AESC	*Annales, Économies, Sociétés, Civilizations*
HAHR	*Hispanic American Historical Review*
JGSWGL	*Jahrbuch für Geschichte von Staat, Wirtschaft und Gesellschaft Lateinamerikas*
RHA	*Revista de Historia de América*
RIHGB	*Revista do Instituto Histórico e Geográfico Brasileiro*

1. PORTUGUESE SETTLEMENT, 1500–1580

The best overall introduction to the sources and the literature of colonial Brazilian history is provided in José Honório Rodrigues' *História da história do Brasil, 1ª parte: historiografia colonial* (2nd edn, São Paulo, 1979); his more detailed but older *Historiografía del brasil, siglo XVI* (Mexico, 1957) deals exclusively with the sixteenth century. Also useful is Rubens Borba de Moraes, *Bibliografia Brasileira do período colonial* (São Paulo, 1969), a 'catalog with commentaries of works published before 1808 by authors born in Brazil'. Many important sources have been transcribed and published as appendixes to the various chapters of Carlos Malheiro Dias (ed.), *História da colonização Portuguesa do Brasil* (hereafter cited as *HCPB*), 3 vols. (Porto, 1921–4). Other major collections of source material can be found scattered throughout the *Anais da Biblioteca Nacional do Rio de Janeiro* (Rio de Janeiro, 1876–) and the volumes of the series *Documentos Históricos* (Rio de Janeiro, 1928–) published by the same institution. Many relevant documents have also appeared scattered throughout the volumes of *As gavetas da Torre do Tombo*, 11 vols. to date (Lisbon, 1960–).

Standard accounts of Brazilian history all treat, in varying degrees, the subjects touched upon in the chapter. Among the more useful are Pedro Calmon, *História do Brasil*, 7 vols. (Rio de Janeiro, 1959); Sérgio Buarque de Holanda (ed.), *História geral da civilização Brasileira*, I, 2 vols. (São Paulo, 1960); and Francisco Adolfo Varnhagen's nineteenth-century classic (enriched with notes by Capistrano de Abreu and Rodolfo Garcia): *História geral do Brasil*, 5 vols. (5th edn, São Paulo, 1948). *HCPB*, Carlos Malheiro Dias (ed.), a collaborative work that reflects the best Portuguese scholarship of its generation, stops at the year 1580; while João Capistrano de Abreu's classic, *Capítulos de história colonial* (4th edn, Rio de Janeiro, 1954) goes up to 1800. A survey of the period to 1580 with emphasis on the economic relations between settlers and Indians is provided by Alexander Marchant in *From barter to slavery* (Baltimore, 1942). Eulália M. L. Lobo has written an excellent overview of Brazilian colonial administration and enriched it by comparison with Spanish examples: *Processo administrativo ibero-americano* (Rio de Janeiro, 1962). Sérgio B. de Holanda gives an attractive account of one aspect of imperial ideology in his *Visão do Paraíso; os motivos edênicos no descobrimento e colonização do Brasil* (Rio de Janeiro, 1959), and Eduardo Hoornaert has edited a collection of studies of the colonial Brazilian church: *História da igreja no Brasil, primeira época* (Petropolis, 1977).

Portugal's thrust into the Atlantic during the fifteenth century has generated a large literature, separate from that of colonial Brazil and too vast to cover in detail. For a general introduction to the field, see Vitorino Magalhães Godinho, *A economia dos descobrimentos henriquinos* (Lisbon, 1962) with an excellent critical bibliography; this may be supplemented by the more exhaustive list provided in Bailey W. Diffie and George D. Winius, *Foundations of the Portuguese Empire, 1415–1580* (Minneapolis, 1977), 480–516. The essential facts of the expansion are given in Damião Peres' standard work, *História dos descobrimentos Portugueses* (2nd edn, Coimbra, 1960), and in Luís de Albuquerque, *Introdução a história dos descobrimentos* (Coimbra, 1962). Contrasting poles of interpretation are offered by Duarte Leite's *História dos descobrimentos* (2 vols., Lisbon, 1958–61) – critical, sceptical and debunking – and by Jaime Cortesão's two-volume synthesis, *Os descobrimentos Portugueses* (Lisbon, 1958–61), which gives greater rein to the historical imagination with sometimes dubious results. The various studies of Teixeira da Mota, dispersed in many journals, are valuable, as is Manuel Nuno Dias' *O capitalismo monárquico Português*, 2 vols. (Coimbra, 1963–4), for its wealth of data, not always fully digested. A stimulating essay that attempts to define some fundamental characteristics of colonial Brazilian life and discover their Iberian provenance has been written by Sérgio B. de Holanda, *Raízes do Brasil* (6th edn, Rio de Janeiro, 1971).

Metropolitan events during the sixteenth century can be approached via A. H. de Oliveira Marques' excellent and interpretive *História de Portugal*, 2 vols. (Lisbon, 1973) – to be preferred to the earlier edition in English – as well as through an older collaborative work edited by

Damião Peres, *et al.*, *História de Portugal*, 7 vols. (Barcelos, 1931–5); most recent is Joaquim Veríssimo Serrão, *História de Portugal*, III (*1498–1580*) (Lisbon, 1978), of value primarily for its wealth of bibliographical citations. For the reign of King Manuel 'The Fortunate', a good secondary study is lacking, but earlier accounts are fundamental: Damião de Góis, *Crónica do Felicíssimo Rei D. Manuel*, edited by David Lopes, 4 vols. (Coimbra, 1949–55) and Jerónimo Osório, *Da vida e feitos d'El Rey D. Manuel*, 3 vols. (Lisbon, 1804–6), a translation of his *De rebus Emmanuelis gestis* (Lisbon, 1571). For the reign of Manuel's successor we have Alfredo Pimenta's *D. João III* (Porto, 1936) as well as two seventeenth-century accounts: Fr. Luís de Sousa, *Anais de D. João III*, edited by M. Rodrigues Lapa, 2 vols. (Lisbon, 1938), and Francisco d'Andrada, *Chronica de... Dom João III...* 4 vols. (Coimbra, 1796). In addition much of the correspondence about imperial affairs between João III and the count of Castanheira has been edited and published (in the original Portuguese) by J. D. M. Ford and L. G. Moffatt, *Letters of John III, King of Portugal, 1521–1557* (Cambridge, Mass., 1931). King Sebastião and his successor, cardinal-King Henrique, have found their biographer in Queiroz Velloso, whose *D. Sebastião, 1554–1578* (3rd edn, Lisbon, 1945) and *O reinado do Cardeal D. Henrique* (Lisbon, 1946) give the essential story.

Vitorino Magalhães Godinho has examined the structure and functioning of the empire, taken as a whole, in various articles printed in his collected *Ensaios II: Sobre a história de Portugal*, 2nd edn (Lisbon, 1978), and more comprehensively in his *Os descobrimentos e a economia mundial*, 2 vols. (Lisbon, 1963), while José Sebastião da Silva Dias has dealt with sixteenth-century Portuguese culture and intellectual life in an excellent study, *A política cultural da época de D. João III*, 2 vols. (Coimbra, 1969). An older work by Hernani Cidade, *A literatura Portuguesa e a expansão ultramarina*, I (2nd edn, Coimbra, 1963), is still useful.

Cabral's discovery of Brazil has generated much controversy cogently summarized by the late Samuel Eliot Morison in *The European discovery of America: the southern voyages 1492–1616* (New York, 1974), 210–35; the voyages that followed Cabral's have been carefully sorted out by Max Justo Guedes in the *História naval Brasileira* (hereafter cited as *HNB*), 2 vols. (Rio de Janeiro, 1975–9), I: I, 179–245. Both Marchant, *From barter to slavery*, and the *HCPB* provide good accounts of the voyage of the *Bretoa*, while Rolando Laguarda Trías clarifies the

Spanish–Portuguese conflict over the La Plata region in the *HNB*, I: 1, 249–348. His account of the voyages of Christóvão Jaques revises the earlier account of António Baião and C. Malheiro Dias in the *HCPB*, III, 59–94. He is also responsible for the best recent account of the expedition of Martim Afonso da Sousa, the primary source for which – a diary of the voyage by Martim's brother, Pero Lopes de Sousa – has been lavishly edited with supplementary documentation by Eugénio Castro (ed.), *Diario da navegação de Pero Lopes de Sousa (1530–1532)*, 2 vols. (Rio de Janeiro, 1940).

The period of settlement is probably the least well studied of the various phases of Brazil's sixteenth-century history and good analyses are lacking. Some of the donatarial grants are printed in the *HCPB*, III, 257–83, 309–423, and competently analysed by Paulo Merêa in an accompanying chapter; the subsequent histories of the captaincies are touched upon in all the general accounts, but the topic still lacks an up-to-date synthesis. One can meanwhile consult the works of João Fernando de Almeida Prado, *Primeiros povoadores do Brasil, 1500–1530* (São Paulo, 1935); *Pernambuco e as capitanias do nordeste do Brasil*, 4 vols. (São Paulo, 1941); *Bahía e as capitanias do centro do Brasil, 1530–1626*, 3 vols. (São Paulo, 1945–50); *São Vicente e as capitanias do sul do Brasil, 1501–1531* (São Paulo, 1961); *A conquista da Paraíba* (São Paulo, 1964). An uncritical, but competent, general account is Elaine Sanceu, *Captains of Brazil* (Barcelos, 1965). Of the earlier writers, Vicente do Salvador, Soares de Sousa and Fernão Cardim give the most information on the post-settlement development of the various captaincies. José António Gonçalves de Melo has re-edited (in collaboration with Cleonir Xavier de Albuquerque) the letters of Duarte Coelho, donatary of Pernambuco: *Cartas de Duarte Coelho a el Rei* (Recife, 1967) with a valuable introductory study, while many of the other letters about the early settlements that were sent back to Portugal have been published as appendixes to various chapters of the *HCPB*, III, 257–83, 309–23.

Post-discovery relations between Indians and Portuguese can now be followed in the excellent and detailed survey (with full bibliography) of John Hemming, *Red gold: the conquest of the Brazilian Indians, 1500–1760* (London, 1978), while the evolution of Portuguese policy toward the Brazilian natives is outlined by Georg Thomas, *Die portugiesische Indianerpolitik in Brasilien, 1500–1640* (Berlin, 1968). The Jesuits' role in the conversion and acculturation of the Tupi is related in detail by Serafim Leite, *História da Companhia de Jesus no Brasil*, 10 vols.

(Lisbon–Rio de Janeiro, 1938–50), while the principal sources – the Jesuit missionaries' letters – have been edited in four volumes by the same scholar: *Monumenta Brasiliae* (Rome, 1956–60). This prolific historian has also given us (*inter alia*) Nóbrega's *corpus* in *Cartas do Brasil e mais escritos do P. Manuel da Nóbrega* (Coimbra, 1955), as well as a study of the foundation and early history of São Paulo, so closely linked to Jesuit activity: *Nóbrega e a fundação de São Paulo* (Lisbon, 1953). More references to the Jesuits will be found in *CHLA* 1, bibliographical essay 15. Other works on the early history of São Paulo are Jaime Cortesão, *A fundação de São Paulo – capital geográfica do Brasil* (Rio de Janeiro, 1955), and Vitorino Nemésio, *O campo de São Paulo. A Companhia de Jesus e o plano Português do Brasil, 1528–1563* (Lisbon, 1954).

A short, introductory overview is Michel Mollat's 'As primeiras relações entre a França e o Brasil: dos Verrazano a Villegagnon', *Revista de História* (São Paulo), 24 (1967), 343–58. More detail is given in Paul Gaffarel, *Histoire de Brésil français au XVIe siècle* (Paris, 1878), and, recently, in Charles-André Julien, *Les Voyages de découverte et les premiers établissements (XV–XVI siècles)* (Paris, 1948). For the rise and fall of Villegaignon's settlement at Rio de Janeiro, we now have a comprehensive, up-to-date study from Philipe Bonnichon and Gilberto Ferrez, 'A França Antártica', *HNB*, 11, 402–71. Two famous contemporary accounts of the colony (which also provide much first-hand information about the Indians) are the Calvinist, Jean de Léry's *Histoire d'un Voyage faict en la terre du Brésil* (La Rochelle, 1578) and *Les Singularitéz de la France Antartique autrement nommée Amérique* (Paris and Antwerp, 1558) by the Franciscan, André Thevet, who sailed out with Villegaignon in 1555.

In addition to the contemporary sources mentioned in the footnotes to the chapter, valuable information on Brazilian society and economy, *c.* 1580, is given in Frédéric Mauro's classic study of the 'sugar cycle', *Le Portugal et l'Atlantique au xviie siècle, 1570–1670* (Paris, 1960), and in Roberto Simonsen's pioneering *História econômica do Brasil, 1550–1820* (4th edn, São Paulo, 1962). A. J. R. Russell-Wood's *Fidalgos and Philanthropists: the Santa Casa da Misericordia of Bahia, 1550–1755* (Berkeley, 1968), and Arnold Wiznitzer's, *Jews in colonial Brazil* (New York, 1960), deal with important aspects of early Brazilian society. Stuart B. Schwartz has examined the composition of the labour force and work practices on some late sixteenth-century sugar plantations in his article, 'Indian labor and New World plantations: European demands and Indian responses in northeastern Brazil', *American Historical Review*, 83/1 (1978), 43–79.

2. POLITICAL AND ECONOMIC STRUCTURES OF EMPIRE, 1580–1750

The following general histories of Portugal are indispensable: in English, H. V. Livermore, *A new history of Portugal* (London, 1966); in Portuguese, A. de Oliveira Marques, *Historia de Portugal*, 2 vols. (Lisbon, 1972–3) (trans. into English and French), and J. Verissimo Serrão, *Historia de Portugal*, 9 vols. (Lisbon, 1980); in French, A. A. Bourdon, *Histoire de Portugal* (Paris, 1970), short but very good, and Y. Bottineau, *Le Portugal et sa vocation maritime. Histoire et civilisation d'une nation* (Paris, 1977), written with style and subtlety, preserving the balance between underlying structures and events. Mention must also be made of the very useful *Dicionario de historia de Portugal*, ed. Joel Serrão, 4 vols. (Lisbon, 1961–71), Damião Peres' great *Historia de Portugal*, 8 vols. (Barcelos, 1929–35), and vols. III and V of Fortunato de Almeida, *Historia de Portugal* (Coimbra, 1922–31), which consist of a description of Portuguese institutions and their development. A. Silbert, *Le Portugal méditerranéen à la fin de l'Ancien Régime*, 2 vols. (Paris, 1966) is very useful for the study of agrarian and social structures. On the Portuguese empire, a start can be made with C. R. Boxer, *The Portuguese seaborne empire 1415–1825* (London, 1973), and *Four centuries of Portuguese expansion 1415–1825: a succinct survey* (Johannesburg, 1965). V. Magalhães Godinho, *L'Économie de l'empire portuguais aux XVe et XVIe siècles* (Paris, 1969), has been expanded for the Portuguese, *Os descobrimentos e a economia mundial*, 2 vols. (Lisbon, 1963–5; 2nd edn, 4 vols., 1983). See also V. Magalhães Godinho's contributions to the *New Cambridge Modern History*: 'Portugal and her empire', *NCMH*, V, 384–97, and 'Portugal and her empire 1680–1720', *NCMH*, VI (1970), 509–40. F. Mauro, *Le Portugal et l'Atlantique au XVIIe siècle 1570–1670. Étude économique* (Paris, 1960; 2nd edn, 1983) is fundamental and has a convenient bibliography to which reference can be made. See also V. Magalhães Godinho, 'Le Portugal – les flottes du sucre et les flottes de l'or (1670–1770)', *AESC*, April–June (1950), 184–97, reprinted in *Ensaios*, II (Lisbon, 1968), 293–315. For complementary material, see B. T. Duncan, *Atlantic Islands...in the XVIIth century* (Chicago, 1972).

João Lúcio de Azevedo, *Épocas de Portugal económico* (2nd edn, Lisbon, 1973) remains very useful. For Brazil, F. Mauro, *Le Brésil du XVe à la fin du XVIIIe siècle* (Paris, 1977), brings the subject up to date and gives bibliographical information. See also F. Mauro's brief *Histoire du Brésil* (2nd edn, Paris, 1978).

There are also a number of monographs essential for an understanding of Portugal's role in America and its repercussions in the Old World. For Portugal's Atlantic policy, see C. R. Boxer, *Salvador de Sá and the struggle for Brazil and Angola 1602–1686* (2nd edn, Westport, 1975), and *The Golden Age of Brazil, 1695–1750* (Berkeley, 1962), and Dauril Alden, *Royal government in colonial Brazil* (Berkeley, 1968), a major part of which is devoted to matters of diplomacy and war. For a study of Portuguese administration in America, see Stuart B. Schwartz, *Sovereignty and society in colonial Brazil: the judges of the High Court of Bahia, 1586–1750* (Berkeley, 1974); also J. N. Joyce, 'Spanish influence on Portuguese administration: a study of the Conselho da Fazenda and Habsburg Brazil' (University of South California, Ph.D., 1974). On Portuguese political economy and the part played in it by Brazil, J. B. de Macedo, *Problemas de historia da industria Portuguesa no seculo XVIII* (Lisbon, 1963) is important. Also the new edition of V. M. Godinho, *Ensaios II. Sobre historia de Portugal* (Lisbon, 1978). An important recent contribution is Carl Hanson, *Economy and society in Baroque Portugal, 1668–1703* (Minneapolis, 1981). On Portuguese diplomacy in America, the following should be consulted: A. P. Canabrava, *O comércio português no Río da Prata 1580–1640* (São Paulo, 1944), Luis Ferrand de Almeida, *A diplomacia portuguesa e os limites meridionais do Brasil*, I, 1493–1700 (Coimbra, 1957), J. Cortesão, *Raposo Tavares e a formação territorial do Brasil* (Rio de Janeiro, 1958), and J. Cortesão, *Alexandre de Gusmão e o Tratado de Madrid* (8 vols., Rio de Janeiro, 1950–9). For the north, see H. C. Palmatory, *The river of the Amazonas. Its discovery and early exploration 1500–1743* (New York, 1965), and Mario Meireles, *Historia do Maranhão* (São Luis, 1960).

On nautical questions, see the sundry publications of the various Portuguese congresses, such as the Congresso da Historia da Expansão Portuguesa no Mundo, Congresso do Mundo Português, Congresso dos Descobrimentos Henriquinos; also A. Marques Esparteiro, *Galeotas e bergantins reais* (Lisbon, 1965); N. Steensgaard, *Carracks, caravans and companies* (Copenhagen, 1973), a new edition of which has appeared under the title: *The Asian trade revolution of the seventeenth century. The East*

India companies and the decline of the caravan trade (Chicago, 1974); Sousa Viterbo, *Trabalhos nauticos dos Portugueses nos seculos XVI e XVII* (Lisbon, 1900); H. Leitão and J. V. Lopes, *Dicionario da linguagem de Marinha Antiga e Actual* (2nd edn, Lisbon, 1974); Fontoura da Costa, *A marinharia dos Descobrimentos* (Lisbon, 1933); the work of Virginia Rau on foreign merchants in Lisbon, for example, 'Os mercadores e banqueiros estrangeiros em Portugal no tempo de D. João III (1521–1587)', in *Estudios de Historia Economica* (Lisbon, 1961), 35–62; finally, all the studies which have appeared in the publications of the *Junta de Investigações Cientificas do Ultramar*, particularly those of the Centro de Estudos de Cartografia Antiga, Secção de Coimbra e Secção de Lisboa.

On the exports from Brazil, especially sugar and gold, see *CHLA* II, bibliographical essays 12 and 14.

On the slave trade to Brazil the following should be noted: M. Goulart, *Escravidão africana no Brasil* (São Paulo, 1950); G. Scelle, *Histoire politique de la traite négrière aux Indes de Castille*, 2 vols. (Paris, 1906); Philip Curtin, *The Atlantic slave trade* (Madison, 1969); H. S. Klein, 'The Portuguese slave trade from Angola in the 18th century', *Journal of Economic History*, 33/4 (1972), 894–917, and *The Middle Passage. Comparative studies in the Atlantic slave trade* (Princeton, 1978); E. G. Peralta Rivera, *Les Mécanismes du commerce esclavagiste XVIIe siècle* (3rd cycle thesis EHESS, Paris, 1977); P. Verger, *Flux et reflux de la traite des nègres entre le golfe du Bénin et Bahia de Todos os Santos du XVIIe au XIXe siècle* (Paris, 1968), and 'Mouvements de navires entre Bahia et le Golfe de Bénin XVIIe–XIXe siècles', *Revue Française d'Histoire d'Outre-Mer* (Paris), 55 (1968), 5–36; E. Vila Vilar, *Hispano-America y el comercio de esclavos. Los asientos portugueses* (Seville, 1977); finally, K. Polanyi, *Dahomey and the slave trade: an analysis of an archaic economy* (Washington, 1966).

On money, see Teixeira de Aragão, *Descripção geral e historica das moedas cunhadas em nome dos reis de Portugal*, 3 vols. (Lisbon, 1874–80), and, among others, N. C. da Costa, *Historia das moedas do Brasil* (Porto Alegre, 1973). On wars at sea, Botelho de Sousa, *Subsidios para a historia das guerras da Restauração no Mar e no Alem Mar*, I, (Lisbon, 1940), and W. J. van Hoboken, *Witte de With in Brazilie 1648–1649* (Amsterdam, 1955). For institutions, Marcelo Caetano, *Do Conselho Ultramarino ao Conselho do Imperio colonial* (Lisbon, 1943); *Regimento das Casas das Indias e Minas*, ed. Damião Peres (Coimbra, 1947); Gustavo de Freitas, *A Companhia Geral do Comercio do Brasil* (São Paulo, 1951).

For foreign relations, the two classic works are E. Prestage, *The diplomatic relations of Portugal with France, England and Holland from 1640 to 1668* (Watford, 1925), and E. Brasâo, *A Restauração. Relacões diplomaticas de Portugal de 1640 à 1668* (Lisbon, 1939). See also Charles Verlinden, *Les Origines de la civilisation atlantique* (Paris, 1966), and F. Mauro, *Études économiques sur l'expansion portugaise 1500–1900* (Paris, 1970). For Spain and the Spanish empire, see the works of E. J. Hamilton, P. and H. Chaunu, and others, cited in *CHLA* I, bibliographical essays 6, 9 and 10. As regards France, there is no comprehensive work, only chapters or articles in various publications. See, in particular, the numerous articles by J. Soares de Azevedo on French trade in Lisbon. I. S. Revah, *Le Cardinal de Richelieu at la Restauration de Portugal* (Lisbon, 1950) also deserves mention.

On the relations of Portugal with England, many works are available: V. M. Shillington and A. B. Wallis Chapman, *The commercial relations of England and Portugal* (London, 1908; reprinted New York, 1970), the standard work; Sir Richard Lodge, 'The English factory at Lisbon', *Transactions of the Royal Historical Society* (4th ser., 16 (1933), 210–47; A. R. Walford, *The British factory in Lisbon* (Lisbon, 1940); Alan K. Manchester, *British preeminence in Brazil, its rise and decline* (Chapel Hill, 1933); R. Davis, 'English foreign trade 1660–1700', *Economic History Review*, VII (1954), 150–66, and 'English foreign trade, 1700–1774', *EconHR*, XV (1962), 285–303; Elizabeth Boody Schumpeter, *English overseas trade statistics (1697–1808)* (Oxford, 1960); H. E. S. Fisher, *The Portugal trade: a study of Anglo-Portuguese commerce 1700–1770* (London, 1971); A. D. Francis, *The Methuens and Portugal 1691–1708* (Cambridge, 1966); S. Sideri, *Trade and Power: informal colonialism in Anglo-Portuguese relations* (Rotterdam, 1970); C. R. Boxer, 'Brazilian gold and British traders in the first half of the eighteenth century', *HAHR*, 49/3 (1969), 454–72; and, most recently, Virgílio Noya Pinto, *O ouro brasileiro e o comercio anglo-português (uma contribuicão aos estudos de economia atlantica no seculo XVIII* (São Paulo, 1979).

As regards the Dutch, their trade with Portugal can be studied in J. Nanninga Uitterdijk, *Een Kamper Handelshuis te Lisabon 1572–1594* (Zwolle, 1904); A. E. Christensen, *Dutch trade to the Baltic about 1600* (The Hague, 1941); and N. W. Posthumus, *Inquiry into the history of prices in Holland* (Leiden, 1946). For the diplomatic and political aspects of the Dutch presence in Brazil, see C. R. Boxer, *The Dutch in Brazil* (2nd edn, Hamden, 1973); P. Agostinho, 'A politica Vieira e a entrega de Pernambuco', *Espiral* (January–March 1965), 122–34; C. R. Boxer,

'Portuguese and Dutch colonial rivalry', *Studia*, 2 (1958), 7–42;
J. M. Campos, *A restauração em Portugal e no Brasil* (Lisbon, 1962);
V. Rau, 'A embaixada de Tristão de Mendonça Furtado e os arquivos
holandeses', *Anais da Academia Portuguesa de Historia*, 2nd ser., 8 (1958),
93–160; G. D. Winius, 'India or Brazil. Priority for imperial survival
during the wars of the Restoration', *Journal of the American-Portuguese
Cultural Society*, 1/4–5 (1967), 34–42. Finally, A. Wiznitzer, *Jews in
Colonial Brazil* (New York, 1960), deserves mention.

3. PLANTATIONS AND PERIPHERIES, *c.* 1580 – *c.* 1750

Guides, general histories, collections

The works of José Honório Rodrigues are fundamental tools. *Historiografía del Brasil, siglo XVI* (Mexico, 1957) and *Historiografía del Brasil,
siglo XVII* (Mexico, 1963) discuss the major sources. *História da história
do Brasil*, 1: *Historiografia colonial* (São Paulo, 1979) covers the eighteenth
century as well. The sources and scholarship in English are contained
with annotations in Francis A. Dutra, *A guide to the history of Brazil,
1500–1822* (Santa Barbara, 1980). Rubens Borba de Moraes, *Bibliografia
brasileira do período colonial* (São Paulo, 1969) is a catalogue of works
by Brazilians published before 1808. A good specialized bibliography
is Robert Conrad, *Brazilian slavery: an annotated research bibliography*
(Boston, 1977).

Sérgio Buarque de Holanda (ed.), *História geral da civilização brasileira,
I A época colonial* (2 vols., São Paulo, 1960) provides a succinct
survey of major themes. Pedro Calmon, *História do Brasil* (7 vols., Rio
de Janeiro, 1959) has the most detailed colonial sections of the many
modern histories. The classic *História geral do Brasil* (6 vols.; 7th edn,
São Paulo, 1962) by Francisco Adolfo de Varnhagen, originally
published in 1857, is still valuable. Together, C. R. Boxer's *Salvador de
Sá and the struggle for Brazil and Angola, 1602–1686* (London, 1952), and
his *The Golden Age of Brazil, 1695–1750* (Berkeley and Los Angeles,
1964) provide the best available overview in English of Brazilian history
for the period. Frédéric Mauro, *Le Brésil du XVe à la fin du XVIIIe siècle*
(Paris, 1977) is a brief survey based on recent scholarship. Dauril Alden
(ed.), *Colonial roots of modern Brazil* (Berkeley and Los Angeles, 1973)
presents an important collection of papers on colonial themes.
A. J. R. Russell-Wood (ed.), *From colony to nation* (Baltimore, 1975), is

primarily concerned with the post-1750 period but does have a number of articles pertinent to the earlier era. The *Anais do Congresso Comemorativo do Bicentenário da Transferência da Sede do Governo do Brasil* (4 vols., Rio de Janeiro, 1966), contains many items of interest, as do the various publications of the Luso-Brazilian Colloquium (1st Proceedings or *Actas* published in Nashville, 1953).

Government and economy

The structure of Portuguese government in Brazil is summarized in Eulália Maria Lahmeyer Lobo, *Processo administrativo Ibero-Americano* (Rio de Janeiro, 1962). Dauril Alden, *Royal government in colonial Brazil* (Berkeley and Los Angeles, 1968), contains much useful material. Stuart B. Schwartz, *Sovereignty and society in colonial Brazil* (Berkeley and Los Angeles, 1973), discusses the judicial structure of the colony. A useful collection of royal instructions is Marcos Carneiro de Mendonça, *Raízes da formação administrativa do Brasil* (2 vols., Rio de Janeiro, 1972). A provocative interpretative essay that touches on the early colonial era is Raymundo Faoro, *Os donos do poder* (1st edn, Rio de Janeiro, 1958). Other works on the organs of colonial government in Portugal itself are cited in *CHLA* 1, Bibliographical Essay 12.

General studies of the colonial economy are few. Frédéric Mauro's invaluable *Portugal et l'Atlantique* (Paris, 1960) is an essential quantitative study of Brazil within the Atlantic system. For other works on the Atlantic economy, again see *CHLA* 1, Bibliographical Essay 12. Mauro has also published important collections of essays such as *Nova história e nôvo mundo* (São Paulo, 1969). Roberto Simonsen, *História económica do Brasil* (São Paulo, 1937) is still valuable although many of the figures presented need revision. A number of volumes by Mircea Buescu, such as his *300 anos da inflação* (Rio de Janeiro, 1973), make good use of colonial economic data. The synthesis of Caio Prado Júnior, *Colonial background* (see *CHLA* 11, Bibliographical Essay 15) and Celso Furtado, *The economic growth of Brazil* (Berkeley and Los Angeles, 1963) provide excellent overviews. Especially provocative is Fernando Novais, *Estrutura e dinâmica do sistema colonial* (Lisbon, 1975) which has also appeared in a Brazilian edition.

Various economic activities have received monographic attention, although the record here is spotty. A major difficulty that the chapter reflects is a lack of serial economic data for the period prior to 1750.

There are no adequate studies of manioc- or tobacco-farming for this period. A good study of the ranching society in the north-east is provided by Luiz Mott, 'Fazendas de gado do Piauí (1697–1762)', *Anais do VII Simpósio Nacional de Professores Universitários de História* (São Paulo, 1976), 343–69. On this topic Lycurgo Santos Filho, *Uma comunidade rural no Brasil antigo* (São Paulo, 1956), is also useful. The best single monograph on sugar is Wanderley Pinho, *História de um engenho no Recôncavo* (Rio de Janeiro, 1946). Unfortunately, similar studies do not exist for the engenhos of Rio de Janeiro and Pernambuco. António Barros de Castro, 'Escravos e senhores nos engenhos do Brasil' (Ph.D. thesis, University of Campinas, 1976), is an excellent overview based on printed primary sources. Still indispensable for any study of the colonial economy is André João Antonil (pseudonym of Antonio Giovanni Andreoni, S.J.), *Cultura e opulência do Brasil por suas drogas e minas* (Lisbon, 1711), a work whose value has been greatly increased by the notes and introduction provided by Andrée Mansuy in the Paris edition of 1968. Myriam Ellis has contributed solid studies such as *Aspectos da pesca da baleia no Brasil colonial* (São Paulo, 1958), and Alice P. Canabrava's analysis of Brazilian trade in the Río de la Plata, *O comércio português no Rio da Prata, 1580–1640* (São Paulo, 1944) remains essential reading.

Slavery

A lively debate is being conducted in Brazil over the nature of the colonial economy and the role of slavery within it. Jacob Gorender, *O escravismo colonial* (São Paulo, 1978) is a major statement based on a wide reading of printed sources. It has produced considerable reaction as is demonstrated in the group of essays in José Roberto do Amaral Lapa (ed.), *Modos do produção e realidade brasileira* (Petrópolis, 1980). An earlier essay by Ciro Flamarion S. Cardoso, 'El modo de producción esclavista colonial en América', in *Modos de producción en América Latina* (Buenos Aires, 1973), is still an important theoretical formulation of the problem.

The form of labour and its relation to the social and economic structures of the colony has been a major theme in Brazilian history. The most complete study of Portuguese Indian policy is Georg Thomas, *Die portugiesische Indianerpolitik in Brasilien, 1500–1640* (Berlin, 1968), but it should be used in conjunction with Kieman's book on Indian policy in the Amazon (cited below) and with the works of Father Serafim Leite on the Jesuits. John Hemming, *Red gold. The conquest of the Brazilian Indians 1500–1760* (London, 1978) is a well-written narrative account. Stuart B. Schwartz, 'Indian labor and New World plantations: European demands and Indian responses in northeastern Brazil', *American Historical Review*, 83/1 (February 1978), 43–79, deals with Bahia, but studies of other regions are sorely needed.

Despite the centrality of African slavery to colonial Brazil, the coverage of the topic is very uneven. To some extent this is a problem of sources available for the pre-1750 period. Some of the best books about slavery in Brazil often have little information on the early colonial period and are forced to infer the previous history. Such is the case with Gilberto Freyre's classic, *The masters and the slaves* (New York, 1946), originally published in 1933 in Brazil. Present concerns have also oriented research. Thus, we have a large and growing literature on slave resistance and especially Palmares as is represented by Edison Carneiro, *O quilombo dos Palmares* (3rd edn, Rio de Janeiro, 1966), but little on the early slave trade. On that topic Maurício Goulart, *A escravidão africana no Brasil* (São Paulo, 1949) is still a good starting point.

Portuguese attitudes towards slavery have been studied by A. J. R. Russell-Wood, 'Iberian expansion and the issue of black slavery', *American Historical Review*, 83/1 (February 1978), 16–42, and David Sweet, 'Black robes and black destiny: Jesuit views of African slavery in 17th-century Latin America', *RHA*, 86 (July–December 1978), 87–133; but many other issues need investigation. Questions concerning the profitability, demography, family structure and internal organization of Brazilian slavery in this period all remain to be studied. An example of what can be done is provided by Francisco Vidal Luna, *Minas Gerais: Escravos e senhores* (São Paulo, 1981), an essentially quantitative study of slave ownership. On slave culture, Roger Bastide, *The African religions of Brazil* (Baltimore, 1978) remains the essential introduction. A useful popular survey that incorporates the best recent scholarship is Katia M. de Queiros Mattoso, *Être esclave au Brésil XVIᵉ–XIXᵉ siècle* (Paris, 1979).

Social aspects

In some ways the literature on free people of colour and race relations is better developed than that on slavery itself. A. J. R. Russell-Wood, 'Colonial Brazil', in David W. Cohen and Jack P. Greene (eds.), *Neither slave nor free: the freedman of African descent in the slave societies of the New World* (Baltimore, 1972), incorporates much of the author's own work and follows the approach of Charles R. Boxer, *Race relations in the Portuguese colonial empire* (Oxford, 1963). Stuart Schwartz, 'The manumission of slaves in colonial Brazil: Bahia 1684–1745' (*HAHR*, 54/4 (1974), 603–65) is a quantitative study. A. J. R. Russell-Wood, 'Black and mulatto brotherhoods in colonial Brazil', *HAHR*, 54/4 (1974), 567–602, is a good general discussion, but it should be used together with Patricia Mulvey, 'The black lay brotherhoods of colonial Brazil: a history' (Ph.D. thesis, City University of New York, 1976), and Manoel S. Cardozo, 'The lay brotherhoods of colonial Bahia', *The Catholic Historical Review*, 33/1 (April 1947), 12–30.

Social change and social groups before 1750 have received little attention. Francis Dutra has produced a number of studies of institutional response to social change of which 'Membership in the Order of Christ in the seventeenth century', *The Americas*, 27/1 (July 1970), 3–25, is a good example. The role of women remains mostly unstudied except for chapters by Susan Soeiro and A. J. R. Russell-Wood in Asunción Lavrin (ed.), *Latin American women: historical perspectives* (Westport, 1978), 60–100, 173–97. Various social groups have been best studied in Bahia (see below), but many important topics need to be examined. We have, for example, no studies of wage labourers or artisan organizations in the early period.

One social group, the New Christians, has received extensive treatment. Arnold Wiznitzer, *The Jews in colonial Brazil* (New York, 1960), is a general study. Anita Novinsky, *Cristãos novos na Bahia* (São Paulo, 1972) brings a great deal of new material into the debate about the Judaism of the New Christians. Regional studies like José Gonçalves Salvador, *Os cristãos-novos. Povoamento e conquista do solo brasileiro* (São Paulo, 1976), on the southern captaincies, and the excellent piece by Gonsalves de Mello, 'A nação judaica do Brasil holandês', *Revista do Instituto Arqueológico, Histórico e Geográfico de Pernambuco* [*RIAHGP*], 49 (1977), 229–393, on Pernambuco, have deepened our understanding of their story. The history of the New Christians was intimately, if unfortunately, tied to that of the Inquisition. A good recent study of that institution and especially of its structure and operation is Sónia A. Siqueira, *A inquisição portuguesa e a sociedade colonial* (São Paulo, 1978).

On the Brazilian cities and towns, the fundamental work is Nestor Goulart Reis Filho, *Evolução urbana do Brasil (1500–1720)* (São Paulo,

1968). Also useful are Edmundo Zenha, *O município no Brasil* (São Paulo, 1948), and Nelson Omegna, *A cidade colonial* (Rio de Janeiro, 1961). A recent thesis with emphasis on the late colonial era is Roberta Marx Delson, 'Town planning in colonial Brazil' (Ph.D. thesis, Columbia University, 1975). An excellent interpretative essay is Richard M. Morse, 'Brazil's urban development: colony and empire', in Russell-Wood, *From colony to nation*, 155–81.

Regional studies

The historiography of the period before 1750 is regionally unbalanced. Bahia has received far more attention than other areas. Thus, many generalizations contained in the chapter are based on findings for Bahia which remain to be demonstrated for other areas.

For Bahia there are excellent social and institutional studies. A. J. R. Russell-Wood, *Fidalgos and philanthropists* (Berkeley and Los Angeles, 1968), studies the Misericórdia. Susan Soeiro, 'A baroque nunnery: the economic and social role of a colonial convent: Santa Clara de Desterro, Salvador, Bahia, 1677–1800' (Ph.D. thesis, New York University, 1974), is good on women in society and the financial role of that institution. C. R. Boxer's chapter on the câmara of Salvador in *Portuguese society in the tropics* (Madison, 1965) is particularly valuable. David G. Smith, 'The mercantile class of Portugal and Brazil in the seventeenth century: a socio-economic study of the merchants of Lisbon and Bahia, 1620–1690' (Ph.D. thesis, University of Texas, 1975), is the most thorough study of merchants. Rae Flory, 'Bahian society in the mid-colonial period: the sugar planters, tobacco growers, merchants, and artisans of Salvador and the Recôncavo, 1680–1725' (Ph.D. thesis, University of Texas, 1978), is based on notarial records. Stuart B. Schwartz, 'Free farmers in a slave economy: the *lavradores de cana* of colonial Bahia', in Alden (ed.), *Colonial roots*, 147–97, looks at that group based on plantation records. José Roberto do Amaral Lapa, *A Bahia e a carreira da Índia* (São Paulo, 1968), deals with Salvador as a port and shipyard. Thales de Azevedo, *Povoamento da Cidade do Salvador* (3rd edn, Bahia, 1968), and Afonso Ruy, *História política e administrativa da cidade do Salvador* (Bahia, 1949), are still invaluable.

For Pernambuco and its adjacent areas the situation is in general much worse. José Antônio Gonsalves de Mello has done much in *RIAHGP* to rectify this situation. Also valuable is Francis A. Dutra, *Matias de*

Albuquerque (Recife, 1976). On the war of the Mascates, see Norma Marinovic Doro, 'Guerra dos Mascates – 1710' (Master's thesis, University of São Paulo, 1979), and J. A. Gonsalves de Mello's excellent 'Nobres e mascates na câmara de Recife', *RIAHGP* (forthcoming).

The best recent scholarship on the Dutch occupation of the north-east is represented by C. R. Boxer's *The Dutch in Brazil, 1624–54* (Oxford, 1957) on military and political affairs; José Antônio Gonsalves de Mello, *Tempo dos Flamengos* (2nd edn, Recife, 1978), on social matters; and Evaldo Cabral de Mello, *Olinda Restaurada* (São Paulo, 1975), on the economy. These works incorporate the earlier classic studies. In addition, the above authors have all edited important documents of the period. Representative of them and extremely valuable is J. A. Gonsalves de Mello (ed.), *Relatório sôbre as capitanias conquistadas* by Adriaen van der Dussen (Rio de Janeiro, 1947). E. van den Boogaart (ed.), *Johan Maurits van Nassau-Siegen, 1604–1679* (The Hague, 1979), presents recent Dutch and Brazilian scholarship on the period.

Modern social and economic history on Rio de Janeiro before 1750 is virtually nonexistent. Joaquim Veríssimo Serrão, *O Rio de Janeiro no século XVI* (2 vols., Lisbon, 1965), is valuable for the documents it reproduces. Vivaldo Coaracy, *O Rio de Janeiro no século XVII* (2nd edn, Rio de Janeiro, 1965), contains useful information. The many works of Alberto Lamego on the sugar economy of Rio de Janeiro were extensively used by William Harrison, in 'A struggle for land in colonial Brazil: the private captaincy of Paraiba do Sul, 1533–1753' (Ph.D. thesis, University of New Mexico, 1970), but much remains to be done.

There is an extensive historiography on São Paulo, although much of it concentrates on the exploits of the bandeiras and was written prior to 1950, thus reflecting older historical concerns. A provocative essay on the early history of São Paulo is Florestan Fernandes, *Mudanças sociais no Brasil* (São Paulo, 1960), 179–233. There are a number of histories of the region of which Afonso d'Escragnolle Taunay, *História seiscentista da Vila de São Paulo* (4 vols., São Paulo, 1926–9) is the most thorough. Taunay is also the dean of bandeira studies, and his *História geral das bandeiras paulistas* (11 vols., São Paulo, 1924–50), is the basic study. Alfredo Ellis Júnior, *Meio século de bandeirismo* (São Paulo, 1948) and Jaime Cortesão, *Rapôso Tavares e a formação territorial do Brasil* (Rio de Janeiro, 1958) are standard works by other specialists. There has been in recent years considerable interest in the society of São Paulo in the period after 1750, but for the early times the literature is limited. Alcântara Machado, *Vida e morte do bandeirante* (São Paulo, 1930), uses the series *Inventários e testamentos* (São Paulo, 1920–) to evoke everyday life. The works of Sérgio Buarque de Holanda, such as *Caminhos e fronteiras* (Rio de Janeiro, 1957) and *Visão do paraíso* (Rio de Janeiro, 1959), are indispensable. Richard M. Morse (ed.), *The Bandeirantes: the historical role of the Brazilian pathfinders* (New York, 1965) presents excerpts from many important works. Suggestive essays are contained in Jaime Cortesão's *Introdução à história das bandeiras* (2 vols., Lisbon, 1964).

On the extreme south, José Honório Rodrigues, *O continente do Rio Grande* (Rio de Janeiro, 1954) provides a succinct essay. Guillermino César, *História do Rio Grande so Sul* (Pôrto Alegre, 1970) has interesting social information. Dauril Alden, *Royal government*, provides the best summary in English.

For the Brazilian north prior to 1750 the bibliography is not large. J. Lúcio de Azevedo, *Os Jesuitas no Grão-Pará: suas missões e a colonização* (Coimbra, 1930) is still valuable. Mathias Kieman, *The Indian policy of Portugal in the Amazon region, 1614–1693* (Washington, D.C., 1954) remains indispensable. Artur Cezar Ferreira Reis, *História do Amazonas* (Manaus, 1935) is representative of his many works on the region. João Francisco Lisboa's *Crônica do Brasil Colonial: Apontamentos para a história do Maranhão* (Petropolis, 1976), is a republication of an earlier and still useful work. Two articles by Colin MacLachlan, 'The Indian labor structure in the Portuguese Amazon', in Alden, *Colonial Roots*, 199–230, and 'African slave trade and economic development in Amazonia, 1700–1800', in Robert Toplin (ed.), *Slavery and Race Relations in Latin America* (Westport, Conn., 1974), 112–45, are useful. On the economy, Sue Ellen Anderson Gross, 'The economic life of the Estado do Maranhão e Grão-Pará, 1686–1751' (Ph.D. thesis, Tulane University, 1969) provides a survey. Dauril Alden, 'The significance of cacao production in the Amazon region during the late colonial period: an essay in comparative economic history', *Proceedings of the American Philosophical Society*, 120/2 (April 1976), 103–35, is the best study of that topic. On the society of the Amazon region, the most thorough study to date is David Sweet, 'A rich realm of nature destroyed: the middle Amazon valley, 1640–1750' (Ph.D. thesis, University of Wisconsin, 1974).

4. INDIANS ANL THE FRONTIER

Literature on Brazilian Indians is far richer for the sixteenth than for subsequent centuries. On contemporary authors and secondary literature, see Hemming *CHLA* 1, chapter 5, and *CHLA* 1 Bibliographical Essay 5.

On the west and the south in the seventeenth century, the fundamental study, although sometimes confusing, is Afonso de Escragnolle Taunay, *História geral das bandeiras paulistas* (11 vols., São Paulo, 1924–50). The majority of documents about bandeirante–Jesuit conflict are in the seven volumes edited by Jaime Cortesão and Hélio Vianna, *Manuscritos da Coleção De Angelis* (Rio de Janeiro, 1951–70), and in Jaime Cortesão, *Rapôso Tavares e a formação territorial do Brasil* (Rio de Janeiro, 1958) and *Introdução à história das bandeiras* (2 vols., Lisbon, 1964). See also Alfredo Ellis Júnior, *Meio século de bandeirismo* (São Paulo, 1948), José de Alcântara Machado, *Vida e morte do bandeirante* (São Paulo, 1943), and the works of Sérgio Buarque de Holanda. Many key sources have been translated in Richard M. Morse (ed.), *The Bandeirantes: the historical role of the Brazilian pathfinders* (New York, 1965). There is contemporary information on the bandeirantes in Pedro Tacques de Almeida Paes Leme, *Nobiliarchia Paulistana* and *Historia da Capitania de S. Vicente* (1772) and in collections of documents such as: *Actas da Câmara Municipal de S. Paulo* (São Paulo, 1914–), *Inventários e testamentos* (São Paulo, 1920–) and the large but disorganized *Documentos interessantes para a história e costumes de São Paulo* (86 vols., São Paulo, 1894–1961). Aurélio Porto, *História das missões orientais do Uruguai* (Rio de Janeiro, 1943) is important, and the history of the Jesuits' Paraguayan missions is documented in Nicolau del Techo, S.J., *Historia de la Provincia del Paraguay* (Liège, 1673), José Sánchez Labrador, S.J., *El Paraguay católico* [1770] (3 vols., Buenos Aires, 1910–17), and Antonio Ruiz de Montoya, S.J., *Conquista espiritual...en las provincias del Paraguay, Paraná, Uruguay y Tapi* (Madrid, 1639), and, among modern accounts, Pablo Pastells, S.J., *Historia de la Compañía de Jesús en la Provincia del Paraguay* (8 vols., Madrid, 1912–59), Magnus Mörner, *The political and economic activities of the Jesuits in the La Plata region* (Stockholm, 1953), and Guillermo Fúrlong, *Misiones y sus pueblos de guaraníes* (Buenos Aires, 1962).

For Bahia and the north-east in the seventeenth century, Diogo de Campos Moreno, *Livro que da razão do Estado do Brasil* [1612] (Recife, 1955) is useful, as are André João Antonil, *Cultura e opulência do Brasil...*(Lisbon, 1711; modern edns, São Paulo, 1923 and Paris, 1968), and Ambrosio Fernandes Brandão, *Os diálogos das grandezas do Brasil* [*c.* 1618] (Recife, 1962). The Franciscan Martin of Nantes wrote an interesting chronicle of his mission with the Bahia Cariri: *Relation succinte et sincère*... (Quimper, *c.* 1707; Salvador, 1952). There is some good material in Barão de Studart (ed.), *Documentos para a história do Brasil e especialmente a do Ceará* (4 vols., Fortaleza, 1908–21), but by far the most material is in the vast and disorganized *Documentos históricos da Biblioteca Nacional do Rio de Janeiro* (Rio de Janeiro, 1928–). In English, see Charles Boxer, *Salvador de Sá and the struggle for Brazil and Angola, 1602–1686* (London, 1952); and Stuart B. Schwartz, 'Indian labor and New World plantations: European demands and Indian responses in northeastern Brazil', *American Historical Review*, 83/1, February 1978, 43–79.

The impact of the Dutch wars on the Indians of the north-east is reported in the contemporary works of Caspar Barlaeus, *Rerum in Brasilia gestarum historia* (Cleef, 1660; Rio de Janeiro, 1940), Roulox Baro, *Relation du voyage...au pays des Tapuies* [1647], Adriaen van der Drussen, *Report on the conquered captaincies in Brazil* [1639] (Rio de Janeiro, 1947); various letters and reports by Gedeon Morris de Jonge in *RIHGB* 58/1 (1895), and Joannes de Laet, *Novus Orbis* (Leyden, 1633; French trans. *Histoire du Nouveau Monde*, Leyden, 1640) and *Historie ofte Iaerlick Verhael van de Verrichtinghen der Geotroyeerde West-Indische Compagnie* (Leyden, 1644; trans. *ABNRJ*, 30–42 (1908–20)). From the Portuguese side: Diogo Lopes de Santiago, 'Historia da guerra de Pernambuco...' [1655], *RIHGB*, 38–9 (1875–6), Raphael de Jesus, *Castrioto Lusitano* (Lisbon, 1679), and papers in *Documentos holandeses* (Rio de Janeiro, 1945). For modern works on the Dutch in north-east Brazil, see *CHLA* II, Bibliographical Essay 12.

For Maranhõ and the Amazon, the basic contemporary history is Bernardo Pereira de Berredo, *Annaes historicos do Estado do Maranhão* (Lisbon, 1749). The 'Livro grosso do Maranhão', *ABNRJ*, 66–7 (1948) is full of good information. The *Anais* of the Biblioteca Nacional also published early reports by Jacomé Raimundo de Noronha, Simão Estácio da Sylveira and others. For the later seventeenth century, there are João de Sousa Ferreira, 'America abreviada, suas noticias e de seus naturaes, e em particular do Maranhão' [1686], *RIHGB*, 57/1 (1894), and Francisco Teixeira de Moraes, 'Relação histórica e política dos tumultos que sucederam na cidade de S. Luiz do Maranhão' [1692], *RIHGB*, 40/1 (1877).

As usual, missionaries produced the bulk of written material on the

Amazon region. Venâncio Willeke has recorded the activities of the early Franciscans, *Missões Franciscanos no Brasil, 1500–1975* (Petrópolis, 1974). But the Jesuits were the most active, and their mission was inspired by António Vieira, for whom the basic sources are: *Obras escolhidas* (12 vols., Lisbon 1951–4, of which vol. 5 deals with Indians); *Cartas* (3 vols., Coimbra, 1925–8); and *Sermões* (14 vols., Lisbon, 1679–1710, or 3 vols., Pôrto, 1908); André de Barros, *Vida do apostólico Padre António Vieyra* (Lisbon, 1745). Two vivid and important memoirs by missionaries are: João Felipe Bettendorf, 'Chronica da missão dos Padres da Companhia de Jesus no Estado do Maranhão' [1699], *RIHGB*, 72/1 (1901), and João Daniel, 'Thesouro descoberto no maximo rio Amazonas', *RIHGB*, 2–3, 41 (1840–1, 1878). There is also a history of the Jesuits and a *Memorial sobre o Maranhão* by the eighteenth-century Jesuit José de Moraes, in Cândido Mendes de Almeida, *Memórias para a história do extincto Estado do Maranhão* (2 vols., do Brasil, 1: *Historiografia colonial* (São Paulo, 1979) covers the eighteenth century as well. The sources and scholarship in English are contained with annotations in Francis A. Dutra, *A guide to the history of Brazil, 1500–1822* (Santa Barbara, 1980). Rubens Borba de Moraes, *Bibliografia brasileira do período colonial* (São Paulo, 1969) is a catalogue of works by Brazilians published before 1808. A good specialized bibliography is Robert Conrad, *Brazilian slavery: an annotated research bibliography* (Boston, 1977).

Sérgio Buarque de Holanda (ed.), *História geral da civilização brasileira, I A época colonial* (2 vols., São Paulo, 1960) provides a succinct survey of major themes. Pedro Calmon, *História do Brasil* (7 vols., Rio de Janeiro, 1959) has the most detailed colonial sections of the many modern histories. The classic *História geral do Brasil* (6 vols.; 7th edn, São Paulo, 1962) by Francisco Adolfo de Varnhagen, originally published in 1857, is still valuable. Together, C. R. Boxer's *Salvador de Sá and the struggle for Brazil and Angola, 1602–1686* (London, 1952), and his *The Golden Age of Brazil, 1695–1750* (Berkeley and Los Angeles, 1964) provide the best available overview in English of Brazilian history for the period. Frédéric Mauro, *Le Brésil du XVᵉ à la fin du XVIIIᵉ siècle* (Paris, 1977) is a brief survey based on recent scholarship. Dauril Alden (ed.), *Colonial roots of modern Brazil* (Berkeley and Los Angeles, 1973) presents an important collection of papers on colonial themes. A. J. R. Russell-Wood (ed.), *From colony to nation* (Baltimore, 1975), is primarily concerned with the post-1750 period but does have a number of articles pertinent to the earlier era. The *Anais do Congresso Comemorativo do Bicentenário da Transferência da Sede do Governo do Brasil* (4 vols., Rio de Janeiro, 1966), contains many items of interest, as do the various publications of the Luso-Brazilian Colloquium (1st Proceedings or *Actas* published in Nashville, 1953).

Government and economy

The structure of Portuguese government in Brazil is summarized in Eulália Maria Lahmeyer Lobo, *Processo administrativo Ibero-Americano* (Rio de Janeiro, 1962). Dauril Alden, *Royal government in colonial Brazil* (Berkeley and Los Angeles, 1968), contains much useful material. Stuart B. Schwartz, *Sovereignty and society in colonial Brazil* (Berkeley and Los Angeles, 1973), discusses the judicial structure of the colony. A useful collection of royal instructions is Marcos Carneiro de Mendonça, *Raízes* An interesting report on Indian policy at the end of the century is José Arouche de Toledo Rendon, 'Memoria sôbre as aldeas de índios da Provincia de São Paulo' [1798], *RIHGB*, 4 (1842).

Most interest in Indians was in southern Brazil. For the Guaicurú and Paiaguá, who harassed convoys to Cuiabá, see José Sánchez Labrador, *El Paraguay católico*, Manuel Felix de Azara, *Viajes por la America Meridional* [1809] (Madrid, 1923), Francisco Rodrigues do Prado, 'História dos índios Cavalleiros ou da nação Guaycurú' [1795], *RIHGB*, 1 (1839), Martin Dobrizhoffer, *Geschichte der Abiponer...* (3 vols., Vienna, 1783–4; Eng. trans., London, 1822), Ricardo Franco de Almeida Serra, 'Parecer sôbre o aldêamento dos índios uaicurús e guanás...' [1803], *RIHGB*, 7 and 13 (1845 and 50) and 'Discripção geographica da Provincia de Matto Grosso' [1797], *RIHGB*, 6 (1844). For Bororo and other tribes near Cuiabá, Antonio Pires de Campos, 'Breve noticia...do gentio barbaro que ha na derrota...do Cuyabá' [1727], *RIHGB*, 25 (1862). A general history of that region is Joseph Barbosa de Sá, 'Relação das povoações do Cuyabá e Matto Grosso...' [1775], *ABNRJ*, 23 (1904).

For the War of the Sete Povos, the Treaty of Madrid and the expulsion of the Jesuits, Jacintho Rodrigues da Cunha, 'Diario da expedição de Gomes Freire de Andrade às missões do Uruguai' [1756], *RIHGB*, 16 (1853), Thomaz da Costa Corrêa Rebello e Silva, 'Memoria sobre a Provincia de Missões', *RIHGB*, 2 (1840), Jaime Cortesão, *Do Tratado de Madri à conquista dos Sete Povos (1750–1802)* (Rio de Janeiro,

1969) and *Alexandre de Gusmão e o Tratado de Madri* (8 vols., Rio de Janeiro, 1950–9), and works on the Jesuits already cited. Among modern works, Guillermo Kratz, *El tratado hispano-portugués de Límites de 1750 y sus consecuencias* (Rome, 1954), deserves mention. A comprehensive treatment of the Indians and the expansion of the frontiers up to the expulsion of the Jesuits is John Hemming, *Red gold. The conquest of the Brazilian Indians* (London, 1978).

5. THE GOLD CYCLE, c. 1690–1750

Studies on the 'golden age' of Brazil have focused on only one area – Minas Gerais, which was the major gold-producing region of the colonial period. There has been an erroneous assumption that what was true for Minas Gerais was equally applicable to auriferous zones of Bahia, São Paulo, Goiás, Mato Grosso, Pernambuco and Espírito Santo. Readers should be cautious of generalizations based on the Mineiro experience and recognize that differences in topography, chronology, demography, racial composition, political importance, degree of effective crown administration and relative importance within the overall economic context resulted in wide variations between the gold-bearing regions of Brazil. The diamond industry lies beyond the scope of this chapter, but an excellent introduction is provided by Augusto de Lima Júnior, *História dos diamantes nas Minas Gerais* (Lisbon and Rio de Janeiro, 1945) and Joaquim Felício dos Santos, *Memórias do Distrito Diamantino da Comarca do Serro do Frio* (3rd edn, Rio de Janeiro, 1956).

Many contemporary or near-contemporary accounts of gold strikes, exploitation, consolidation and decline are available. André João Antonil (pseudonym of Antonio Giovanni Andreoni, S.J.) is valuable for the early years in Minas Gerais, although it is doubtful if he ever visited the region. Available in a modern edition (edited by Andrée Mansuy, Paris, 1968), his *Cultura e opulência do Brasil por suas drogas e minas* (Lisbon, 1711), especially part 3, contains information not available elsewhere. It remains unsurpassed for bringing to the reader the intensity and raw emotions of the initial gold rush. Dr Caetano Costa Matoso's notes form the basis for the *Relatos sertanistas. Colectânea*, with introduction and notes by Afonso de Escragnolle Taunay (São Paulo, 1953). A commentary on the medical state of the captaincy is Luís Gomes Ferreira's *Erário mineral dividido em doze tratados* (Lisbon, 1735), based on his residence for two decades in Minas Gerais. Charles Boxer has made some of the few studies of the author and his medical treatise:

see *The Indiana University Bookman*, 10 (November 1969), 49–70; 11 (November 1973), 89–92. The moral tract *Compendio narrativo do peregrino da America* (Lisbon, 1728) of Nuno Marques Pereira, whose literary Maecenas was none other than the *sertanista* Manuel Nunes Viana, contains many insights. See also *Notícias das minas de São Paulo e dos sertões da mesma capitania, 1597–1772* (3rd edn, São Paulo, 1954) by the Paulista Pedro Taques de Almeida Paes Leme (1714–77). The intensely spiritual life of the captaincy is revealed in the *Triunfo Eucharistico exemplar da Christandade Lusitana*...by Simão Ferreira Machado (Lisbon, 1734). There are numerous memoranda, of which the most penetrating was penned by José João Teixeira Coelho, an eleven-year resident as crown judge: 'Instrucção para o governo da Capitania de Minas Gerais (1780)', first published in *RIHGB*, 15/3 (1852), 257–463, reprinted in *Revista do Arquivo Público Mineiro* [*RAPM*], 8/1–2 (January–June 1903), 399–581, and translated in part by E. Bradford Burns (ed.), *A documentary history of Brazil* (New York, 1966), 155–63. Other commentaries, many of them published in *RAPM* (Ouro Prêto, 1896– ; Belo Horizonte, 1903–), focus on the decline of the economy of Minas Gerais. The best overview is undoubtedly the *Pluto Brasiliensis* of the German mining engineer Baron Wilhelm Ludwig von Eschwege (Berlin, 1833), portions of which have been published in *RAPM* and in the *História e Memória da Academia Real das Ciencias de Lisboa*, 4/1 (1815), 219–29, as 'De uma memória sobre a decadencia das minas de ouro de Capitania de Minas Gerais e sobre outros objetos montanísticos'. Technical aspects of processing gold and silver were the subject of a monograph by António da Silva, *Directorio practico da prata e ouro, em que se mostram as condiçõens, com que se devem lavrar estes dous nobilissimos metaes; para que se evitem nas obras os enganos, e nos artifices os erros* (Lisbon, 1720). For Minas Gerais such accounts may be complemented by those of nineteenth-century travellers; e.g. John Mawe, *Travels in the interior of Brazil, particularly in the gold and diamond districts* (London, 1812), Johann Baptist von Spix and Carl Friedrich von Martius, *Reise in Brasilien in den Jahren 1817 bis 1820* (3 vols., Munich, 1823–31), of which a partial English translation by H. E. Lloyd is available (2 vols., London, 1824).

Other mining captaincies have been less favoured than was Minas Gerais by contemporary chroniclers and commentators, although a great deal can be found, for example, in the pages of *RIHGB* and *Revista do Instituto Histórico e Geográfico de São Paulo* [*RIHGSP*] in the nineteenth and early twentieth centuries.

Contemporary scholarship has been fascinated by the Brazilian pathfinders, the *bandeirantes*, and the frontier. Myriam Ellis, 'As bandeiras na expansão geográfica do Brasil', in *História geral da civilisação brasileira, I A época colonial* (2 vols., São Paulo, 1960), and her essay in *Revista de História de São Paulo* [*RHSP*], 36 (1958), 429–67, survey the field. For fuller discussion of the literature, see *CHLA* II, Bibliographical Essay 13. On the search for gold, more particularly in the period before the so-called 'golden age', see: Myriam Ellis Austregésilo, 'Pesquisas sobre a existência do ouro e da prata no planalto paulista nos séculos XVI e XVII', *RHSP*, 1 (1950), 51–72; Lucy de Abreu Maffei and Arlinda Rocha Nogueira, 'O ouro na capitania de São Vicente nos séculos XVI e XVII', *Anais do Museu Paulista* (1966); Joaquim José Gomes da Silva, 'História das mais importantes minas de ouro do Estado do Espírito Santo', *RIHGB*, 55/2 (1893), 35–58; Madalena da Câmara Fialho, 'Muragem do oiro nas capitanias do norte do Brasil', *Congresso do mundo português*, 10/2, 2a secção, 1a pte (Lisbon, 1940), 85–94.

Manoel da Silveira Cardozo describes the roller-coaster nature of the crown's hopes in 'Dom Rodrigo de Castel-Blanco and the Brazilian El Dorado, 1673–1682', *The Americas*, 7/2 (October 1944), 131–59. Well-publicized but abortive attempts to discover significant mineral deposits brought acute embarrassment to both the king and to Afonso Furtado de Castro do Rio de Mendonça during his governorship of Brazil (1671–5); a manuscript by a mysterious Spaniard Juan Lopes Sierra, acquired by the Bell Library of the University of Minnesota, has been translated into English by Ruth E. Jones and edited with notes by Stuart B. Schwartz under the title *A governor and his image in baroque Brazil* (Minneapolis, 1979). Cardozo has surveyed the Minas Gerais phase of the initial gold rush in his classic article 'The Brazilian gold rush', *The Americas*, 3/2 (October 1946), 137–60. Routes from São Vicente and Rio de Janeiro are described by Richard P. Momsen, Jr., *Routes Over the Serra do Mar* (Rio de Janeiro, 1964). Several authors have discussed the relationship between Brazilian gold strikes and moves to the west in the first half of the eighteenth century. The most succinct account in English is David M. Davidson, 'How the Brazilian West was won: freelance and state on the Mato Grosso frontier, 1737–1752', in D. Alden (ed.), *Colonial roots of modern Brazil* (Berkeley and Los Angeles, 1973), 61–106. In Portuguese there is Capistrano de Abreu, *Caminhos antigos e povoamento do Brasil* (4th edn, Rio de Janeiro, 1975); Sérgio Buarque de Holanda, *Monções* (Rio de Janeiro, 1945) and *Caminhos e fronteiras* (Rio de Janeiro, 1957); Taunay, *Relatos monçoeiros* (São Paulo, 1953), and his 'Demonstração dos diversos caminhos de que os moradores de S. Paulo se servem para os rios de Cuiabá e Província de Cochiponé', *Anais do Museu Paulista*, 1 (1922), 459–79. Francisco Tavares de Brito's account of travel from Rio de Janeiro to Minas Gerais (Seville, 1732) was republished in *RIHGB*, 230 (January–March 1956), 428–41. Exploration, settlement and consolidation in Goiás occupied Taunay in *Os primeiros anos de Goyaz, 1722–1748* (São Paulo, 1950), *separata* from vol. 11 of his *História geral* (*q.v.*).

Crown government and the fiscal administration of the mining areas has received remarkably little attention from scholars, and what few studies there are have focused on Minas Gerais. The first governor of Minas Gerais and São Paulo was chronicled by Aureliano Leite in his *António de Albuquerque Coelho de Carvalho, capitão-general de São Paulo e Minas do Ouro no Brasil* (Lisbon, 1944). Francisco de Assis Carvalho Franco's *História das minas de São Paulo. Administradores gerais e provedores, séculos XVI e XVII* (São Paulo, 1964) holds useful information: the most penetrating study of a local crown administrator is Marcos Carneiro de Mendonça, *O Intendente Câmara. Manuel Ferreira da Câmara Bethancourt e Sá, Intendente geral das minas e diamantes, 1764–1835* (São Paulo, 1958). Early minutes of the town council of Vila Rica have been published in the *Annaes da Biblioteca Nacional*, 49 (1927; published in 1936), 199–391, and in *RAPM*, 25/2 (1937), 3–166. The struggle between officialdom and *poderosos do sertão* is described by A. J. R. Russell-Wood, 'Manuel Nunes Viana: paragon or parasite of empire?', *The Americas*, 37/4 (April 1981), 479–98. Augusto de Lima Júnior focused on the establishment of municipalities in Minas Gerais in several of his many works: *A Capitania das Minas Gerais (Origens e formação)* (3rd edn, Belo Horizonte, 1965); *As primeiras vilas do Ouro* (Belo Horizonte, 1962), *Vila Rica do Ouro Prêto. Síntese histórica e descritiva* (Belo Horizonte, 1957). See also Yves Leloup, *Les villes de Minas Gerais* (Paris, 1970) and A. J. R. Russell-Wood, 'Local government in Portuguese America: a study in cultural divergence', *Comparative Studies in Society and History*, 16/2 (March 1974), 187–231. Francisco Iglesias has placed the events in Minas Gerais in broader context in 'Minas e a imposição do estado no Brasil', *RHSP*, 50/100 (October–December 1974), 257–73. If the administration of mining areas has not received the attention it deserves, the same cannot be said of the legal aspects of mining, especially the collection of the royal fifths: as to the former, indispensable are

Francisco Ignácio Ferreira, *Repertorio juridico do Mineiro. Consolidação alphabetica e chronologica de todas as disposições sobre Minas comprehendendo a legislação antiga e moderna de Portugal e do Brasil* (Rio de Janeiro, 1884) and João Pandiá Calógeras, *As Minas do Brasil e sua legislação* (3 vols., Rio de Janeiro, 1904–5). Information on the fifths is contained in C. R. Boxer, *The Golden Age of Brazil, 1695–1750* (Berkeley and Los Angeles, 1969); Kenneth Maxwell, *Conflicts and conspiracies: Brazil and Portugal, 1750–1808* (Cambridge, 1973); and Virgílio Noya Pinto, *O ouro brasileiro e o comércio anglo-português* (São Paulo, 1979). Manoel de Silveira Cardozo's early studies are still the best available: 'Alguns subsídios para a história da cobrança do quinto na capitania de Minas Gerais até 1735' (Lisbon, 1938; reprint from *1 Congresso da história da expansão portuguesa no mundo*, 3a secção (Lisbon, 1937)); 'The collection of the fifths in Brazil, 1695–1709', *HAHR*, 20/3 (August 1940), 359–79; 'Os quintos do ouro em Minas. Gerais (1721–1732)', *1 Congresso do mundo português*, 10/2, 2a secção, 1a pte (Lisbon, 1940), 117–28. Robert White focused on the capitation tax of 1735 in 'Fiscal policy and royal sovereignty in Minas Gerais', *The Americas*, 34/2 (October 1977), 207–29. Cardozo returned to fiscal aspects in his later article 'Tithes in colonial Minas Gerais', *Catholic Historical Review*, 38/2 (July 1952), 175–82.

For the social history of the mining areas the articles of Donald Ramos are of great interest: 'Marriage and the family in colonial Vila Rica', *HAHR*, 55/2 (May 1975), 200–25; 'Vila Rica: profile of a colonial Brazilian urban centre', *The Americas* 35/4 (April 1979), 495–526; 'City and country: the family in Minas Gerais, 1804–1838', *Journal of Family History*, 3/4 (winter 1975), 361–75. On the slave trade, see *CHLA* I, Bibliographical Essay 12. A. J. R. Russell-Wood, *The black man in slavery and freedom in colonial Brazil* (London, 1982), 104–27, examines the impact of gold mining on the slave trade, and the institution of slavery in the mining regions. Studies of persons of African descent have focused on two very different areas, namely religious brotherhoods and runaways. The former have been studied by Fritz Teixeira de Salles, *Associações religiosas no ciclo do ouro* (Belo Horizonte, 1963), Julita Scarano, *Devoção e escravidão: A irmandade de Nossa Senhora do Rosário dos prêtos no Distrito Diamantino no século XVIII* (São Paulo, 1976), and A. J. R. Russell-Wood, 'Black and mulatto brotherhoods in colonial Brazil: a study in collective behavior', *HAHR*, 54/4 (November 1974), 567–602. Runaways are discussed in Waldemar de Almeida Barbosa, *Negros e quilombos em Minas Gerais* (Belo

Horizonte, 1972). An interesting dialogue between a sometime miner and a lawyer on the evils of slavery has been translated by C. R. Boxer under the title 'Negro slavery in Brazil. A Portuguese pamphlet (1764)', *Race*, 5/3 (January 1964), 38–47. A general survey is Aires da Mata Machado Filho, *O Negro e o garimpo em Minas Gerais* (2nd edn, Rio de Janeiro, 1964).

There are no satisfactory general surveys in English of life in mining communities. Chapters in Boxer's *The Golden Age* on the gold rush to Minas Gerais, the struggle between Paulistas and Emboabas and life in eighteenth-century Vila Rica have yet to be bettered. General surveys include: João Camillo de Oliveira Tôrres, *História de Minas Gerais* (5 vols., Belo Horizonte, 1962); Francisco Adolpho de Varnhagen, *História geral do Brasil* (5 vols., 9th edn, São Paulo, 1975), especially vol. 4; Miran de Barros Latif, *As Minas Gerais* (2nd edn, Rio de Janeiro, 1960). Afonso de Escragnole Taunay's monograph *Sôb el Rey Nosso Senhor. Aspectos da vida setecentista brasileira, sobretudo em São Paulo* (São Paulo, 1923; an earlier version appeared in the *Anais do Museu Paulista*, 1 (1922)) can still be read with profit. Mário Leite, *Paulistas e mineiros. Plantados de cidades* (São Paulo, 1961) is useful. Much can be gleaned on events in central Minas Gerais from an excellent account of the Diamond District: Aires da Mata Machado Filho, *Arraial do Tijuco. Cidade Diamantina* (2nd edn, São Paulo, 1957).

Much ink has been expended on two incidents in the history of Minas Gerais in the first half of the eighteenth century: one so-called 'war' and one revolt. The first was the War of the Emboabas, for which there is adequate material for thought in Manoel da Silveira Cardozo's 'The *Guerra dos Emboabas*: civil war in Minas Gerais, 1708–1709', *HAHR*, 22/3 (August 1942), 470–92, and the scholarly chapter in Boxer's *The Golden Age* together with the references there cited. The second was the 1720 revolt in Vila Rica, also treated by Boxer, and in more detail by P. Xavier da Veiga, *A revolta de 1720 em Vila Rica, discurso histórico-político* (Ouro Prêto, 1898).

If the social history of the mining areas has yet to receive its due from historians, no such neglect has been present in treating the spiritual, intellectual, musical, architectural and artistic vitality of Minas Gerais in the eighteenth century. The *Triunfo Eucharístico* (Lisbon, 1734) and the *Aúreo Trono Episcopal* (Lisbon, 1749) have been reproduced, with introduction and notes by Affonso Avila, under the title *Resíduos seiscentistas em Minas. Textos do século do ouro e as projeções do mundo barroco*

(2 vols., 2nd edn, Belo Horizonte, 1967). Diogo de Vasconcelos, *História do bispado de Mariana* (Belo Horizonte, 1935) and Cônego Raimundo Trindade's *Arquidiocese de Marianna. Subsídios para a sua história* (2 vols., 2nd edn, Belo Horizonte, 1953 and 1955) provide an introduction. Intellectual life is addressed in José Ferreira Carrato, *Igreja, iluminismo, e escolas mineiras coloniais (Notas sobre a cultura da decadência mineira setecentista)* (São Paulo, 1968) and his earlier *As Minas Gerais e os primórdios do Caraça* (São Paulo, 1963); Eduardo Frieiro, *O diabo na livraria do cônego* (Belo Horizonte, 1957), and E. Bradford Burns, 'The Enlightenment in two colonial Brazilian libraries', *The Journal of the History of Ideas*, 25/3 (July–September 1964), 430–8. Resurrection of a long-forgotten musical tradition in eighteenth-century Minas Gerais is attributable to the unflagging efforts of Francisco Curt Lange: see *CHLA* II, Bibliographical Essay 19. The greatest scholarly interest has focused on baroque art and architecture in Minas Gerais: see *CHLA* II, Bibliographical Essay 18.

Turning from the social and cultural history of the mining areas to the economic aspect, the reader is better supplied. The mining process is well described by Antonil (*Cultura e opulência*, pt 3, ch. 14 and elsewhere); Calógeras, *As minas*, I, 111–32; and Eschwege. To these contemporary accounts can be added Mawe, *Travels*, and Paul Ferrand, *L'or à Minas Gerais (Brésil)* (2 vols., Belo Horizonte, 1913), especially I, 21–67. Labour arrangements occupied Lucinda Coutinho de Mello Coelho, 'Mão-de-obra escrava na mineração e tráfico negreiro no Rio de Janeiro', *Anais do VI simpósio nacional dos professores de história*, I (São Paulo, 1973), 449–89. Productivity of slaves in Goiás was studied by Luís Palacin, 'Trabalho escravo: produção e produtividade nas minas de Goiás', *Anais do VI simpósio*, I, 433–48. Estimates as to actual production vary enormously: see Eschwege; Calógeras; Roberto C. Simonsen, *História económica do Brasil, 1500–1820* (4th edn, São Paulo, 1962); Visconde de Carnaxide, *Brasil na administração pombalina* (São Paulo, 1940); Adolph G. Soetbeer, *Edelmetall-Produktion and Werthverhältnis zwischen Gold und Silber seit der Entdeckung Amerikas bis zur Gegenwart* (Gotha, 1819). Revenue yields for Minas Gerais are contained in appendices to Boxer, *The Golden Age* and Maxwell, *Conflicts and conspiracies*. The most recent study of the subject is Noya Pinto, *O ouro brasileiro*, 39–117. Numismatists may wish to consult A. C. Teixeira de Aragão, *Descripção geral e histórica das moedas cunhadas em nome dos reis, regentes e governadores de Portugal* (3 vols., Lisbon, 1874–80); K. Prober,

Catálogo das moedas brasileiras (São Paulo, 1966); Vitorino de Magalhães Godinho, *Prix et monnaies au Portugal, 1750–1850* (Paris, 1955); Alvaro de Salles Oliveira, *Moedas do Brasil. I. Moedas e barras de ouro. Elementos para o seu estudo* (São Paulo, 1944); Severino Sombra, *História monetária do Brasil colonial. Repertório com introdução, notas e carta monetária* (enlarged edn, Rio de Janeiro, 1938); Alvaro da Veiga Coimbra. *Noções de numismática brasileira – Brasil colônia* and *Noções de numismática – Brasil independente*, reprints 18 and 21 in the series Coleção da Revista de História (São Paulo).

The economies and commerce of the mining areas have been the subjects of fewer studies. Problems of supply lines and the domestic economy were well described by Antonil and, more recently, by the well-documented studies of Myriam Ellis, *Contribuição ao estudo do abastecimento das áreas mineradoras do Brasil no século XVIII* (Rio de Janeiro, 1961) and Mafalda P. Zemella, *O abastecimento da capitania das Minas Gerais no século XVIII* (São Paulo, 1951). The cattle industry is mentioned by Rollie E. Poppino, 'Cattle industry in colonial Brazil', *Mid-America*, 31/4 (October 1949), 219–47. The importance of muleteers is described by Basílio de Magalhães, 'The pack trains of Minas-Gerais', *Travel in Brazil*, 2/4 (1942), 1–7, 33. The most detailed study of any single commercial activity is by Miguel Costa Filho, *A cana-de-açúcar em Minas Gerais* (Rio de Janeiro, 1963).

General studies of the Brazilian economy include sections on mining: the reader is referred to the still useful *Obras económicas* of J. J. da Cunha de Azeredo Coutinho, available in a modern edition (São Paulo, 1966) edited by Sérgio Buarque de Holanda; Roberto Simonsen, *História económica*; Caio Prado Jr., *História económica do Brasil* (8th edn, São Paulo, 1963); P. Pereira dos Reis, *O colonialismo português e a conjuração mineira* (São Paulo, 1964). There is extensive literature on the Atlantic trade in gold and its impact on Portugal and on Anglo-Portuguese relations; see *CHLA* 1, Bibliographical Essays 12 and 13.

6. IMPERIAL RE-ORGANIZATION, 1750–1808

For a general approach to the Portuguese empire during the period 1750–1808, there are two fundamental works by C. R. Boxer, *The Portuguese seaborne empire, 1415–1815* (London, 1969), chapters VI and VII, and *The Golden Age of Brazil 1695–1750. Growing pains of a colonial society* (Berkeley, 1962), the last chapter. Useful textbooks include A. H. Oliveira Marques, *História de Portugal desde os tempos mais remotos até ao governo do Sr. Marcelo Caetano*, 2 vols. (Lisbon, 1972), I, chapters VIII and IX, and *História geral da civilização Brasileira*, ed. Sérgio Buarque de Holanda (São Paulo, 1960–), I: *A época colonial* (2 vols., 1960), and II: *O Brasil monárquico*, I, *O processo de emancipação* (1962). There are also certain studies of individual reigns which, despite the limitations of their time and genre, deserve mention: Simão José da Luz Soriano, *História do reinado de El-Rei D. José e da administrado do Marquês de Pombal*, 2 vols. (Lisbon, 1867); João Lúcio d'Azevedo, *O Marquês de Pombal e sua época* (2nd edn, Lisbon, 1922), an early critical study; Alfredo Duarte Rodrigues, *O Marquês de Pombal e os seus biógrafos* (Lisbon, 1947), which summarizes the early literature; Caetano Beirão, *Dona Maria I (1777–1792)* (4th edn, Lisbon, 1944), still unfortunately the best work on the post-Pombal years; and Angelo Pereira, *D. João VI Príncipe e Rei*, 4 vols. (Lisbon, 1953–7), I: *A retirada da família real para o Brasil (1807)*. More recently, there are several excellent works based on extremely important archival research. Dauril Alden, *Royal government in colonial Brazil, with special reference to the administration of the Marquis of Lavradio, viceroy, 1769–1779* (Berkeley, 1968) is particularly concerned with the structure of royal power in Brazil in the Pombal era and the activities of an enlightened administrator, and, more generally, with the political, military and economic history of the captaincies of the South. Kenneth R. Maxwell, *Conflicts and conspiracies: Brazil and Portugal 1750–1808* (Cambridge, 1973), makes a new contribution to the study of the tensions between the metropolis and the colony and of the first moves towards Brazilian independence, notably in 1789. Fernando A. Novais, *Portugal e Brasil na crise do antigo sistema colonial (1777–1808)* (São Paulo, 1979), gives us an important survey of mercantilist colonialism and of the economic policies of the Portuguese government at the end of the eighteenth and beginning of the nineteenth century. Like Boxer's *Golden Age* for the preceding period, these last three penetrating analyses are a landmark in the historiography of Brazil.

More specifically, on the territorial redefinition of Brazil, J. Cortesão, *Alexandre de Gusmão e o Tratado de Madrid (1750)*, 10 vols. (Rio de Janeiro, 1952–63), gives an extremely full documentation for the Treaty of Madrid, its antecedents and some of its consequences, together with a commentary which is often polemical. Alden, *Royal government*, already cited, pp. 59–275, makes an extremely lucid and detached analysis of the same subject, especially concerned with all the negotiations and military operations from the Treaty of Madrid to the Treaty of San Ildefonso (1778) and after. On the occupation, defence and colonization of the Amazon region and the government's Indian policy, the fundamental documents were published in Marcos Carneiro de Mendonça, *A Amazônia na era pombalina (correspondência inédita do Governador e Capitão General do Estado do Grão Pará e Maranhão, Francisco Xavier de Mendonça Furtado, 1751–1759*, 3 vols. (Rio de Janeiro, 1963); see also João Lúcio de Azevedo, *Os Jesuítas no Grão Pará* (Lisbon, 1901), and 'Política de Pombal relativa ao Brasil', in *Novas Epanáforas. Estudos de história e literatura* (Lisbon, 1932), 7–62; more recently, Manuel Nunes Dias, 'Política pombalina na colonização da Amazonia 1755–1777', *Studia*, 23 (1968), 7–32, together with his exhaustive study of one of the instruments of Pombal's policy, the commercial company of Grão Pará e Maranhão (see below). Among the works of Arthur Cezar Ferreira Reis, see especially *A política de Portugal no valle amazônico* (Belém, 1940).

On the reorganization of political institutions, a good general study is lacking. This is a major lacuna in Portuguese historiography and there is no alternative to recourse to the sources. The best general essay is the chapter on administration, justice and the army in Caio Prado Júnior, *Formação do Brasil contemporâneo: Colônia* (8th edn, São Paulo, 1965), translated by Suzette Macedo, as *The colonial background of modern Brazil* (Berkeley, 1967). See also the works by Alden and Maxwell cited above. Despite its many omissions so far as the description and analysis of administrative structures are concerned, the *Dicionário de História de Portugal* (ed. Joel Serrão), 4 vols. (Lisbon, 1961–71) has its uses. There are also the articles of Marcelo Caetano, 'As Reformas pombalinas e post-pombalinas respeitantes ao Ultramar. O novo espírito em que são concebidas', *História da expansão Portuguesa no mundo*, 3 vols. (Lisbon, 1940), III, 251–60, and José Gonçalo de Santa Ritta, 'Organização da administração ultramarina no século XVIII', *Congresso do mundo Português* (Lisbon, 1940), VIII, 123–53.

The fundamental importance of the texts of laws and decrees, of which much use has been made in this chapter, should be underlined. In the absence of a complete edition, it is necessary to turn to compilations such as: *Collecção das Leys, Decretos e Alvarás que comprehende o feliz Reinado del Rey Fidelissimo D. José I Nosso Senhor, desde o anno de 1750 até o de 1777*, 4 vols. (Lisbon, 1777), and António Delgado da Silva, *Collecção da Legislação Portugueza desde a ultima compilação das Ordenações. Legislação de 1756 a 1820*, 6 vols. (Lisbon, 1830–5).

On the reorganization of the economy, besides consulting manuscript sources it is indispensable to go to contemporary accounts, among which, see especially the following: *Memorias Economicas da Academia Real das Sciencias de Lisboa para o adiantamento da Agricultura, das Artes e da Industria em Portugal e suas Conquistas*, 5 vols. (Lisbon, 1789–1815), analysed by Abílio Carlos d'Ascensão Diniz Silva, 'La Formulation d'une politique de développement économique au Portugal à la fin du XVIIIe siècle' (Mémoire for the Diploma in Sciences Économiques, University of Paris 1, 1969); *Obras Econômicas de J. J. da Cunha de Azeredo Coutinho* (1794–1804), edited by Sérgio Buarque de Holanda (São Paulo, 1966); Jacome Ratton, *Recordaçoens de...sobre occurrencias do seu tempo em Portugal... de Maio 1744 a Setembro de 1810* (London, 1813); Dom Rodrigo de Souza Coutinho, speeches, memoranda, reports and letters, published by the Marquis of Funchal, *O Conde de Linhares, Dom Rodrigo Domingos Antonio de Souza Coutinho* (Lisbon, 1908), and by Marcos Carneiro de Mendonça, *O Intendente Câmara, Manoel Ferreira da Câmara Bethencourt e Sá, Intendente Geral das Minas e dos Diamantes, 1764–1835* (Rio de Janeiro, 1933); Adrien Balbi, *Essai statistique sur le Royaume de Portugal et d'Algarve*, 2 vols. (Paris, 1822); José Accursio das Neves, *Noções historicas, economicas e administrativas sobre a produção e manufactura das sedas em Portugal...*(Lisbon, 1827), and *Variedades sobre objectos relativos às artes, commercio e manufacturas*, 2 vols. (Lisbon, 1814–17).

Among the studies of economic history dating from the first half of the twentieth century, two classics should not be forgotten: João Lúcio de Azevedo, *Epocas de Portugal económico* (2nd edn, Lisbon, 1973), and Roberto C. Simonsen, *História econômica do Brasil 1500–1820* (6th edn, São Paulo, 1969).

Among recent works dealing with the whole period, two well-documented studies have made a fundamental contribution: the pioneering work of quantitative history, Vitorino Magalhães Godinho, *Prix et monnaies au Portugal 1750–1850* (Paris, 1955), and Kenneth R. Maxwell, *Conflicts and conspiracies* (cited above).

Apart from these, it is necessary to have recourse to books dealing with specific subjects and specific periods, of which the Pombal era is by far the most thoroughly studied, notably by Jorge Borges de Macedo, *A situacão económica no tempo de Pombal.* (1951; 2nd edn, Lisbon, 1982), a suggestive and well-documented work, and by the Viscount of Carnaxide, *O Brasil na administração pombalina (Economia e política externa)* (São Paulo, 1940), a controversial study. See also J. Borges de Macedo, 'Portugal e a economia "pombalina". Temas e hipoteses',

Revista de História (São Paulo), 19 (1954), 81–99. On the fleet system, see V. Magalhães Godinho, 'Portugal, as frotas do açúcar e as frotas do ouro 1670–1770', *Ensaios*, II (Lisbon, 1968), 293–315 (original in French in *AESC* (1950), 184–97). See also Eulália Maria Lahmeyer Lobo, 'As frotas do Brasil', *JGSWGL*, 4 (1967), 465–88; Albert-Alain Bourdon, 'Le Marquis de Pombal et la réorganisation des flottes de commerce entre le Portugal et le Brésil (1753–1766)', Universidade de Lisboa, *Revista da Faculdade de Letras*, 3rd ser., 6 (1962), 182–97; and especially Virgílio Noya Pinto, *O ouro brasileiro e o comércio anglo-português (Uma contribução aos estudos de economia atlântica no século XVIII)* (São Paulo, 1979). For the post-Pombal period, there is now Fernando A. Novais, *Portugal e Brasil na crise do antigo sistema colonial* (cited above), as well as José Jobson de A. Arruda, *O Brasil no comércio colonial* (São Paulo, 1980), which is a detailed analysis of the trade balances of the last years of the period.

On commercial companies and monopolies, besides the exhaustive studies by Manuel Nunes Dias, *Fomento e mercantilismo. A Companhia Geral de Comércio do Grão Pará e Maranhão (1755–1778)* (São Paulo, 1971), and José Ribeiro Júnior, *Colonização e monopólio no Nordeste Brasileiro. A Companhia Geral de Pernambuco e Paraíba (1759–1780)* (São Paulo, 1976), see the article by Jorge Borges de Macedo, 'Companhias commerciais', in *Dicionário de História de Portugal*, I, 637–44, which provides both a synthesis and a good bibliography, and two penetrating studies by Myriam Ellis: *O monopólio do sal nos Estados do Brasil (1631–1801)* (Universidade de São Paulo, 1955) and *A Baleia no Brasil colonial* (São Paulo, 1969). For the slave trade, see the works cited in *CHLA* I, bibliographical essay 12, and, more particularly for the late eighteenth century, Antonio Carreira, *As companhias pombalinas de Grão-Pará e Maranhão e Pernambuco e Paraíba* (2nd edn, Lisbon, 1983).

On industrial policy, Jorge Borges de Macedo, *Problemas de história da indústria portuguesa no século XVIII* (1963; 2nd edn, Lisbon, 1982), and the analysis of Fernando A. Novais, 'A Proibição das manufacturas no Brasil e a política econômica portuguesa do fim do século XVIII', *Revista de História* (São Paulo), XXXIII, 67 (1966), 145–66. On the policy of developing traditional and new colonial products, see *CHLA* II, bibliographical essay 15.

Portugal's international trade, notably with England, has been the object of several good analyses, such as H. E. S. Fisher, *The Portugal trade. A study of Anglo-Portuguese commerce, 1700–1770* (London, 1971), whose statistics may be supplemented, for the years 1770–1808, with those in E. B. Schumpeter, *English overseas trade statistics (1697–1808)* (Oxford, 1962), 17–18; see also Sandro Sideri, *Trade and power. Informal colonialism in Anglo-Portuguese relations* (Rotterdam, 1970), and the very recent study of Virgílio Noya Pinto, *O ouro brasileiro e o comércio anglo-português* (cited above). For reference, José de Almada, *A aliança inglesa. Subsídios para o seu estudo*, 2 vols. (Lisbon, 1946). The short- and long-term consequences of the famous Methuen Treaty have been the subject of violent controversy. See the solid study by A. D. Francis, *The Methuens and Portugal 1691–1708* (Cambridge, 1966), and the survey by Jorge Borges de Macedo, 'Methuen', in *Dicionário de história de Portugal*, III, 49–55. On Franco-Portuguese trade, which has been studied less intensively, Vitorino Magalhães Godinho, *Prix et monnaies* (cited above), 321–71, and Frédéric Mauro, 'L'Empire portugais et le commerce franco-portugais au milieu du XVIIIe siècle', in his *Études économiques sur l'expansion portugaise* (Paris, 1970), 81–95. On the very end of the period, Jorge Borges de Macedo, *O bloqueio continental. Economia e guerra peninsular* (Lisbon, 1962).

As regards quantitative history, besides the work of Magalhães Godinho, Novais and Arruda, there are three conference papers published in *L'Histoire quantitative du Brésil de 1800 à 1930* (Colloques Internationaux du C.N.R.S., Paris, 11–15 Octobre 1971) (Paris, 1973): Fernando A. Novais, 'Notas para o estudo do Brasil no comércio internacional do fim do século XVIII e início do século XIX (1796–1808)', 59–75, Harold B. Johnson, Jr, 'Money and prices in Rio de Janeiro (1760–1820)', 39–57, and Kátia M. de Queirós Mattoso, 'Os preços na Bahia de 1750 a 1930', 167–82. Queiriós Mattoso has also written 'Conjoncture et société au Brésil à la fin du XVIIIe siècle', *Cahiers des Amériques Latines*, 5 (1970), 33–53, while Johnson is also the author of 'A preliminary enquiry into money, prices and wages 1763–1823', in *The colonial roots of modern Brazil*, edited by Dauril Alden (Berkeley, 1972).

On Pombal the majority of the works already mentioned have something to say. See also Francisco José Calazans Falcon, *A Epoca pombalina (Política econômica e Monarquia ilustrada)* (São Paulo, 1982). A number of valuable publications appeared on the occasion of the two hundredth anniversary of Pombal's death in 1982, notably: *O Marquês de Pombal e o seu tempo*, edited by the Instituto de História e Teoria das Ideias of the Faculdade de Letras de Coimbra (*Revista de*

História das Ideias, IV, 1982); *Como interpretar Pombal? No bicentenário da sua morte*, edited by *Brotéria* (Lisbon, 1983), and Joaquim Veríssimo Serrão, *O Marquês de Pombal: o homem, o diplomata e o estadista* (Lisbon, 1982). Martinho de Mello e Castro has not been the subject of any monograph, but Dom Rodrigo de Souza Coutinho is currently being studied by Andrée Mansuy-Diniz Silva.

7. LATE COLONIAL BRAZIL, 1750–1808

For reference material on the colonial period as a whole, see Bibliographical Essay 12. To the bibliographies cited there, that compiled by Abeillard Barreto, *Bibliografia sul-riograndense* (2 vols., Rio de Janeiro, 1976), easily the best regional survey, might be added.

The forthcoming volume of Joaquim Veríssimo Serrão, *Historia de Portugal*, 5 vols. to date (Lisbon, 1972–80) will include the late colonial period and may be expected to be as comprehensive as are the preceding volumes. Other general histories of the period, such as Fortunato de Almeida, *História de Portugal*, IV (*1580–1816*) (Coimbra, 1926), and Damião Peres (ed.), *História de Portugal* (8 vols., Barcelos, 1928–66), are badly dated but may still be profitably consulted. Although uneven in quality, there are many informative essays in Joel Serrão (ed.), *Dicionário de história de Portugal* (4 vols., Lisbon, 1962–7, and a later, expanded printing). For more specialized studies of Portugal under Pombal and his successors, see *CHLA* I, Bibliographical Essay 13.

For a century and a quarter the classic history of colonial Brazil has been Francisco Adolfo de Varnhagen, *História geral do Brasil* (7th edn, 6 vols., São Paulo, 1962). While it continues to be worth consulting because of the sources utilized by the author and added to by subsequent editors, it is unsatisfactory as a synthesis for this period because of its defective organization. More readable is the fourth volume of Pedro Calmon, *História do Brasil* (7 vols., Rio de Janeiro, 1959), but the treatment of the post-1750 years in Sérgio Buarque de Holanda (ed.), *História geral da civilização brasileira*, I *A época colonial* (2 vols., São Paulo, 1960) is woefully incomplete and generally disappointing. No modern study supersedes the seminal analysis and range of insights supplied by Caio Prado Júnior, *The colonial background of modern Brazil*, translated by Suzette Macedo (Berkeley and Los Angeles, 1967), first published in Portuguese more than three decades ago.

On peninsular aspects of the Luso-Brazilian economic relationship during this period, the fleet system, and the Pombaline monopoly companies, see *CHLA* I, Bibliographical Essay 13.

Two recent Ph.D. dissertations, one already published, examine the emergence of Rio de Janeiro as Brazil's chief entrepot in this period: Corcino Madeiros dos Santos' conscientiously researched *Relações comerciais do Rio de Janeiro com Lisboa (1763–1808)* (Rio de Janeiro, 1980), and Rudolph William Bauss' industriously prepared 'Rio de Janeiro: the rise of late-colonial Brazil's dominant emporium, 1777–1808' (Tulane University, 1977). Additional details may be found in the opening chapter of Eulália Maria Lahmeyer Lobo's encyclopaedic *História do Rio de Janeiro (Do capital comercial ao capital industrial e financeiro)* (2 vols., Rio de Janeiro, 1978), but we await comparable studies of other Brazilian seaports.

On the slave trade, see *CHLA* I, Bibliographical Essay 12 and, for the late eighteenth century, Jean Mettas, 'La traite portugaise en haute Guinée, 1758–1797: problèmes et méthodes', *Journal of African History*, 16/3 (1975), 343–63, and J. C. Miller, 'Mortality in the Atlantic slave trade: statistical evidence on causality', *Journal of Interdisciplinary History*, 11/3 (Winter, 1981), 385–423, which demonstrate what the archives and modern methodologies are able to tell us. Joseph C. Miller (compiler), *Slavery: a comparative teaching bibliography* (Waltham, Mass., 1977) and supplements, reports on most of the known literature concerning this vast topic.

On the treatment of slaves in colonial Brazil and the socio-economic status of emancipated slaves, especially mulattos, which warrants further investigation, see *CHLA* II, Bibliographical Essay 12.

Apart from Caio Prado Júnior's incisive essays in *Colonial background*, no reliable history of Brazil's agricultural development during these years exists. Luiz Amaral, *História geral da agricultura brasileira* (2nd edn, 2 vols., São Paulo, 1958), remains standard but is badly digested and does not reflect newer, archive-based findings. Though primarily concerned with the nineteenth century, Eulália Maria Lahmeyer Lobo, *História político-administrativa da agricultura brasileira 1808–1889* (Brasília, 1980) is useful for its bibliography and for some of its details.

In spite of their vital importance to the Brazilian diet, no modern study of the beginnings of wheat or manioc cultivation and trade exists. We are better served with respect to the tobacco industry. Its origins have been deftly traced by Rae Jean Flory, 'Bahian society in the mid-colonial period: the sugar planters, tobacco growers, merchants, and artisans of Salvador and the Recôncavo, 1680–1725' (Ph.D. dissertation, University of Texas, 1978), ch. 5, and its further development analysed by Catherine Lugar, 'The Portuguese tobacco trade and tobacco growers of Bahia in the late colonial period', in D. Alden and Warren Dean (eds.), *Essays concerning the socioeconomic history of Brazil and Portuguese India* (Gainesville, 1977), 26–70; see also José Roberto do Amaral Lapa (ed.), 'O tabaco brasileiro no século xviii (Anotações aos estudos sobre o tabaco de Joaquim de Amorim Castro)', *Studia*, 29 (April 1970), 57–144, reprinted in *Economia colonial* (São Paulo, 1973), 141–230. Geancarlo Belotte, 'Le tabac brésilien aux xviiiᵉ siècle' (Thèse pour le doctorat de 3ᵐᵉ cycle, Université de Paris-Nanterre, 1973), organizes most of the known statistics but is otherwise unimpressive.

The socio-economic background for the revival of the sugar industry in Bahia is closely examined by Flory (see above), but its development there, in Pernambuco, and in Rio de Janeiro during the years after 1750 requires further study. See, however, Alberto Lamego, 'Os engenhos de açúcar nos recôncavos do Rio de Janeiro, em fins do século xvii[i]', *Brasil Açucareiro* (March 1965), 18–25; José Honório Rodrigues, 'Agricultura e economia açucareiras no século xviii', *Brasil Açucareiro*, 26 (July 1945), and portions of Alberto Lamego's chaotically organized *A terra Goitacá a luz de documentos inéditos* (8 vols., Rio de Janeiro, 1913–47), for the spectacular rise of sugar in the Campos district of Rio de Janeiro. Maria Thereza Schorer Petrone, *A lavoura canavieira em São Paulo* (São Paulo, 1968), is a model study.

The literature on other aspects of the agricultural renaissance is fragmentary. José Ribeiro Júnior has promised a study of the cotton industry of Pernambuco. We badly need it and a comparable monograph on the cotton industry of Maranhão. Some features of the cattle industry in the interior of the north-east have been explored by Luiz R. B. Mott in several essays, including 'Fazendas de gado do Piauí (1697–1762) [*sic* for 1772]', *Anais do VIII Simpósio Nacional dos Professores Universitários de História* (São Paulo, 1976), but no comparable account of stock raising in other key areas, especially Minas Gerais and Rio Grande do Sul, has been published. The beginnings of rice cultivation have been examined by D. Alden, 'Manoel Luis Vieira: an entrepreneur in Rio de Janeiro during Brazil's…agricultural renaissance', *HAHR*, 34/4 (November 1959), 521–37. The only study of the production of dyestuffs in this period is D. Alden, 'The growth and decline of indigo production in colonial Brazil: a study in comparative economic history', *Journal of Economic History*, 25 (March 1965), 35–60. Surprisingly, no adequate history of the beginnings of Brazilian coffee has appeared, but see Afonso de Escragnolle Taunay, *História do café no Brasil*, 11 (Rio de Janeiro, 1939). For the development of cacao, see D. Alden, 'The significance of cacao production in the Amazon in the late colonial period', American Philosophical Society, *Proceedings* (April 1976), 120/2. Myriam Ellis, *O monopólio do sal no estado do Brasil (1631–1801)* (São Paulo, 1955) remains unsurpassed.

The economic decline of the interior during this period has never been adequately assessed. A masterful account of efforts by royal and private enterprise to link the back-country with the seacoast is David M. Davidson's 'Rivers and empire: the Madeira route and the incorporation of the Brazilian far west, 1737–1808' (Ph.D. dissertation, Yale University, 1970), of which the only published excerpt is 'How the Brazilian west was won: freelance and state on the Mato Grosso frontier, 1737–1752', in D. Alden (ed.), *Colonial roots of modern Brazil* (Berkeley and Los Angeles, 1973), 61–106. The transportation and marketing problems of the backlands at this time warrant systematic explication.

Another vital economic activity that scholars have ignored is colonial Brazil's coastal fishing industry. Only whaling has received attention: see Myriam Ellis, *Aspectos da pesca da baleia no Brasil colonial* (São Paulo, 1958), and D. Alden, 'Yankee sperm whalers in Brazilian waters, and the decline of the Portuguese whale fishery (1773–1801)', *The Americas*, 20 (January 1964), 267–88.

We will obtain a far better understanding of how particular branches of the Brazilian economy fared during this period when we possess adequate price histories for major markets. Two pioneering studies are Harold B. Johnson, Jr. 'A preliminary inquiry into money, prices, and wages in Rio de Janeiro, 1763–1823', in Alden, *Colonial roots*, 231–83, and Kátia M. de Queirós Mattoso, 'Conjuncture et société au Brésil à la fin du XVIIIe siècle: prix et salaires à la veille de la révolution des alfaiates – Bahia 1798', *Cahiers des Amériques Latines*, no. 5 (Paris, 1970), 33–53.

Colonial administration during this period is discussed in detail in D. Alden, *Royal government in colonial Brazil* (Berkeley and Los Angeles,

1968), and more briefly by Caio Prado Júnior in the final chapter of *Colonial background*. A more favourable appraisal of the religious policy of the Pombaline regime than that offered here is Henrique Schaefer, *Historia de Portugal,* 5 (Porto, 1899), 208–13; see also Fortunato de Almeida, *História da igreja em Portugal,* new edn by Damião Peres, vol. 3 (Porto, 1970), which is a mine of useful data. See also Thales de Azevedo, *Igreja e estado em tensão e crise* (São Paulo, 1978). No one is likely to improve significantly upon the meticulously researched, carefully organized, forcefully presented works by Serafim Leite, S.J. His *História da companhia de Jesús no Brasil* (10 vols., Rio de Janeiro, 1938–50) is one of the major works ever produced on Brazil's colonial experience and appears in a condensed version as *Suma histórica da companhia de Jesús no Brasil...1549–1760* (Lisbon, 1965). See also D. Alden, 'Economic aspects of the expulsion of the Jesuits from Brazil: a preliminary report', in Henry H. Keith and S. F. Edwards (eds.), *Conflict and continuity in Brazilian society* (Columbia, S.C., 1969), 25–65. A recent study of the role of parish priests is Eugenio de Andrade Veiga, *Os parocos no Brasil no período colonial 1500–1822* (Salvador, 1977). The cultural role of the church in the interior is analysed by José Ferreira Carrato, *Igreja, iluminismo e escolas mineiras coloniais* (São Paulo, 1968), while the ubiquitous black brotherhoods have been restudied by Patricia A. Mulvey, 'Black brothers and sisters: membership in the black lay brotherhoods of colonial Brazil', *Luso-Brazilian Review,* 17/2 (1980), 253–79. For additional bibliography, see *CHLA* II, Bibliographical Essay 12, and *CHLA* I, Bibliographical Essay 15.

Without question the best serial runs of demographic evidence for this period pertain to São Paulo. They have been analysed closely in two recent dissertations: Maria Luiza Marcílio, *La ville de São Paulo 1750–1850: peuplement et population* (Rouen, 1968), and Elizabeth Anne Kuznesof, 'Household economy and composition in an urbanizing community: São Paulo 1765 to 1836' (University of California at Berkeley, 1976). The latter of these particularly demonstrates what can be done with adequate resources, sound methodolgy and access to computer time. See also Kuznesof, 'The role of the female-headed household in Brazilian modernization: São Paulo 1765 to 1836', *Journal of Social History,* 13 (Summer 1980), 589–613, and 'The role of merchants in the economic development of São Paulo 1765–c. 1850', *HAHR,* 60/4 (November 1980), 571–92. While demographic materials are less extensive for other parts of Brazil, much remains in Brazilian and

Portuguese archives to challenge future scholars. See also *CHLA* II, Bibliographical Essay 2.

The opening chapter of Lobo's *História do Rio de Janeiro* helps to fill the gap that exists concerning the urban history of that city during this period. We have better coverage for Bahian society and the city of Salvador than we do for any other part of Brazil during the eighteenth and early nineteenth centuries. In addition to the outstanding dissertation by Flory, there is David Grant Smith and Rae Jean Flory, 'Bahian merchants and planters in the seventeenth and early eighteenth centuries', *HAHR*, 58/4 (November 1978), 571–94; John Norman Kennedy's 'Bahian elites, 1750–1822', *HAHR*, 53/3 (August 1973), 415–39; and two well-researched dissertations that span the late eighteenth and early nineteenth centuries: F. W. O. Morton, 'The conservative revolution of independence, Bahia 1790–1840' (Oxford, 1974), the first half of which concerns the years before 1808, and Catherine Lugar, 'The merchant community of Salvador, Bahia 1780–1830' (SUNY at Stony Brook, 1980). Still valuable is Thales de Azevedo, *Povoamento da cidade de Salvador* (3rd edn, Bahia, 1968). Would that we possessed studies for other major cities comparable to Kátia M. de Queirós Mattoso's sophisticated, carefully researched and lucidly presented *Bahia: a cidade do Salvador e seu mercado no século XIX* (Salvador, 1978), portions of which concern the late colonial period. The curious emergence of Brazilian Levittowns, i.e., planned, model communities, in the Amazon, the far west and the south-east, mostly established between 1716 and 1775, is examined by Roberta Marx Delson, *New towns for colonial Brazil* (Ann Arbor, 1979). Still useful is Paulo F. Santos, 'Formação de cidades no Brasil colonial', v Colóquio Internacional de Estudos Luso-brasileiros, *Actas*, 5 (Coimbra, 1968), 7–116.

For a detailed analysis that places the conspiracies of this period within a broad context, see Kenneth R. Maxwell, *Conflicts and conspiracies: Brazil and Portugal 1750–1808* (Cambridge, 1973), which is mainly concerned with the Mineiro plot. The Tailors' insurrection has inspired several fascinating studies: Afonso Ruy, *A primeira revolução social brasileira* (2nd edn, Bahia, 1951); Kátia M. de Queirós Mattoso, *Presença francesca no movimento democrático Baiano de 1798* (Salvador, 1969); and Luis Henrique Dias Tavares, *História da sedição intentada na Bahia em 1798* ('*A conspiração dos alfaiates*') (São Paulo, 1975) are the major Brazilian studies, but the outstanding chapter in Morton's thesis should not be missed. In addition to Buarque de Holanda's fine introduction to

Azeredo Coutinho's works, see E. Bradford Burns, 'The role of Azeredo Coutinho in the enlightenment of Brazil', *HAHR*, 44 (May 1964), 145–60, and Manoel Cardozo, 'Azeredo Coutinho and the intellectual ferment of his times', in Keith and Edwards, *Conflicts and continuity*, 72–112.

INDEX